6 Practice Tests for the
DIGITAL SAT®

2026 Edition

The Staff of The Princeton Review

PrincetonReview.com

Penguin
Random
House

The Princeton Review
110 East 42nd Street, 7th Floor
New York, NY 10017

ISBN: 978-0-593-51820-5
ISSN: 2377-7273

This book is the 2026 edition of Princeton Review SAT Practice Questions. Some material in this book was previously published in Princeton Review PSAT Prep 2024, a trade paperback respectively published by Random House LLC in 2023.

Editor: Patricia Murphy
Production Editors: Sarah Litt, Emma Parker
Production Artist: Jason Ullmeyer
Content Developer: Amy Minster

Printed in the United States of America.

10 9 8 7 6 5 4 3 2 1

2026 Edition

The Princeton Review Publishing Team
Rob Franek, Editor-in-Chief
David Soto, Senior Director, Data Operations
Stephen Koch, Senior Manager, Data Operations
Deborah Weber, Director of Production
Jason Ullmeyer, Production Design Manager
Jennifer Chapman, Senior Production Artist
Selena Coppock, Director of Editorial
Aaron Riccio, Director, Editorial Admissions Content
Orion McBean, Senior Editor
Meave Shelton, Senior Editor
Chris Chimera, Editor
Patricia Murphy, Editor
Laura Rose, Editor
Isabelle Appleton, Editorial Assistant

Penguin Random House Publishing Team
Tom Russell, VP, Publisher
Alison Stoltzfus, Senior Director, Publishing
Emily Hoffman, Associate Managing Editor
Mary Ellen Owens, Assistant Director of Production
Suzanne Lee, Senior Designer
Eugenia Lo, Publishing Assistant

For customer service, please contact **editorialsupport@review.com**, and be sure to include:

- full title of the book
- ISBN
- page number

Acknowledgments

An SAT course is much more than clever techniques and powerful computer score reports. The reason our results are great is that our teachers care so much about their students. Many teachers have gone out of their way to improve the course, often going so far as to write their own materials, some of which we have incorporated into our course manuals as well as into this book. The list of these teachers could fill this page.

Special thanks to all those who contributed to this year's edition: Kenneth Brenner, Sara Kuperstein, Amy Minster, Scott O'Neal, Aleksei Alferiev, Brittany Budzon, Tania Capone, Remy Cosse, Stacey Cowap, Wazhma Daftanai, Harrison Foster, Beth Hollingsworth, Adam Keller, Kevin Keogh, Ali Landreau, Aaron Lindh, Jomil London, Sweena Mangal, Sionainn Marcoux, Valerie Meyers, Acacia Nawrocik-Madrid, Gabby Peterson, Kathy Ruppert, Jess Thomas, Jimmy Williams, and Suzanne Wint.

We are also, as always, very appreciative of the time and attention given to each page by Jason Ullmeyer, Sarah Litt, and Emma Parker.

Finally, we would like to thank the people who truly have taught us everything we know about the SAT: our students.

Contents

Get More (Free) Content

at **PrincetonReview.com/prep**

As easy as 1·2·3

1 Go to PrincetonReview.com/prep or scan the **QR code** and enter the following ISBN to register your book:
9780593518205

2 Answer a few simple questions to set up an exclusive Princeton Review account. *(If you already have one, you can just log in.)*

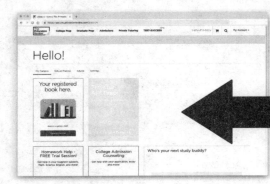

3 Enjoy access to your **FREE** content!

Once you've registered, you can...

- Test yourself with two additional online Digital SAT practice tests

- Take a full-length practice Digital SAT and/or ACT

- Get valuable advice about the college application process, including tips for writing a great essay and where to apply for financial aid

- Get our take on any recent or pending updates to the Digital SAT

- If you're still choosing between colleges, use our searchable rankings of *The Best 390 Colleges* to find out more information about your dream school

- Check to see if there have been any corrections or updates to this edition

Need to report a potential **content** issue?

Contact **EditorialSupport@review.com** and include:

- full title of the book
- ISBN
- page number

Need to report a **technical** issue?

Contact **TPRStudentTech@review.com** and provide:

- your full name
- email address used to register the book
- full book title and ISBN
- Operating system (Mac/PC) and browser (Chrome, Firefox, Safari, etc.)

Part I
Introduction

WHAT'S INSIDE

Welcome to *6 Practice Tests for the Digital SAT*. As you've probably already guessed, this book contains practice tests for the Digital SAT, which we at The Princeton Review have created based on the information released by the College Board. We've rigorously analyzed available tests, and our content development teams have tirelessly worked to ensure that our material accurately reflects what you will see in terms of design, structure, style, and, most importantly, content on test day. We continually evaluate the data on each question to ensure validity, and refine the level of difficulty within each test to match that of the Digital SAT even more closely. Reach out to EditorialSupport@review.com if you feel something is amiss.

We are confident that if you work through these questions and evaluate your performance with our comprehensive explanations, you'll improve the skills that you need to score higher on the Digital SAT. Register your book at PrincetonReview.com to gain access to detailed, interactive score reports. Track your overall performance so that you get the most out of your test prep, and make sure to read the in-depth explanations that not only explain how to get the right answer but also why the other choices are incorrect. Through careful self-assessment, you can correct any recurring mistakes, as well as identify any weaknesses or gaps in knowledge that you can then focus your attention on studying.

But before we go any further, let's talk about the Digital SAT itself.

What's on the Digital SAT?

The Digital SAT is 2 hours and 14 minutes long.

The test consists of the following sections, in this order:

- Reading and Writing (2 modules, each 27 questions in 32 minutes)
    o All questions in the Reading and Writing (RW) section are multiple-choice.
    o Two questions in each module are experimental and are not scored.
- a 10-minute break
- Math (2 modules, each 22 questions in 35 minutes)
    o Most questions in the Math section are multiple-choice.
    o The rest are "student-produced responses" (fill-ins).
    o Two questions in each module are experimental and are not scored.

Scoring on the Digital SAT

Scores from the Digital SAT will be reported in a matter of days, not weeks, as was the case with the paper-and-pencil test. Your score report for the Digital SAT will feature scores for each of the following:

- **Total Score:**
    the sum of the two section scores (Reading and Writing, Math), ranging from 400 to 1600
- **Section Scores:**
    1. Reading and Writing, ranging from 200 to 800
    2. Math, also ranging from 200 to 800

The following table summarizes the structure and scoring of the Digital SAT.

Category	Digital SAT
Time Overall	134 minutes plus 10-minute break
Components	• Reading and Writing section • Math section
Number of Questions	• Reading and Writing: 54, including 4 experimental questions • Math: 44, including 4 experimental questions
Answer Choices	• Reading and Writing: all multiple-choice with 4 answers per question • Math: 75% multiple-choice with 4 answers per question, 25% student-produced responses
Time by Section	• Reading and Writing: 64 minutes in two 32-minute modules • Math: 70 minutes in two 35-minute modules
Relationship Between Modules	• Module 1 has a broad mix of levels of difficulty. • Performance on Module 1 determines the difficulty of Module 2. • Students who do well on Module 1 will get a Module 2 that is harder, on average. • Students who do less well on Module 1 will get a Module 2 that is easier, on average.
Scoring	• The score is based on the number of correctly answered questions and the difficulty of those questions. • There is no penalty for wrong answers or leaving questions blank, so it's in your best interest to guess rather than leave a question blank. • Students who do well on Module 1 are put into a higher bracket of possible scores. • Students who do less well on Module 1 are put into a lower bracket of possible scores. • Section scores range from 200 to 800. • Total score is the sum of the section scores and ranges from 400 to 1600.

HOW TO USE THIS BOOK

There are two ways that you can use the content in this book: you can take full-length practice tests or you can focus on honing your skills on specific concepts. You can even do a bit of both.

The questions in this book are laid out as tests in the way that you'll encounter them on the Digital SAT. Each section (Reading and Writing or Math) begins with a module of mixed difficulty, and your performance on that module determines whether you will get the second module that is easier or harder on average. On the real Digital SAT, you'll automatically be given an easier or harder second module based on your performance on the first module of each subject. In this book, we've included both options for the second module, so if you'd like to take a full test, be sure to follow the guidelines provided at the start of each practice test so that you can mimic the length and difficulty level of the computer-based test as realistically as possible. (For Practice Tests 5 and 6 in your online student tools, the test will automatically send you to the correct second module in each section.)

Use the paper tests in this book (Practice Tests 1–4) to work on your content knowledge and pace, and when you're ready to mimic the real digital testing experience, block off about 140 minutes to take Practice Tests 5 and 6 in your online student tools. You can also work on a test a single module at a time to perfect your pacing. Don't forget to carefully review our detailed explanations! Whether you get a question right or not, its explanation is packed full of our powerful Digital SAT strategies and techniques and might help you to save time on future questions or to clarify where you might have gotten the right answer for the wrong reason.

Calculator use is allowed on all Math questions on the Digital SAT. The testing app includes a built-in Desmos calculator. For the tests printed in this book (Practice Tests 1–4), practice by using the calculator at Desmos.com. For the online-only test found in your student tools (Practice Tests 5 and 6), use our testing app's built-in calculator.

WHEN YOU TAKE A TEST

Here are some suggestions for working through this book:

1. Keep track of your performance. Whether you're working through individual modules or taking each test as a whole, be sure to use the answer key to score yourself. For the printed tests, you'll want to do this after each Module 1 so that you can determine which of the two Module 2s to complete. It's also a good idea to log the time and date of each practice session so that you can track your progress on the in-book Practice Tests 1–4.

2. The Digital SAT is a timed test. You may be a star test-taker when you have all the time in the world to mull over the questions, but can you perform as well when the clock is ticking? Timing yourself will ensure you are prepared for the constraints of the actual test, just as our strategy-filled explanations can help you to discover faster methods for solving questions.

3. Don't cram it all in at once. It's hard enough to concentrate throughout one Digital SAT test—don't burn yourself out by taking multiple tests in a row. You wouldn't run two marathons back-to-back, so why treat your brain (which is like a muscle) in that way? Give yourself at least a couple of months before your anticipated "real" test date so that you can learn from any mistakes that were made on these practice tests.

4. Accordingly, take time to analyze your performance between tests or practice modules. As you actively review your work, your mind will be subtly taking notes and tweaking the way it handles future questions of a similar nature, shaving seconds off its processing time as it grows more accustomed to particular wordings or presentations.

Answers and Explanations

This section is split into two parts, an answer key and then a detailed set of explanations that breaks down things such as the type of question, our recommended method for tackling that type, and the correct answer. By reading the explanations, you'll learn not only why the correct answer is right but, when applicable, what makes the wrong answers incorrect. Begin by checking off the questions that you got right; for each one you got wrong, take the time to read the explanation and understand where you went wrong in order to learn from those mistakes. Don't just rush to the next section. Take your time to not only analyze what you got wrong and why, but to be sure that you completely understand why you got each question *right*. This is what will truly give you the experience necessary to improve your skills and be as prepared as possible for the Digital SAT.

> **Common Acronyms**
>
> Some strategies are explained with terms such as FOIL and SOHCAHTOA. If you're unfamiliar with these and need more help understanding how these work, our SAT Prep book offers more practice tests and a guide to the test's content.

Other Important Terms

As you read through the explanations for the Reading and Writing Modules, you will also see some capitalized terms describing the question types. We identify these by name to help you learn to recognize not only what they look like but also where to find them in the modules and how to approach them. Although you may not see all of the following 8 Reading question types or 3 Writing question types on every module, the ones you do see will appear in this order. Question types listed on the same line may be mixed together within a module.

> **Reading Question Types**
> Vocabulary
> Purpose
> Dual Texts
> Retrieval and Main Idea
> Claims and Charts
> Conclusions
>
> **Writing Question Types**
> Rules
> Transitions
> Rhetorical Synthesis

For the Math explanations, you will see some strategies used repeatedly. We've included a brief description of these here, but see our other titles such as *SAT Prep* if you'd like more information.

Bite-Sized Pieces

When dealing with complicated math questions, take it one little piece at a time. We call this strategy Bite-Sized Pieces. If you try to do more than one step at a time, especially if you do it in your head, you are likely to make mistakes or fall for trap answers. After each step, take a look at the answer choices and determine whether you can eliminate any.

Plugging In

When the question has variables in the answer choices, you can often plug in your own numbers for the unknowns and do arithmetic instead of algebra. When you plug in, use "good" numbers—ones that are simple to work with and that make the problem easier to manipulate: 2, 5, 10, or 100 are generally easy numbers to use. Work the steps of the problem and get an answer. Then plug the same number(s) for the variable(s) into all four answer choices, and eliminate ones that don't match the answer you found.

Plugging In the Answers

Plugging In the Answers is a useful technique for solving word problems in which the answer choices are all numbers. When a multiple-choice question asks for a specific value using words like "how much" or "what is the value of," skip the process of setting up the algebra by simply checking the four possible solutions. One of these is the correct answer. Try them out to see if the math works, stopping when you find the right one. Most of the time, you will only have to try a couple of the answers, saving yourself even more time.

Built-in Calculator

The calculator that is available in the testing app for every math question is often the most efficient way to answer a question. Look for ways to use it when solving for a variable, calculating statistical measures, and especially working with graphs in the coordinate plane.

GOOD LUCK!

We know that the Digital SAT may seem intimidating at first glance—but then again, after using this book, you'll be well beyond that first glance, so you're headed in the right direction. Also, as you prepare, whether you're stressed or relaxed, remember this key point: the Digital SAT doesn't measure the stuff that matters. It measures neither intelligence nor the depth and breadth of what you're learning in high school. It doesn't predict college grades as well as your high school grades do, and colleges know there is more to you as a student—and a person—than how you fare on a single test administered on a random day. This is a high-stakes test, and you should absolutely work hard and prepare. But don't treat it like it's some mythical monster or earth-shattering event. It's just a test, and we at The Princeton Review know tests. We're here for you every step of the way.

Part II
Practice Tests

Chapter 1
Practice Test 1

HOW TO EMULATE THE DIGITAL SAT ON PAPER

Practice Tests 5 and 6 are available in your online student tools in a digital, adaptive environment. The four tests in this physical book are printed on paper, but otherwise emulate the digital test in every way: test style, difficulty, and content. Please use the checklist below to ensure that you are able to emulate the adaptive nature of the test and get the preparation that you need for test day. Feel free to use the versions of Module 2 that you do not take during your test as additional practice.

- ☐ Take Reading and Writing (RW) Module 1, allowing yourself 32 minutes to complete it.

- ☐ Go to the answer key on page 74 and determine the number of questions you got correct in RW Module 1.

- ☐ If you get fewer than 15 questions correct, take RW Module 2 – Easier, which starts on page 22. If you get 15 or more questions correct, take RW Module 2 – Harder, which starts on page 33.

- ☐ Whichever RW Module 2 you take, start immediately and allow yourself 32 minutes to complete it.

- ☐ Take a 10-minute break between RW Module 2 and Math Module 1.

- ☐ Take Math Module 1, allowing yourself 35 minutes to complete it.

- ☐ Go to the answer key on page 74 and determine the number of questions you got correct in Math Module 1.

- ☐ If you get fewer than 14 questions correct, take Math Module 2 – Easier, which starts on page 56. If you get 14 or more questions correct, take Math Module 2 – Harder, which starts on page 64.

- ☐ Whichever Math Module you take, start it immediately and allow yourself 35 minutes to complete it.

- ☐ After you finish the test, check your answers to RW Module 2 and Math Module 2.

- ☐ Only after you complete the entire test should you read the explanations for the questions, which start on page 75.

Test 1—Reading and Writing
Module 1

Turn to Section 1 of your answer sheet to answer the questions in this section.

DIRECTIONS

The questions in this section address a number of important reading and writing skills. Each question includes one or more passages, which may include a table or graph. Read each passage and question carefully, and then choose the best answer to the question based on the passage(s).

All questions in the section are multiple-choice with four answer choices. Each question has a single best answer. Fill in the circle with the answer letter for the answer you think is best.

---

1 ☐ Mark for Review

The religious ceremony Gẹlẹdẹ (performed by the Yoruba people of West Africa) _____ female ancestors, village elders, and goddesses in multiple ways: for instance, one part of the ceremony celebrates the fertility of women as a power over life itself.

Which choice completes the text with the most logical and precise word or phrase?

(A) soothes

(B) critiques

(C) praises

(D) neglects

2 ☐ Mark for Review

In the years following James Watson's and Francis Crick's 1953 discovery of the double helix structure of DNA, scientists developed new processes to determine how many bases made up each codon (sequence of DNA). For example, a _____ experiment in 1961 by scientists Marshall W. Nirenberg and J. Heinrich Matthaei successfully decoded the first codon.

Which choice completes the text with the most logical and precise word or phrase?

(A) dubious

(B) pioneering

(C) redundant

(D) prior

CONTINUE →

3 ⎙ Mark for Review

Alfons Mucha's *Slav Epic* is a series of twenty paintings heralded as a masterwork by art critics but often described as confusing by casual observers. This disparity may be due to the _____ nature of the work, as the paintings are meant to be analyzed as one piece but are sometimes displayed individually in galleries.

Which choice completes the text with the most logical and precise word or phrase?

(A) elusive

(B) collective

(C) painstaking

(D) miniature

4 ⎙ Mark for Review

A recent study presents neurological evidence suggesting that greater density of white matter in the brain's left corticospinal tract produces a _____ of the symptoms of ADHD (attention-deficit/hyperactivity disorder). As research subjects aged, those experiencing ADHD remission demonstrated greater white matter density than those not in remission.

Which choice completes the text with the most logical and precise word or phrase?

(A) glorification

(B) visualization

(C) progression

(D) reduction

5 ⎙ Mark for Review

The Turkish word *yakamoz*—meaning "the reflection of moonlight in water"—was recently declared "the most beautiful word in any language" by a panel of German journalists and TV presenters. Using measurements such as originality and cultural specificity, the jury explained that the use of a single word to describe such a visually striking effect creates a sense of _____, especially considering that most languages need to use several words to describe the same phenomenon.

Which choice completes the text with the most logical and precise word or phrase?

(A) elegance

(B) agitation

(C) confusion

(D) convolution

CONTINUE ➤

6 ☐ Mark for Review

In North America, wolves have surprisingly varied diets—including plant matter like blueberries—despite being known carnivores. Wolves mostly prey on hoofed herbivorous mammals, but periods of scarcity compel these pack hunters to look, or listen, beyond their usual food sources. When wolves can't use their sharp eyesight, their acute hearing seems to help: <u>they can hear prey moving in or around bodies of water</u>. Indeed, in 2018, Tom Gables and his colleagues at Voyageurs National Park captured footage of wolves fishing at night by listening for splashes on the surface of a creek.

Which choice best describes the function of the underlined portion in the text as a whole?

(A) It explains how wolves might use their hearing to expand their diets.

(B) It illustrates how periods of scarcity affect the group dynamics of North American wolf packs.

(C) It reinforces the idea that North American wolves have almost entirely carnivorous diets.

(D) It establishes why wolves prefer to hunt in water rather than on land.

7 ☐ Mark for Review

Residents of Athens, Georgia, commonly know the Jackson Oak as "the tree that owns itself." A newspaper article from 1890 describes how Colonel William Henry Jackson deeded the tree ownership of both itself and the land surrounding it. However, under US common law, trees lack the legal capacity to accept property. Furthermore, it's unclear whether the Oak was actually on Jackson's property at all and, therefore, whether the tree was his to deed ownership to in the first place. Regardless, the tree's self-ownership status is acknowledged by the residents and municipal officials of Athens-Clarke County, with neighbors and aid groups serving as stewards and advocates for the tree's continued care.

Based on the text, what can be concluded about the status of the Jackson Oak?

(A) The public's designation of the Jackson Oak may be influenced by factors other than legal definitions.

(B) As the surrounding property changed hands, the legality of the Jackson Oak's self-ownership came into question.

(C) The local popularity of the Jackson Oak likely predates the 1890 newspaper article.

(D) Although trees can't legally own themselves, Athens municipal officials changed the law for the Jackson Oak.

CONTINUE

---

8 ☐ Mark for Review

In the 1800s through the 1930s, paleontological excavations on the Texas Coastal Plain revealed the fossils of what is now recognized as a 15-million-year-old species of beaver. However, while the initial excavations yielded some basic information, such as skeletal structure and likely diet, much of what scientists know about the species, *Anchitheriomys buceei*, comes from a more recent partial skull discovery in Burkesville, Texas. According to paleontologist Matthew Brown and his colleagues, sediment in this particular fossil fused brain matter to bone, preserving many anatomical details of the brain that could only be brought into view by high-resolution X-ray technology, which wasn't developed until late in the twentieth century.

What does the text indicate about the discovery of *Anchitheriomys buceei*?

Ⓐ The partial skull would not have been uncovered without high-resolution X-ray technology.

Ⓑ Scientists used findings from multiple time periods to help understand the species.

Ⓒ The discovery supplements data on the skeletal structures of modern beaver species from the Coastal Plain.

Ⓓ *Anchitheriomys buceei* would not have been identified without Matthew Brown and his colleagues.

9 ☐ Mark for Review

Researchers have found that fifty species of turtles previously thought to be mute actually vocalize sounds such as purring, hissing, clicking, and chirping. By employing specialized underwater recording equipment, biologist Gabriel Jorgewich-Cohen and his team have predicted that such complex repertoires of sounds indicate "communicative meaning" amongst species like *Podocnemis expansa*. The team further suggested that while these and other sound-producing reptile species have adapted differently from each other, they may share common ancestors known as choanate vertebrates, or vertebrates with lungs, from which they have inherited the ability to vocalize.

Which choice best states the main idea of the text?

Ⓐ Researchers compared the vocalizations of *Podocnemis expansa* with those of other species to better understand their communicative meanings.

Ⓑ Jorgewich-Cohen and his colleagues discovered a new species of turtle through its unique vocalizations.

Ⓒ An examination of turtle vocalizations proves that these species communicate with clicks, chirps, purrs, and hisses.

Ⓓ The recordings of turtle vocalizations provide new insights on the ancestry of certain reptile species.

CONTINUE ➡

10 ☐ Mark for Review

Travels in Alaska is a 1915 travel and exploration book by John Muir. In the book, which describes the experience of exploring the Alaskan wilderness, Muir emphasizes the beauty of a landscape that he believes is without parallel: _____

Which quotation from *Travels in Alaska* most effectively illustrates the claim?

(A) "I shall see as much as possible of the glacier, and I know not how long it will hold me."

(B) "The starlight was so full that I distinctly saw not only the berg-filled bay, but most of the lower portions of the glaciers, lying pale and spirit-like amid the mountains."

(C) "In the evening, after witnessing the unveiling of the majestic peaks and glaciers and their baptism in the down-pouring sunbeams, it seemed inconceivable that nature could have anything finer to show us."

(D) "For those who really care to get into hearty contact with the coast region, travel by canoe is by far the better way."

11 ☐ Mark for Review

In her 1850 collection of poems *Sonnets from the Portuguese*, Elizabeth Barrett Browning wrote and arranged her works in a sonnet cycle. This method groups sonnets in such a way that they can be read either individually or as a single collection and are written around a common theme. Barrett Browning wrote the sonnets centered on the theme of love but was hesitant to publish them, fearing that they were too personal. To address this, Barrett Browning published her collection under a title that suggested the works were not hers but rather translations of foreign sonnets. Upon release, the collection received critical acclaim for its handling of the theme of love and for the multiple ways in which the work could be read. This response suggests that _____

Which choice most logically completes the text?

(A) Browning influenced other poets to create collections utilizing a sonnet cycle.

(B) most critics didn't realize Browning's goal for *Sonnets from the Portuguese*.

(C) Browning's use of a sonnet cycle contributed to the success of *Sonnets from the Portuguese*.

(D) *Sonnets from the Portuguese* is one of Browning's most famous works.

CONTINUE ➜

12 ☐ Mark for Review

By developing a high-resolution computer simulation to model the formation of the Moon, Jacob Kegerreis and colleagues show that the Moon likely formed in a matter of hours rather than months or years as was previously believed. The team suggests that an object called Theia struck proto-Earth with an extreme amount of force, breaking off enough material for moon formation. Due to the ferocity of the collision, this material would have been expelled violently into space, acting as a catalyst for the rapid formation of the satellite. In one of the simulations, the team delayed the formation of the Moon to months rather than hours and encountered the same issues as previous theories: such a delay did not produce a moon with the same mass, orbit, and composition as our current moon. The team therefore hypothesizes that _____

Which choice most logically completes the text?

(A) the collision with Theia actually affected the Earth's composition, not just that of the Moon.

(B) the Moon formed more slowly in the time following the collision than the team's simulations suggested.

(C) the speed at which the Moon formed played a critical role in its current position and physical features.

(D) if the collision between Theia and the proto-Earth had been less violent, all of the material broken off in the collision would have remained closer to Earth.

13 ☐ Mark for Review

American literary regionalism was a movement that arose following the American Civil War. According to a 1993 essay, the purpose of the movement was to preserve regional culture at a time when the United States was pushing towards a more national and urban identity. However, critics of the movement claim that it created an inequity between those who embraced the new national identity, calling themselves "realists," and those who wished to hold on to regional traditions, disparagingly called "regionalists" by the first group. Both sides agree that a key feature of regionalist stories is a strong emphasis on setting to such a degree that the actual plot of the story is minimized. By emphasizing the local setting, customs, and dialects associated with their chosen region, regionalist authors were also _____

Which choice most logically completes the text?

(A) helping future generations within a region have access to the histories of their ancestors.

(B) adapting stories from one particular region so that they may be understood at a national level.

(C) expanding the gap between realists and regionalists by focusing only on one of the two groups.

(D) recording the local flavor of a region at a time when some worried such things may soon be lost.

CONTINUE ➡

14 ☐ Mark for Review

Aboard the *Voyager 1* and *Voyager 2* spacecraft are the Voyager Golden Records, which hold images and sounds meant to convey the diversity of life and culture on Earth. While the records are intended to communicate with any extraterrestrial life forms that may find _____ the spacecraft are not heading for any particular destinations as they travel through interstellar space.

Which choice completes the text so that it conforms to the conventions of Standard English?

(A) them, and

(B) them,

(C) them

(D) them and

15 ☐ Mark for Review

American author Justin Torres's novel *We the Animals* is a semi-autobiographical story about growing up in rural upstate New York. The novel depicts the _____ and how he eventually broke away from his family.

Which choice completes the text so that it conforms to the conventions of Standard English?

(A) protagonist's childhood with his two brothers'

(B) protagonists childhood with his two brothers

(C) protagonists childhood with his two brothers'

(D) protagonist's childhood with his two brothers

16 ☐ Mark for Review

Many sundials have a motto inscribed on the dial _____ these mottos usually reference human mortality and the passing of time, although some are more humorous in nature, such as "I count only the sunny hours."

Which choice completes the text so that it conforms to the conventions of Standard English?

(A) face;

(B) face,

(C) face

(D) face and

17 ☐ Mark for Review

The first woman to receive a pilot's license in the United _____ Harriet Quimby, successfully flew across the English Channel on April 16, 1912. However, her accomplishment received little attention, as the *Titanic* sank the day before her flight.

Which choice completes the text so that it conforms to the conventions of Standard English?

(A) States:

(B) States

(C) States,

(D) States;

CONTINUE ➡

18 ☐ Mark for Review

Known as a leader of the Harlem Renaissance, poet Langston Hughes was an early innovator of jazz _____ his writing career also included plays, short stories, nonfiction books, and a weekly newspaper column in *The Chicago Defender*.

Which choice completes the text so that it conforms to the conventions of Standard English?

- (A) poetry. Though
- (B) poetry: though
- (C) poetry, though
- (D) poetry; though

19 ☐ Mark for Review

Sunbeams that occur when the Sun is above or below a layer of clouds are known as crepuscular _____ occurring around sunrise and sunset, they received their name from the Latin word for twilight, *crepusculum*.

Which choice completes the text so that it conforms to the conventions of Standard English?

- (A) rays and generally
- (B) rays. Generally
- (C) rays, generally
- (D) rays generally

20 ☐ Mark for Review

In a photo taken in 1921 at the University of Chicago's Yerkes Observatory, several male scientists are easily recognizable, including physicist Albert Einstein and astronomer Edward E. Barnard. _____ the eight women in the photo were unknown to present-day researchers until librarian Andrea Twiss-Brooks and her team uncovered the women's stories.

Which choice completes the text with the most logical transition?

- (A) Similarly,
- (B) By contrast,
- (C) In fact,
- (D) Thus,

21 ☐ Mark for Review

For hundreds of years, the gorkon, a type of stone pot, was used to cook foods in northern Pakistan. _____ the arrival of modern appliances and easier cooking techniques led to the decreased popularity of the gorkon. Nevertheless, some restaurants have started using the traditional pot again.

Which choice completes the text with the most logical transition?

- (A) However,
- (B) Consequently,
- (C) Indeed,
- (D) For example,

CONTINUE ➤

22 ☐ Mark for Review

Coast Guard employee Sally Snowman is known as the last official lighthouse keeper in the United States. The lighthouse she tended, Boston Light Beacon, was recently sold by the US government to a private owner. _____ Snowman retired from her position after twenty years of service.

Which choice completes the text with the most logical transition?

Ⓐ Instead,

Ⓑ In other words,

Ⓒ However,

Ⓓ Consequently,

23 ☐ Mark for Review

People who live in hotter countries tend to eat spicier food than do people living in colder countries. _____ Indonesia, Thailand, and Kenya all have hot climates and some of the spiciest food in the world. The reason for this correlation is still under investigation, although researchers have suggested several possible theories.

Which choice completes the text with the most logical transition?

Ⓐ For example,

Ⓑ Likewise,

Ⓒ Furthermore,

Ⓓ Therefore,

24 ☐ Mark for Review

Until recently, scientists believed that the genus *Cyclopes* consisted of one species, the silky anteater. Scientist Flávia Miranda studied the DNA of the silky anteater and found that there may be more than one species in the genus. _____ Miranda and her team proposed that there are seven distinct species of silky anteaters.

Which choice completes the text with the most logical transition?

Ⓐ Still,

Ⓑ Nevertheless,

Ⓒ Specifically,

Ⓓ Furthermore,

CONTINUE ➔

_ _

25 ☐ Mark for Review

While researching a topic, a student has taken the following notes:

- Stephanie Wilson became a NASA astronaut in 1996.
- She participated in three space missions.
- She spent over 42 days in space.
- Jessica Watkins became a NASA astronaut in 2017.
- She participated in one space mission.
- She spent over 120 days in space.

The student wants to compare the lengths of time the two women spent in space. Which choice most effectively uses relevant information from the notes to accomplish this goal?

(A) Astronaut Stephanie Wilson participated in three space missions and spent over 42 days in space.

(B) Some of the astronauts at NASA have spent over a month in space.

(C) Both Stephanie Wilson and Jessica Watkins became astronauts with NASA and spent time in space.

(D) Astronaut Jessica Watkins spent over 120 days in space, while astronaut Stephanie Wilson spent over 42 days in space.

26 ☐ Mark for Review

While researching a topic, a student has taken the following notes:

- Ursula Vernon is an American writer and artist who writes books for adults under the pen name T. Kingfisher.
- Her fantasy novel _Nettle and Bone_ was published in 2022.
- _Nettle and Bone_ is a fairy tale that focuses on the character Marra.
- Marra must go through a series of trials in order to rescue her sister Kania.

The student wants to describe _Nettle and Bone_ to an audience unfamiliar with Ursula Vernon. Which choice most effectively uses relevant information from the notes to accomplish this goal?

(A) Marra is a character in Vernon's _Nettle and Bone_ who is trying to rescue her sister.

(B) In _Nettle and Bone_, a 2022 fantasy novel by American writer Ursula Vernon, the character Marra must undergo a series of trials to rescue her sister Kania.

(C) Vernon's 2022 novel _Nettle and Bone_, which is a fantasy book, is about Marra rescuing her sister Kania.

(D) Ursula Vernon's novel _Nettle and Bone_ was published in 2022.

CONTINUE ➡

27 Mark for Review

While researching a topic, a student has taken the following notes:

- African penguins have unique patterns of black dots on their white bellies.
- In a recent study, Luigi Baciadonna investigated whether African penguins can recognize each other using the dots.
- He presented a penguin with a photo of its mate and a photo of another penguin from the colony.
- The penguins in the study spent more time looking at and standing next to the photos of their mates.
- When the pattern of dots on the penguins' bellies was removed from the photos, the penguins didn't spend time with either one.
- The findings suggest that the penguins use the patterns of dots to recognize each other.

The student wants to present the study and its findings. Which choice most effectively uses relevant information from the notes to accomplish this goal?

(A) The patterns of dots on African penguins' bellies was the focus of a recent study.

(B) In a recent study, Baciadonna wanted to find out whether African penguins could recognize each other based on their patterns of dots.

(C) A recent study by Baciadonna suggested that African penguins could recognize their mates by looking at the unique patterns of dots on their bellies.

(D) In a recent study, Baciadonna presented African penguins with photos of both their mates and other members of their colony.

YIELD
Once you've finished (or run out of time for) this section, use the answer key to determine how many questions you got right. If you got fewer than 14 questions right, move on to Module 2—Easier, otherwise move on to Module 2—Harder.

Test 1—Reading and Writing
Module 2—Easier

Turn to Section 1 of your answer sheet to answer the questions in this section.

---

1 ☐ Mark for Review

The Bair Hugger, a temperature regulation system employed in hospital surgical theaters, is manufactured by the 3M Corporation. While the system requires disposable components such as warming blankets, the main component of the system is a warming unit, which is reusable. The warming unit of the Bair Hugger operates using both convection and radiation, each of which works to _____ warm air across the patient's skin.

Which choice completes the text with the most logical and precise word or phrase?

(A) conduct

(B) chill

(C) diminish

(D) withdraw

2 ☐ Mark for Review

Studying how recreation affects mental state, Yesol Kim, Soomin Hong, and Mona Choi found that older adults who play "serious games" were less _____ than those who do not incorporate such games into their routine. Serious games, a type of digital intervention involving the use of video games for rehabilitation and education, can be combined with physical activity, and patients who chose to include physical activity into their serious games experienced an even greater reduction in feelings of sadness than those who played the games without physical activity.

Which choice completes the text with the most logical and precise word or phrase?

(A) ruthless

(B) truthful

(C) depressed

(D) organized

CONTINUE

3 ☐ Mark for Review

Born in 1938, engineer and artist Alfred H. Qöyawayma works as a sculptor and potter of the Hopi Nation, and many of his stunning creations are centered on maize (corn) and its central role in Hopi religion and culture. One of Qöyawayma's pots, featuring a motif of this culturally _____ crop, was taken aboard a mission to the International Space Station in 2002.

Which choice completes the text with the most logical and precise word or phrase?

Ⓐ sustainable

Ⓑ significant

Ⓒ unassuming

Ⓓ puzzling

4 ☐ Mark for Review

Damage tolerance, a term used in civil, mechanical, and aerospace engineering, refers to the capacity of a structure to withstand defects and still serve its purpose until it can be mended. A structure can be considered damage tolerant if there is in place a maintenance program that will _____ and repair any damage (such as corrosion or cracks due to fatigue) that would reduce the residual strength to unsafe levels. Under the damage tolerance definition, the program must also be able to alert personnel to any damage that it has flagged but cannot repair on its own.

Which choice completes the text with the most logical and precise word or phrase?

Ⓐ empty

Ⓑ disrupt

Ⓒ withhold

Ⓓ detect

5 ☐ Mark for Review

Examining data involving both second-hand smoke and asthma, researchers Jiacheng Liu and Dinh Bui found _____: using previously published data on the familial histories of 1,689 children who grew up in Tasmania, Liu and Bui calculated that the risk of non-allergenic asthma in a child increases by 59% if the child's father was exposed to secondhand smoke and by 72% if the child's father was exposed to secondhand smoke and then becomes a smoker himself.

Which choice completes the text with the most logical and precise word or phrase?

Ⓐ an obstacle

Ⓑ an inconsistency

Ⓒ a correlation

Ⓓ a curiosity

6 ☐ Mark for Review

The following text is adapted from Horace Walpole's 1764 novel *The Castle of Otranto*.

Manfred's impatience for this ceremonial was remarked by his family and neighbours. The former, indeed, apprehending the severity of their Prince's disposition, did not dare to utter their surmises on this precipitation.

As used in the text, what does the word "apprehending" most nearly mean?

Ⓐ Recognizing

Ⓑ Supporting

Ⓒ Ignoring

Ⓓ Questioning

CONTINUE ▶

7 ☐ Mark for Review

Occurring 252 million years ago, an extinction event known commonly as the "Great Dying" eliminated over ninety percent of living species. A recent study of a reptile fossil from that time might offer new understanding about the Great Dying's aftermath. A team of scientists used tomographic scanning technology and microscopy to produce 3D renderings of a *Palacrodon* specimen from Antarctica. Kelsey Jenkins, lead author of the study, claims that these replications could bridge gaps in our understanding of evolutionary development. *Palacrodon* had a transitional form of hearing, between the vibration-detecting ear of earlier reptiles and the modern reptile ear capable of hearing high frequencies.

Which choice best describes the function of the underlined portion in the text as a whole?

Ⓐ It emphasizes a contrast between two theories regarding an extinction event.

Ⓑ It presents Kelsey Jenkins's remarks about an obstacle that she and her colleagues faced.

Ⓒ It introduces an assertion that explains the significance of the study.

Ⓓ It highlights the unexpected nature of the determination of the study.

8 ☐ Mark for Review

The following text is adapted from Ann Radcliffe's 1794 novel *The Mysteries of Udolpho*. Monsieur Quesnel was speaking in private with Monsieur St. Aubert, who now returns to the room where his wife Madame St. Aubert is.

The subject of this conversation was not known; but, whatever it might be, St. Aubert, when he returned to the supper-room, seemed much disturbed, and a shade of sorrow sometimes fell upon his features that alarmed Madame St. Aubert. When they were alone she was tempted to enquire the occasion of it, but the delicacy of mind, which had ever appeared in his conduct, restrained her: she considered that, if St. Aubert wished her to be acquainted with the subject of his concern, he would not wait on her enquiries.

Which choice best describes the main purpose of the text?

Ⓐ To explain the reason that Madame St. Aubert is alarmed and describe how her husband comforts her

Ⓑ To demonstrate that a wife desires to ask what is troubling her husband but ultimately decides against doing so

Ⓒ To show that Madame St. Aubert does not dare to enquire of her husband any questions during supper time

Ⓓ To stress that Monsieur St. Aubert will eventually reveal the reason that he is feeling sorrow following the conversation with Monsieur Quesnel

CONTINUE ➤

9 ☐ Mark for Review

Text 1

For decades, musicologists have discussed the heritage of Flamenco, a musical tradition dating back to the 18th century. Some assert that Flamenco is defined by its origins in Andalusia, the southernmost region of peninsular Spain, making the art form a Spanish tradition. Such proponents of the "Andalusian thesis" maintain that Flamenco draws heavily from both Andalusian folklore and the Spanish language and has been a national symbol of Spanish identity since the Francoist dictatorship.

Text 2

Flamenco isn't purely a product of Spain. In fact, the tradition of Flamenco music has roots in the Romani people, whose ancestors settled in the Andalusian region of Southern Spain after migrating from the Indian subcontinent centuries ago. Since the 1700s, *Gitanos*, or the Romani people of Spain, have taught their own particular family styles of Flamenco in the home and played Flamenco to celebrate weddings and traditional crafts such as metalsmithing.

Based on the texts, how would the author of Text 2 most likely regard the perspective of the Andalusian thesis proponents, as described in Text 1?

(A) As incomplete, because the Andalusian thesis doesn't account for the entire scope of influences on Flamenco

(B) As insensitive, because the Andalusian thesis disregards other Spanish musical traditions

(C) As improbable, since the Andalusian thesis proponents have no way of supporting their assertions

(D) As irrational, since the Andalusian thesis proponents don't consider Andalusia part of Spain

10 ☐ Mark for Review

The following text is from Amy Lowell's 1916 book *Men, Women and Ghosts*, a collection of narrative poems.

> I walk down the patterned garden-paths
> In my stiff, brocaded gown.
> With my powdered hair and jewelled fan,
> I too am a rare pattern.
> Just a plate of current fashion,
> Tripping by in high-heeled, ribboned shoes.
> Not a softness anywhere about me,
> Only whalebone and brocade.
> And I sink on a seat in the shade
> Of a lime tree. For my passion
> Wars against the stiff brocade.

Based on the text, in what way is the narrator's attire like the garden?

(A) It is memorable despite conflicting aesthetics.

(B) It becomes increasingly brittle from exposure to the elements.

(C) It draws attention from onlookers.

(D) It incorporates elements of structure into its design.

CONTINUE

11 ☐ Mark for Review

Moon Disc Visibility by Lunar Phase

Lunar phase	Portion illuminated by sunlight	Visibility timeframe
New moon	0%	(during solar eclipse only)
Waxing crescent	0–50%	late morning to after dusk
First quarter	50.1%	afternoon and early evening
Waxing gibbous	50–100%	late afternoon and early nighttime
Full moon	100%	nighttime

For a research project, an astronomy student needs to determine in which lunar phase the moon has afternoon visibility and is no more than half illuminated by sunlight. Based on the attributes of five lunar phases, she decides to choose the _____

Which choice most effectively uses data from the table to complete the text?

(A) full moon.

(B) waxing gibbous.

(C) first quarter.

(D) waxing crescent.

12 ☐ Mark for Review

Springhaven is an 1887 novel by R. D. Blackmore. In the novel, Blackmore portrays Miss Dolly Darling as having undergone a transformation in her demeanor: _____

Which quotation from *Springhaven* most effectively illustrates the claim?

(A) "She was always longing for something sweet and thrilling and romantic, and what chance of finding it in this dull place, even with the longest telescope? For the war, with all its stirring rumors and perpetual motion on shore and sea, and access of gallant visitors, was gone for the moment, and dull peace was signed."

(B) "Although she pretended to be so merry, and really was so self-confident (whenever anybody wanted to help her), Miss Dolly Darling, when left to herself, was not like herself, as it used to be. For although she was not given, any more than other young people are, to plaguesome self-inspection, she could not help feeling that she was no longer the playful young Dolly that she loved so well."

(C) "[She] let young Dolly take the course of her own stubbornness. Dolly had a good start, and growing much excited with the petulance of the wind and with her own audacity, crossed the mouth of the brook at a very fine pace, with the easterly gusts to second her."

(D) "Miss Dolly Darling could not be happy without a little bit of excitement, though it were of her own construction. Her imagination, being bright and tender and lively, rather than powerful, was compelled to make its own material, out of very little stuff sometimes."

CONTINUE →

---

13 ☐ Mark for Review

The Importance of Being Earnest is an 1895 play by Oscar Wilde. Jack, a country boy and the play's main character, chooses to live a double life as Ernest, a member of high-society. As he prepares to reveal this ruse to a woman with whom he has fallen in love, he attempts to distance himself from his chosen disguise, when he says to her _____

Which quotation from *The Importance of Being Earnest* most effectively illustrates the claim?

Ⓐ "For heaven's sake, don't try to be cynical. It's perfectly easy to be cynical."

Ⓑ "Merriman, order the dog-cart at once. Mr. Ernest has been suddenly called back to town."

Ⓒ "Personally, darling, to speak quite candidly, I don't much care about the name of Ernest...I don't think the name suits me at all."

Ⓓ "When one is placed in the position of guardian, one has to adopt a very high moral tone on all subjects."

CONTINUE ➤

Participant Responses When Surveyed on Their Experiences Wearing Continuous Glucose Monitors (CGM)

Statement	Disagree (%)	Neutral (%)	Agree (%)	Strongly Agree (%)
Gave me insight into my body's reaction to food	0	0	35	65
Was valuable to my medical education	0	0	15	85
Will help me better serve patients	0	0	25	75
Encouraged me to change my eating behavior	5	30	50	15
Medical students should get the opportunity to wear a CGM	0	0	20	80

14 ☐ Mark for Review

Harvard Medical School researcher Nicholas G. Norwitz and colleagues studied ways to integrate nutrition instruction into already dense medical school curricula. They recruited medical school students to wear continuous glucose monitors (CGM) and report the impact of the experience on their understanding and perspective on nutrition. Participants all agreed that the educational benefit was positive, but not all agreed that it would lead them to a lifestyle change; for example, _____.

Which choice most effectively uses data from the table to complete the example?

(A) 80% of participants strongly agreed that future medical students should get the opportunity to wear a CGM, and another 20% of participants agreed with this statement.

(B) 100% of participants agreed or strongly agreed that wearing a CGM gave them insight into their body's reaction to food, but 35% didn't agree that it would encourage them to change their own eating behavior.

(C) 65% of participants agreed or strongly agreed that wearing a CGM encouraged them to change their own eating behavior, but 35% of participants were either neutral or disagreed with this statement.

(D) 100% of participants agreed or strongly agreed that wearing a CGM was valuable to their medical education, and 85% of these responses strongly agreed with this statement.

CONTINUE ➡

15 ☐ Mark for Review

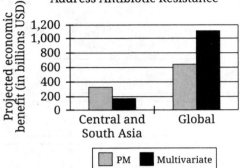

Projected Economic Benefits in 2050
of Applying Two Different Methods to
Address Antibiotic Resistance

Antibiotic resistance is a growing global concern, resulting in millions of deaths worldwide every year, and particulate matter (PM) pollution is believed to be a significant factor in global antibiotic resistance. A study done by Zhenchao Zhou and colleagues analyzed global data and ran models to predict antibiotic resistance trends until 2050 based on two potential courses of preventative measures: limiting only the amount of PM air pollution or instead applying a multivariate combination of increasing health expenditure, reducing antibiotic use, providing basic drinking water services, and applying PM pollution control. The team found that while multivariate factors would lead to the largest possible economic benefit due to reduced antibiotic resistance on a global scale, PM control alone was the better option for certain regions of the world.

Which choice best describes data from the graph that support Zhou and colleagues' conclusion?

(A) PM control in Central and South Asia predicted about half of the economic benefit as PM control did globally.

(B) Multivariate control in Central and South Asia predicted a significantly lower economic benefit than multivariate control at the global scale.

(C) PM control in Central and South Asia predicted a greater economic benefit than did multivariate control in that region.

(D) Multivariate control in Central and South Asia predicted a greater economic benefit than PM control in Central and South Asia.

16 ☐ Mark for Review

Cysteine is an amino acid used in many important biological processes and was thought to only be produced by the cystathionine β-synthase (*CBS*) enzyme in the *CBS* gene. A study led by Dr. Octavio Salazar generated a high-quality genome of the coral *Acropora loripes*, which was believed to have lost the *CBS* gene and thus the ability to synthesize cysteine; however, the resulting genome found that the coral was able to synthesize cysteine, even though it lacked the *CBS* gene. The researchers hypothesized that the genetic makeup of *A. loripes* allows it to produce the needed *CBS* enzyme without the presence of the *CBS* gene.

Which finding, if true, would most directly support the researchers' hypothesis?

(A) When examined, *A. loripes* contains no traces of the amino acid cysteine.

(B) Other corals of the same genus were found to have the ability to synthesize cysteine and contained the *CBS* gene.

(C) Though *A. loripes* was able to synthesize cysteine, it did not produce the amino acid in similar quantities found in other corals.

(D) The suspected cysteine-producing gene found in *A. loripes* was found in other organisms that can produce cysteine but similarly lack the *CBS* gene.

CONTINUE ➤

---

17 ☐ Mark for Review

One feature consistent with each of the Egyptian pyramids is a central shaft that extends from the pharaoh's main burial chamber through the top of the pyramid. Some historians have suggested that this shaft provided a path for the pharaoh's soul to reach the afterlife, since the Egyptians believed that the night sky was a gateway to the heavens, but others claim that the shaft was merely symbolic and not intended as an actual physical pathway. The fact that the shaft is always included in the same orientation in each pyramid, however, _____

Which choice most logically completes the text?

(A) creates a challenge for those attempting to understand the pyramid's construction.

(B) may mean that the shaft had some significance to the Egyptians.

(C) suggests that the pharaoh's soul required a path to reach the afterlife.

(D) removes the possibility that the shaft was merely symbolic.

18 ☐ Mark for Review

Navajo physicist Fred Begay, also known as Clever Fox, had a research career in the laser program at Los Alamos National Laboratory that spanned nearly 30 years. Much of his work _____ on the use of lasers to control nuclear fusion reactions.

Which choice completes the text so that it conforms to the conventions of Standard English?

(A) to focus

(B) focused

(C) focusing

(D) having focused

19 ☐ Mark for Review

Despite their association with Chinese cuisine, fortune cookies actually _____ their way from Japan to California sometime between the 1880s and early 1900s.

Which choice completes the text so that it conforms to the conventions of Standard English?

(A) made

(B) will make

(C) have made

(D) were making

20 ☐ Mark for Review

The nesting strategies of mourning doves, small-headed doves with soft, long calls that are common across North America, can vary widely depending on habitat availability. While these birds usually nest in trees, they also inhabit environments with limited tree availability, _____ them to adapt and construct nests on the ground or on human-made structures.

Which choice completes the text so that it conforms to the conventions of Standard English?

(A) spurred

(B) spurs

(C) to spur

(D) spurring

CONTINUE ➡

21 ⚑ Mark for Review

People with Restless Leg Syndrome—also known as Willis-Ekbom Disease—experience unpleasant sensations in their legs that often result in uncontrollable leg movements. These uncomfortable sensations are often most severe at night, and _____ can severely disrupt sufferers' sleeping patterns.

Which choice completes the text so that it conforms to the conventions of Standard English?

- (A) it
- (B) they
- (C) one
- (D) you

22 ⚑ Mark for Review

Senegalese dancer and choreographer Germaine Acogny is often referred to as "the mother of African contemporary dance." Audiences worldwide have applauded her _____ that transcend language barriers.

Which choice completes the text so that it conforms to the conventions of Standard English?

- (A) works' deeply expressive messages'
- (B) works deeply expressive messages
- (C) works deeply expressive messages'
- (D) works' deeply expressive messages

23 ⚑ Mark for Review

Geneticist Jennifer Doudna co-developed CRISPR-Cas9, a gene-editing technology that enables precise modifications to DNA sequences and holds immense potential for medical _____ other scientists have voiced ethical concerns due to the possibility of unintended consequences in the use of such a powerful tool for altering the building blocks of life.

Which choice completes the text so that it conforms to the conventions of Standard English?

- (A) advancements, but
- (B) advancements
- (C) advancements,
- (D) advancements but

24 ⚑ Mark for Review

In her captivating photography series "Fa'a fafine: In a Manner of a Woman," Samoan artist Shigeyuki Kihara employs visual storytelling _____ the complex experiences and identities of fa'a fafine individuals, who are considered a third gender in Samoan culture.

Which choice completes the text so that it conforms to the conventions of Standard English?

- (A) explored
- (B) explores
- (C) to explore
- (D) is exploring

CONTINUE ➡

25 🔖 Mark for Review

When a cat is confronted by a bear, the cat's physiological response is characterized by an increase in heart rate, elevated levels of stress hormones, and heightened muscle tension until this state of heightened arousal _____ a cascade of aggressive behaviors, including snarling, unsheathing its claws, and lunging forward, as the cat instinctively prepares to defend itself against the perceived threat.

Which choice completes the text so that it conforms to the conventions of Standard English?

- Ⓐ will trigger
- Ⓑ had triggered
- Ⓒ triggers
- Ⓓ triggered

26 🔖 Mark for Review

The Family and Medical Leave Act (FMLA) guarantees eligible employees up to 12 weeks of unpaid leave each year to care for a newborn, a newly adopted child, or a seriously ill family member. This act was proposed in Congress every year from 1984 to 1993 but faced fierce opposition from business interests. _____ the FMLA was signed into law by President Bill Clinton on February 5, 1993.

Which choice completes the text with the most logical transition?

- Ⓐ Finally,
- Ⓑ Additionally,
- Ⓒ Instead,
- Ⓓ Likewise,

27 🔖 Mark for Review

Hundreds of millions of years ago, an ancestral mammalian lineage evolved viviparity, or live birth. Some scientists have theorized that viviparity provides evolutionary benefits over egg laying, including protection from parasites and predators. However, not all mammals give birth to live offspring. The duck-billed platypus, _____ lays its eggs in a burrow.

Which choice completes the text with the most logical transition?

- Ⓐ meanwhile,
- Ⓑ in addition,
- Ⓒ for example,
- Ⓓ nevertheless,

STOP
**If you finish before time is called, you may check your work on this module only.
Do not turn to any other module in the test.**

Test 1—Reading and Writing
Module 2—Harder

Turn to Section 1 of your answer sheet to answer the questions in this section.

DIRECTIONS

The questions in this section address a number of important reading and writing skills. Each question includes one or more passages, which may include a table or graph. Read each passage and question carefully, and then choose the best answer to the question based on the passage(s).

All questions in the section are multiple-choice with four answer choices. Each question has a single best answer. Fill in the circle with the answer letter for the answer you think is best.

---

1 ☐ Mark for Review

The research done by chemical engineer Frances Arnold is intended to make the production and development of enzymes less _____ to the environment. Arnold's work focuses on accelerating the natural processes by which enzymes are produced, and the end goal of such acceleration is to limit the damage done to the ecosystem when such production takes place over a longer period of time.

Which choice completes the text with the most logical and precise word or phrase?

(A) detrimental

(B) favorable

(C) fundamental

(D) palliative

2 ☐ Mark for Review

Scientists have predicted that speech patterns and socialization often _____, as humans rely on verbal and non-verbal feedback from others as a way to learn, grow, and recreate. Jonathan Harrington and his colleagues at the Institute of Phonetics and Speech Processing in Germany tested this hypothesis by analyzing the speech patterns of a group of individuals who were isolated together at a research station in Antarctica: the analysis revealed that each subject had developed hints of a similar accent to each other during the isolation period that quickly dissipated once each individual returned to society at large.

Which choice completes the text with the most logical and precise word or phrase?

(A) correlate

(B) triumph

(C) capitulate

(D) diverge

CONTINUE

---

3 🔖 Mark for Review

Most scientists had believed that the earliest evidence of hominid (human ancestor) cooking dates from 170,000 years ago, but a team of researchers from three different universities claims that the presence of fish remains at an Israeli archaeological site _____ a need for an adjustment to that belief. The remains, which date back 780,000 years, show clear signs of having been exposed to flame and bear hominid teeth marks.

Which choice completes the text with the most logical and precise word or phrase?

Ⓐ circumvents

Ⓑ refutes

Ⓒ suppresses

Ⓓ indicates

4 🔖 Mark for Review

A psychological phenomenon known as the anchoring effect explains how a person's judgments are affected by a referential "anchor." An example of anchoring is the practice of positioning an item for sale near a more expensive one to _____ the customer into thinking the item's price is reasonable or even inexpensive, whether or not it actually is.

Which choice completes the text with the most logical and precise word or phrase?

Ⓐ extort

Ⓑ persuade

Ⓒ reprimand

Ⓓ counsel

CONTINUE ➡

5 ☐ Mark for Review

The following text is adapted from Thomas Hardy's 1874 novel *Far from the Madding Crowd*. The main character, Gabriel Oak, has just been introduced to a woman named Bathsheba with whom he becomes smitten.

"I am sorry," he said, the instant after, regretfully.

"What for?"

"Letting your hand go so quickly."

"You may have it again if you like; there it is." She gave him her hand again.

Oak held it longer this time—indeed, <u>curiously</u> long. "How soft it is—being winter time, too—not chapped or rough or anything!" he said.

"There—that's long enough," said she, though without pulling it away. "But I suppose you are thinking you would like to kiss it? You may if you want to."

As used in the text, what does the word "curiously" most nearly mean?

(A) Demandingly

(B) Imploringly

(C) Disinterestedly

(D) Notably

6 ☐ Mark for Review

In 1966, computer scientist Joseph Weizenbaum developed a computer program known as ELIZA that was capable of having text conversations with human users. Upon its release, ELIZA succeeded remarkably well in drawing out emotional reactions from those conversing with it. According to Weizenbaum, many human users erroneously described ELIZA's algebraic computations as "knowing," "thinking," or "understanding." Weizenbaum later wrote of his surprise that such fleeting exposure to a computer program would result in illogical conclusions drawn by test subjects deemed to be logical thinkers. This projection of human characteristics onto a computer program would later be called the ELIZA Effect.

Which choice best states the main purpose of the text?

(A) To emphasize how popular ELIZA was

(B) To detail how computer programs function

(C) To describe both Weizenbaum's work with ELIZA and the ELIZA effect

(D) To call attention to Weizenbaum's computer development background

CONTINUE ➡

7 ☐ Mark for Review

The following text is from the 1812 poem "If Sometimes in the Haunts of Men" by English poet Lord Byron.

> Oh, pardon that in crowds awhile
> I waste one thought I owe to thee,
> And self-condemned, appear to smile,
> Unfaithful to thy memory:
>
> Nor deem that memory less dear,
> That then I seem not to repine;
> I would not fools should overhear
> One sigh that should be wholly *thine*.

Which choice best states the main purpose of the text?

(A) To convey how responsibility for the death of a loved one has contributed to a feeling of guilt

(B) To ponder whether positive emotions experienced as part of a crowd are more powerful than the negative emotions one can feel when alone

(C) To clarify that a momentary lapse in focus does not diminish the gravity of emotion felt towards another

(D) To discount the possibility that memories are less important than new experiences are

8 ☐ Mark for Review

On the Thursday preceding each Easter Sunday, a night procession known as *Za križen* takes place on Hvar, a Croatian island in the Adriatic Sea. Conducted regularly for over 500 years, the ceremony holds special religious and cultural significance for the inhabitants of central Hvar. Taking eight hours and covering 25 kilometers, the procession has as its centerpiece the *Gospin plač*, or Lady's Weeping: a fifteenth-century sung text that tells the story of Jesus's crucifixion. The tradition was added to UNESCO's List of Intangible Cultural Heritage in 2009.

Which choice best describes the function of the underlined portion in the text as a whole?

(A) It offers additional insight into lives of the inhabitants of Hvar mentioned earlier in the text.

(B) It further describes a central component of a celebration discussed earlier in the text.

(C) It presents an illustration of a social dynamic of the island of Hvar given earlier in the text.

(D) It emphasizes a possible inconsistency with the length and breadth of the ceremony discussed earlier in the text.

CONTINUE →

9 ☐ Mark for Review

Text 1

Citing previous studies that have found correlations between poverty and increased risk of death, Aaron Richterman and colleagues found that subsidy payments from governments to citizens led to significantly lower mortality rates among women and children under five years old and the reduction in mortality rate increased roughly correlated to the monetary value of the payment. Richterman claimed that the team's findings lend support to the use of government anti-poverty programs such as cash transfers, employed by an increased number of countries since the COVID-19 pandemic, in order to increase overall population well-being.

Text 2

Economist Eeshani Kandpal argues against increasing government cash transfer payments uninhibitedly. The natural desire to protect members of one's own species is understandable, but Kandpal claims that cash transfers have negative benefits for nonbeneficiaries. For example, Kandpal showed that targeted cash transfers greatly raised prices of protein-rich foods that were perishable, which resulted in a 34% increase in stunted growth among nonbeneficiary children.

Based on the texts, how would Kandpal (Text 2) respond to the claim made by Richterman (Text 1)?

Ⓐ By asserting that the cash transfer payments discussed in Text 1 are actually examples of beneficial government subsidies rather than harmful ones

Ⓑ By conceding that it is more natural to want to protect members of one's own species than those of another species

Ⓒ By questioning the logic in Text 1, as it has not been verified that government subsidies can protect an individual family

Ⓓ By cautioning against unwaveringly supporting an initiative, as there are possible consequences to the practice of that initiative

10 ☐ Mark for Review

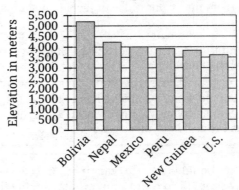

Countries with the Highest Approximate Elevation of Alpine Tree Line

The tree lines of alpine, or mountainous, regions are primarily determined by environmental limits such as high winds, extreme cold, and heavy snowfall. Excessive snow cover shortens the growing season, but a moderate amount of snow insulates and hydrates, so even some cold, snowy habitats at high elevations can support trees. According to a survey conducted by the National Institute of Health, the elevation of the alpine tree line of Bolivia is over 5,000 meters, and that of _____

Which choice most effectively uses data from the graph to complete the text?

Ⓐ Peru is between 4,500 and 5,000 meters.

Ⓑ the US is between 3,500 and 4,000 meters.

Ⓒ Mexico is less than 3,000 meters.

Ⓓ Nepal and that of New Guinea are each greater than 4,000 meters.

CONTINUE

11 🔖 Mark for Review

In "Hyperion," an 1820 poem by John Keats, the author directly addresses his Muse, imploring her to narrow his focus from many possible subjects to just one: _____

Which quotation from "Hyperion" most effectively illustrates the claim?

(A) "O tell me, lonely Goddess, by thy harp / That waileth every morn and eventide / Tell me why thus I rave, about these groves!"

(B) "Why should I tell thee what thou so well seest? / Why should I strive to show what from thy lips / Would come no mystery?"

(C) "I see, astonished, that severe content / Which comes of thought and musing: give us help!"

(D) "O leave them, Muse! O leave them to their woes / For thou art weak to sing such tumults dire / A solitary sorrow best befits thy lips."

12 🔖 Mark for Review

In 1903, an approximately 10,000-year-old human male skeleton was excavated from Gough's Cave in Somerset, England. Although many think that the humans who migrated to the British Isles over 45,000 years ago soon adapted light-colored eyes and pale skin to protect against UV light and maintain vitamin D levels, recent DNA testing of the fossilized remains indicates that the two adaptations may not have occurred together. The fossil has genetic markers for blue-green eye color and dark skin; according to one researcher, this suggests that the region's Mesolithic humans exhibited the phenotype of light eyes significantly earlier than that of light complexions.

Which finding, if true, would most directly weaken the underlined claim?

(A) A different set of Mesolithic human remains discovered in the area dates to the same time period and had DNA profiles consistent with blue eyes and light skin.

(B) Light-colored eyes were a common adaptation for the Mesolithic humans who migrated to Europe.

(C) More than a dozen DNA samples from modern Somerset residents have genetic links to the human male remains excavated from Gough's Cave.

(D) It would have taken many centuries for light complexions to become the dominant phenotype amongst people who had migrated from sub-Saharan Africa.

CONTINUE ➡

13 ☐ Mark for Review

Maximum Sea Levels Before and After an
18.61-Year Diurnal Lunar Cycle

Bioregion	Mean sea level, 1993–2020	Maximum sea level, 1993–2020	Maximum sea level, 1993–2006	Maximum sea level, 2007–2020
Gulf of Carpentaria (linear rate of change from previous year, in mm)	3.43	3.47	6.97	−25.29
Carnarvon (linear rate of change from previous year, in mm)	5.37	2.19	−14.12	6.17

After an 18.61-year lunar nodal cycle ended in 2006, a nodal diurnal tide maxima (a type of high tide) occurred on Australia's coastlines, along which are the Gulf of Carpentaria and the town of Carnarvon. Analysis showed that this tide maxima led to increased sea levels for years afterwards. However, on the Gulf of Carpentaria, an atypically-weak monsoon wet season in 2015–2016 resulted in reduced rainfall for the area. Geomorphologists Monica Mulrennan and Colin Woodruffe believe that the weak monsoon season counteracted the effects of the tide maxima on sea levels for the Gulf of Carpentaria, given that _____

Which choice most effectively uses data from the table to complete the statement?

Ⓐ from 1993–2020, the Gulf bioregion experienced a general increase in mean sea level and a general decrease in maximum sea level, which suggests a reversal of the tide maxima.

Ⓑ for both the Gulf bioregion and Carnarvon, mean and maximum sea levels generally increased from 1993–2020 despite the 2006 nodal diurnal tide maxima and the weak 2015–2016 monsoon wet season.

Ⓒ for the Gulf bioregion, maximum sea levels decreased from 2007–2020 while maximum sea levels increased for Carnarvon during the same time period.

Ⓓ from 1993–2020, the mean sea level was substantially lower for the Gulf bioregion than it was for Carnarvon, but the Gulf bioregion had a higher maximum sea level.

CONTINUE →

14 ☐ Mark for Review

With over 50 honorary degrees, Maya Angelou was widely recognized for her civil rights activism and her works of both fiction and nonfiction. In an essay on Angelou's writing, a student claims that Angelou blended multiple genres by infusing her autobiographies with elements of music, poetry, and storytelling.

Which quotation from a literary critic best supports the student's claim?

Ⓐ "Angelou's first autobiography depicts her introduction to poetry by Mrs. Bertha Flowers, a schoolteacher and family friend, and how reading and eventually reciting poetry with Mrs. Flowers helped Angelou overcome a fear of speaking aloud."

Ⓑ "For one book, an autobiographical work describing the author's youth, Angelou approached her narrative like a balladeer, drawing from oral traditions such as personal testimonies, recitations of poetry, African-American folklore, and even the Blues."

Ⓒ "Angelou gained widespread recognition for her eight autobiographies, including *I Know Why the Caged Bird Sings*, long before being invited to recite her poem 'On the Pulse of Morning' at the 1993 American presidential inauguration."

Ⓓ "Many of Angelou's poems are marked by the writer's use of style elements usually associated with autobiographies, such as a first-person point of view and the incorporation of chronology."

CONTINUE →

---

15 ☐ Mark for Review

Glow Worm Signal Detection in Y-Maze Under Increasing Illumination Intensities

Illumination level	Illumination intensity (lumens per square meter)	Probability of reaching signal	Average number of males reaching signal per trial	Average time to reach signal (seconds)
Bright light	90	0.233	6.0	136.55
Low light	45	0.467	15.0	48.25
Darkness	0	0.855	28.0	27.8

Zoologist Jeremy Niven and colleagues explored artificial lighting's impacts on the nocturnal mating behavior of common glow worms (*Lampyris noctiluca*), a species whose females employ a bioluminescent glow to "signal" males. The researchers tested *L. noctiluca* males' ability to detect female-mimicking LED light sources in a *y*-maze under increasing illumination intensities. Based on the results, the researchers concluded that higher illumination intensity reduced the likelihood of detection while prolonging the time taken for successful detections.

Which choice uses data from the table to most effectively support the researchers' conclusion?

Ⓐ The lowest number of males successfully reached the LED signal in darkness, but the probability of reaching the signal increased as illumination intensity increased.

Ⓑ The difference in average time taken to reach the signal was smaller between the low light and darkness conditions and larger between the low light and bright light conditions.

Ⓒ Males in low light and darkness needed less time to reach the signal and had a greater probability of reaching the signal than did those in bright light.

Ⓓ Males in bright light conditions experienced double the illumination intensity compared with males in low light but took substantially longer to successfully reach the LED signal than males in low light did.

CONTINUE

16 🔖 Mark for Review

In her research on the psychology of learning, Shana Carpenter explores spacing, or the inverse of the "cramming" approach. This strategy entails learning less content in each study session and extending the time between sessions—even extending the time long enough to forget some material. As Carpenter notes, leaving enough time to forget material before returning to it may seem counterintuitive to learners, especially high-level learners like doctoral candidates. But according to Carpenter's study, medical students who completed surgical training in a single day remembered less both one week and one year post-training than did their counterparts who completed equivalent training in abbreviated sessions over three weeks. Thus, the spacing method may _____

Which choice most logically completes the text?

(A) prove effective for retaining complex information long-term despite short-term setbacks.

(B) more strongly foster data retention in learners than traditional methods of studying do.

(C) hold broader appeal for medical students than for other postgraduates.

(D) lead many students who use the method to pursue more rigorous coursework and higher-level degree programs over time.

17 🔖 Mark for Review

Environmental scientists at McGill University compiled data on how people around the world typically allocate time—and energy—to model a "global human day." Most people spend roughly an hour each day on transportation but cover vastly different distances in that same amount of time as their methods, and thus their energy expenditures, are highly dependent on both the local economy and the environment. The model suggests that focusing on decreasing the energy spent moving about by the hour rather than by the kilometer could help improve sustainability efforts worldwide. Therefore, to reduce human transportation's environmental impact, _____

Which choice most logically completes the text?

(A) people who typically spend significantly more than an hour each day on transportation will need to adapt to a global human day.

(B) local governments should offer incentives for developing more time-efficient methods of public transportation.

(C) people may need to limit time spent using energy for transportation.

(D) similar studies that model energy expenditures of transportation methods by time and distance may need to be implemented worldwide.

CONTINUE ➡

18 ☐ Mark for Review

The cellulose nitrate-based film used to record many early motion pictures _____ spontaneously if improperly stored, causing over 70 percent of American movies from the Silent Era to have been irretrievably lost.

Which choice completes the text so that it conforms to the conventions of Standard English?

(A) combusts

(B) have combusted

(C) combust

(D) were combusting

19 ☐ Mark for Review

Art Deco architecture, which rose in popularity in the 1920s, represented an optimistic and forward-looking style that utilized modern materials such as stainless steel and aerodynamic lines inspired by the latest technology. Other influences were much _____ many of the decorative elements found on Art Deco façades were drawn from the art of ancient Egyptian and Mayan civilizations.

Which choice completes the text so that it conforms to the conventions of Standard English?

(A) older, however;

(B) older, however,

(C) older, however

(D) older; however,

20 ☐ Mark for Review

The three most familiar types of volcanoes are shield volcanoes, which produce gentle flows of liquid _____ stratovolcanoes, which produce viscous lava and erupt violently; and cinder cones, made up of rock fragments called scoria formed during the eruption of magma rich in gas.

Which choice completes the text so that it conforms to the conventions of Standard English?

(A) lava,

(B) lava:

(C) lava;

(D) lava

21 ☐ Mark for Review

The first step in acrylic painting is the application of _____ layers of pre-mixed pigment that coat the canvas and ensure that the paint adheres properly.

Which choice completes the text so that it conforms to the conventions of Standard English?

(A) gesso. Successive

(B) gesso: successive

(C) gesso; successive

(D) gesso successive

CONTINUE

- -

22 ☐ Mark for Review

In 1966, labor activist Dolores Huerta cofounded the United Farm Workers, formed as a merger of two smaller unions in response to the Delano grape strike, which _____ the year before. Huerta served as the lead negotiator on behalf of the striking farmworkers and managed to obtain significant concessions from the California grape-growing companies that were the targets of the strike.

Which choice completes the text so that it conforms to the conventions of Standard English?

Ⓐ begins

Ⓑ had begun

Ⓒ was beginning

Ⓓ will begin

23 ☐ Mark for Review

A recent research study by neuroscientist Melanie Furrer and colleagues explains how reindeer are able to feed nearly constantly during the long days of the Arctic _____ the deer examined in the study continued to chew on vegetation as they entered a state of non-REM sleep, as measured by electrodes attached to their heads.

Which choice completes the text so that it conforms to the conventions of Standard English?

Ⓐ summer,

Ⓑ summer while

Ⓒ summer

Ⓓ summer:

24 ☐ Mark for Review

Fusion reactors have long been proposed as a source of abundant energy with a number of safety advantages over existing nuclear power plants, but their use has been hampered by the difficulty of achieving net energy gain. _____ as currently designed, fusion reactors require more energy to achieve the high temperatures needed to initiate fusion than the energy they produce.

Which choice completes the text with the most logical transition?

Ⓐ Nevertheless,

Ⓑ Furthermore,

Ⓒ That is,

Ⓓ For instance,

CONTINUE →

25 ▢ Mark for Review

While researching a topic, a student has taken the following notes:

- Roman politician Marcus Junius Brutus led a conspiracy to assassinate Julius Caesar in 44 BCE.
- Brutus was a character in Italian poet Dante Alighieri's most famous work, the *Divine Comedy*, completed around 1321 CE.
- The *Divine Comedy* portrays Brutus as a traitor to Caesar and the Roman state.
- Irish author Jonathan Swift included the ghost of Brutus as a character in his 1726 work *Gulliver's Travels*.
- *Gulliver's Travels* depicts Brutus as a heroic rebel against tyranny.

The student wants to emphasize a difference between two literary portrayals of Brutus. Which choice most effectively uses relevant information from the notes to accomplish this goal?

(A) While Dante Alighieri portrayed Brutus as a traitor, Jonathan Swift depicted him as a heroic rebel against tyranny.

(B) The leader of a plot to assassinate Julius Caesar, Brutus is portrayed as a traitor by Dante Alighieri.

(C) Marcus Junius Brutus is a controversial historical figure, with different later authors portraying his character in different ways.

(D) Jonathan Swift portrayed Brutus as a heroic rebel in his work *Gulliver's Travels*.

26 ▢ Mark for Review

While researching a topic, a student has taken the following notes:

- Homer Hans Bryant is the founder and artistic director of the Chicago Multicultural Dance Center.
- He has been credited with the invention of hiplet, a fusion of ballet and hip-hop dancing.
- The term "hiplet" was coined in 2009.
- In 1992, Hans Bryant choreographed a dance called "Rap Ballet."
- "Rap Ballet" was the first work recognized as belonging to the genre of hiplet.

The student wants to explain the significance of one of Hans Bryant's works. Which choice most effectively uses relevant information from the notes to accomplish this goal?

(A) Hiplet dancing was first choreographed in 1992, although the term itself was only coined in 2009.

(B) Homer Hans Bryant, founder and artistic director of the Chicago Multicultural Dance Center, choreographed the dance "Rap Ballet."

(C) Hiplet was first performed in 1992 and was invented by Hans Bryant.

(D) Hans Bryant choreographed "Rap Ballet," the first work belonging to the genre of hiplet, which fuses ballet and hip-hop dancing.

CONTINUE ➡

---

27 ☐ Mark for Review

While researching a topic, a student has taken the following notes:

- Some biologically important molecules are amphiphilic, meaning that they have both polar and nonpolar parts.

- These molecules often form special 3D structures when dissolved in water.

- Many amphiphilic molecules contain long hydrocarbon chains.

- Fatty acid salts are amphiphilic molecules that contain one hydrocarbon chain and a carboxylate group.

- Phospholipids are amphiphilic molecules that contain two hydrocarbon chains and a phosphate group.

The student wants to emphasize a similarity between two types of molecules. Which choice most effectively uses relevant information from the notes to accomplish this goal?

(A) Molecules with both polar and nonpolar parts often form special 3D structures in a water solution.

(B) Many amphiphilic molecules contain hydrocarbon chains, but the number of these chains varies depending on the type of molecule.

(C) Like many other amphiphilic molecules, both fatty acid salts and phospholipids contain hydrocarbon chains.

(D) While fatty acid salts contain a carboxylate group, phospholipids contain a phosphate group instead.

STOP
**If you finish before time is called, you may check your work on this module only.
Do not turn to any other module in the test.**

THIS PAGE LEFT INTENTIONALLY BLANK.

Test 1—Math
Module 1

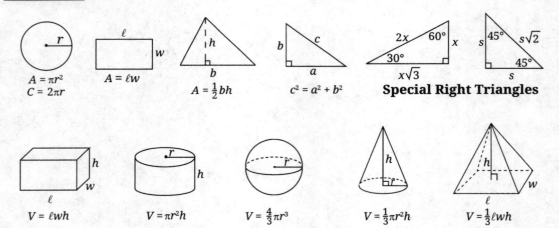

CONTINUE

——

For multiple-choice questions, solve each problem, choose the correct answer from the choices provided, and then fill in the circle with the answer letter. Enter only one answer for each question. You will not get credit for questions with more than one answer entered or for questions with no answers entered.

For student-produced response questions, solve each problem and write your answer in the test book as described below.

- Enter your answer into the box provided.
- If you find **more than one correct answer**, enter only one answer.
- Your answer can be up to 5 characters for a **positive** answer and up to 6 characters (including the negative sign) for a **negative** answer.
- If your answer is a **fraction** that is too long (over 5 characters for positive, 6 characters for negative), write the decimal equivalent.
- If your answer is a **decimal** that is too long (over 5 characters for positive, 6 characters for negative), truncate it or round at the fourth digit.
- If your answer is a **mixed number** (such as $3\frac{1}{2}$), write it as an improper fraction (7/2) or its decimal equivalent (3.5).
- Don't enter **symbols** such as a percent sign, comma, or dollar sign in your answer.

CONTINUE ➡

1 ☐ Mark for Review

$$8, 11, 11, 15, 16, 23$$

What is the mean of the data shown?

(A) 11

(B) 13

(C) 14

(D) 15

2 ☐ Mark for Review

Which of the following expressions is equivalent to $90z - (10z - 40z)$?

(A) $40z$

(B) $60z$

(C) $80z$

(D) $120z$

3 ☐ Mark for Review

If $56 - 4a = 24$, what is the value of $14 - a$?

[____]

4 ☐ Mark for Review

A car moves at a constant speed of 55 miles per hour with no stops. At this rate, how many miles will the car have traveled after 7 hours?

(A) 48

(B) 62

(C) 385

(D) 547

5 ☐ Mark for Review

	Striped	Speckled	Solid	Total
Fish	0	3	13	16
Insect	3	6	4	13
Bird	2	11	8	21
Total	5	20	25	50

The table shows the distribution of animal type and pattern for a deck of 50 flashcards that each display a picture of one animal. If one card is selected at random, what is the probability that the animal on the card is speckled? (Express your answer as a decimal or a fraction, not as a percent.)

[____]

CONTINUE →

6 Mark for Review

What is the value of $7p$ if $5(7p + 6) + 2p = 30p - 5$?

_____

7 Mark for Review

The function f is defined by the equation $f(x) = x^2 + 5$. Which table gives three values of x and their corresponding values of $f(x)$ for function f?

Ⓐ

x	$f(x)$
–2	9
–1	6
0	5

Ⓑ

x	$f(x)$
–2	1
–1	3
0	5

Ⓒ

x	$f(x)$
–2	3
–1	4
0	5

Ⓓ

x	$f(x)$
–2	9
–1	6
0	6

8 Mark for Review

A rower crosses a lake with a width of 1.2 miles while rowing directly from one shore to another at a constant rate of 5 miles per hour. Which of the following function types best represents the relationship between the rower's distance from the starting shore and the time rowed?

Ⓐ Decreasing exponential

Ⓑ Decreasing linear

Ⓒ Increasing exponential

Ⓓ Increasing linear

9 Mark for Review

Out of a school of 300 students, 50 were chosen at random and asked to sample a new flavor of an energy drink and provide their opinions in a survey. Based on the results of the survey, it is estimated that 66% of students in the school dislike the flavor, with an associated margin of error of 9%. Based on these results, which of the following is a reasonable value for the total number of students in the school who dislike the new flavor?

Ⓐ 17

Ⓑ 33

Ⓒ 114

Ⓓ 188

CONTINUE

10 Mark for Review

What is the negative solution to the equation

$x + 1 = \frac{72}{x}$?

_____

11 Mark for Review

The ratio of a certain parallelogram's height to its base is 40 to 75. If the parallelogram's base is decreased by 9 inches, how must the height change to maintain the same ratio?

(A) It must decrease by 4.8 inches.

(B) It must increase by 4.8 inches.

(C) It must decrease by 9 inches.

(D) It must increase by 9 inches.

12 Mark for Review

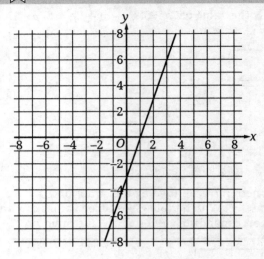

The graph of $y = h(x) - 12$ is shown. Which of the following equations defines the function h?

(A) $h(x) = 3x - 15$

(B) $h(x) = 3x + 9$

(C) $h(x) = 3x - 3$

(D) $h(x) = 3x + 12$

CONTINUE

13 🔖 Mark for Review

$$-5x^2 + y = -578$$
$$20x = 7 - y$$

The graphs of the equations in the given system of equations intersect at the point (x, y) in the xy-plane. Which of the following is a possible value of y?

Ⓐ −13

Ⓑ 4

Ⓒ 173

Ⓓ 267

14 🔖 Mark for Review

Distance (meters)	Relative sound intensity
0	80.00
1	20.00
2	5.00
3	1.25

A sound technician is identifying the safest location to place speakers for an event. The table shows the relationship between the distance d, in meters, that the technician is from the source of the sound and the relative sound intensity I of the sound. Which of the following equations best represents the relationship between d and I if nothing other than the distance is adjusted?

Ⓐ $I = 0.75(1 - 80)^d$

Ⓑ $I = (1 - 80)^d$

Ⓒ $I = (1 - 0.75)^d$

Ⓓ $I = 80(1 - 0.75)^d$

15 🔖 Mark for Review

$$-7(-10 - 30x) = 30(7x + 2)$$

How many solutions does the given equation have?

Ⓐ Zero

Ⓑ Exactly one

Ⓒ Exactly two

Ⓓ Infinitely many

16 🔖 Mark for Review

What is the volume, in cubic feet, of a right rectangular pyramid with a base length of 10 feet, a base width of 15 feet, and a height of 20 feet?

Ⓐ 45

Ⓑ 1,000

Ⓒ 3,000

Ⓓ 9,000

CONTINUE ➡

---

17 ☐ Mark for Review

$$7a - 3b = c$$

The given equation relates the numbers a, b, and c. Which equation correctly expresses b in terms of a and c?

(A) $b = \frac{7}{3}a - c$

(B) $b = \frac{7a - c}{3}$

(C) $b = \frac{-7a - c}{3}$

(D) $b = -3c - 7a$

18 ☐ Mark for Review

Circle O and circle P are graphed in the xy-plane. Circle O has the equation $(x-3)^2 + (y+3)^2 = 81$, and circle P has the equation $(x-12)^2 + (y+12)^2 = 9$. The length of the radius of circle O is how many times the length of the radius of circle P?

☐

19 ☐ Mark for Review

In triangle ABC, angle B is a right angle. If $\sin(A) = \frac{40}{41}$, what is the value of $\sin(C)$?

☐

20 ☐ Mark for Review

In function g, $g(-1) = -5$ and $g(0) = -2$. Which equation defines linear function g?

(A) $g(x) = -2x - 2$

(B) $g(x) = 3x$

(C) $g(x) = 3x - 2$

(D) $g(x) = 3x - 5$

21 ☐ Mark for Review

An online store has a promotion in which the first 5 pairs of sunglasses that a customer buys cost $39 each and each additional pair of sunglasses costs $13. If a customer buys p pairs of sunglasses, and $p \geq 5$, which function h gives the total cost, in dollars, for all the sunglasses the customer buys?

(A) $h(p) = -65 + 52p$

(B) $h(p) = 39 + 13p$

(C) $h(p) = 130 + 13p$

(D) $h(p) = 195 + 13p$

22 ☐ Mark for Review

In the xy-plane, a parabola has the equation $y = -3x^2 + 5x$. If a line with the equation $3y = k$ intersects the parabola at exactly one point, and k is a constant, what is the value of k?

YIELD

Once you've finished (or run out of time for) this section, use the answer key to determine how many questions you got right. If you got fewer than 14 questions right, move on to Module 2—Easier, otherwise move on to Module 2—Harder.

THIS PAGE LEFT INTENTIONALLY BLANK.

Test 1—Math
Module 2—Easier

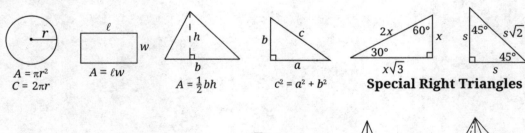
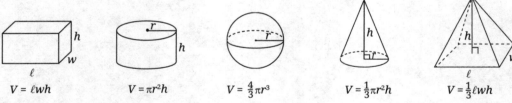
CONTINUE

_____

For multiple-choice questions, solve each problem, choose the correct answer from the choices provided, and then fill in the circle with the answer letter. Enter only one answer for each question. You will not get credit for questions with more than one answer entered or for questions with no answers entered.

For student-produced response questions, solve each problem and write your answer in the test book as described below.

- Enter your answer into the box provided.
- If you find **more than one correct answer,** enter only one answer.
- Your answer can be up to 5 characters for a **positive** answer and up to 6 characters (including the negative sign) for a **negative** answer.
- If your answer is a **fraction** that is too long (over 5 characters for positive, 6 characters for negative), write the decimal equivalent.
- If your answer is a **decimal** that is too long (over 5 characters for positive, 6 characters for negative), truncate it or round at the fourth digit.
- If your answer is a **mixed number** (such as $3\frac{1}{2}$), write it as an improper fraction (7/2) or its decimal equivalent (3.5).
- Don't enter **symbols** such as a percent sign, comma, or dollar sign in your answer.

---

1 ☐ Mark for Review

What is the value of x if $35 + x = 75$?

2 ☐ Mark for Review

A shipment of chocolate bars contains 8,000 chocolate bars, and 2,000 of the chocolate bars contain nuts. What percentage of the chocolate bars in the shipment contains nuts?

Ⓐ 25%

Ⓑ 40%

Ⓒ 60%

Ⓓ 75%

3 ☐ Mark for Review

A triangle has a base of 6 inches (in) and a height of 11 in. What is the area of the triangle?

Ⓐ 17 in²

Ⓑ 33 in²

Ⓒ 66 in²

Ⓓ 289 in²

4 ☐ Mark for Review

$$5y^3 + 12y^2 - 4y^2$$

Which expression is equivalent to the given expression?

Ⓐ $5y^3 - 48y^4$

Ⓑ $5y^3 + 8y^2$

Ⓒ $13y^3$

Ⓓ $17y^3 - 4y^2$

5 ☐ Mark for Review

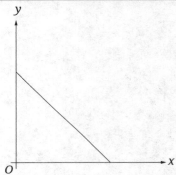

The graph represents the total distance a marathon runner is from home, in kilometers, after x minutes of a practice run. The runner starts the run at a park and ends the run at her home. She runs at a constant rate for her entire practice run. In this context, what is the best interpretation of the y-intercept of the graph?

Ⓐ The distance the runner is from her home at the end of the run

Ⓑ The runner's rate of speed

Ⓒ The minimum distance the runner is from home during the run

Ⓓ The distance the park is from the runner's home

CONTINUE ➤

---

6 ⬛ Mark for Review

In triangle XYZ, if angle Z measures $32°$ and angle Y measures $103°$, what is the measure of angle X?

Ⓐ $19°$

Ⓑ $45°$

Ⓒ $71°$

Ⓓ $135°$

7 ⬛ Mark for Review

In a group of 200 campers, 65% brought their own sleeping bags. How many campers brought their own sleeping bags?

[　　　]

8 ⬛ Mark for Review

$$g(x) = -3 + x^2$$

The function g is defined by the given equation. What is the value of $g(4)$?

Ⓐ -12

Ⓑ 3

Ⓒ 5

Ⓓ 13

9 ⬛ Mark for Review

Anna decides to make 36 free throws as part of her basketball warmup. She makes an average of 3 free throws per minute. For how many minutes must Anna shoot free throws in order to reach her goal?

Ⓐ 3

Ⓑ 8

Ⓒ 12

Ⓓ 36

10 ⬛ Mark for Review

If $18 - 7(x-2) = -6(x-2)$, what is the value of $x - 2$?

Ⓐ 16

Ⓑ 18

Ⓒ 19

Ⓓ 20

CONTINUE ➡

_____

11 ☐ Mark for Review

Ismael is working on a novel. He handwrites for h minutes, types for t minutes, and writes a total of 1,065 words. He can handwrite 20 words per minute and type 40 words per minute. Which of the following equations best represents this situation?

Ⓐ $\frac{1}{20}h + \frac{1}{40}t = 17.75$

Ⓑ $\frac{1}{20}h + \frac{1}{40}t = 1,065$

Ⓒ $20h + 40t = 1,065$

Ⓓ $20h + 40t = 63,900$

12 ☐ Mark for Review

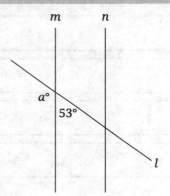

Note: Figure not drawn to scale

In the figure, parallel lines m and n are intersected by line l. What is the value of a?

13 ☐ Mark for Review

$$f(x) = 4x - 5$$

The function f is defined by the given equation. What is the value of $f(x)$ when $x = 5$?

Ⓐ 4

Ⓑ 5

Ⓒ 15

Ⓓ 25

14 ☐ Mark for Review

$$\frac{8x + 40}{64}$$

The expression $\frac{x + a}{8}$, where a is a constant, is equivalent to the given expression. What is the value of a?

Ⓐ $\frac{1}{8}$

Ⓑ 5

Ⓒ 56

Ⓓ 320

CONTINUE

15 ☐ Mark for Review

The equation $4x - 10y = 45$ is graphed in the xy-plane. The x intercept is $(c, 0)$, and the y-intercept is $(0, k)$, where c and k are constants. What is the value of $\frac{c}{k}$?

Ⓐ $-\frac{5}{2}$

Ⓑ $-\frac{2}{5}$

Ⓒ $\frac{2}{5}$

Ⓓ $\frac{5}{2}$

16 ☐ Mark for Review

Which of the following expressions is equivalent to $x^2 - 16x + 28$?

Ⓐ $(x - 2)(x - 14)$

Ⓑ $(x + 2)(x + 14)$

Ⓒ $(x + 4)(x + 7)$

Ⓓ $(x - 4)(x - 7)$

17 ☐ Mark for Review

$$22F + 12T = 500$$

In a certain video game, players can make combinations of cards that are worth different numbers of coins depending on the number of cards the combination contains. One player earned a total of 500 coins by making F four-card combinations and T three-card combinations. If the given equation represents this game situation, how many fewer coins is a three-card combination worth than a four-card combination?

[   ]

18 ☐ Mark for Review

The number of water hyacinths in a pond decreases by $\frac{1}{3}$ every week after the start of winter. There are 2,200 water hyacinths in the pond at the start of winter. If $0 < w < 7$, which equation represents the number of water hyacinths, h, in the pond w weeks after the start of winter?

Ⓐ $h = \frac{2}{3}(2{,}200)^w$

Ⓑ $h = 3(2{,}200)^w$

Ⓒ $h = 2{,}200\left(\frac{2}{3}\right)^w$

Ⓓ $h = 2{,}200(3)^w$

19 ☐ Mark for Review

A work site requires at least 81,000 kg of concrete. The concrete is delivered by 32 mixer trucks. Due to losses, each mixer truck delivers 9% less concrete than it was loaded with initially. Which of the following is closest to the minimum mass of concrete, in kg, that needs to be loaded in each truck initially for the work site to receive enough concrete?

Ⓐ 2,250

Ⓑ 2,303

Ⓒ 2,531

Ⓓ 2,782

CONTINUE ➤

- -

20 ☐ Mark for Review

In the equation $0 = 45x^2 + 60x + c$, c is a constant. If the equation has no real solutions, which of the following is a possible value of c?

Ⓐ -20

Ⓑ 15

Ⓒ 20

Ⓓ 25

21 ☐ Mark for Review

$$q = \frac{23}{17 + r}$$

The given equation relates the numbers q and r, where $r < 17$ and $q \neq 0$. Which equation correctly expresses r in terms of q?

Ⓐ $r = \frac{23}{q} - 17$

Ⓑ $r = 17 - \frac{23}{q}$

Ⓒ $r = \frac{17 - q}{23}$

Ⓓ $r = \frac{23}{17 - q}$

22 ☐ Mark for Review

x	$h(x)$
-3	41
-2	0
-1	-41

Three values of x and their corresponding values of $h(x)$ for function h are shown in the table. If function h is defined by the equation $h(x) = px + q$, where p and q are constants, what is the value of $p + q$?

Ⓐ -123

Ⓑ -82

Ⓒ -43

Ⓓ 0

STOP

**If you finish before time is called, you may check your work on this module only.
Do not turn to any other module.**

THIS PAGE LEFT INTENTIONALLY BLANK.

Test 1—Math
Module 2—Harder

The questions in this section address a number of important math skills.
Use of a calculator is permitted for all questions.

NOTES

Unless otherwise indicated:

- All variables and expressions represent real numbers.
- Figures provided are drawn to scale.
- All figures lie in a plane.
- The domain of a given function f is the set of all real numbers x for which $f(x)$ is a real number.

REFERENCE

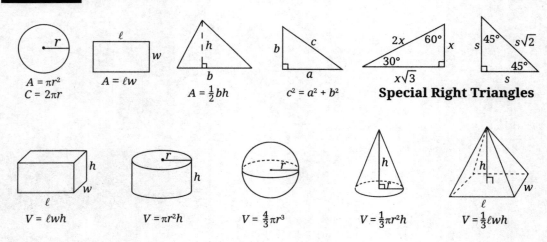

$A = \pi r^2$
$C = 2\pi r$

$A = \ell w$

$A = \frac{1}{2}bh$

$c^2 = a^2 + b^2$

Special Right Triangles

$V = \ell wh$

$V = \pi r^2 h$

$V = \frac{4}{3}\pi r^3$

$V = \frac{1}{3}\pi r^2 h$

$V = \frac{1}{3}\ell wh$

The number of degrees of arc in a circle is 360.
The number of radians of arc in a circle is 2π.
The sum of the measures in degrees of the angles of a triangle is 180.

CONTINUE

For multiple-choice questions, solve each problem, choose the correct answer from the choices provided, and then fill in the circle with the answer letter. Enter only one answer for each question. You will not get credit for questions with more than one answer entered or for questions with no answers entered.

For student-produced response questions, solve each problem and write your answer in the test book as described below.

- Enter your answer into the box provided.
- If you find **more than one correct answer**, enter only one answer.
- Your answer can be up to 5 characters for a **positive** answer and up to 6 characters (including the negative sign) for a **negative** answer.
- If your answer is a **fraction** that is too long (over 5 characters for positive, 6 characters for negative), write the decimal equivalent.
- If your answer is a **decimal** that is too long (over 5 characters for positive, 6 characters for negative), truncate it or round at the fourth digit.
- If your answer is a **mixed number** (such as $3\frac{1}{2}$), write it as an improper fraction (7/2) or its decimal equivalent (3.5).
- Don't enter **symbols** such as a percent sign, comma, or dollar sign in your answer.

1 ☐ Mark for Review

$$61, 61, 72, 75, 75, 75, 81, 81$$

Which of the following frequency tables correctly represents the data listed?

Ⓐ

Number	Frequency
122	61
72	72
225	75
162	81

Ⓑ

Number	Frequency
61	2
72	1
75	3
81	2

Ⓒ

Number	Frequency
2	61
1	72
3	75
2	81

Ⓓ

Number	Frequency
61	122
72	72
75	225
81	162

2 ☐ Mark for Review

The number a is 47 greater than the number b. Which equation represents this situation?

Ⓐ $a = \frac{1}{47}b$

Ⓑ $a = b - 47$

Ⓒ $a = b + 47$

Ⓓ $a = 47b$

3 ☐ Mark for Review

x	y
-3	-12
0	-6
3	0
6	6

The table shows four values of x and their corresponding values of y. Which of the following linear equations represents the relationship between x and y?

Ⓐ $y = -3x - 6$

Ⓑ $y = 2x - 6$

Ⓒ $y = -3x - 12$

Ⓓ $y = 2x - 12$

CONTINUE ▶

4 ☐ Mark for Review

The anticipated profit $p(x)$, in dollars, of a lemonade stand that sells x cups of lemonade can be modeled by the function $p(x) = 0.5x - 12$. According to this model, what is the anticipated profit, in dollars, of selling 120 cups of lemonade at this stand?

(A) 48

(B) 72

(C) 84

(D) 108

5 ☐ Mark for Review

The function h is defined by the equation $h(x) = (7.5)(5)^x$. What is the y-intercept of the graph of $y = h(x)$ in the xy-plane?

(A) $(0, 0)$

(B) $(0, 5)$

(C) $(0, 7.5)$

(D) $(0, 37.5)$

6 ☐ Mark for Review

A bookstore has 118,400 books for sale. The bookstore has 12 regular sections and 3 children's sections. The equation $12x + 3y = 118,400$ represents this situation. Which of the following is the best interpretation of x in this context?

(A) The total number of books in the regular sections

(B) The total number of books in the children's sections

(C) The average number of books per children's section

(D) The average number of books per regular section

7 ☐ Mark for Review

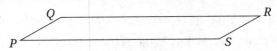

Note: Figure not drawn to scale

In parallelogram $PQRS$, the length of $\overline{PQ}$ is one-fourth the length of $\overline{PS}$. If the perimeter of the parallelogram is 60 inches, what is the length, in inches, of $\overline{RS}$?

(A) 6

(B) 12

(C) 15

(D) 24

---

8 ☐ Mark for Review

The equation $4x - 10y = 45$ is graphed in the xy-plane. The x intercept is $(c, 0)$, and the y-intercept is $(0, k)$, where c and k are constants. What is the value of $\frac{c}{k}$?

Ⓐ $-\frac{5}{2}$

Ⓑ $-\frac{2}{5}$

Ⓒ $\frac{2}{5}$

Ⓓ $\frac{5}{2}$

9 ☐ Mark for Review

$$\frac{8x + 40}{64}$$

The expression $\frac{x + a}{8}$, where a is a constant, is equivalent to the given expression. What is the value of a?

Ⓐ $\frac{1}{8}$

Ⓑ 5

Ⓒ 56

Ⓓ 320

10 ☐ Mark for Review

Rectangle $ABCD$ has an area of 140 square inches. If the width of the rectangle is z inches, and its length is 4 inches greater than its width, what is the value of z?

Ⓐ 10

Ⓑ 14

Ⓒ 24

Ⓓ 35

11 ☐ Mark for Review

Samantha saved a total of $320 to buy a prom dress. She first saved a gift of $75 that she received from her grandparents, and then saved $5 dollars a day for d days. Which of the following equations represents this situation?

Ⓐ $5d - 75 = 320$

Ⓑ $5d + 75 = 320$

Ⓒ $75d - 5 = 320$

Ⓓ $75d + 5 = 320$

CONTINUE

12 ☐ Mark for Review

$$y = 3x - 4$$
$$2y = 6x + 20$$

In the xy-plane, at how many points do the graphs of the given equations intersect?

(A) Exactly one

(B) Exactly two

(C) Infinitely many

(D) Zero

13 ☐ Mark for Review

$$7x + 2y = 28$$
$$13x + 4y = 52$$

If (x, y) is the solution to the given system of equations, what is the value of x?

(A) −4

(B) 0

(C) 4

(D) 8

14 ☐ Mark for Review

The function g is defined by the equation $g(x) = -3x^2 - 27x - 74$. For what value of x does $g(x)$ reach its maximum?

15 ☐ Mark for Review

$$4x - \frac{1}{5} = 3ky$$
$$8x - 45y = 1 - 12x$$

The given system of equations has infinitely many solutions. If k is a constant, what is the value of k?

16 ☐ Mark for Review

The equation $v = -\frac{1}{2}m^2 + 15m + 6$ represents the value v, in thousands of dollars, of a business investment m months after the initial investment was made. In this context, which number represents the initial value, in thousands of dollars, of the business investment?

(A) $-\frac{1}{2}$

(B) 0

(C) 6

(D) 15

CONTINUE →

17 ☐ Mark for Review

$$AB = 99$$
$$BC = 168$$
$$CA = 195$$

The side lengths of right triangle ABC are given. Triangle DEF is similar to triangle ABC, where B corresponds to E and C corresponds to F. What is the value of $\cos(D)$?

(A) $\frac{33}{65}$

(B) $\frac{33}{56}$

(C) $\frac{56}{65}$

(D) $\frac{65}{33}$

18 ☐ Mark for Review

The quadratic function g is graphed in the xy-plane, where $y = g(x)$. The vertex of the graph is $(2, -11)$ and one of its x-intercepts is $\left(\frac{16}{3}, 0\right)$. If the other x-intercept is at (x, y), what is the value of x?

(A) $-\frac{22}{3}$

(B) $-\frac{16}{3}$

(C) $-\frac{4}{3}$

(D) $\frac{10}{3}$

19 ☐ Mark for Review

The hypotenuse of a certain right triangle has a length of 72 units. The acute angles measure 60° and 30°. What is the perimeter, in units, of this triangle?

(A) $36\sqrt{3}$

(B) $72 + 36\sqrt{3}$

(C) $72 + 72\sqrt{3}$

(D) $108 + 36\sqrt{3}$

20 ☐ Mark for Review

When graphed in the xy-plane, line d passes through the origin and is perpendicular to the line represented by the equation $y = -2x + 3$. What is the value of a if line d also passes through the point $(a, 14)$?

CONTINUE ➤

---

21 ☐ Mark for Review

There are exactly 8 positive integers greater than 10 in data set D. The list shown gives 7 of the integers from data set D.

$$18, 25, 17, 19, 27, 26, 29$$

The mean of these 7 integers is 23. If the mean of data set D is an integer that is less than 23, what is the value of the smallest integer from data set D?

22 ☐ Mark for Review

In triangles ABC and DEF, $AC = 11$, $DF = 55$, and angles B and E each measure $85°$. Which additional piece of information is sufficient to prove that triangles ABC and DEF are similar?

Ⓐ The measures of angles A and D are $30°$ and $35°$, respectively.

Ⓑ The measures of angles A and F are $30°$ and $65°$, respectively.

Ⓒ $BC = 6$ and $EF = 6$

Ⓓ $BC = 6$ and $EF = 30$

STOP

**If you finish before time is called, you may check your work on this module only.
Do not turn to any other module.**

Chapter 2
Practice Test 1:
Answers and
Explanations

PRACTICE TEST 1: ANSWER KEY

Reading and Writing		
Module 1	Module 2 (Easier)	Module 2 (Harder)
1. C	1. A	1. A
2. B	2. C	2. A
3. B	3. B	3. D
4. D	4. D	4. B
5. A	5. C	5. D
6. A	6. A	6. C
7. A	7. C	7. C
8. B	8. B	8. B
9. D	9. A	9. D
10. C	10. D	10. B
11. C	11. D	11. D
12. C	12. B	12. A
13. D	13. C	13. C
14. B	14. B	14. B
15. D	15. C	15. C
16. A	16. D	16. A
17. C	17. B	17. C
18. C	18. B	18. A
19. B	19. A	19. A
20. B	20. D	20. C
21. A	21. B	21. B
22. D	22. D	22. B
23. A	23. A	23. D
24. C	24. C	24. C
25. D	25. C	25. A
26. B	26. A	26. D
27. A	27. C	27. C

Math		
Module 1	Module 2 (Easier)	Module 2 (Harder)
1. C	1. 40	1. B
2. D	2. A	2. C
3. 6	3. B	3. B
4. C	4. B	4. A
5. $\dfrac{20}{50}, \dfrac{2}{5},$ or .4	5. D	5. C
6. −35	6. B	6. D
7. A	7. 130	7. A
8. D	8. D	8. A
9. D	9. C	9. B
10. −9	10. B	10. A
11. A	11. C	11. B
12. B	12. 127	12. D
13. D	13. C	13. C
14. D	14. B	14. -4.5
15. A	15. A	15. 3
16. B	16. A	16. C
17. B	17. 10	17. A
18. 3	18. C	18. C
19. $\dfrac{9}{14},$ .2195, 0.219, or 0.220	19. D	19. D
20. C	20. D	20. 28
21. C	21. A	21. 15
22. 6.25 or $\dfrac{25}{4}$	22. A	22. B

PRACTICE TEST 1—READING AND WRITING EXPLANATIONS

Module 1

1. **C** This is a Vocabulary question, as it asks for a *logical and precise word or phrase* to fill in the blank. The blank should describe how the ceremony treats female ancestors, village elders, and goddesses, so look for and highlight clues in the passage about that interaction. Highlight that *one part of the ceremony celebrates the fertility of women as a power over life itself.* A good word for the blank to enter in the annotation box would be "celebrates" or "honors."

    - (A) is wrong because *soothes* doesn't match "celebrates."

    - (B) and (D) are wrong because *critiques* and *neglects* are the **Opposite** tone of "celebrates."

    - (C) is correct because *praises* matches "celebrates."

2. **B** This is a Vocabulary question, as it asks for a *logical and precise word or phrase* to fill in the blank. The blank should describe the experiment conducted by Nirenberg and Matthaei, so look for and highlight clues in the passage about that experiment. Highlight that *scientists developed new processes to determine how many bases made up each codon.* A good word for the blank to enter in the annotation box would be "new" or "first of its kind."

    - (A) and (C) are wrong because *dubious* and *redundant* are the **Opposite** tone of "new," which is being used positively here.

    - (B) is correct because *pioneering* (trailblazing) matches "new."

    - (D) is wrong because *prior* is the **Opposite** of the chronology of the text—the experiment by Nirenberg and Matthaei comes after the experiment by Watson and Frick, not before.

3. **B** This is a Vocabulary question, as it asks for a *logical and precise word or phrase* to fill in the blank. The blank should describe the nature of the work, so look for and highlight clues in the passage about Mucha's *Slav Epic*. Highlight that *the paintings are meant to be analyzed as one piece but are sometimes displayed individually in galleries.* Note also that *Slav Epic* is actually made up of *twenty paintings*, so a good word for the blank to enter in the annotation box would be "grouped" or "unified."

    - (A) is wrong because *elusive* (mysterious) is **Right Answer, Wrong Question**—casual observers who find the work *confusing* might consider it mysterious, but the blank refers to the author's description of the work from the second sentence, not the observers' opinion of the work from the first sentence.

    - (B) is correct because *collective* (a number of things considered as a one group) matches "grouped."

- (C) is wrong because *painstaking* (extremely thorough) goes **Beyond the Text**—Mucha may have needed to be careful and thorough when making *Slav Epic*, but the passage does not state that.

- (D) is wrong because *miniature* is the **Opposite** of something being described as a large collection.

4. **D**   This is a Vocabulary question, as it asks for a *logical and precise word or phrase* to fill in the blank. The blank should describe the interaction between white matter and the symptoms of ADHD, so look for and highlight clues in the passage about that interaction. Highlight *those experiencing ADHD remission demonstrated greater white matter density than those not in remission*. Since *remission* means "a decrease of," a good word for the blank to enter in the annotation box would be "lessening" or "decrease."

- (A) and (C) are wrong because *glorification* and *progression* are the **Opposite** of "lessening."

- (B) is wrong because *visualization* doesn't match "lessening."

- (D) is correct because *reduction* matches "lessening."

5. **A**   This is a Vocabulary question, as it asks for a *logical and precise word or phrase* to fill in the blank. The blank should describe the sense created by the use of the word *yakamoz*, so look for and highlight clues in the passage about the word and the feelings it evokes. Highlight that *most languages need to use several words to describe the same phenomenon*, but *yakamoz* is just a *single word*. Therefore, *yakamoz* does something in a single word that most languages need several words for. A good word for the blank to enter in the annotation box would be "simplicity" or "refinement."

- (A) is correct because *elegance* matches "simplicity" in this context—the word is being praised in the passage for capturing a *visually striking effect* with one word.

- (B), (C), and (D) are wrong because *agitation* (anxiety), *confusion*, and *convolution* (complication) are the **Opposite** tone or meaning of the positive way the word *yakamoz* is described.

6. **A**   This is a Purpose question, as it asks for the *function of the underlined portion* in the passage. Read the passage and highlight clues in the sentences before or after that can help understand the function of the underlined phrase. The earlier part of the sentence states that *When wolves can't use their sharp eyesight, their acute hearing seems to help*. The underlined phrase explains this further by offering a specific example. Therefore, a good function of the underlined sentence to enter in the annotation box would be "explain how wolves use their hearing."

- (A) is correct because it's consistent with the highlighting and annotation.

- (B) is wrong because it contains **Recycled Language**—it misuses *periods of scarcity* from the second sentence, and the passage offers no information about the *group dynamics* of wolf packs.

- (C) is wrong because it's the **Opposite** of what's stated in the first sentence—wolves have *surprisingly varied diets*, not *almost entirely carnivorous diets*.

- (D) is wrong because it goes **Beyond the Text**—the passage offers an example of wolves using their hearing to hunt in *water* but doesn't claim they *prefer to hunt in water rather than on land*.

7. **A** This is a Retrieval question, as it asks for a detail about the *status of the Jackson Oak*. Look for and highlight information about the tree. Since the entire passage refers to the Jackson Oak and its legal status, go straight to the answers after reading the passage and use Process of Elimination. The correct answer should be as consistent as possible with the details presented in the passage.

  - (A) is correct because it's consistent with the final three sentences—while under *US common law* the tree is ineligible to own itself, the *residents and...officials of Athens-Clarke County* have *acknowledged* its self-ownership status, indicating that something other than *legal definitions* is guiding the public's decision.

  - (B) is wrong because it's **Half-Right**—the legality of the Jackson's Oak's self-ownership has come *into question*, but the passage doesn't state that *the surrounding property changed hands*.

  - (C) is wrong because it goes **Beyond the Text**—it's not stated whether or not the tree was popular before the 1890 newspaper article.

  - (D) is wrong because it's **Extreme Language**—while the *municipal officials* have *acknowledged* the tree's self-ownership status, this does not mean they actually *changed the law* for the tree.

8. **B** This is a Retrieval question, as it asks for a detail about the *discovery of Anchitheriomys buceei*. Look for and highlight information about this beaver species. The passage states that the species was first discovered during a period of excavations from *the 1800s through the 1930s*, but after a *more recent partial skull discovery*, much more about the species was discovered using *high-resolution X-ray technology, which wasn't developed until late in the twentieth century*. The correct answer should be as consistent as possible with these details.

  - (A) is wrong because it's **Extreme Language**—the passage does not claim that the *partial skull* would *not have been uncovered* without *high-resolution X-ray technology*. In fact, the technology wasn't said to have been part of the discovery of *A. buccei* at all—rather, it contributed to the analysis of the species.

  - (B) is correct because it's consistent with the highlighted sentences—there were two different time periods in which fossils of *A. buccei* were discovered that each contributed to the understanding of the species.

  - (C) is wrong because it's **Recycled Language**—it misuses *Coastal Plain* and *skeletal structure* from different parts of the passage to make an unsupported claim.

  - (D) is wrong because it's also **Extreme Language**—it's not possible to know from the passage that *A. buccei* would *not have been identified* at all without any one specific individual or team.

9. **D** This is a Main Idea question, as it asks for the *main idea of the text*. Look for and highlight information that can serve as the main idea. The passage states *Researchers have found that fifty species of turtles previously thought to be mute actually vocalize sounds such as purring, hissing, clicking, and chirping*. Since the other sentences explain the process by which this was determined and what its implications may be, the first sentence serves as the main idea. The correct answer should be as consistent as possible with this portion of the passage.

- (A) is wrong because it's **Recycled Language**—it misuses *Podocnemis expansa*, *vocalize*, and *communicative meanings* to create a statement that sounds like something the research team would logically do but not something it actually did in the passage.

- (B) is wrong because it's not stated that any of the species of turtles examined in the passage are *new* discoveries or have *unique* vocalizations.

- (C) is wrong because it's **Right Answer, Wrong Question**—while turtles do vocalize these sounds and the team seems to indicate that this is some form of communication, this is not the main idea of the entire passage. Additionally, *proves* would be **Extreme Language** as the team has only *predicted* and *suggested* certain things about *P. expansa*.

- (D) is correct because it's consistent with the opening sentence, as well as the details regarding both how the team did its research in the second sentence as well as the possible *common ancestors* in the last sentence.

10. **C** This is a Claims question, as it asks which choice *would most effectively illustrate the claim*. Look for and highlight the claim in the passage, which is that *Muir emphasizes the beauty of a landscape that he believes is without parallel*. The correct answer should be as consistent as possible with this claim.

- (A) and (D) are wrong because they're both irrelevant to the claim—stating that he will *see as much as possible of the glacier* or recommending *travel by canoe* addresses neither the *beauty* of the Alaskan landscape nor that such beauty is *without parallel*.

- (B) is wrong because it's **Half-Right**—it describes the Alaskan landscape and implies the author enjoys looking at it but does not say anything strong enough that could support that Muir believes the landscape's beauty is *without parallel*.

- (C) is correct because it's consistent with the highlighted claim—*majestic peaks and glaciers* could be the beauty of the landscape, and *it seemed inconceivable that nature could have anything finer to show us* could mean that Muir believes that the beauty of the Alaskan landscape is *without parallel*.

11. **C** This is a Conclusions question, as it asks what *most logically completes the text*. Look for the main focus of the passage, which is the sonnet cycle method utilized by Browning. Then, highlight the main points made regarding this focus: first, the *method groups sonnets in such a way that they can be read either individually or as a single collection and are written around a common theme*. The passage also states that *the collection received critical acclaim...for the multiple ways in which the work could be read*.

Therefore, Browning was successful in her application of the sonnet cycle method in *Sonnets from the Portuguese*. The correct answer must be as consistent as possible with this conclusion.

- (A) is wrong because it goes **Beyond the Text**—no *other poets* are mentioned, even if it's logical that Browning probably influenced others.

- (B) is wrong because it also goes **Beyond the Text**—it's not stated how aware of Browning's goal the critics were, but they all praised the end result.

- (C) is correct because it's consistent with what the highlighted sentences say about the sonnet cycle method and how it was received.

- (D) is wrong because it's **Extreme Language**—while *Sonnets* was well received, it's not known that is one of Browning's *most* famous works.

12. **C** This is a Conclusions question, as it asks what *most logically completes the text*. Look for the main focus of the passage, which is the theory that the Moon likely formed in a matter of hours. Then, highlight the main points made regarding this focus: first, *Due to the ferocity of the collision, this material would have been expelled violently into space, acting as a catalyst for the rapid formation of the satellite*. The passage also states that when Kegerreis and colleagues tried a simulation with a slower formation time, the result *did not produce a moon with the same mass, orbit, and composition as our current moon*. Therefore, the time it took the moon to form directly affected its mass, orbit, and composition. The correct answer must be as consistent as possible with this conclusion.

- (A) is wrong because it goes **Beyond the Text**—to what extent, if any, Theia *affected the Earth's composition* is not addressed in the passage.

- (B) is wrong because it's the **Opposite** of the passage—the team's simulations suggest that the Moon formed quickly, not more slowly as other theories had posited.

- (C) is correct because it's consistent with what the highlighted sentences say about the Moon's formation and the importance of its formation's timing.

- (D) is wrong because it's **Extreme Language**—while a slower collision may not have expelled the material from Earth as violently, it's impossible to know if *all* of the material would have remained closer to Earth.

13. **D** This is a Conclusions question, as it asks what *most logically completes the text*. Look for the main focus of the passage, which is the American literary regionalist movement. Then, highlight the main points made regarding this focus: first, *the purpose of the movement was to preserve regional culture at a time when the United States was pushing towards a more national and urban identity*. The passage also states that *a key feature of regionalist stories is a strong emphasis on setting*. Therefore, whether the movement was a good or a bad thing, at least some people believed that regionalist stories tried to preserve regional culture by focusing on local settings and all the things associated with them. The correct answer must be as consistent as possible with this conclusion.

- (A) is wrong because it goes **Beyond the Text**—while regionalist stories might preserve some aspects of local culture, it's impossible to say it would preserve the *histories* of any specific individuals.

- (B) is wrong because it's the **Opposite** of what's supported by the passage—regionalist stories were about preserving regional culture, not adapting stories for a broader, or *national*, audience.

- (C) is wrong because it's **Recycled Language**—the words *realists* and *regionalists* and the *inequity* (gap) between them is discussed in the third sentence, but the passage doesn't claim that regionalist authors were *expanding* this gap by publishing their stories.

- (D) is correct because it's consistent with what the highlighted sentences say about the American literary movement and how it was viewed, at least by the author of the 1993 essay and anyone who supports it.

14. **B** In this Rules question, punctuation is changing in the answer choices. The first part of the sentence says *While the records are intended to communicate with any extraterrestrial life forms that may find them*, which is a dependent clause. The rest of the sentence is an independent clause. Eliminate any answer that doesn't correctly connect a dependent + an independent clause.

- (A) and (D) are wrong because a coordinating conjunction (*and*) can't be used with a dependent clause.

- (B) is correct because a comma should be used after the dependent clause.

- (C) is wrong because it doesn't use a comma after the dependent clause.

15. **D** In this Rules question, apostrophes with nouns are changing in the answer choices. Determine whether each word possesses anything. The *protagonist* possesses the *childhood*, but the *brothers* don't possess anything. Eliminate any answer that doesn't match this.

- (A) and (C) are wrong because *brothers* shouldn't be possessive.

- (B) is wrong because *protagonist* should have an apostrophe.

- (D) is correct because *protagonist* is possessive and *brothers* is not.

16. **A** In this Rules question, punctuation is changing in the answer choices. Look for independent clauses. The first part of the sentence says *Many sundials have a motto inscribed on the dial face*, which is an independent clause. The second part says *these mottos usually reference human mortality and the passing of time…*, which is also an independent clause. Eliminate any answer that can't correctly connect two independent clauses.

- (A) is correct because a semicolon can connect two independent clauses.

- (B) is wrong because a comma without a coordinating conjunction (FANBOYS) can't connect two independent clauses.

- (C) is wrong because some type of punctuation is needed in order to connect two independent clauses.

- (D) is wrong because a coordinating conjunction (*and*) without a comma can't connect two independent clauses.

17.　**C**　In this Rules question, punctuation is changing in the answer choices. The first part of the sentence says *The first woman to receive a pilot's license in the United States,* which is a describing phrase. Noun phrases are always Extra Information and should be set off with commas. Eliminate answers that do not have a comma.

- (A) and (D) are wrong because the first part isn't an independent clause, and a semicolon or colon can only follow an independent clause.

- (B) is wrong because a comma is needed for Extra Information.

- (C) is correct because it uses a comma after the Extra Information.

18.　**C**　In this Rules question, punctuation is changing in the answer choices. Look for independent clauses. The first part of the sentence says *...poet Langston Hughes was an early innovator of jazz poetry,* which is an independent clause. The second part of the sentence says *though his writing career also included plays, short stories, nonfiction books, and a weekly newspaper column...,* which is a dependent clause. Eliminate any option that doesn't correctly connect an independent + a dependent clause.

- (A), (B), and (D) are wrong because independent + dependent cannot be connected with punctuation other than a comma.

- (C) is correct because independent + dependent can be connected with a comma.

19.　**B**　In this Rules question, punctuation is changing in the answer choices. Look for independent clauses. The first part of the sentence says *Sunbeams that occur when the Sun is above or below a layer of clouds are known as crepuscular rays,* which is an independent clause. The second part says *generally occurring around sunrise and sunset, they received their name from the Latin word for twilight...,* which is also an independent clause. Eliminate any answer that can't correctly connect two independent clauses.

- (A) and (D) are wrong because some type of punctuation is needed in order to connect two independent clauses.

- (B) is correct because the period makes each independent clause its own sentence, which is fine.

- (C) is wrong because a comma without a coordinating conjunction (FANBOYS) can't connect two independent clauses.

20. **B** This is a Transitions question, so follow the basic approach. Highlight ideas that relate to each other. The preceding sentence states that in a photo *several male scientists are easily recognizable*, and this sentence states that *the eight women in the photo were unknown*. These ideas disagree, so an opposite-direction transition is needed. Make an annotation that says "disagree." Eliminate any answer that doesn't match.

- (A), (C), and (D) are wrong because they are same-direction transitions.

- (B) is correct because it is an opposite-direction transition.

21. **A** This is a Transitions question, so follow the basic approach. Highlight ideas that relate to each other. The preceding sentence states that *For hundreds or years, the gorkon...was used to cook foods*, and this sentence states that *the arrival of modern appliances...led to the decreasing popularity of the gorkon*. These ideas disagree, so an opposite-direction transition is needed. Make an annotation that says "disagree." Eliminate any answer that doesn't match.

- (A) is correct because it is an opposite-direction transition.

- (B), (C), and (D) are wrong because they are same-direction transitions.

22. **D** This is a Transitions question, so follow the basic approach. Highlight ideas that relate to each other. The preceding sentence states that *The lighthouse she tended...was recently sold*, and this sentence states that *Snowman retired from her position*. These ideas agree, so a same-direction transition is needed. Make an annotation that says "agree." Eliminate any answer that doesn't match.

- (A) and (C) are wrong because they are opposite-direction transitions.

- (B) is wrong because this sentence is not a restatement of the preceding one.

- (D) is correct because it is a same-direction transition and accurately portrays the cause-and-effect relationship between the two sentences, as it's logical that the sale of the lighthouse could lead to her retirement.

23. **A** This is a Transitions question, so follow the basic approach. Highlight ideas that relate to each other. The preceding sentence states that *People who live in hotter countries tend to eat spicier food than do people living in colder countries*, and this sentence lists some hot countries where spicy food is common. These ideas agree, so a same-direction transition is needed. Make an annotation that says "agree." Eliminate any answer that doesn't match.

- (A) is correct because this sentence contains examples supporting the preceding sentence.

- (B) and (C) are wrong because the second sentence is not a similar or an additional point.

- (D) is wrong because the second sentence is not a consequence of the first.

24. **C** This is a Transitions question, so follow the basic approach. Highlight ideas that relate to each other. The preceding sentence states that *Scientist Flávia Miranda…found that there may be more than one species in the genus*, and this sentence states that *there are seven distinct species of silky anteaters*. These ideas agree, so a same-direction transition is needed. Make an annotation that says "agree." Eliminate any answer that doesn't match.

- (A) and (B) are wrong because they are opposite-direction transitions.

- (C) is correct because this sentence specifies the number of species, as the preceding sentence merely stated that there were more than one.

- (D) is wrong because this sentence isn't a new point; it's providing more specific information about Miranda's results as stated in the preceding sentence.

25. **D** This is a Rhetorical Synthesis question, so follow the basic approach. Highlight the goal(s) stated in the question: *compare the lengths of time the two women spent in space*. Eliminate any answer that doesn't fulfill this purpose.

- (A) is wrong because it only discusses one woman's time *spent in space*.

- (B) is wrong because it doesn't specifically mention either of the women.

- (C) is wrong because it doesn't include a comparison of the women's time *spent in space*.

- (D) is correct because it includes both women's time *spent in space*.

26. **B** This is a Rhetorical Synthesis question, so follow the basic approach. Highlight the goal(s) stated in the question: *describe Nettle and Bone to an audience unfamiliar with Ursula Vernon*. Eliminate any answer that doesn't *describe Nettle and Bone* in a way that assumes the audience is *unfamiliar with Ursula Vernon*.

- (A), (C), and (D) are wrong because they don't provide background information about *Ursula Vernon*, and the audience is unfamiliar with her, so this information is needed.

- (B) is correct because it describes *Nettle and Bone* and provides information about *Ursula Vernon*.

27. **C** This is a Rhetorical Synthesis question, so follow the basic approach. Highlight the goal(s) stated in the question: *present the study and its findings*. Eliminate any answer that doesn't fulfill this purpose.

- (A), (B), and (D) are wrong because they don't provide the study's *findings*.

- (C) is correct because it discusses *the study and its findings*.

Module 2 – Easier

1. **A**   This is a Vocabulary question, as it asks for a *logical and precise word or phrase* to fill in the blank. The blank should describe what convection and radiation do to warm air, so look for and highlight clues in the passage about that interaction. Highlight that *the main component of the system is a warming unit.* So, however the unit operates, it should be warming the patient. A good word for the blank to enter in the annotation box would be "spread" or "distribute."

    - (A) is correct because *conduct* matches "spread."

    - (B), (C), and (D) are wrong because they are the **Opposite** of "spreading" warm air.

2. **C**   This is a Vocabulary question, as it asks for a *logical and precise word or phrase* to fill in the blank. The blank should describe a characteristic of older adults who play "serious games," so look for and highlight clues in the passage about these individuals. Highlight *patients who chose to include physical activity into their serious games experienced an even greater reduction in feelings of sadness than those who played the games without physical activity.* This clue means that even those who played serious games without physical activity would experience some level of reduction in feelings of sadness, even if that reduction were to be made greater by using physical activity as well. A good word for the blank to enter in the annotation box would be that those who play serious games, then, are less "sad" or "unhappy."

    - (A), (B), and (D) are wrong because *ruthless*, *truthful*, and *organized* don't match "sad."

    - (C) is correct because *depressed* matches "sad."

3. **B**   This is a Vocabulary question, as it asks for a *logical and precise word or phrase* to fill in the blank. The blank should describe a crop (in this case maize, or corn), so look for and highlight clues in the passage about that crop. Highlight that the crop has a *central role in Hopi religion and culture.* A good word for the blank to enter in the annotation box would be "central" or "important."

    - (A) is wrong because *sustainable* goes **Beyond the Text**—it's common to think of crops along with the concept of sustainability, but the passage offers no information about how sustainable maize is or why that would be important to the artist's work.

    - (B) is correct because *significant* matches "central."

    - (C) and (D) are wrong because *unassuming* and *puzzling* don't match "central."

4. **D**   This is a Vocabulary question, as it asks for a *logical and precise word or phrase* to fill in the blank. The blank should describe what maintenance programs might do about damage to a structure, so look for and highlight clues in the passage about that interaction. Highlight that *the program must also be able to alert personnel to any damage that it has flagged but cannot repair on its own.* Since there are two actions the maintenance program takes in regard to damage (the second of which is *repair*), *flagged* in this clue would refer to the first action. A good word for the blank to enter in the annotation box would be "notice" or "find."

- • (A), (B), and (C) are wrong because *empty*, *disrupt*, and *withhold* don't match "notice."

- • (D) is correct because *detect* matches "notice."

5. **C** This is a Vocabulary question, as it asks for a *logical and precise word or phrase* to fill in the blank. The blank should describe something that the researchers found, so look for and highlight clues in the passage about the researchers' findings. Highlight that *the risk of non-allergenic asthma in a child increases by 59% if the child's father was exposed to second hand-smoke and by 72% if the child's father was exposed to second-hand smoke and then becomes a smoker himself.* These findings suggest a link between second-hand smoke and asthma, so a good word for the blank to enter in the annotation box would be "link" or "connection."

- • (A) is wrong because *obstacle* doesn't match "link."

- • (B) is wrong because an *inconsistency* is the **Opposite** of a "link."

- • (C) is correct because *correlation* matches "link."

- • (D) is wrong because *curiosity* goes **Beyond the Text**—the author does not claim that the link was curious, or interesting, just that there was a link.

6. **A** This is a Vocabulary question, as it asks what a word *most nearly means*. Treat *apprehending* as if it were a blank—the blank should describe how Manfred's family (*the former* means to look at the first group given in a list of two) reacts to Manfred's attitude, or disposition. Look for and highlight clues in the passage about this interaction. Highlight that the family *remarked* on Manfred's impatience and *did not dare to utter their surmises on this precipitation.* Even if some of the words here are unfamiliar, it's clear that the family was aware of how impatient Manfred was and chose not to say anything in this case. A good phrase for the blank to enter in the annotation box would be "aware that he's impatient."

- • (A) is correct because *Recognizing* matches being "aware that he's impatient."

- • (B) is wrong because *Supporting* goes **Beyond the Text**—the family being aware of how Manfred feels about this ceremonial does not mean that they support his attitude.

- • (C) and (D) are wrong because they're the **Opposite** of the passage—the family is aware of Manfred's patience, not *Ignoring* it, and they are choosing not to say anything rather than *Questioning* Manfred in any way.

7. **C** This is a Purpose question, as it asks for the *function of the underlined portion* in the passage. Read the passage and highlight clues in the sentences before or after that can help understand the function of the underlined sentence. The sentence before states that *A team of scientists used tomographic scanning technology and microscopy to produce 3D renderings of a Palacrodon specimen from Antarctica.* The underlined sentence then states that *these replications could bridge gaps in our understanding of evolutionary development.* Therefore, a good function of the underlined sentence to enter in the annotation box would be "explain why replications could be important."

- (A) is wrong because the passage does not offer *two theories* about the Great Dying.

- (B) is wrong because the claim by Jenkins in the underlined portion does not reference an *obstacle* that the team faced.

- (C) is correct because it's consistent with the highlighting and annotation.

- (D) is wrong because while the lines after the underlined portion do discuss what the team determined, it's not stated that this determination was *unexpected* or surprising to anyone.

8. **B** This is a Purpose question, as it asks for the *main purpose* of the passage. Read the passage and high-light clues that can help determine the main purpose. The last sentence states that *she was tempted to enquire the occasion of it, but the delicacy of mind…restrained her.* In other words, Madame St. Aubert wants to ask her husband something but decides not to. Therefore, a good main purpose to enter in the annotation box would be "explain that she wanted to ask something but didn't."

- (A) is wrong because it's **Half-Right**—Madame St. Aubert is *alarmed* in the passage, but her husband does not comfort her.

- (B) is correct because it's consistent with the highlighting and annotation.

- (C) is wrong because it's also **Half-Right**—Madame St. Aubert does decide *not to enquire of her husband in the passage*, but it's not specifically during *supper* time, which is misused from the first sentence.

- (D) is wrong because it goes **Beyond the Text**—it's not stated that Monsieur St. Aubert *will eventually reveal* what has him upset at all, just that if he did wish for his wife to know, she believes that he would tell her.

9. **A** This is a Dual Texts question, as it asks how *the author of Text 2* would regard *the perspective of the Andalusian thesis proponents* from Text 1. Read Text 1 and focus on the perspective of these propo-nents, which is that *Flamenco draws heavily from both Andalusian folklore and the Spanish language and has been a national symbol of Spanish identity since the Francoist dictatorship.* Then, read Text 2 and highlight what its author says about the same topic. The author claims that *Flamenco isn't purely a product of Spain* and that it *has roots in the Romani people.* Therefore, the author of Text 2 would claim that Flamenco's origins go beyond just those in Spain. Enter "disagree—Flamenco also from Romani" into the annotation box.

- (A) is correct because it's consistent with the annotated relationship between the passages— the author of Text 2 claims that the origins of Flamenco extend beyond Spain.

- (B) is wrong because it's **Extreme Language**—while the author of Text 2 does believe the per-spective from Text 1 is missing an element, there is no evidence to support that it's *insensitive*.

- (C) is wrong because the author of Text 2 does not address the Andalusian thesis proponents' ability to support their assertion or not.

- (D) is wrong because it's the **Opposite** of Text 1—Text 1 directly states that Andalusia is *the southernmost region of peninsular Spain.*

10. **D** This is a Retrieval question, as it asks for a detail *based on the text*. Look for and highlight information about the *garden* and the narrator's *attire* that is similar. The passage states that the narrator is walking on *patterned garden-paths*, and that her gown is *stiff* and supported by *whalebone and brocade*. The correct answer should be as consistent as possible with these details.

    - (A) is wrong because the only conflict in the passage is between the narrator's passion and her dress in the final two lines—neither the garden nor her attire is said to have *conflicting aesthetics*.

    - (B) is wrong because it goes **Beyond the Text**—while it's easy to imagine that both gardens and attire won't fare well when exposed to bad weather, there is nothing to this effect in the passage.

    - (C) is wrong because it also goes **Beyond the Text**—while both the garden and especially the narrator's attire could be visually striking, there is no reference to *attention from onlookers* in the passage.

    - (D) is correct because it's consistent with the highlighted details about the garden and the attire—the pattern of the garden paths and stiffness of the gown are both elements of *structure*.

11. **D** This is a Charts question, as it asks for *data from the table* that will *complete the text*. Read the title and variables from the table. Then, read the text and highlight the statement containing the same information, which is that the *student needs to determine in which lunar phase the moon has afternoon visibility and is no more than half illuminated by sunlight*. The correct answer should offer accurate information from the table that is consistent with this statement.

    - (A), (B), and (C) are wrong because each has 50% or more of the moon illuminated by sunlight, which is the **Opposite** of what the student needs in the passage.

    - (D) is correct because it's consistent with both the table and the highlighted statement.

12. **B** This is a Claims question, as it asks which quotation *most effectively illustrates the claim*. Look for and highlight the claim in the passage, which is that *Blackmore portrays Miss Dolly Darling as having undergone a transformation in her demeanor*. The correct answer should address and be consistent with each aspect of this claim.

    - (A), (C), and (D) are wrong because they're each **Half-Right**—while each address aspects of Dolly's *demeanor* (*longing for something*, *excited*, and *not be happy without a little bit of excitement*, respectively), none of these answers demonstrates a *transformation* in Dolly's demeanor.

    - (B) is correct because it's consistent with the highlighted claim—the transformation could be that Dolly *was not like herself, as it used to be* and that Dolly *was no longer the playful young Dolly that she loved so well*.

13.   **C**   This is a Claims question, as it asks which quotation *most effectively illustrates the claim*. Look for and highlight the claim in the passage, which is that Jack *attempts to distance himself from his chosen disguise* as he *prepares to reveal this ruse to a woman with whom he has fallen in love*. The correct answer should address and be consistent with each aspect of this claim—note that the claim does not state that Jack must reveal his disguise in the correct quotation, but only that he must do something that could be perceived as distancing himself from the disguise of Ernest.

- (A) and (D) are wrong because they're each irrelevant to the claim—each does not directly reference Jack's disguise.

- (B) is wrong because it goes **Beyond the Text**—while Jack acknowledges the existence of Ernest in this quotation, there is no support in the quotation that Jack is attempting to *distance himself* from the disguise or *reveal* it to anyone.

- (C) is correct because it's consistent with the highlighted claim—in this quotation, Jack is declaring that he does not like the name Ernest, which could support that he is distancing himself from the name in preparation to reveal his disguise.

14.   **B**   This is a Charts question, as it asks for *data from the table* that will *complete the example*. Read the title and variables from the table. Then, read the text and highlight the statement containing the same information, which is that the *Participants all agreed that the educational benefit was positive, but not all agreed that it would lead them to a lifestyle change*. The correct answer should offer accurate information from the table that is consistent with this statement.

- (A) and (D) are wrong because they're **Half-Right**—they each only reference an *educational benefit* but make no reference to a *lifestyle change* (such as eating behavior).

- (B) is correct because it's consistent with the table and with both aspects of the highlighted statement.

- (C) is wrong because it also **Half-Right**—it only references a *lifestyle change* but not an *educational benefit*.

15.   **C**   This is a Charts question, as it asks for *data from the graph* that will *support Zhou and colleagues' conclusion*. Read the title, key, variables, and units from the graph. Then, read the text and highlight Zhou and colleagues' conclusion, which is that *while multivariate factors would lead to the largest possible economic benefit due to reduced antibiotic resistance on a global scale, PM control alone was the better option for certain regions of the world*. The correct answer should offer accurate information from the graph that is consistent with this conclusion.

- (A) and (B) are wrong because they're consistent with the graph but irrelevant to the claim—each answer focuses only on one control method rather than comparing PM control to multivariate control as the passage does.

- (C) is correct because it's consistent with both the graph and the highlighted statement—if PM control outperformed multivariate control in *Central and South Asia*, this would support that PM control may be *the better option for certain regions of the world*.

- (D) is wrong because it's the **Opposite** of the graph—multivariate control predicted a lower, not greater, economic benefit for Central and South Asia than did PM control.

16. **D** This is a Claims question, as it asks which finding *would most directly support the researchers' hypothesis*. Look for and highlight the hypothesis in the passage, which is that *the genetic makeup of A. loripes allows it to produce the needed CBS enzyme without the presence of the CBS gene*. The correct answer should address and be consistent with each aspect of this claim.

    - (A) is wrong because it's the **Opposite** of the passage, which acknowledges that *A. loripes* can indeed *synthesize cysteine*.

    - (B) is wrong because it's irrelevant to the hypothesis—it's acknowledged in the passage that the *CBS* gene leads to the production of cysteine, but this has nothing to do with the *unique genetic makeup* of *A. loripes*, which lacks this gene.

    - (C) is wrong because it's also irrelevant to the hypothesis—the *quantities* of cysteine produced by either *A. loripes* or *other corals* is not addressed by the claim.

    - (D) is correct because it's consistent with the highlighted claim—if *other organisms* that *lack the CBS gene* but can still *produce cysteine* as well as contain the same *suspected cysteine-producing gene* as the one found in *A. loripes*, this would support that there is something in the *genetic makeup* of *A. loripes* that allows it to *synthesize cysteine*.

17. **B** This is a Conclusions question, as it asks what *most logically completes the text*. Look for the main focus of the passage, which is the shaft present in each Egyptian pyramid. Then, highlight the main points made regarding this focus: first, *Some historians have suggested that this shaft provided a path for the pharaoh's soul to reach the afterlife*. The passage also states that *others claim that the shaft was merely symbolic and not intended as an actual physical pathway*. Therefore, regardless of whether the shaft serves a physical or only a symbolic function, both groups suggest some importance to the shaft. The correct answer must be as consistent as possible with this conclusion.

    - (A) is wrong because it goes **Beyond the Text**—the passage doesn't support that the shaft provides any type of *challenge* for those seeking to understand the construction, only that the shaft's meaning is a debate for historians.

    - (B) is correct because it's consistent with what the highlighted sentences say about the shaft's possible importance.

    - (C) is wrong because it's **Right Answer, Wrong Question**—while this is consistent with what was suggested by one group of historians, it fails to capture the debate about the shaft's meaning present in the passage.

    - (D) is wrong because it's the **Opposite** of what's claimed in the passage—the second group of historians directly states that the shaft is *merely symbolic*, not that the position of the shaft *removes* this possibility.

18. **B** In this Rules question, verb forms are changing in the answer choices, so it's testing sentence structure. The subject of the sentence is *Much of his work*, and there is no main verb, so the answer must provide the main verb. Eliminate any answer that isn't in the correct form to be the main verb.

- (A) is wrong because a "to" verb can't be the main verb in a sentence.

- (B) is correct because it's in the right form to be the main verb.

- (C) and (D) are wrong because an *-ing* verb can't be the main verb in a sentence.

19. **A** In this Rules question, verbs are changing in the answer choices, so it's testing consistency with verbs. Find and highlight the subject, *fortune cookies*, which is plural, so a plural verb is needed. All of the answers work with a plural subject, so look for a clue regarding tense. The sentence includes the phrase *between the 1880s and early 1900s*. Highlight that phrase and write an annotation that says "past." Eliminate any answer not in past tense.

- (A) is correct because it's in past tense.

- (B) is wrong because it's in future tense.

- (C) is wrong because *have made* suggests time going up to the present, but the text describes something that ended by the early 1900s.

- (D) is wrong because *were making* suggests an event in progress, but there is no reason to refer to the movement of the fortune cookies as being in progress.

20. **D** In this Rules question, verb forms are changing in the answer choices, so it's testing sentence structure. The sentence already contains an independent clause followed by a comma. Thus, the phrase after the comma must be a phrase that describes the *limited tree availability* and isn't an independent clause. Eliminate any answer that does not correctly form this phrase.

- (A) and (B) are wrong because they are in main verb form, which isn't appropriate for a describing phrase.

- (C) is wrong because *to spur* does not clearly indicate what is spurring the birds' adaptation.

- (D) is correct because it correctly describes the *limited tree availability* as *spurring* the birds to take a certain action.

21. **B** In this Rules question, pronouns are changing in the answer choices, so it's testing consistency with pronouns. Find and highlight the word the pronoun refers back to, *uncomfortable sensations*, which is plural, so a plural pronoun is needed. Write an annotation saying "plural." Eliminate any answer that isn't plural or doesn't clearly refer back to the *uncomfortable sensations*.

- (A) and (C) are wrong because they are singular.

- (B) is correct because *they* is plural and is consistent with *uncomfortable sensations*.

- (D) is wrong because *you* isn't consistent with *uncomfortable sensations*.

22. **D** In this Rules question, apostrophes with nouns are changing in the answer choices. Determine whether each word possesses anything. The *works* possess the *messages*, but the *messages* don't possess anything. Eliminate any answer that doesn't match this.

- (A) is wrong because *messages* shouldn't be possessive.

- (B) and (C) are wrong because *works* is possessive and should have an apostrophe.

- (D) is correct because *works* is possessive and *messages* is not.

23. **A** In this Rules question, punctuation is changing in the answer choices. Look for independent clauses. The first part of the sentence says *Geneticist Jennifer Doudna co-developed CRISPR-Cas9...*, which is an independent clause. The second part says *other scientists have voiced ethical concerns due to the possibility of unintended consequences...*, which is also an independent clause. Eliminate any answer that can't correctly connect two independent clauses.

- (A) is correct because it connects the independent clauses with a comma + a coordinating conjunction (FANBOYS), which is acceptable.

- (B) is wrong because some type of punctuation is needed in order to connect two independent clauses.

- (C) is wrong because a comma without a coordinating conjunction (FANBOYS) can't connect two independent clauses.

- (D) is wrong because a coordinating conjunction (*but*) without a comma can't connect two independent clauses.

24. **C** In this Rules question, verb forms are changing in the answer choices, so it's testing sentence structure. The sentence already contains a main verb (*employs*) for the subject (*Kihara*), so this verb should introduce a phrase that describes how and why Kihara *employs visual storytelling*, and it shouldn't be in main verb form. Eliminate any answer that does not make the phrase clear and correct.

- (A), (B), and (D) are wrong because they are in main verb form, which isn't needed here.

- (C) is correct because it states that Kihara *employs visual storytelling to explore the complex experiences and identities...*, which provides a clear and correct meaning.

25. **C** In this Rules question, verbs are changing in the answer choices, so it's testing consistency with verbs. Find and highlight the subject, *state*, which is singular, so a singular verb is needed. All of the answers work with a singular subject, so look for a clue regarding tense. The rest of the sentence uses present tense verbs: *is confronted*, *is characterized*, and *prepares*. Highlight those verbs and write an annotation that says "present." Eliminate any answer not in present tense.

- (A) is wrong because it's in future tense.

- (B) and (D) are wrong because they're in past tense.

- (C) is correct because it's in present tense.

26. **A** This is a Transitions question, so follow the basic approach. Highlight ideas that relate to each other. The preceding sentence states that *This act was proposed in Congress every year from 1984 to 1993*, and this sentence describes how the law was eventually *signed* in 1993. These ideas represent a time change, so write an annotation that says "time change." Eliminate any answer that doesn't match.

- (A) is correct because *Finally* is used to indicate a time-change transition.

- (B) and (D) are wrong because this sentence isn't an additional point beyond the previous one.

- (C) is wrong because this sentence doesn't provide an alternative.

27. **C** This is a Transitions question, so follow the basic approach. Highlight ideas that relate to each other. The previous sentence says *not all mammals give birth to live offspring*, and this sentence provides an example of such a mammal, the duck-billed platypus, which *lays its eggs in a burrow*, so a same-direction transition is needed. Make an annotation that says "agree." Eliminate any answer that doesn't match.

- (A) is wrong because this sentence doesn't refer to something that happened at the same time as something else.

- (B) is wrong because this sentence isn't an additional point beyond the previous one.

- (C) is correct because the *platypus* is an example of a mammal that doesn't *give birth to live offspring*.

- (D) is wrong because it is an opposite-direction transition.

Module 2 – Harder

1. **A** This is a Vocabulary question, as it asks for a *logical and precise word or phrase* to fill in the blank. The blank should describe a lessening of some impact that enzymes can have on the environment, so look for and highlight clues in the passage about this impact. Highlight that *the end goal of such acceleration is to limit the damage done to the ecosystem*. A good word for the blank to enter in the annotation box would be "damaging" or "harmful."

- (A) is correct because *detrimental* means "damaging."

- (B), (C), and (D) are wrong because *favorable*, *fundamental*, and *palliative* (soothing) are all positive words that are the **Opposite** tone of "damaging."

2. **A** This is a Vocabulary question, as it asks for a *logical and precise word or phrase* to fill in the blank. The blank should describe some interaction between speech patterns and socialization in society, so look for and highlight clues in the passage about this interaction. Highlight that *the analysis revealed that each subject had developed hints of a similar accent to each other during the isolation period that quickly dissipated once each individual returned to society at large*. This clue supports a link between speech patterns and socialization in two ways: that the individuals developed similar

accents to each other when in isolation and that the accents disappeared when the individuals were allowed to socialize with the broader community once more. A good word for the phrase to enter in the annotation box would be that speech patterns and socialization are often "connected" or "linked."

- (A) is correct because *correlate* (relate) matches "connected."

- (B) and (C) are wrong because *triumph* and *capitulate* (surrender) don't match "connected."

- (D) is wrong because *diverge* (differ) is the **Opposite** of "connected."

3. **D** This is a Vocabulary question, as it asks for a *logical and precise word or phrase* to fill in the blank. The blank should describe how the presence of fish remains affects a belief regarding when hominids started cooking, so look for and highlight clues in the passage about that interaction. Highlight that the remains *date back 780,000 years* and *show clear signs of having been exposed to flame and bear hominid teeth marks*. Also note the transition word *but*, which indicates a contrast. Therefore, a good word for the blank to enter in the annotation box would be that the presence of these fish remains "suggests" or "may require" an adjustment to the previous belief that hominids first cooked 170,000 years ago.

- (A), (B), and (C) are wrong because *circumvents* (avoids), *refutes* (contradicts), and *suppresses* (destroys) would all mean that there is not a need to adjust the current belief, which is the **Opposite** of what's stated in the passage.

- (D) is correct because *indicates* matches "suggests."

4. **B** This is a Vocabulary question, as it asks for a *logical and precise word or phrase* to fill in the blank. The blank should describe how anchoring might affect a customer, so look for and highlight clues in the passage about that interaction. Highlight that *the practice of positioning an item for sale near a more expensive one* might make the customer think that *the item's price is reasonable or even inexpensive, whether or not it actually is*. A good word for the blank to enter in the annotation box would be "influence" or "affect."

- (A) is wrong because *extort* is **Extreme Language**—while the act of anchoring may influence a customer's evaluation of an item, nothing in the passage supports that customers are being extorted, or forced to agree to something under duress.

- (B) is correct because *persuade* matches "influence."

- (C) is wrong because *reprimand* (scold) doesn't match "influence."

- (D) is wrong because *counsel* (advise) goes **Beyond the Text**—the act of anchoring may influence the customer's decision, but an act is not capable of giving anyone advice.

5. **D** This is a Vocabulary question, as it asks for what a word *most nearly means*. Treat *curiously* as if it were a blank—the blank should describe the length of time that Oak held the woman's hand, so look for and highlight clues in the passage about the length of time. The woman in the passage states that Oak has held her hand *long enough*. Since the woman felt it was long enough that it was worth commenting on, a good word for the blank would be "particularly" or "markedly."

    •   (A) and (B) are wrong because *Demandingly* and *Imploringly* (pleadingly) don't match "particularly."

    •   (C) is wrong because *Disinterestedly* is the **Opposite** of the way Oak is described while holding the woman's hand—he is interested in the woman and is not a neutral party in this interaction.

    •   (D) is correct because *Notably* matches "particularly."

6. **C** This is a Purpose question, as it asks for the *main purpose* of the passage. Read the passage and highlight clues that can help determine the main purpose. The second sentence states that *ELIZA succeeded remarkably well in drawing out emotional reactions from those conversing with it*, while the third sentence states that *According to Weizenbaum, many human users erroneously described ELIZA's algebraic computations as "knowing," "thinking," or "understanding."* Therefore, a good main purpose to enter in the annotation box would be "describe ELIZA and what Weizenbaum had to say about it."

    •   (A) is wrong because ELIZA's popularity is not discussed in the passage.

    •   (B) and (D) are wrong because they're each **Right Answer, Wrong Question**— it's explained that ELIZA functions using *algebraic computations*, but the passage does not discuss any other computer programs or *how computer programs function* in general. Similarly, Weizenbaum is called a *computer scientist* in the first sentence, but the passage fails to elaborate any more about his *computer development background*.

    •   (C) is correct because it's consistent with the highlighting and annotation.

7. **C** This is a Purpose question, as it asks for the *main purpose* of the passage. Read the passage and highlight clues that can help determine the main purpose. The first four lines say *pardon that in crowds awhile / I waste one thought I owe to thee / And self-condemned, appear to smile, / Unfaithful to thy memory.* These lines mean that the speaker has, for a moment, thought of something or someone that made him smile and doesn't want a person he has promised to remember to think that he's been unfaithful by not thinking of the person in that moment. Therefore, a good main purpose to enter in the annotation box would be "explain that speaker is not being unfaithful to person's memory."

    •   (A) is wrong because the passage does not imply that the speaker is in any way responsible *for the death of a loved one.*

    •   (B) is wrong because it's **Recycled Language**—it misuses *crowd* from the first line. The passage also does not compare *positive emotions* to *negative emotions.*

- (C) is correct because it's consistent with the highlighting and annotation.

- (D) is wrong because *new experiences* are not discussed in the passage, nor is it discussed whether those experiences are more or *less important* than *memories*.

8. **B**   This is a Purpose question, as it asks for the *function of the underlined portion* in the passage. Read the passage and highlight clues in the sentences before or after that can help understand the function of the underlined portion. The sentence before the colon states that *the procession has as its centerpiece the Gospin plač, or Lady's Weeping*. Since the underlined portion after the colon describes the subject matter of the Lady's Weeping, a good function of the underlined sentence to enter in the annotation box would be "explain a key aspect of the ceremony."

- (A) and (C) are wrong because they each go **Beyond the Text**—learning what subject a text focuses on does not by itself give *additional insight* or illustrate a *social dynamic* of those who use the text as part of a celebration.

- (B) is correct because it's consistent with the highlighting and annotation.

- (D) is wrong because it's **Recycled Language**—no connection between the *length* (eight hours) or *breadth* (25 kilometers) and the subject matter of the Lady's Weeping is made in the passage.

9. **D**   This is a Dual Texts question, as it asks how *Kandpal* from Text 2 would respond to the *claim made by Richterman* in Text 1. Read Text 1 and focus on Richterman's claim, which is that *the team's findings lend support to the use of government anti-poverty programs such as cash transfers…in order to increase overall population well-being*. Then, read Text 2 and highlight what Kandpal says about the same topic. Kandpal *argues against increasing government cash transfer payments uninhibitedly* and says that *cash transfers have negative benefits for nonbeneficiaries*. Therefore, Kandpal would not completely agree with Richterman's claim, as helping some groups could hurt others. Enter "disagree—cash transfers can hurt nonbeneficiaries" into the annotation box.

- (A) is wrong because it's the **Opposite** of Kandpal's view in Text 2, which is that cash transfers can indeed have negative, or harmful, effects.

- (B) is wrong because it goes **Beyond the Text**—as logical as this may sound, neither passage discusses any other *species* besides humans.

- (C) is wrong because Kandpal does not claim that government subsidies cannot *protect an individual family* or that this idea needs to be *verified*, but rather that helping or protecting one family may harm other families.

- (D) is correct because it's consistent with the annotated relationship between the passages—notice that in the first sentence of Text 2, Kandpal argues against increasing government cash transfer payments *uninhibitedly* (without limit), which is a synonym for *unwaveringly*.

10.   **B**   This is a Charts question, as it asks for *data from the graph* that will *complete the text*. Read the title and variables from the graph. Then, read the text and highlight the statement containing the same information, which is that under the right conditions, *even some cold, snowy habitats at high elevations can support trees*. The correct answer should offer accurate information from the graph that is as consistent with this statement as possible.

- (A), (C), and (D) are wrong because each is inconsistent with the graph—Peru's tree line elevation is not between 4,500 and 5,000 meters, Mexico's is higher than 3,000 meters, and while Nepal's tree line elevation is over 4,000 meters, New Guinea's is not.

- (B) is correct because it's the only answer that's consistent with the graph.

11.   **D**   This is a Claims question, as it asks which quotation *most effectively illustrates the claim*. Look for and highlight the claim in the passage, which is that *the author directly addresses his Muse, imploring her to narrow his focus from many possible subjects to just one*. The correct answer should address and be consistent with each aspect of this claim.

- (A) and (C) are wrong because they're each **Half-Right**—the author *addresses his Muse* and seeks her help in these quotes but does not specifically ask her to *narrow his focus from many possible subjects to just one*.

- (B) is wrong because it's irrelevant to the claim—it's not clear that the author is even addressing his Muse here, and no part of the quotation seems to be a request for help.

- (D) is correct because it's consistent with the highlighted claim—the author's statement that a *solitary sorrow* best suits his Muse could be a statement that he wants *just one* tale to focus on.

12.   **A**   This is a Claims question, as it asks which finding would *most directly weaken the underlined claim*. Highlight the underlined claim in the passage, which is that *the region's Mesolithic humans exhibited the phenotype of light eyes significantly earlier than that of light complexions*. The correct answer should offer evidence that is as inconsistent with this claim as possible.

- (A) is correct because it's inconsistent with the claim—if a different set of remains *discovered in the area* dates to the *same time period* and has evidence of both *blue eyes and light skin*, this would weaken the suggestion that *light eyes* developed in Mesolithic humans *significantly earlier* than light complexions.

- (B) is wrong because it's irrelevant to the claim—it's consistent with the reasoning given for why Mesolithic humans may have developed light eyes but does not address whether light eyes or light complexions developed earlier.

- (C) is wrong because it's also irrelevant to the claim—the fact that some *modern Somerset residents have genetic links* to remains discovered at Gough's Cave does not address whether light eyes or light complexions developed earlier.

- (D) is wrong because it's the **Opposite** of the question task—such evidence would strengthen, not weaken, the claim that light complexions developed later than light eyes.

13. **C** This is a Charts question, as it asks for *data from the table* that will *complete the statement*. Read the title and variables from the table. Then, read the text and highlight the statement containing the same information, which is that *the weak monsoon season counteracted the effects of the tide maxima on sea levels for the Gulf of Carpentaria*. The correct answer should offer accurate information from the table that is consistent with this statement.

- (A) is wrong because it's the **Opposite** of what's shown in the table—from 1993–2020, the Gulf of Carpentaria experienced an increase (3.47) rather than a decrease (which would be shown as a negative) in maximum sea level.

- (B) and (D) are wrong because they're consistent with the table but irrelevant to the claim— neither addresses the idea that the weak monsoon season in the Gulf of Carpentaria in 2015– 2016 (which should decrease the sea level due to less rainfall) *counteracted the effects* of the tide maxima, which should increase sea level, according to the passage.

- (C) is correct because it's consistent with the table and the claim in the passage—since the 2015–2016 weak monsoon season would occur between 2007–2020, showing that there was a decrease of 25.29 mm in seal level in the Gulf of Carpentaria would be consistent with the weak monsoon season counteracting the effects of the tide maxima, which should have raised the sea level during that period (and did in Carnarvon).

14. **B** This is a Claims question, as it asks which quotation *best supports the student's claim*. Look for and highlight the claim in the passage, which is that *Angelou blended multiple genres by infusing her autobiographies with elements of music, poetry, and storytelling*. The correct answer should address and be consistent with each aspect of this claim.

- (A) is wrong because it's **Half-Right**—it references the use of *poetry* in Angelou's biographies but not *music* or storytelling.

- (B) is correct because it's consistent with the highlighted claim—a *balladeer* (singer of ballads) and *the Blues* address *music*, *recitations of poetry* addresses *poetry*, and *African-American folklore* addresses *storytelling*.

- (C) and (D) are wrong because they're each *irrelevant* to the claim and use **Recycled Language**—while both mention *autobiographies* and a *poem* or *poetry*, neither claims that Angelou's autobiographies used poetry in them, nor does either discuss *music* or *storytelling*.

15. **C** This is a Charts question, as it asks for *data from the table* that will *most effectively support the researchers' conclusion*. Read the title, variables, and units from the table. Then, read the text and highlight the researchers' conclusion, which is that *higher illumination intensity reduced the likelihood of detection while prolonging the time taken for successful detections*. The correct answer should offer accurate information from the table that is consistent with this conclusion.

- (A) is wrong because it's the **Opposite** of the information presented in the table—the highest (28.0 on average), not the *lowest*, number of males reached the signal in darkness, and the probability of reaching the signal decreased, not *increased*, as illumination intensity increased.

- (B) and (D) are wrong because they're consistent with the table but irrelevant to the claim—neither addresses the *likelihood* (or probability in the table) *of detection* that is part of the claim in the passage.

- (C) is correct because it's consistent with both the table and the highlighted claim.

16. **A** This is a Conclusions question, as it asks what *most logically completes the text*. Look for the main focus of the passage, which is the spacing method. Then, highlight the main points made regarding this focus: first, *leaving enough time to forget material before returning to it may seem counterintuitive to learners*. However, the passage goes on to say that *medical students who completed surgical training in a single day remembered less both one week and one year post-training than did their counterparts who completed equivalent training in abbreviated sessions over three weeks*. Therefore, despite it not seeming logical, the spacing method helped the second group of students remember more of their surgical training. The correct answer must be as consistent as possible with this conclusion.

- (A) is correct because it's consistent with what the highlighted sentences say about the spacing method—it does lead to a *short-term setback*, the loss of some learned information, but it may potentially help with *long-term* data retention.

- (B) is wrong because it goes **Beyond the Text**—the passage only compares *spacing* to *cramming*, not to any other *traditional methods of studying*.

- (C) and (D) are wrong because they also go **Beyond the Text**—no comparison is made between *medical students* and *other postgraduates* in the passage, nor is it known what students who use the spacing method might go on to *pursue* in terms of their education.

17. **C** This is a Conclusions question, as it asks what *most logically completes the text*. Look for the main focus of the passage, which is the model of the "global human day." Then, highlight the main points made regarding this focus: first, *Most people…cover vastly different distances in that same amount of time as their methods, and thus their energy expenditures, are highly dependent on both the local economy and the environment*. The passage also states that *focusing on decreasing the energy spent moving about by the hour rather than the kilometer could help improve sustainability efforts worldwide*. Therefore, to reduce human transportation's environmental impact, the focus should be on decreasing the time spent traveling rather than the distance traveled. The correct answer must be as consistent as possible with this conclusion.

- (A) is wrong because it goes **Beyond the Text**—it's not known from the passage that the "global human day" is anything more than a model or something that anyone would have to *adapt* to in the future.

- (B) is wrong because it's **Extreme Language**—the passage does not make a recommendation that local governments should specifically *offer incentives* to anyone for developing more time-efficient methods of transportation.

- (C) is correct because it's consistent with what the highlighted sentences say about the "global human day" model.

- (D) is wrong because it goes **Beyond the Text**—the passage does not recommend that the rest of the world adopts models similar to the one used by the scientists at McGill University.

18. **A** In this Rules question, verbs are changing in the answer choices, so it's testing consistency with verbs. Find and highlight the subject, *film*, which is singular, so a singular verb is needed. Write an annotation saying "singular." Eliminate any answer that is not singular.

- (A) is correct because it's singular.

- (B), (C), and (D) are wrong because they are plural.

19. **A** In this Rules question, punctuation with a transition is changing in the answer choices. Look for independent clauses. The first part of the sentence says *Other influences were much older.* There is an option to add *however* to this independent clause. This statement does contrast with the previous sentence, which states that *Art Deco architecture…rose in popularity in the 1920s,* so *however* belongs in the first part of the sentence. Eliminate options with *however* in the second part.

- (A) is correct because it puts *however* with the first independent clause and puts a semicolon between the two independent clauses.

- (B) and (C) are wrong because the sentence contains two independent clauses, which cannot be connected with commas alone.

- (D) is wrong because it puts *however* with the second independent clause, but the second part of the sentence agrees with the first.

20. **C** In this Rules question, commas and semicolons are changing in the answer choices. The sentence already contains a semicolon near the end, and the part after it is not an independent clause, which suggests that the sentence contains a list separated by semicolons. Use the third example to determine the structure of each item: Type of Volcano, Comma, Description. Make an annotation of this pattern and eliminate any answer that doesn't follow it.

- (A), (B), and (D) are wrong because they don't have a semicolon after the first item.

- (C) is correct because it follows the pattern of the third item.

21. **B** In this Rules question, punctuation is changing in the answer choices. Look for independent clauses. The first part of the sentence says *The first step in acrylic painting is the application of gesso*, which is an independent clause. The second part of the sentence says *successive layers of pre-mixed pigment…*, which is a phrase that isn't an independent clause and that states what gesso is. Eliminate any option that doesn't correctly connect the independent clause to the explanation.

- (A) and (C) are wrong because the period and semicolon make *successive layers of pre-mixed pigment* its own sentence, which doesn't work because it's not an independent clause.

- (B) is correct because a colon can be used when the second part of the sentence elaborates on the first.

- (D) is wrong some type of punctuation is needed to separate the explanation from the independent clause.

22. **B** In this Rules question, verbs are changing in the answer choices, so it's testing consistency with verbs. Find and highlight the subject, *Delano grape strike*, which is singular, so a singular verb is needed. All of the answers work with a singular subject, so look for a clue regarding tense. The sentence says *the year before*. Highlight that phrase and write an annotation that says "past." Eliminate any answer not in past tense.

- (A) is wrong because it's in present tense.

- (B) is correct because it's in past tense and *had begun* suggests an event that occurred before another past event, which is correct because the strike happened before the merger and the merger happened in the past, in 1966.

- (C) is wrong because *was beginning* suggests an event in progress, but there is no reason to refer to the strike as being in progress.

- (D) is wrong because it's in future tense.

23. **D** In this Rules question, punctuation is changing in the answer choices. Look for independent clauses. The first part of the sentence says *A recent research study…explains how reindeer are able to feed nearly constantly…*, which is an independent clause. The second part of the sentence says *the deer…continued to chew on vegetation as they entered a state of non-REM sleep…*, which is also an independent clause. Eliminate any answer choice that can't connect two independent clauses.

- (A) is wrong because a comma alone can't connect two independent clauses.

- (B) is wrong because *while* suggests a contrast, but the two parts of the sentence agree.

- (C) is wrong because some type of punctuation is needed in order to connect two independent clauses.

- (D) is correct because a colon can be used to connect two independent clauses when the second part explains the first, as it does here.

24. **C** This is a Transitions question, so follow the basic approach. Highlight ideas that relate to each other. The preceding sentence states that *Fusion reactors have long been proposed* but that they haven't been successfully used, and this sentence expands on this by explaining the problem with them. These ideas agree, so a same-direction transition is needed. Make an annotation that says "agree." Eliminate any answer that doesn't match.

- (A) is wrong because *Nevertheless* is an opposite-direction transition.

- (B) is wrong because this sentence isn't an additional point; it expands on the same point.

- (C) is correct because this sentence clarifies and specifies the point from the preceding sentence.

- (D) is wrong because this sentence isn't an example of the previous one.

25. **A** This is a Rhetorical Synthesis question, so follow the basic approach. Highlight the goal(s) stated in the question: *emphasize a difference between two literary portrayals of Brutus.* Eliminate any answer that doesn't fulfill this purpose.

- (A) is correct because it contrasts two different *literary portrayals of Brutus.*

- (B) and (D) are wrong because they each mention only one literary portrayal of Brutus.

- (C) is wrong because it doesn't mention any particular *portrayals.*

26. **D** This is a Rhetorical Synthesis question, so follow the basic approach. Highlight the goal(s) stated in the question: *explain the significance of one of Hans Bryant's works.* Eliminate any answer that doesn't fulfill this purpose.

- (A) is wrong because it doesn't mention *Hans Bryant.*

- (B) and (C) are wrong because they don't include the *significance* of one of Bryant's works.

- (D) is correct because it describes *"Rap Ballet"* and its *significance.*

27. **C** This is a Rhetorical Synthesis question, so follow the basic approach. Highlight the goal(s) stated in the question: *emphasize a similarity between two types of molecules.* Eliminate any answer that doesn't fulfill this purpose.

- (A) is wrong because it doesn't mention *two types of molecules.*

- (B) is wrong because it discusses only one type of molecule.

- (C) is correct because it mentions two types of molecules, *fatty acid salts* and *phospholipids,* and provides a similarity, that they both *contain hydrocarbon chains.*

- (D) is wrong because it describes a difference instead of a *similarity.*

PRACTICE TEST 2—MATH EXPLANATIONS

Module 1

1. **C**   The question asks for the mean, or average, of a data set. For averages, use the formula $T = AN$, in which T is the *Total*, A is the *Average*, and N is the *Number of things*. There are 6 values, so $N = 6$. Find the *Total* by adding the six integers to get $T = 8 + 11 + 11 + 15 + 16 + 23 = 84$. The average formula becomes $84 = (A)(6)$. Divide both sides of the equation by 6 to get $A = 14$, making (C) correct.

    It is also possible to calculate the mean of a list of numbers using the built-in calculator. Enter *mean(8,11,11,15,16,23)* in an entry field, and the mean of 14 is shown in the lower right corner of the entry field, so (C) is correct.

    Using either of these methods, the correct answer is (C).

2. **D**   The question asks for an equivalent form of an expression. Every term includes the variable z multiplied by a different number, called a coefficient. Work with the coefficients, and remember the order of operations, PEMDAS, which stands for Parentheses, Exponents, Multiply, Divide, Add, Subtract. Start inside the parentheses: $10z - 40z = -30z$. The expression becomes $90z - (-30z)$. Remember that subtracting a negative is the same thing as adding, so the expression becomes $90z + 30z$, and then $120z$. The correct answer is (D).

3. **6**   The question asks for the value of an expression given an equation. When an SAT question asks for the value of an expression, there is usually a straightforward way to solve for the expression without needing to completely isolate the variable. Since 56 is four times 14 and $4a$ is four times a, divide the entire equation $56 - 4a = 24$ by 4 to get $14 - a = 6$. The correct answer is 6.

4. **C**   The question asks for a value given a rate. Begin by reading the question to find information about the rate. The question states that the car *moves at a constant speed of 55 miles per hour*. Set up a proportion to determine how many miles the car will travel in 7 hours, being sure to match up units. The proportion is $\dfrac{55 \text{ miles}}{1 \text{ hour}} = \dfrac{x \text{ miles}}{7 \text{ hours}}$. Cross-multiply to get $(1)(x) = (55)(7)$, or $x = 385$. The correct answer is (C).

5. $\dfrac{20}{50}, \dfrac{2}{5},$ **or .4**

    The question asks for a probability based on data in a table. Probability is defined as $\dfrac{\text{\# of outcomes that fit requirements}}{\text{total \# of outcomes}}$. Read the table carefully to find the numbers to make the probability. There are 50 total flashcards, so that is the *total # of outcomes*. Of the animals on the 50 flashcards, 20 are speckled, so that is the *# of outcomes that fit requirements*. Therefore, the probability that a card selected at random will have a speckled animal on it is $\frac{20}{50}$. This fraction fits in the fill-in box, so there is no need to reduce it. The reduced form, $\frac{2}{5}$, or the decimal form, .4, would also be accepted as correct. The correct answer is $\frac{20}{50}$ or an equivalent form.

6. **–35** The question asks for the value of a term based on an equation. Start solving by distributing the number outside the parentheses on the left side of the equation. The equation becomes $35p + 30 + 2p = 30p - 5$. Combine like terms on the left side of the equation to get $37p + 30 = 30p - 5$. Subtract $30p$ from both sides of the equation to get $7p + 30 = -5$, and then subtract 30 from both sides of the equation to get $7p = -35$. The question asks for the value of $7p$, so stop here. The correct answer is –35.

7. **A** The question asks for correct values in a function. When given a function and asked for the table of values, plug values from the answer choices into the function and eliminate answers that don't work. Start with $x = -1$ because two answers pair it with $y = 6$ and two pair it with other numbers, so this will eliminate at least two of the answer choices. Plug $x = -1$ into the function to get $f(-1) = (-1)^2 + 5$, which becomes $f(-1) = 1 + 5$, and then $f(-1) = 6$. Eliminate (B) and (C) because they do not have $f(x) = 6$ for the x-value of –1. The first pair of values are the same in (A) and (D), so try the third pair of values and plug $x = 0$ into the function. The function becomes $f(0) = 0^2 + 5$, and then $f(0) = 5$. Eliminate (D) because it does not have $f(x)$ as 5 for the x-value of 0. The correct answer is (A).

8. **D** The question asks for a description of a function that models a specific situation. Compare the answer choices. Two choices say the function is increasing, and two say it is decreasing. Since the rower is crossing the lake directly, the distance between the rower and the starting shore is increasing over time. Eliminate (A) and (B) because they describe a decreasing function. The difference between (C) and (D) is whether the function is linear or exponential. Since the rower rows at a constant rate, the distance between the rower and the starting shore changes by a constant amount during each unit of time. Thus, the relationship between the rower's distance from the starting shore and the time rowed is linear. Eliminate (C) because it describes an exponential function. The correct answer is (D).

9. **D** The question asks for a reasonable number based on survey results and a margin of error. Work in bite-sized pieces and eliminate after each piece. Work with the survey results first. Start by applying the percentage of students in the survey who did not like the flavor to the entire population of students. Take 66% of the entire student population to get $\left(\frac{66}{100}\right)(300) = 198$ students. Eliminate (A) and (B) because they are not close to this value and do not represent a reasonable number of students who would not like the flavor. Now deal with the margin of error, which expresses the

amount of random sampling error in a survey's results. The margin of error is 9%, meaning that results within a range of 9% above and 9% below the estimate are reasonable. A 9% margin of error will not change the result very much, and (D) is the only answer choice close to 198. Since 188 is less than 198, check (D) by calculating the lower limit of the range based on the margin of error. To find the lower limit, subtract 9% from 66% to get 57%. Next, find 57% of the total population to get a lower limit of $\left(\dfrac{57}{100}\right)(300) = 171$ students. The value in (C) is less than the lower limit, so it is not a reasonable number of students who would dislike the new flavor. Choice (D) contains a value between 171 and 198, so it is a reasonable number of students based on the survey results and the margin of error. The correct answer is (D).

10. **–9** The question asks for the negative solution to an equation. The most efficient approach is to use the built-in calculator. Enter the equation as written into an entry field, and then scroll and zoom as needed to see vertical lines that indicate the x-intercepts at –9 and 8. The question asks for the negative solution, which is –9.

To solve for x algebraically, start by multiplying both sides of the equation by x to get $x(x + 1) = 72$. Next, distribute on the left side of the equation to get $x^2 + x = 72$. Finally, subtract 72 from both sides of the equation to get $x^2 + x - 72 = 0$. Now that the equation is a quadratic in standard form, which is $ax^2 + bx + c$, factor it to find the solutions. Find two numbers that multiply to –72 and add to 1. These are 9 and –8, so the factored form of the quadratic is $(x + 9)(x - 8) = 0$. Now set each factor equal to 0 to get two equations: $x + 9 = 0$ and $x - 8 = 0$. Subtract 9 from both sides of the first equation to get $x = -9$. This is negative, so stop here.

Using either of these methods, the correct answer is –9.

11. **A** The question asks for the change in a value given a proportion. The question is superficially about geometry, but the important part is the ratio. No specific numbers are given for the base or the height, so plug in. Use the numbers in the ratio, and make the height 40 inches and the base 75 inches. The base decreases by 9 inches, so the new base is $75 - 9 = 66$ inches. To find the new height, set up a proportion as $\dfrac{height}{base} : \dfrac{40}{75} = \dfrac{x}{66}$. Cross-multiply to get $(75)(x) = (40)(66)$, which becomes $75x = 2,640$. Divide both sides of the equation by 75 to get $x = 35.2$. Since the original height was 40, the change is $40 - 35.2 = 4.8$. The new height is less than the original height, so it decreased by 4.8. The correct answer is (A).

12. **B** The question asks for an equation that represents a function given the graph of a related function. To find the best equation, compare features of the graph to the answer choices. The answer choices are all in slope-intercept form, $y = mx + b$, in which m is the slope and b is the y-intercept. All of the answer choices have the same slope, so focus on the y-intercept. The graph shown in the question has been translated from the graph of function h. Adding or subtracting outside the parentheses shifts the graph up or down. Thus, the given graph of $h(x) - 12$ is shifted 12 units down from the graph of $h(x)$. Undo this by adding 12 to translate the given graph back to $h(x)$. The graph of $h(x) -$ 12 has its y-intercept at $(0, -3)$. Move the y-intercept up 12 units to get a y-intercept of $(0, 9)$. Eliminate (A), (C), and (D) because the equations have the wrong y-intercept, leaving (B) as correct.

Another method is to use the built-in calculator. Enter $y = h(x) - 12$ into an entry field, but do not open the slider for h. Instead, enter the equation in (A) into a separate entry field. The graph of $y = h(x) - 12$ does not match the graph in the question, so eliminate (A). Next, enter the equation in (B). Now the graph of $y = h(x) - 12$ matches the graph in the question. Additionally, the y-intercept of the graph of $h(x) - 12$ is at $(0, -3)$ while the y-intercept of the graph of $h(x)$ is at $(0, 9)$. This means that the first graph is correctly translated down 12 units from the second graph, so (B) is correct.

Using either of these methods, the correct answer is (B).

13. **D** The question asks for the value of the y-coordinate of the solution to a system of equations. The most efficient method is to enter both equations into the built-in calculator, and then scroll and zoom as needed to find the points of intersection. The graph shows two points of intersection, at $(-13, 267)$ and $(9, -173)$, so the y-coordinate is either 267 or -173. Only 267 is in an answer choice, so choose (D).

Since there are numbers in the answer choices and the algebra is complicated, another method is to plug in the answers. Start with (C), 173, and plug $y = 173$ into the easier second equation first to get $20x = 7 - 173$, which becomes $20x = -166$. Divide both sides of the equation by 20 to get $x = -8.3$. Then plug these values for x and y into the first equation to see if it is true: $-5(8.3)^2 + 173 = -578$ is not true, so eliminate (C). Try (D) next, and plug $y = 267$ into the second equation to get $20x = 7 - 267$, which becomes $20x = -260$. Divide both sides of the equation by 20 to get $x = -13$. Plug $x = -13$ and $y = 267$ into the first equation to get $-5(-13)^2 + 267 = -578$. Simplify the left side of the equation to get $-5(169) + 267 = -578$, then $-845 + 267 = -578$, and finally $-578 = -578$. Since both equations are true when $y = 267$, (D) is correct.

Using either of these methods, the correct answer is (D).

14. **D** The question asks for an equation that represents the relationship between two variables. When given a table of values and asked for the correct equation, plug values from the table into the answer choices to see which one works. According to the table, when $d = 2$, $I = 5$. Plug these values into the answer choices and eliminate any that are not true. Choice (A) becomes $5 = 0.75(1 - 80)^2$, then $5 = 0.75(-79)^2$, and finally $5 = 4,680.75$. This is not true, so eliminate (A). Choice (B) becomes $5 = (1 - 80)^2$, then $5 = (-79)^2$, and finally $5 = 6,241$; eliminate (B). Choice

(C) becomes $5 = (1 - 0.75)^2$, then $5 = (0.25)^2$, and finally $5 = 0.0625$; eliminate (C). Choice (D) becomes $5 = 80(1 - 0.75)^2$, then $5 = 80(0.25)^2$, and finally $5 = 5$. This is true, so keep (D). Only (D) worked with the first pair of values, so stop here. The correct answer is (D).

15.　**A**　The question asks for the number of solutions to an equation. Distribute on both sides of the equation to get $70 + 210x = 210x + 60$. The two sides of the equation have the same x-terms but different constants, so there are no solutions. To check algebraically, subtract $210x$ from both sides of the equation to get $70 = 60$. This is not true, so the equation has no solutions. The correct answer is (A).

16.　**B**　The question asks for the volume of a geometric figure. Use the Geometry Basic Approach. Start by drawing a pyramid on the scratch paper as best as possible, and then label the figure with the given information. Look up the formula for the volume of a pyramid on the reference sheet and write it down: $V = \frac{1}{3} lwh$. Plug in the values given in the question for the length, the width, and the height to get $V = \frac{1}{3} (10)(15)(20)$. Simplify the right side of the equation to get $V = \frac{1}{3} (3,000)$, and simplify again to get $V = 1,000$. The correct answer is (B).

17.　**B**　The question asks for an equation in terms of a specific variable. The question asks about the relationship among variables and there are variables in the answer choices, so one option is to plug in. That might get messy with three variables, and all of the answer choices have b by itself, so the other option is to solve for b. Start to isolate b by subtracting $7a$ from both sides of the equation to get $-3b = -7a + c$. Since b is positive in the answer choices, multiply both sides of the equation by -1 to get $3b = 7a - c$. Divide both sides of the equation by 3 to get $b = \frac{7a - c}{3}$. The correct answer is (B).

18.　**3**　The question asks for the relationship between radii given information about circles in the coordinate plane. The equation of a circle in standard form is $(x - h)^2 + (y - k)^2 = r^2$, where (h, k) is the center and r is the radius. In the equation given for circle O, $r^2 = 81$. Take the positive square root of both sides of the equation to get $r = 9$. In the equation given for circle P, $r^2 = 9$. Take the positive square root of both sides of the equation to get $r = 3$. Divide the radius of circle O, 9, by the radius of circle P, 3, to determine that the radius of circle O is $\frac{9}{3} = 3$ times the radius of circle P. The correct answer is 3.

19. $\dfrac{9}{41}$, .2195, 0.219, or 0.220

The question asks for the value of a trigonometric function. Use the Geometry Basic Approach. Begin by drawing a triangle and labeling the vertices. Label angle B as a right angle. The drawing should look something like this:

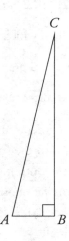

Next, write out SOHCAHTOA to remember the trig functions. The SOH part defines the sine as $\dfrac{opposite}{hypotenuse}$, and the question states that $\sin(A) = \dfrac{40}{41}$, so label the side opposite angle A, which is $\overline{BC}$, as 40 and the hypotenuse, which is $\overline{AC}$, as 41. To find the length of the third side, use the Pythagorean Theorem: $a^2 + b^2 = c^2$. Plug in the known values to get $40^2 + b^2 = 41^2$. Square the numbers to get $1{,}600 + b^2 = 1{,}681$, then subtract 1,600 from both sides of the equation to get $b^2 = 81$.

Take the positive square root of both sides of the equation to get $b = 9$. With all three side lengths labeled, the drawing looks like this:

To find sin(C), use the SOH part of SOHCAHTOA again. The side opposite angle C is 9, and the hypotenuse is 41, so sin(C) = $\dfrac{9}{41}$. On fill-in questions, a fractional answer can also be entered as a decimal. When the answer is positive, there is room in the fill-in box for five characters, including the decimal point. In this case, $\dfrac{9}{41} \approx 0.2195122$, which is too long. Either stop when there's no more room and enter .2195 or round the last digit, which in this case also becomes .2195. It is allowed but not required to put a 0 in front of the decimal point, which would make the answer 0.219 or 0.220, but do not shorten it more than that. The correct answer is $\dfrac{9}{41}$ or an equivalent form.

20. **C** The question asks for the equation that defines a function. In function notation, the number inside the parentheses is the x-value that goes into the function, or the input, and the value that comes out of the function is the y-value, or the output. The question provides two pairs of input and output values, so plug those into the answer choices and eliminate answers that don't work with both pairs. Start by plugging $x = -1$ and $g(x) = -5$ into the answer choices. Choice (A) becomes $-5 = -2(-1) - 2$, then $-5 = 2 - 2$, and finally $-5 = 0$. This is not true, so eliminate (A). Choice (B) becomes $-5 = 3(-1)$, and then $-5 = -3$; eliminate (B). Choice (C) becomes $-5 = 3(-1) - 2$, then $-5 = -3 - 2$, and finally $-5 = -5$. This is true, so keep (C). Choice (D) becomes $-5 = 3(-1) - 5$, then $-5 = -3 - 5$, and finally $-5 = -8$; eliminate (D). Only (C) worked with the first pair of values, so stop here. The correct answer is (C).

21. **C** The question asks for the function that represents a certain situation. There are variables in the answer choices, and the question asks about the relationship between the total cost and the number of pairs of sunglasses bought, so plug in. Make $p = 10$ to include both $39 pairs and $13 pairs of sunglasses. The first 5 pairs of sunglasses bought cost $39 each, for a total of $(5)(39) = \$195$. The 5 additional pairs of sunglasses cost $13 each, for a total of $(5)(13) = \$65$. The total cost for all 10 pairs of sunglasses is $\$195 + \$65 = \$260$. This is the target value; write it down and circle it.

Now plug $p = 10$ into the answer choices and eliminate any that do not match the target value. Choice (A) becomes $h(10) = -65 + 52(10)$, then $h(10) = -65 + 520$, and finally $h(10) = 455$. This does not match the target value, so eliminate (A). Choice (B) becomes $h(10) = 39 + 13(10)$, then $h(10) = 39 + 130$, and finally $h(10) = 169$; eliminate (B). Choice (C) becomes $h(10) = 130 + 13(10)$, then $h(10) = 130 + 130$, and finally $h(10) = 260$. This matches the target value, so keep (C), but check the remaining answer just in case. Choice (D) becomes $h(10) = 195 + 13(10)$, then $h(10) = 195 + 130$, and finally $h(10) = 325$; eliminate (D). The correct answer is (C).

22. **6.25 or $\dfrac{25}{4}$**

The question asks for a value in a system of equations. One method is to use the built-in calculator, although it will take some experimentation. Start by entering each equation into a separate entry field. The slider for k does not appear, so subtract k from both sides of the second equation and enter $3y - k = 0$. It might be necessary to delete "=0" to show the slider and then add it back to see the graph of the line. Click on the slider for k, and then move left and right to see when the line intersects the parabola at exactly one point. Click on the "$k =$" equation above the slider to expand or narrow the range of the slider to find the exact value of k when the system of equations has exactly one solution. Click on either equation to see a gray dot at the point of intersection. This happens when $k = 6.25$, so the correct answer is 6.25.

Another option is to use the discriminant. The discriminant is the part of the quadratic formula under the square root sign, and it can be written as $D = b^2 - 4ac$. When the discriminant is positive, the quadratic has exactly two real solutions; when the discriminant is 0, the quadratic has exactly one real solution; and when the discriminant is negative, the quadratic has no real solutions. In this case, the quadratic has exactly one real solution, so the discriminant must equal 0. First, isolate y in the first equation by dividing both sides of the equation by 3 to get $y = \frac{k}{3}$. Now that each equation equals y, set the right sides of the two equations equal to each other to get $\frac{k}{3} = -3x^2 + 5x$. Add $3x^2$ to both sides of the equation and subtract $5x$ from both sides of the equation to get $3x^2 - 5x + \frac{k}{3} = 0$. With the equation in standard form, which is $ax^2 + bx + c = 0$, $a = 3$, $b = -5$ and $c = \frac{k}{3}$. Plug these values into the discriminant formula and set it equal to 0 to get $(-5)^2 - 4(3)\left(\frac{k}{3}\right) = 0$. Simplify the left side of the equation to get $25 - 12\left(\frac{k}{3}\right) = 0$, and then $25 - 4k = 0$. Add $4k$ to both sides of the equation to get $25 = 4k$, and then divide both sides of the equation by 4 to get $\frac{25}{4} = k$. The decimal equivalent, 6.25, will also be accepted as correct.

Using either of these methods, the correct answer is 6.25 or $\frac{25}{4}$.

Module 2 – Easier

1. **40**   The question asks for the value of a variable based on an equation. Solve for x by subtracting 35 from both sides of the equation to get $x = 40$. The correct answer is 40.

2. **A**   The question asks for a percentage based on a specific situation. Start by ballparking: half of 8,000 is 4,000, so 2,000 is less than 50%. Eliminate (C) and (D) because they are greater than 50%. Next, plug in one of the two remaining answer choices to see whether it works. Try (A), 25%. *Percent* means out of 100, so 25% can be represented as $\frac{25}{100}$. Multiply this by the total number of chocolate bars to get $\frac{25}{100}(8,000) = 2,000$. This matches the number of chocolate bars containing nuts given in the question, so stop here. The correct answer is (A).

3. **B** The question asks for the area of a geometric figure. Use the Geometry Basic Approach. Start by drawing a triangle on the scratch paper, and then label the figure with the given information. Label the base as 6 and the height at 11. The question asks for the area of the triangle, so write out the formula for the area of a triangle, either from memory or after looking it up on the reference sheet: $A = \frac{1}{2} bh$. Plug in the given values to get $A = \frac{1}{2} (6)(11)$. Simplify the right side of the equation to get $A = 33$. The correct answer is (B).

4. **B** The question asks for an equivalent form of an expression. Use bite-sized pieces and the Process of Elimination to tackle this question. The only term with y^3 is $5y^3$, so it cannot be combined with any other terms and must appear in the correct answer. Eliminate (C) and (D) because they do not include $5y^3$. Combine the two terms with y^2 to get $12y^2 - 4y^2 = 8y^2$. Eliminate (A) because it does not include $8y^2$. The correct answer is (B).

5. **D** The question asks for the best interpretation of part of a graph representing a certain situation. Start by reading the final question, which asks for the best interpretation of the y-intercept of the graph. In a linear graph that represents an amount over time, the y-intercept represents the initial amount. In this case, it represents the distance the marathon runner is from home at the start of the run, or after 0 minutes on the x-axis. Since the runner starts at the park, this is the same as the distance from the park to the runner's home. The correct answer is (D).

6. **B** The question asks for the value of the measure of an angle on a geometric figure. Use the Geometry Basic Approach. Start by drawing a triangle on the scratch paper. Then label the figure with the given information. Label angle Z as 32°, angle Y as 103°, and angle X without a number. Since the measures of the angles in a triangle have a sum of 180°, set up the equation 32° + 103° + X = 180°, which becomes 135° + X = 180°. Subtract 135° from both sides of the equation to get X = 45°. The correct answer is (B).

7. **130** The question asks for a value based on a percentage. Translate the English to math in bite-sized pieces. *Percent* means out of 100, so translate 65% as $\frac{65}{100}$. Translate *how many* as a variable, such as c for campers. Translate *of* as multiplication. The equation becomes $c = \frac{65}{100} (200)$. Solve the equation by hand or with the built-in calculator to get $c = 130$. The correct answer is 130.

8. **D** The question asks for the value of a function. In function notation, the number inside the parentheses is the x-value that goes into the function, or the input, and the value that comes out of the function is the y-value, or the output. The question provides an input value, so plug $x = 4$ into the function to get $g(4) = -3 + 4^2$, which becomes $g(4) = -3 + 16$, and then $g(4) = 13$. The correct answer is (D).

9. **C** The question asks for a value given a rate. Begin by reading the question to find information about the rate. The question states that *Anna makes an average of 3 free throws per minute.* Set up a proportion to determine how many minutes it will take Anna to make 36 free throws. The proportion is $\frac{3 \text{ free throws}}{1 \text{ minute}} = \frac{36 \text{ free throws}}{x \text{ minutes}}$. Cross-multiply to get $(3)(x) = (1)(36)$, or $3x = 36$. Divide both sides of the equation by 3 to get $x = 12$. The correct answer is (C).

10. **B** The question asks for the value of an expression based on an equation. When an SAT question asks for the value of an expression, there is usually a straightforward way to solve for the expression without needing to completely isolate the variable. Start by adding $7(x - 2)$ to both sides of the equation to get $18 = 7(x - 2) - 6(x - 2)$. Combine the terms with $(x - 2)$ to get $18 = (7 - 6)(x - 2)$, which becomes $18 = 1(x - 2)$, or $18 = x - 2$. The question asks for the value of $x - 2$, so stop here and pick (B).

Another method is to use the built-in calculator. Enter the equation as written, and then scroll and zoom as needed to see the value of x indicated by a vertical line at $x = 20$. Read carefully: the question asks for the value of $x - 2$, which is $20 - 2$, or 18, making (B) correct.

Using either of these methods, the correct answer is (B).

11. **C** The question asks for an equation that represents a specific situation. Translate the information in bite-sized pieces and eliminate after each piece. One piece of information says that Ismael *writes a total of 1,065 words*, so the right side of the equation must equal 1,065. Eliminate (A) and (D) because they have the wrong number on the right side of the equation. Another piece of information says that Ismael *can handwrite 20 words per minute*. Handwriting at a rate of 20 words per minute for h minutes can be represented by the term $20h$. Eliminate (B) because it does not contain this term. Choice (C) also correctly translates the total number of words that Ismael types as $40t$. The correct answer is (C).

12. **127** The question asks for the value of an angle on a geometric figure. Use the Geometry Basic Approach. Start by redrawing the figure on the scratch paper, and then label the figure with the given information. The fact that two of the lines are parallel will be important on some questions about lines and angles, but here it is unnecessary information. Instead, since the angle marked as a and the angle marked as 53° make up a straight line and there are 180° in a line, $a + 53 = 180$. Subtract 53 from both sides of the equation to get $a = 127$. The correct answer is 127.

13. **C** The question asks for the value of a function. In function notation, the number inside the parentheses is the x-value that goes into the function, or the input, and the value that comes out of the function is the y-value, or the output. The question provides an input value, so plug $x = 5$ into the function to get $f(5) = 4(5) - 5$, which becomes $f(5) = 20 - 5$ and then $f(5) = 15$. The correct answer is (C).

14. **B** The question asks for the value of a constant given two equivalent expressions. One method is to use the built-in calculator. Enter $\dfrac{(8x+40)}{64}$ and $\dfrac{(x+a)}{8}$ into separate entry fields, and then click on the slider for a. Equivalent expressions result in the same graph, so either use the slider tool or enter each answer one at a time into the "$a =$" equation until the same line is graphed twice. This happens when $a = 5$, so (B) is correct.

To solve algebraically, start by rewriting the expressions with an equals sign between them to get $\dfrac{8x+40}{64} = \dfrac{x+a}{8}$. Cross-multiply to get $(8x+40)(8) = 64(x+a)$, and then distribute on both sides of the equation to get $64x + 320 = 64x + 64a$. Subtract $64x$ from both sides of the equation to get $320 = 64a$. Divide both sides of the equation by 64 to get $5 = a$, which is (B).

Using either of these methods, the correct answer is (B).

15. **A** The question asks for the value of an expression given the equation of a graph in the xy-plane. One method is to use the built-in calculator. Enter the equation of the line, and then scroll and zoom as needed to find the intercepts. The x-intercept is at $(11.25, 0)$, and the y-intercept is at $(0, -4.5)$. Thus, $c = 11.25$, $k = -4.5$, and $\dfrac{c}{k} = \dfrac{11.25}{-4.5}$, which becomes $\dfrac{c}{k} = -2.5$. Eliminate (C) and (D) because they are positive, and then check (A) and (B) on a calculator. The decimal form of (A) is -2.5; keep (A). The decimal form of (B) is -0.4; eliminate (B), which makes (A) correct.

Another option is to plug the given points into the equation of the line. Start with the x-intercept, $(c, 0)$, and plug in $x = c$ and $y = 0$ to get $4c - 10(0) = 45$, or $4c = 45$. Divide both sides of the equation by 4 to get $c = \dfrac{45}{4}$. Next, use the y-intercept, $(0, k)$, and plug in $x = 0$ and $y = k$ to get $4(0) - 10k = 45$, or $-10k = 45$. Divide both sides of the equation by -10 to get $k = -\dfrac{45}{10}$. Both c and k have 45 in the numerator of the fraction, so do not reduce the k fraction. Divide the two values to get $\dfrac{c}{k} = \dfrac{\frac{45}{4}}{-\frac{45}{10}}$. When dividing fractions, multiply the fraction in the numerator by the reciprocal of the fraction in the denominator. This becomes $\dfrac{c}{k} = \left(\dfrac{45}{4}\right)\left(-\dfrac{10}{45}\right)$. The 45s cancel out, leaving $\dfrac{c}{k} = -\dfrac{10}{4}$. This reduces to $\dfrac{c}{k} = -\dfrac{5}{2}$, which matches (A).

Using either of these methods, the correct answer is (A).

16. **A** The question asks for an equivalent form of an expression. One approach is to use the built-in calculator. Enter the expression given in the question, and then enter the expressions from the answer choices one at a time and stop when one of the answers produces the same graph. Only the graph in (A) matches, so it is correct.

Since the question asks for an equivalent expression and the answer choices contain variables, another approach is to plug in. Make $x = 2$, and plug it into the expression to get $2^2 - 16(2) + 28$, which becomes $4 - 32 + 28$, and then 0. This is the target value; write it down and circle it. Next plug $x = 2$ into each answer choice and eliminate any that do not equal the target value. Choice (A) becomes $(2 - 2)(2 - 14)$, then $(0)(-12)$, and finally 0. This matches the target value, so keep (A), but check the remaining answers just in case. Choice (B) becomes $(2 + 2)(2 + 14)$, then $(4)(16)$, and finally 64. This does not match the target value, so eliminate (B). Choice (C) becomes $(2 + 4)(2 + 7)$, then $(6)(9)$, and finally 54; eliminate (C). Choice (D) becomes $(2 - 4)(2 - 7)$, then $(-2)(-5)$, and finally 10; eliminate (D). Only (A) matched the target value, so it is correct.

Finally, when given a quadratic in standard form, which is $ax^2 + bx + c$, another approach is to factor it. Find two numbers that multiply to 28 and add to -16. These are -2 and -14, so the factored form of the quadratic is $(x - 2)(x - 14)$, which is (A).

Using any of these methods, the correct answer is (A).

17. **10** The question asks for a value given a specific situation. Translate the information in bite-sized pieces. The question states that the *player earned a total of 500 coins*. Since the sum of $22F$ and $12T$ is the number of coins, and F and T are the numbers of four-card and three-card combinations, respectively, 22 and 12 must be the coin values of one F combination and one T combination, respectively. Thus, the difference between the number of coins each combination is worth is $22 - 12 = 10$. The correct answer is 10.

18. **C** The question asks for an equation that represents a specific situation. The number of water hyacinths in the pond is decreasing by a certain fraction over time, so this question is about exponential decay. Write down the growth and decay formula: *final amount = (original amount)$(1 \pm rate)^{\text{number of changes}}$*. In this case, h is the final amount and w is the number of changes. The question states that the original amount was 2,200. Eliminate (A) and (B) because they do not have 2,200 as the original amount in front of the parentheses. Since this situation involves a decrease, the original amount must be multiplied by $1 - rate$. The rate is given as $\frac{1}{3}$, so the value in the parentheses becomes $\left(1 - \frac{1}{3}\right)$, or $\frac{2}{3}$. Eliminate (D) because it does not have this value in the parentheses. The correct answer is (C).

19. **D**   The question asks for a minimum value given a specific situation. Since the question asks for a specific value and the answers contain numbers in increasing order, plug in the answers. Rewrite the answer choices on the scratch paper and label them "concrete per truck." The question asks for a minimum value, so start with (A), 2,250. If each truck is loaded with 2,250 kg of concrete and there are 32 trucks, the total mass of concrete is (2,250)(32) = 72,000 kg. The question states that *each mixer truck delivers 9% less concrete than it was loaded with initially*, so the amount delivered will be less than 72,000 kg. The question also states that the *work site requires at least 81,000 kg of concrete*. The starting amount is already too small, so eliminate (A). The result of (A) was not close, so try (C), 2,531, next. If each truck is loaded with 2,531 kg of concrete, the total mass of concrete is (2,531)(32) = 80,992 kg. This is also less than 81,000, and the trucks will lose concrete along the way, so eliminate (C). A larger initial mass of concrete is needed, so also eliminate (B). The correct answer is (D).

20. **D**   The question asks for the value of a constant in a quadratic equation. One method is to use the built-in calculator and plug in the answers. Enter the equation without "= 0" into an entry field, and then click on the slider tool for *c*. Either move the slider left and right—expanding the range as needed—or enter each answer choice one at a time into the "*c* =" equation. When *c* = –20, there are two vertical lines indicating solutions to the equation. The question states that *the equation has no real solutions*, so eliminate (A). When *c* = 15, there are still two vertical lines at the solutions; eliminate (B). When *c* = 20, there is one vertical line, so the equation has one real solution; eliminate (C). When *c* = 25, there are no vertical lines, so there are no real solutions, and (D) is correct.

To determine when a quadratic equation has no real solutions algebraically, use the discriminant. The discriminant is the part of the quadratic formula under the square root sign and is written as $D = b^2 - 4ac$. When the discriminant is positive, the quadratic has exactly two real solutions; when the discriminant is 0, the quadratic has exactly one real solution; and when the discriminant is negative, the quadratic has no real solutions. Thus, the discriminant of this quadratic must equal a negative number. This quadratic equation is already in standard form, which is $ax^2 + bx + c = 0$. In this case, $a = 45$, $b = 60$, and $c = c$. Plug these into the discriminant formula to get $D = (60)^2 - 4(45)$ (*c*), or $D = 3,600 - 180c$. The result must be negative, so $3,600 - 180c < 0$. Add $180c$ to both sides of the inequality to get $3,600 < 180c$. Divide both sides of the inequality by 180 to get $20 < c$. The only number in the answer choices greater than 20 is 25, so (D) is correct.

Using either of these methods, the correct answer is (D).

21. **A**   The question asks for an equation in terms of a specific variable. Since the question is about the relationship between variables and the answers contain variables, plug in. The fraction on the right side of the equation could make the numbers awkward, so make $r = 6$ to keep things simple. Plug in 6 for r, and the equation becomes $q = \dfrac{23}{17 + 6}$, then $q = \dfrac{23}{23}$, and finally $q = 1$. This means that when $r = 6$, $q = 1$.

Now plug $r = 6$ and $q = 1$ into the answer choices and eliminate any that do not work. Choice (A) becomes $6 = \dfrac{23}{1} - 17$, then $6 = 23 - 17$, and finally $6 = 6$. This is true, so keep (A), but check the remaining answers just in case. Choice (B) becomes $6 = 17 - \dfrac{23}{1}$, then $6 = 17 - 23$, and finally $6 = -6$. This is not true, so eliminate (B). Choice (C) becomes $6 = \dfrac{17 - 1}{23}$, then $6 = \dfrac{16}{23}$; eliminate (C). Choice (D) becomes $6 = \dfrac{23}{17 - 1}$, then $6 = \dfrac{23}{16}$; eliminate (D). The correct answer is (A).

22.   **A**   The question asks for the value of an expression based on information about a function. In function notation, the number inside the parentheses is the x-value that goes into the function, or the input, and the value that comes out of the function is the y-value, or the output. The table gives three pairs of input and output values for the function. To solve for the constants p and q, start by plugging in one of the pairs from the table. Plug $x = -2$ and $h(x) = 0$ into the function to get $0 = -2p + q$. There is no way to solve for $p + q$ using only this equation, so plug in a second pair of values. Plug $x = -1$ and $h(x) = -41$ into the function to get $-41 = -p + q$. There are now two equations with two unknown constants, so find a way to make one of the constants disappear when stacking and adding the equations. Multiply the second equation by -1 to get $41 = p - q$. The q-terms are now the same with opposite signs, so stack and add the two equations.

$$
\begin{aligned}
0 &= -2p + q \\
41 &= \underline{p - q} \\
41 &= -p
\end{aligned}
$$

Divide both sides of the resulting equation by -1 to get $-41 = p$. Plug $p = -41$ into the first equation to get $0 = -2(-41) + q$, or $0 = 82 + q$. Subtract 82 from both sides of the equation to get $-82 = q$. Add the values of the two constants to get $p + q = -41 + (-82)$, which becomes $p + q = -41 - 82$, and then $p + q = -123$, which is (A).

Another method is to recognize that the equation is in slope-intercept form, $y = mx + b$, in which m is the slope and b is the y-intercept. In this case, the constant p is the slope and the constant q is the y-intercept. Find the slope by putting two points from the table, such as $(-3, 41)$ and $(-2, 0)$, into the formula $slope = \dfrac{y_2 - y_1}{x_2 - x_1}$. The formula becomes $slope = \dfrac{41 - 0}{-3 - (-2)}$, then $slope = \dfrac{41}{-1}$, and finally $slope = -41$. Thus, $p = -41$. To find the y-intercept, note that the values of $h(x)$ in the table decrease by 41 each time the x-value increases by 1. Thus, the next row of the table will contain $x = 0$ and $h(x) = -82$. The y-intercept is where $x = 0$, so the y-intercept is -82, and $q = -82$. If $p = -41$ and $q = -82$, the value of $p + q$ is $-41 + (-82)$, which becomes $p + q = -41 - 82$, and then $p + q = -123$, making (A) correct.

Using either of these methods, the correct answer is (A).

Module 2 – Harder

1. **B** The question asks for the frequency table that correctly represents a list of numbers. A frequency table has two columns: the left-hand column contains the values, and the right-hand column contains the number of times each value occurs, or its frequency. Work in bite-sized pieces and eliminate answer choices that do not match the data. The number 61 occurs twice in the list, so its frequency is 2. Eliminate (C) because it shows a frequency of 61 for the number 2 instead of a frequency of 2 for the number 61. Eliminate (D) because it shows a frequency of 122 for the number 61. Next, the number 72 occurs once in the list, so its frequency is 1. Eliminate (A) because it shows a frequency of 2 for the number 72. Choice (B) shows the correct frequency for each value. The correct answer is (B).

2. **C** The question asks for an equation that represents a specific situation. Translate the English to math in bite-sized pieces. Translate *is* as equals, or =. Translate *greater than* as +. Thus, *a is 47 greater than b* translates to $a = b + 47$. The correct answer is (C).

3. **B** The question asks for the equation that represents values given in a table. The table shows pairs of values for x and y, and the correct equation must work for every pair of values. Plug in values from the table and eliminate equations that don't work. Since plugging in 0 often makes more than one answer work, start with the fourth row. Plug $x = 6$ and $y = 6$ into the answer choices. Choice (A) becomes $6 = -3(6) - 6$, then $6 = -18 - 6$, and finally $6 = -24$. This is not true, so eliminate (A). Choice (B) becomes $6 = 2(6) - 6$, then $6 = 12 - 6$, and finally $6 = 6$. This is true, so keep (B), but check the remaining answers with this pair of values. Choice (C) becomes $6 = -3(6) - 12$, then $6 = -18 - 12$, and finally $6 = -30$; eliminate (C). Choice (D) becomes $6 = 2(6) - 12$, then $6 = 12 - 12$, and finally $6 = 0$; eliminate (D). Only (B) worked with this pair of values, so stop here. The correct answer is (B).

4. **A** The question asks for the value of a function that represents a situation. In function notation, the number inside the parentheses is the x-value that goes into the function, or the input, and the value that comes out of the function is the y-value, or the output. The question provides the number of cups of lemonade, which is represented by x, so plug $x = 120$ into the function to get $p(120) = 0.5(120) - 12$, which becomes $p(120) = 60 - 12$, and then $p(120) = 48$. The correct answer is (A).

5. **C** The question asks for the y-intercept of a function. A y-intercept is a point where $x = 0$. In function notation, the number inside the parentheses is the x-value that goes into the function, or the input, and the value that comes out of the function is the y-value, or the output. Together, they represent points on the graph of the function. Plug $x = 0$ into the function to get $h(0) = 7.5(5)^0$. Any value raised to the power of 0 equals 1, so $(5)^0 = 1$, and the equation becomes $h(0) = 7.5(1)$, or $h(0) = 7.5$. Thus, when $x = 0$, $h(x) = 7.5$, and the y-intercept of the graph is at $(0, 7.5)$. The correct answer is (C).

6. **D** The question asks for the interpretation of a value in context. Start by reading the final question, which asks for the best interpretation of x. Then label the parts of the equation with the information given. The question states that *The bookstore has 12 regular sections and 3 children's sections* and

that the total number of books for sale is 118,400. Rewrite the equation with these labels: (number of regular sections)(x) + (number of children's sections)(y) = total books. Next, eliminate answers that are not consistent with the labels. Since x is multiplied by the number of regular sections, it must have something to do with regular sections. Eliminate (B) and (C) because they refer to the children's sections, not the regular sections. Compare the remaining answer choices. The difference is between the average number of books and the total number of books. Since x is multiplied by the number of regular sections in the bookstore, it must represent books per section, not total books. Keep (D) because it is consistent with this information, but eliminate (A) because it refers to a total number. The correct answer is (D).

7. **A** The question asks for the length of a side of a geometric figure. Use the Geometry Basic Approach. Start by redrawing the figure on the scratch paper, and then label the figure with information from the question. Since the question asks for a specific value and the answers contain numbers in increasing order, plug in the answers. Write the answers on the scratch paper, label them "side RS," and start with a middle number. Try (B) and make $RS = 12$. In a parallelogram, opposite sides have the same length, so label RS and PQ with a length of 12 on the figure. The question states that *the length of PQ is one-fourth the length of PS*. Given this, if $PQ = 12$, $PS = 4(12) = 48$, and so does QR. Label this on the figure, which now looks like this:

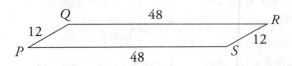

The perimeter of a geometric shape is the sum of the lengths of the sides, so the perimeter of this figure is 12 + 48 + 12 + 48 = 120. This does not match the perimeter of 60 given in the question, so eliminate (B). The result was too large, and a longer side length will make the perimeter even larger, so eliminate (C) and (D), as well. Choice (A) works because, when $RS = 6$, $PQ = 6$, $PS = 4(6) = 24$, and $QR = 24$, so the perimeter is 6 + 24 + 6 + 24 = 60, which matches the information given in the question. The correct answer is (A).

8. **A** The question asks for the value of an expression given the equation of a graph in the xy-plane. One method is to use the built-in calculator. Enter the equation of the line, and then scroll and zoom as needed to find the intercepts. The x-intercept is at (11.25, 0), and the y-intercept is at (0, −4.5). Thus, $c = 11.25$, $k = -4.5$, and $\frac{c}{k} = \frac{11.25}{-4.5}$, which becomes $\frac{c}{k} = -2.5$. Eliminate (C) and (D) because they are positive, and then check (A) and (B) on a calculator. The decimal form of (A) is −2.5; keep (A). The decimal form of (B) is −0.4; eliminate (B), which makes (A) correct.

Another option is to plug the given points into the equation of the line. Start with the x-intercept, $(c, 0)$, and plug in $x = c$ and $y = 0$ to get $4c - 10(0) = 45$, or $4c = 45$. Divide both sides of the equation by 4 to get $c = \dfrac{45}{4}$. Next, use the y-intercept, $(0, k)$, and plug in $x = 0$ and $y = k$ to get $4(0) - 10k = 45$, or $-10k = 45$. Divide both sides of the equation by -10 to get $k = -\dfrac{45}{10}$. Both c and k have 45 in the numerator of the fraction, so do not reduce the k fraction. Divide the two values to get $\dfrac{c}{k} = \dfrac{\frac{45}{4}}{-\frac{45}{10}}$. When dividing fractions, multiply the fraction in the numerator by the reciprocal of the fraction in the denominator. This becomes $\dfrac{c}{k} = \left(\dfrac{45}{4}\right)\left(-\dfrac{10}{45}\right)$. The 45s cancel out, leaving $\dfrac{c}{k} = -\dfrac{10}{4}$. This reduces to $\dfrac{c}{k} = -\dfrac{5}{2}$, which matches (A).

Using either of these methods, the correct answer is (A).

9. **B** The question asks for the value of a constant given two equivalent expressions. One method is to use the built-in calculator. Enter $\dfrac{(8x + 40)}{64}$ and $\dfrac{(x + a)}{8}$ into separate entry fields, and then click on the slider for a. Equivalent expressions result in the same graph, so either use the slider tool or enter each answer one at a time into the "$a =$" equation until the same line is graphed twice. This happens when $a = 5$, so (B) is correct.

To solve algebraically, start by rewriting the expressions with an equals sign between them to get $\dfrac{8x + 40}{64} = \dfrac{x + a}{8}$. Cross-multiply to get $(8x + 40)(8) = 64(x + a)$, and then distribute on both sides of the equation to get $64x + 320 = 64x + 64a$. Subtract $64x$ from both sides of the equation to get $320 = 64a$. Divide both sides of the equation by 64 to get $5 = a$, which is (B).

Using either of these methods, the correct answer is (B).

10. **A** The question asks for a value based on a geometric figure. Use the Geometry Basic Approach. Start by drawing a rectangle on the scratch paper, and then label the figure with the given information. Since the question asks for a specific value and the answers contain numbers in increasing order, plug in the answers. Write the answers on the scratch paper, label them as "z," and start with a middle number. Try (B), 14. Since z represents the width of the rectangle, the width is 14; label this on the figure. The question states that the length of the rectangle *is 4 inches greater than its width*, so the length is $14 + 4 = 18$; label this on the figure. The figure should now look something like this:

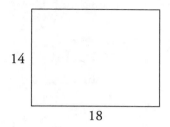

Write down the formula for the area of a rectangle, either from memory or after looking it up on the reference sheet. The formula is $A = lw$. Plug in the length of 18 and width of 14 to get $A = (18)(14)$, or $A = 252$. This does not match the area of 140 given in the question, so eliminate (B).

The result on the right side of the equation was too large, so also eliminate (C) and (D). Choice (A) works because, when the width, z, is 10, the length is $10 + 4 = 14$. The area formula becomes $A = (14)(10)$, or $A = 140$, which matches the area given in the question. The correct answer is (A).

11. **B** The question asks for an equation that represents a specific situation. Translate the information in bite-sized pieces and eliminate after each piece. One piece of information says that Samantha *saved $5 dollars a day for d days*. Since d represents the number of days, it should be multiplied by 5. Eliminate (C) and (D) because they multiply d by 75 instead of by 5. Compare the remaining answer choices. The difference between (A) and (B) is whether 75 is added to $5d$ or subtracted from $5d$. Since Samantha *first saved a gift of $75* and went on to save a total of $320, 75 should be added to $5d$ and set equal to 320. Eliminate (A) because it uses subtraction. The correct answer is (B).

12. **D** The question asks for the number of points of intersection in a system of equations. One method is to enter both equations into the built-in calculator, and then scroll and zoom as needed to see where, if at all, they intersect. The lines are parallel and do not intersect, which means (D) is correct.

To solve algebraically, divide both sides of the second equation by 2 to get $y = 3x + 10$. Now both equations are in slope-intercept form, $y = mx + b$, in which m is the slope and b is the y-intercept. The lines have the same slope, 3, but different y-intercepts, -4 and 10. This means the lines are parallel and do not intersect, and (D) is correct.

Using either of these methods, the correct answer is (D).

13. **C** The question asks for the value of the x-coordinate of the solution to a system of equations. The most efficient method is to enter both equations into the built-in calculator, and then scroll and zoom as needed to find the point of intersection. The point is $(4, 0)$, so the x-coordinate is 4, and (C) is correct.

To solve the system for the x-coordinate algebraically, find a way to make the y-coordinates disappear when stacking and adding the equations. Compare the y-terms: the larger coefficient, 4, is 2 times the smaller one, 2. Multiply the entire first equation by -2 to get the same coefficient with opposite signs on the y terms. The first equation becomes $-14x - 4y = -56$. Now stack and add the two equations.

$$-14x - 4y = -56$$
$$\underline{+\ 13x + 4y = \ \ 52}$$
$$-x \qquad \ \ = -4$$

Divide both sides of the resulting equation by -1 to get $x = 4$, which is (C).

Using either of these methods, the correct answer is (C).

14. **−4.5** The question asks for the value when a quadratic function reaches its maximum. A parabola reaches its minimum or maximum value at its vertex, so find the x-coordinate of the vertex. One method is to enter the equation into the built-in graphing calculator, and then scroll and zoom as needed to find the vertex. The vertex is at $(-4.5, -13.25)$, so the value of the x-coordinate is -4.5.

To solve algebraically, find the value of h, which is the x-coordinate of the vertex (h, k). The equation is in standard form, $ax^2 + bx + c$, in which $h = -\dfrac{b}{2a}$. Since $a = -3$ and $b = -27$, $h = -\dfrac{-27}{2(-3)}$. This becomes $h = -\dfrac{27}{6}$, and then $h = -4.5$. A fractional form that fits in the fill-in box would also be accepted as correct.

Using either of these methods, the correct answer is -4.5 or an equivalent form.

15. **3** The question asks for the value of a constant in a system of equations. When a system of linear equations has infinitely many solutions, the two equations form the same line. One method is to enter both equations into the built-in calculator. Click to add the slider for k, and then move the slider left and right until the two lines are the same. This happens when $k = 3$, so 3 is correct.

To solve for k algebraically, start by making the two equations look similar. First, add $12x$ to both sides of the second equation to get $20x - 45y = 1$. Add $45y$ to both sides of the second equation to get $20x = 45y + 1$, and then subtract 1 from both sides of the second equation to get $20x - 1 = 45y$. Next, multiply both sides of the first equation by 5 to get $20x - 1 = 15ky$. Write the two equations above each other to see how the terms match up.

$$20x - 1 = 15ky$$
$$20x - 1 = 45y$$

Both equations contain $20x$ and -1, so the y-terms must be equal for the system of equations to have infinitely many solutions. Thus, $15ky = 45y$. Divide both sides of this equation by $15y$ to get $k = 3$, so 3 is correct.

Using either of these methods, the correct answer is 3.

16. **C** The question asks for the number in an equation that represents a specific part of a scenario. The question states that *m* represents the number of *months after the initial investment was made* and asks for the initial value of the investment. No months had passed at the time of the initial investment, so plug *m* = 0 into the equation. The equation becomes $v = -\dfrac{1}{2}(0)^2 + 15(0) + 6$. Simplify the right side of the equation to get *v* = 0 + 0 + 6, or *v* = 6. Since the value at the time of 0 months is 6 thousand dollars, that number represents the initial value of the investment, and (C) is correct.

Another method is to use the built-in calculator. Enter the equation into an entry field, and then scroll and zoom as needed to see that the *y*-intercept is at (6, 0). The *y*-intercept represents the amount in the account after 0 months, or at the time the initial investment was made, so (C) is correct.

Using either of these methods, the correct answer is (C).

17. **A** The question asks for the value of a trigonometric function. Use the Geometry Basic Approach. Start by drawing two right triangles that are similar to each other, meaning they have the same proportions but are different sizes. Be certain to match up the corresponding angles that are given in the question, and put the longest side opposite the right angle. Then label the sides of triangle *ABC* with the lengths given in the question. The drawing should look something like this:

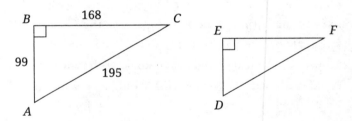

The question asks for the cosine of angle *D*, which corresponds to angle *A*. The sides in similar triangles are proportional, so the trig functions of corresponding angles are equal. Thus, cos(*D*) = cos(*A*), and it is possible to answer the question without knowing any of the side lengths of triangle *DEF*. To find cos(*A*), use SOHCAHTOA to remember the trig functions. The CAH part of the acronym defines the cosine as $\dfrac{adjacent}{hypotenuse}$. The side adjacent to *A* is 99, and the hypotenuse is 195, so cos(*A*) = $\dfrac{99}{195}$. Therefore, cos(*D*) is also $\dfrac{99}{195}$. This is not one of the answer choices, so reduce the fraction by dividing both the numerator and the denominator by 3 to get cos(*D*) = $\dfrac{33}{65}$. The correct answer is (A).

18. **C** The question asks for an *x*-intercept of a parabola. Sketch a graph using the given points, and label those points. The vertex of a parabola is on the axis of symmetry, so the axis of symmetry of this parabola is the line *x* = 2; add this line to the graph. The graph should look something like this:

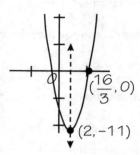

The two *x*-intercepts are an equal distance from the line of symmetry. The *x*-coordinate of the given *x*-intercept is $\frac{16}{3}$, so the distance from the line of symmetry is $\frac{16}{3} - 2$. Use a common denominator to get $\frac{16}{3} - \frac{6}{3}$, and then $\frac{10}{3}$. The *x*-coordinate of the other *x*-intercept is a distance of $\frac{10}{3}$ from the line of symmetry in the other direction, so subtract the *x*-coordinates: $2 - \frac{10}{3}$, which becomes $\frac{6}{3} - \frac{10}{3}$, and then $-\frac{4}{3}$. The correct answer is (C).

19. **D** The question asks for the perimeter of a triangle. Use the Geometry Basic Approach. Start by drawing a right triangle on the scratch paper. Next, label the figure with the information given. Label the hypotenuse 72. An acute angle is an angle with a measure less than 90°. Label one of those angles 60° and the other 30°. The drawing should look something like this:

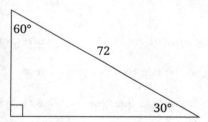

A 30:60:90 triangle is one of the special right triangles that has a specific proportional relationship among the sides. The proportion can be found by clicking open the reference sheet, and it is *x*: $x\sqrt{3}$:2*x*. Since the longest side is 72, 2*x* = 72, so *x* = 36. The other sides are 36 and $36\sqrt{3}$. Label the figure with this information; the figure now looks like this:

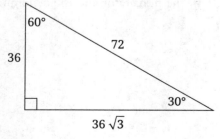

The perimeter of a geometric shape is the sum of the lengths of all of the sides. Add all three side lengths to get $36 + 36\sqrt{3} + 72$. Combine like terms to get $108 + 36\sqrt{3}$. The correct answer is (D).

20. **28**   The question asks for the value of a constant in a point on a line. The question states that the graph of line d and the graph of $y = -2x + 3$ are perpendicular lines, which means they have slopes that are negative reciprocals of each other. Find the slope of $y = -2x + 3$. This equation is in the slope-intercept form of a linear equation, $y = mx + b$, in which m is the slope and b is the y-intercept, so the slope of the given line is -2. The negative reciprocal of -2 is $\frac{1}{2}$, so the slope of line d is $\frac{1}{2}$. The question also states that line d *passes through the origin*, so the line goes through the point $(0, 0)$. This is also the y-intercept, so $b = 0$. Next, use the given point, $(a, 14)$, and plug $x = a$, $y = 14$, $m = \frac{1}{2}$, and $b = 0$ into the slope-intercept equation, $y = mx + b$, to get to get $14 = \frac{1}{2}(a) + 0$. This simplifies to $14 = \frac{1}{2}a$. Multiply both sides of the equation by 2 to get $28 = a$. The correct answer is 28.

21. **15**   The question asks for a value given information about the mean, or average, of a data set. For averages, either use the formula $T = AN$, in which T is the *Total*, A is the *Average*, and N is the *Number of things*, or use the built-in calculator. In the calculator, type the word *mean* followed by the list of numbers inside the parentheses, and the calculated mean will appear in the lower right corner of the entry box. Start with the given list of 7 numbers, and a mean of 23 appears in the lower right corner.

The question asks for the smallest integer that results in the full data set having a mean that is an integer less than 23. Plug in the smallest possible integer and find the mean. The question states that the integers are all greater than 10, so start with 11. In the built-in calculator, add 11 to the list of numbers in the parentheses, and the mean is 21.5. This is not an integer, so keep going. When the eighth integer is 12, the mean is 21.625. When the eighth integer is 13, the mean is 21.75, When the eighth integer is 14, the mean is 21.875. When the eighth integer is 15, the mean is 22. Thus, 15 is the smallest integer value that results in a new mean that is an integer less than 23, which matches the information in the question. The correct answer is 15.

22. **B**   The question asks for information that will provide proof of similar triangles. Use the Geometry Basic Approach. Triangles are similar when they have the same angle measures and proportional side lengths, so draw two triangles on the scratch paper that look similar but are different sizes. Then label the figures with information from the question: label AC as 11, DF as 55, and angles B and E as 85°. The drawing should look something like this.

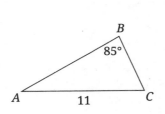
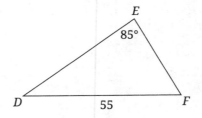

Next, evaluate the answer choices. Some give information about angles while others give information about sides. To start, focus on the rule that similar triangles have the same three angle measures. Try (A), and label angle A as 30° and angle D as 35°. Find the measure of the third angle in each triangle. All triangles contain 180°, so set up equations: $30° + 85° + C° = 180°$, and $35° + 85° + F° = 180°$. Simplify the first equation to get $115° + C° = 180°$, then subtract 115° from both sides of the equation to get $C = 65°$. Simplify the second equation to get $120° + F° = 180°$, then subtract 120° from both sides of the equation to get $F = 60°$. Label the figures with this information, and they now look like this:

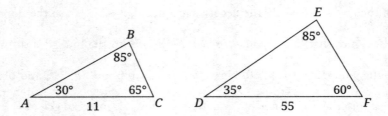

The two triangles do not have three equal angles, so (A) is not sufficient to prove that the triangles are similar; eliminate (A).

Try (B) next, and follow the same steps: label angle A as 30° and angle F as 65°. As with (A), the third angle of triangle ABC is 65°. Find the measure of the third angle in triangle DEF using the equation $65° + 85° + D° = 180°$. Simplify the equation to get $150° + D° = 180°$, then subtract 150° from both sides of the equation to get $D = 30°$. Relabel the figures, which now look like this:

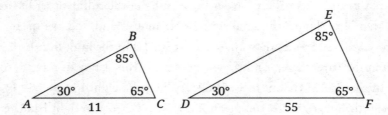

Now the two triangles do have the same three angle measures, so (B) is sufficient to prove that they are similar. Choice (C) is incorrect because there is not enough information to determine whether the two sides with a length of 6 are opposite angles with the same measures or different measures. Choice (D) is incorrect because knowing that two pairs of sides are in proportion without knowing the measures of the angles between them or the lengths of the third pair of sides is insufficient. The correct answer is (B).

Chapter 3
Practice Test 2

HOW TO EMULATE THE DIGITAL SAT ON PAPER

Practice Tests 5 and 6 are available in your online student tools in a digital, adaptive environment. The four tests in this physical book are printed on paper, but otherwise emulate the digital test in every way: test style, difficulty, and content. Please use the checklist below to ensure that you are able to emulate the adaptive nature of the test and get the preparation that you need for test day. Feel free to use the versions of Module 2 that you do not take during your test as additional practice.

- [ ] Take Reading and Writing (RW) Module 1, allowing yourself 32 minutes to complete it.

- [ ] Go to the answer key on page 188 and determine the number of questions you got correct in RW Module 1.

- [ ] If you get fewer than 15 questions correct, take RW Module 2 – Easier, which starts on page 138. If you get 15 or more questions correct, take RW Module 2 – Harder, which starts on page 149.

- [ ] Whichever RW Module 2 you take, start immediately and allow yourself 32 minutes to complete it.

- [ ] Take a 10-minute break between RW Module 2 and Math Module 1.

- [ ] Take Math Module 1, allowing yourself 35 minutes to complete it.

- [ ] Go to the answer key on page 188 and determine the number of questions you got correct in Math Module 1.

- [ ] If you get fewer than 14 questions correct, take Math Module 2 – Easier, which starts on page 170. If you get 14 or more questions correct, take Math Module 2 – Harder, which starts on page 178.

- [ ] Whichever Math Module you take, start it immediately and allow yourself 35 minutes to complete it.

- [ ] After you finish the test, check your answers to RW Module 2 and Math Module 2.

- [ ] Only after you complete the entire test should you read the explanations for the questions, which start on page 189.

Test 2—Reading and Writing
Module 1

Turn to Section 1 of your answer sheet to answer the questions in this section.

DIRECTIONS

The questions in this section address a number of important reading and writing skills. Each question includes one or more passages, which may include a table or graph. Read each passage and question carefully, and then choose the best answer to the question based on the passage(s).

All questions in the section are multiple-choice with four answer choices. Each question has a single best answer. Fill in the circle with the answer letter for the answer you think is best.

---

1 ☐ Mark for Review

Even though no woman pilot had ever successfully crossed the Atlantic Ocean while flying solo when she made her attempt, female aviator Amelia Earhart did not consider this feat _____. Piloting a Lockheed Vega 5B in 1932 completely by herself, Earhart successfully navigated a nonstop transatlantic flight, and she was later presented with the United States Distinguished Flying Cross for this accomplishment.

Which choice completes the text with the most logical and precise word or phrase?

(A) definitive

(B) enigmatic

(C) impracticable

(D) appropriate

2 ☐ Mark for Review

Contemporary composer Max Richter's experimental electronic music is _____ looping and phrasing techniques featuring spoken word pieces and elements of electronica. Drawing from his studies with Luciano Berio, Richter artfully revisualizes traditional classical music by weaving synthesizer sounds with samples, resulting in unique compositions that go beyond either source.

Which choice completes the text with the most logical and precise word or phrase?

(A) portrayed by

(B) coupled with

(C) denoted through

(D) constructed from

CONTINUE ➔

---

3 ☐ Mark for Review

Certain scientists theorize that at least some of the hydrocarbons found in oil that is drilled from deep wells rose up from the mantle that sits below the Earth's crust, suggesting that these hydrocarbons may be _____ in origin: chemically created without having any association with living organisms.

Which choice completes the text with the most logical and precise word or phrase?

Ⓐ flexible

Ⓑ genuine

Ⓒ inorganic

Ⓓ alterable

---

4 ☐ Mark for Review

While Ludwig van Beethoven, a renowned composer, grew increasingly deaf from 1801 until his death in 1827, his musical output was seemingly not substantially _____ his deteriorating hearing: 8 of his 9 symphonies and 15 of his 17 choral works were composed during this period.

Which choice completes the text with the most logical and precise word or phrase?

Ⓐ limited to

Ⓑ inhibited by

Ⓒ developed from

Ⓓ understood in

---

5 ☐ Mark for Review

The following text is adapted from James Fenimore Cooper's 1846 novel *Jack Tier, or the Florida Reef*. Mrs. Budd is traveling by boat with her niece, who has never been on a boat before.

Mrs. Budd had made one voyage previously, and she fancied that she knew all about a vessel. Never did she feel her great superiority over her niece as when discussing boats, about which she did know something.

As used in the text, what does the word "fancied" most nearly mean?

Ⓐ Formulated

Ⓑ Imagined

Ⓒ Conceded

Ⓓ Characterized

CONTINUE →

6 ◻ Mark for Review

The following text is from James Elroy Flecker's 1916 poem "No Coward's Tale."

> I am afraid to think about my death,
> When it shall be, and whether in great pain
> I shall rise up and fight the air for breath
> Or calmly wait the bursting of my brain.
>
> I am no coward who could seek in fear
> A folklore solace or sweet Indian tales:
> I know dead men are deaf and cannot hear
> The singing of a thousand nightingales.
>
> I know dead men are blind and cannot see
> The friend that shuts in horror their big eyes,
> And they are witless—O I'd rather be
> A living mouse than dead as a man dies.

Which choice best describes the overall structure of the text?

(A) The speaker confesses his anxiety about a subject, then explains why his beliefs lead him to a certain preference.

(B) The speaker explains why his fears are intensifying, then outlines his philosophy of life.

(C) The speaker laments his cowardice, then forecasts a deep transformation in his beliefs.

(D) The speaker denies his personal failings, then criticizes the failings of others.

7 ◻ Mark for Review

Dogs can discriminate between the smell of their own urine and that of the urine of another dog, and they act especially interested in their own urine when its scent has been altered by the addition of an odorous chemical. Psychologist Alexandra Horowitz made this determination by assessing dogs' level of interest in an odorous stimulus based on the amount of time dogs spent sniffing their own urine compared to the time spent sniffing their own urine mixed with aniseed oil. Dogs demonstrated some interest when presented with their unadulterated urine, but they demonstrated far more interest when presented with their urine adulterated with another scent.

According to the text, how did Horowitz determine the level of interest shown by dogs in the study?

(A) She noted the way each dog approached its own urine.

(B) She measured the time each dog spent sniffing the scents.

(C) She investigated how each dog responded to the urine of other dogs.

(D) She tested each dog's facial reactions to aniseed oil.

CONTINUE ➡

8 ☐ Mark for Review

The Great Barrier Reef is composed of over 2,900 individual reefs that span more than 1,400 miles. Although the Great Barrier Reef is the world's largest structure made of living entities, marine biologists are concerned that reef coverage has declined significantly since 1950, in part due to land-based chemicals polluting the ocean. These biologists believe that strictly controlling the use of fertilizers, herbicides, and pesticides will allow the Great Barrier Reef to regenerate.

According to the text, why are biologists concerned about the Great Barrier Reef?

(A) Its already huge structure cannot accommodate many more new reefs.

(B) It can't expand into new areas because it requires fertilizer to grow.

(C) It is no longer generating new reefs.

(D) It once spread over a much larger area than it does today.

9 ☐ Mark for Review

Culinary master George Auguste Escoffier may have invented the bouillon cube and designed the operational system of the modern professional kitchen, but it is his first cookbook *Le Guide Culinaire* that makes Escoffier a legend. This 1903 masterpiece was pivotal to the evolution of fine cooking. In this collection of over 5,000 international and French recipes, Escoffier popularized and modernized traditional French cooking methods, embracing seasonal ingredients while rejecting fussy garnishes. Revered by many as the ultimate culinary reference book, *Le Guide Culinaire* is considered one of the leading texts on cuisine to this day.

Which choice best describes the main idea of the text?

(A) Escoffier was an accomplished author whose writings encouraged many readers to create their own recipes.

(B) Escoffier's innovative and influential cookbook *Le Guide Culinaire* wasn't recognized as essential by many until long after it was first released in 1903.

(C) Escoffier is renowned for his many culinary inventions, including the bouillon cube.

(D) Escoffier's extensive cookbook *Le Guide Culinaire* is a highly influential collection of recipes.

CONTINUE ➔

10 ☐ Mark for Review

The Y. M. C. A. Boys of Cliffwood is a 1916 novel by Brooks Henderley. In the novel, Henderley portrays Dick Horner as a good-hearted boy whose adventurous nature can cause him trouble: _____

Which quotation from *The Y. M. C. A. Boys of Cliffwood* most effectively illustrates the claim?

Ⓐ "Dick sighed many times. He somehow was thinking of that golden prize which Mr. Holwell had offered for the best farce, and which would be awarded a few nights after Christmas. If only he had won that, there were so many things he had planned to buy with the twenty-five dollars that would have made the Great Day seem so much more joyful."

Ⓑ "As the evening set in Dick felt his gloomy fears increase rather than diminish. It was strange, too, because as a general thing the boy had always been of a cheery disposition, and able to stand up under all manner of ordinary troubles."

Ⓒ "Dick did not have so bad a reputation in the town as the big bully, Nat Silmore, but all the same the stories that drifted to the ears of his anxious mother often caused her gentle heart pain. Dick, upon being appealed to, always promised to turn over a new leaf, and then in the end his natural overflow of wild spirits led him into some new mischief, for which in turn he would be sorry."

Ⓓ "Dick took the letter and looked hard at it. When he saw it was addressed on a typewriter, and that in the upper left-hand corner there was printed the name of a law firm in New York, somehow he was seized with a sense of coming trouble."

11 ☐ Mark for Review

Hula dancing has been an important Hawaiian tradition for hundreds of years. Deeply spiritual and meaningful, hula dances originally honored gods and chiefs and were used to pass down stories that explained all manners of natural phenomena. Over the last 100 years, commercialized hula dancers have been applauded by millions of tourists. However, to recognize the full significance of hula dancing, audience members must have a strong familiarity with the history and stories behind it. Therefore, _____

Which choice most logically completes the text?

Ⓐ hula dancing is more meaningful to those who understand its traditions than are other forms of dance.

Ⓑ hula dancing is among the most popular of all commercialized traditional dance forms.

Ⓒ those with extensive knowledge of hula dancing generally prefer hula to other forms of artistic expression.

Ⓓ tourists are less likely to appreciate hula dancing as fully as are natives who are well-versed in its traditions.

CONTINUE ➤

12 ☐ Mark for Review

The Riace bronzes are two statues of warriors found buried off the coast of southern Italy in 1972. Many art historians claim that the heightened attention to certain anatomical details in these figures proves that they were cast in the 5th century BCE Greece during the Early Classical period. However, Greek sculpture expert B. S. Ridgway argues that these statues were produced centuries later during a period when artists consciously imitated Early Classical style. The fact that these statues were cast in an Early Classical style, thus, _____

Which choice most logically completes the text?

Ⓐ would be challenging to explain if these statues were not cast in the 5th century BCE.

Ⓑ does not definitively prove that these statues originated in the 5th century BCE.

Ⓒ indicates that later statues typically heightened anatomical detail.

Ⓓ proves that these statues did not originate in the 5th century BCE.

13 ☐ Mark for Review

Most psychology PhD programs require students to complete a dissertation, a research-based paper that asserts theories about a psychology topic. To demonstrate their thorough knowledge of their subjects, students must include an extensive review of related literature and research. Education expert Mark Baron contends that although citations are necessary in any literature review, too many direct quotes can result in a stilted dissertation that is difficult to read; paraphrasing the views of other scientists could consequently _____

Which choice most logically completes the text?

Ⓐ allow students to create dissertations that are linguistically clearer and more comprehensible.

Ⓑ result in psychology dissertations that are more popular among non-scientists.

Ⓒ help students' theories better match the consensus views of most renowned psychologists.

Ⓓ enable students to present their theories without having to include numerous scientific citations.

14 ☐ Mark for Review

An American tennis player considered one of the greatest _____ Althea Gibson was the first African American player to win a Grand Slam title, the French Championship, in 1956.

Which choice completes the text so that it conforms to the conventions of Standard English?

Ⓐ ever:

Ⓑ ever;

Ⓒ ever,

Ⓓ ever

CONTINUE ➡

15 ☐ Mark for Review

A photographer and member of the Swinomish and Tulalip tribes, Matika Wilbur started traveling throughout all 50 US states in 2012 to complete Project _____ a multi-year photography project dedicated to documenting contemporary Indigenous life in the more than 562 federally recognized tribes in the US.

Which choice completes the text so that it conforms to the conventions of Standard English?

Ⓐ 562

Ⓑ 562,

Ⓒ 562 and

Ⓓ 562; and

16 ☐ Mark for Review

Paul Baran's invention of packet switching allowed for a more efficient and cost-effective way to transmit data and forms the basis of the modern _____ packet switching's invention, networks transmitted data by relying on circuit switching, a method that depends on a single physical connection between two points.

Which choice completes the text so that it conforms to the conventions of Standard English?

Ⓐ internet and before

Ⓑ internet. Before

Ⓒ internet, before

Ⓓ internet before

17 ☐ Mark for Review

According to local legend, the wild Chincoteague ponies on Assateague Island in the US are descendants of Spanish horses. Recently, while studying bones at a 16th-century historical site, _____ reveals a genetic link between the ponies and early Spanish horses.

Which choice completes the text so that it conforms to the conventions of Standard English?

Ⓐ the discovery archaeologist Nicolas Delsol made is that a horse tooth

Ⓑ a horse tooth, which archaeologist Nicolas Delsol discovered,

Ⓒ archaeologist Nicolas Delsol's discovery of a horse tooth

Ⓓ archaeologist Nicolas Delsol discovered a horse tooth that

18 ☐ Mark for Review

American Anthony Atala is a doctor and bioengineer whose research is helping people with diseased or damaged organs. Listed as one of *Time* magazine's top ten medical breakthroughs in 2011, _____ has the potential to help the many people waiting for organ donors.

Which choice completes the text so that it conforms to the conventions of Standard English?

Ⓐ the organ developed by Atala was fully lab-grown and

Ⓑ Atala's development of fully lab-grown organs

Ⓒ Atala's team developed fully lab-grown organs, which

Ⓓ Atala developed fully lab-grown organs; this

CONTINUE ➡

19 ☐ Mark for Review

When NASA needed tools that were safe for astronauts to use during the Apollo space missions, American company Black & Decker was tasked with developing those tools. In 1979, the company introduced the DustBuster, which _____ of the larger and bulkier traditional vacuum cleaner.

Which choice completes the text so that it conforms to the conventions of Standard English?

(A) is a cordless, lightweight variation

(B) were cordless, lightweight variations

(C) are cordless, lightweight variations

(D) were a cordless, lightweight variation

20 ☐ Mark for Review

Thomas Herbert Elliot Jackson earned his living as a soldier and a coffee farmer, but he was also keenly interested in lepidopterology, the study of moths and _____ the largest collection of native African butterflies and donating his specimens to museums around the world.

Which choice completes the text so that it conforms to the conventions of Standard English?

(A) butterflies, amassing

(B) butterflies amassing

(C) butterflies. Amassing

(D) butterflies; amassing

21 ☐ Mark for Review

The tidal flats, or mudflats, in Korea provide safe habitats for many different species and are listed as Wetland Protected Areas under the Wetlands Conservation Act. _____ these sites still face a wide variety of threats from humans: construction of bridges, mining, wind farms, and fishing all decrease the biodiversity of the flats.

Which choice completes the text with the most logical transition?

(A) However,

(B) Likewise,

(C) Therefore,

(D) Furthermore,

22 ☐ Mark for Review

James Soong was initially predicted to win the 2000 Taiwanese presidential election until news broke of his potential involvement in corrupt financial practices. _____ Shui-bian Chen was elected president of Taiwan alongside Annette Lu as vice president, ending over 50 years of control by the Chinese Nationalist Party.

Which choice completes the text with the most logical transition?

(A) Specifically,

(B) Likewise,

(C) Moreover,

(D) Afterward,

CONTINUE ➡

23 🔖 Mark for Review

American artist Simone Leigh has stated that her works are intended to put Black women in the forefront and highlight their complex relationships with various societal structures. For her sculpture *Brick House*, Simone created an enormous bronze bust of a Black woman with a torso that resembles a clay house; the sculpture was originally placed in New York City among old and new high-rise buildings. _____ Leigh's exhibition *The Waiting Room* explores an alternative vision of healthcare that is shaped by the African-American female experience.

Which choice completes the text with the most logical transition?

Ⓐ Similarly,

Ⓑ For instance,

Ⓒ Nevertheless,

Ⓓ Therefore,

24 🔖 Mark for Review

While researching a topic, a student has taken the following notes:

- In 1980, video game designers and programmers Roberta and Ken Williams released an adventure game that combined text with images.
- Their game, *Mystery House*, was inspired by author Agatha Christie's mysteries.
- Players of the game find themselves locked in a house that they have to explore.
- As they explore, they meet other characters and learn that they have to find and stop a murderer.
- Images of each location in the house accompanied the text of the game.
- The game was successful because all of the other adventure games at the time only had text.

The student wants to explain an advantage of the format of *Mystery House*. Which choice most effectively uses relevant information from the notes to accomplish this goal?

Ⓐ Using images and text, programmers Roberta and Ken Williams created *Mystery House*, a video game murder mystery.

Ⓑ The format of *Mystery House* was successful because it combined text and images, unlike other video games at the time.

Ⓒ To find and stop the murderer, players explored a house and met other characters.

Ⓓ *Mystery House* contained images of each location of a house that players could explore.

CONTINUE →

25 ⬚ Mark for Review

While researching a topic, a student has taken the following notes:

- Alice Catherine Evans discovered that the bacteria *Bacillus abortus* causes brucellosis in 1917.
- Brucellosis is a disease that can affect cows and humans.
- Evans found that consuming raw, unpasteurized cow milk could lead to infection in humans.
- She recommended pasteurization, treating food with mild heat, for dairy milk.
- Her vital work led to wider acceptance of pasteurization and a reduction in the occurrence of brucellosis.

The student wants to emphasize the significance of Evans's research. Which choice most effectively uses relevant information from the notes to accomplish this goal?

(A) Evans discovered that humans could become infected with the bacteria *Bacillus abortus* from drinking raw, unpasteurized cow milk.

(B) Based on her research into brucellosis, Evans recommended pasteurization, treating food with mild heat, for dairy milk.

(C) Evans made the connection between the bacteria *Bacillus abortus* and the disease brucellosis in 1917.

(D) Evans's 1917 discovery of the connection between *Bacillus abortus* and brucellosis was vital to the public's wider acceptance of pasteurization and reduction in brucellosis infections.

26 ⬚ Mark for Review

While researching a topic, a student has taken the following notes:

- Physicists K. Alex Müller and Georg Bednorz were researching cuprates, a type of material, at IBM.
- In 1986, they observed that the cuprates could superconduct at a temperature of 30 kelvins.
- Superconductive materials carry an electric current without any resistance.
- The first observation of superconductivity was of a mercury wire at 4 kelvins, in 1911.
- Cuprates were labeled "high-temperature superconductors."

The student wants to contrast the superconductivity of mercury wire with that of cuprates. Which choice most effectively uses relevant information from the notes to accomplish this goal?

(A) While mercury wire becomes superconductive at 4 kelvins, cuprates are high-temperature superconductors, becoming superconductive at 30 kelvins.

(B) Cuprates are "high-temperature superconductors," unlike mercury wire, because they superconduct at a temperature of 30 kelvins.

(C) Materials can become superconductive and carry an electric current without any resistance at different temperatures.

(D) Although mercury wire's superconductivity was observed in 1911, cuprates' superconductivity was not observed until over seventy years later.

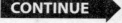
CONTINUE

27 ☐ Mark for Review

While researching a topic, a student has taken the following notes:

- In the 1950s and '60s, the drug thalidomide was used in Europe to treat multiple conditions, including morning sickness experienced in pregnancy.

- The drug, however, was not safe for developing fetuses and led to many negative consequences.

- This situation prompted many countries to adopt better drug regulation and monitoring.

- In the US, the 1962 Kefauver-Harris Amendment added a requirement for a drug to be approved for sale.

- The Amendment required drug manufacturers to provide proof of the effectiveness of the drugs.

The student wants to present the significance of the Kefauver-Harris Amendment to an audience unfamiliar with the medication thalidomide. Which choice most effectively uses relevant information from the notes to accomplish this goal?

(A) Before the Kefauver-Harris Amendment, drug manufacturers were not required to prove a drug's effectiveness.

(B) The negative effects of the use of thalidomide in Europe in the 1950s and '60s led to the 1962 Kefauver-Harris Amendment.

(C) The 1962 Kefauver-Harris Amendment, which requires proof of a drug's effectiveness, was a result of the negative consequences of the morning sickness medication thalidomide.

(D) The medication thalidomide was used to treat morning sickness when the Kefauver-Harris Amendment went into effect.

YIELD

Once you've finished (or run out of time for) this section, use the answer key to determine how many questions you got right. If you got fewer than 14 questions right, move on to Module 2—Easier, otherwise move on to Module 2—Harder.

Test 2—Reading and Writing
Module 2—Easier

Turn to Section 1 of your answer sheet to answer the questions in this section.

---

1 ▯ Mark for Review

Environmental analysts are tasked with _____ the complete ecological evaluation of goods through the use of life-cycle assessments: by looking at the manufacture, distribution, and use of a commercial product, they can find out the environmental impact of a product.

Which choice completes the text with the most logical and precise word or phrase?

- (A) separating
- (B) convincing
- (C) operating
- (D) determining

2 ▯ Mark for Review

For Ghanaian coffin artist Paa Joe, remaining _____ is key to his art form. Customers approach him in a time of grief, hoping to get a custom piece designed to embody meaningful characteristics of their deceased loved ones. After carefully drawing up a design, Joe honors their requests through his work and creates a unique coffin to memorialize the life of the individual who will be placed in it; he believes his designs are a way to carry a piece of life in this world to the afterlife.

Which choice completes the text with the most logical and precise word or phrase?

- (A) compassionate
- (B) hesitant
- (C) assertive
- (D) insensitive

CONTINUE ▶

3 ☐ Mark for Review

In the early 2000s, due to a lack of _____ ways to prevent the disease, the threat of being infected by HIV grew exponentially in South Africa. However, in 2007, South African epidemiologist Quarraisha Abdool Karim was the lead investigator in a study that tested the efficacy of Tenofovir, a gel that was found to lower the risk of contracting HIV by 39%.

Which choice completes the text with the most logical and precise word or phrase?

(A) inefficient

(B) unreasonable

(C) effective

(D) charismatic

4 ☐ Mark for Review

The Birmingham campaign was created in the early 1960s to draw attention to the injustice in the lives of African Americans in Alabama with nonviolent sit-ins, boycotts, and marches. These _____ attempts for change resulted in mass arrests of protestors and physical attacks from police and their dogs.

Which choice completes the text with the most logical and precise word or phrase?

(A) indifferent

(B) peaceful

(C) essential

(D) bland

5 ☐ Mark for Review

Months before the 1998 bombing of the US Embassy in Nairobi, Prudence Bushnell, the US ambassador to Kenya, unsuccessfully requested increased security for her mission several times. When Washington was not able to _____ her appeal, she wrote to US Secretary of State Madeleine Albright pleading for support but was ignored.

Which choice completes the text with the most logical and precise word or phrase?

(A) certify

(B) mistake

(C) approve

(D) demonstrate

6 ☐ Mark for Review

Despite being a best-selling writer, Georgette Heyer continuously _____ to engage in all forms of publicity for her publications after the success of her novel *These Old Shades*. She so believed that her private life was irrelevant to the success of her novels that her fans didn't learn of her married name until after her death.

Which choice completes the text with the most logical and precise word or phrase?

(A) refused

(B) aspired

(C) needed

(D) proceeded

CONTINUE ►

7 ⬚ Mark for Review

In the late 1960s, Dr. Donald Hopkins was hired by the Centers for Disease Control to help implement a program to eradicate smallpox in Sierra Leone. The country had had a major outbreak of the disease one year before Hopkins' arrival and had the highest number of recorded cases in the world. Upon their arrival, Hopkins and his team immediately began mass distribution of the smallpox vaccine, using any means of transportation necessary. Through the use of jet injectors, they were able to vaccinate 1,000 people every 60 minutes.

Which choice best states the main purpose of the text?

(A) To present the effects of smallpox on Sierra Leone

(B) To describe Hopkins' career with the Centers for Disease Control

(C) To highlight the availability of the smallpox vaccine

(D) To explain how Hopkins addressed smallpox in Sierra Leone

CONTINUE

8 ☐ Mark for Review

The following text is from James E. McGirt's 1906 poem "A Sailor's Departure."

> My dearest child, I have no wealth to give you,
> No ring of gold to you can I impart;
> Going, yet why should going grieve you?
> You have my heart.
>
> In calm, in storm, no matter how the weather,
> My one great thought shall ever be of thee;
> Tell me, I pray thee, tell me whether
> You'll think of me?

Which choice best states the main purpose of the text?

- Ⓐ To assure a loved one that she will not be forgotten

- Ⓑ To explain why the speaker loves an individual so dearly

- Ⓒ To justify to a loved one why the speaker is leaving and when he will be back

- Ⓓ To instruct a loved one on what to do while the speaker is gone

9 ☐ Mark for Review

Text 1

The Great Famine of Ireland was an era in Irish history that resulted in hunger and sickness throughout the country. The Irish Lumper potato crop was exposed to the bacteria *Phytophthora infestans* in the 1840s, creating devastating effects. Upon studying the physical impacts of the infestation of the potatoes, scientists originally believed the disease was caused by the US-1 strain of the bacteria. This variety of the bacteria is a very common source of damage to crops and is still responsible for the destruction of crops today.

Text 2

An interested group of researchers tested dried leaves from small, shriveled, inedible potato plants preserved from the Great Famine of Ireland. After collecting the leaves, the researchers were able to analyze them alongside the DNA of modern US-1 strains of the bacteria and found that US-1 was not the cause of the catastrophe. It was concluded that, although the US-1 strain is a common cause of crop loss, a formerly undiscovered strain of the bacteria, HERB-1, was actually at fault for the famine.

Based on the texts, what would the researchers in Text 2 most likely say about the scientists' initial belief in Text 1?

- Ⓐ It is mistaken because the scientists made the assumption that HERB-1 was the strain that caused the famine.

- Ⓑ It is logical because the US-1 strain is similar to the HERB-1 strain but only affects potato crops.

- Ⓒ It is sensible because of how common the US-1 strain is, but the DNA analysis suggests that HERB-1 was to blame.

- Ⓓ It is puzzling because it is unclear why the scientists would think that US-1 caused the famine.

CONTINUE ➡

10 ▢ Mark for Review

The following text is from Amy Lowell's 1912 poem "Diya," originally "Delta-iota-psi-alpha."

> Ah, Dearest, you are good to love me so,
> And yet I would not have it goodness, rather
> Excess of selfishness in you to need
> Me through and through, as flowers need the sun.
> I wonder can it really be that you
> And I are here alone, and that the night
> Is full of hours, and all the world asleep,
> And none can call to you to come away.

Based on the text, in what way is the speaker like the sun?

Ⓐ She shines brightly on others.

Ⓑ She provides something that is needed.

Ⓒ She is completely alone.

Ⓓ She is asleep at night with the rest of the world.

11 ▢ Mark for Review

"The Haunted Orchard" is a 1912 short story by Richard Le Gallienne. In the story, the main character suspects that his orchard is haunted by the spirit of a young girl. As a result, he is eager to help bring peace to the restless spirit, stating _____

Which quotation from "The Haunted Orchard" most effectively illustrates the claim?

Ⓐ "I had lived in the old house for about a month, when one afternoon a strange thing happened to me."

Ⓑ "And the next day I had a curious confirmation of my theory."

Ⓒ "Poor child! tell me of your grief – that I may help your sorrowing heart to rest."

Ⓓ "But, of course, there was no answer; yet that night I dreamed a strange dream."

12 ▢ Mark for Review

Characteristics of Biomes

Type of biome	Maximum temperature (°F)	Annual precipitation
Temperate forest	86	30–59
Desert	100	0–10
Boreal forest	68	12–35
Tropical forest	77	79–394
Grassland	86	20–35

An ecologist is interested in studying the habitats of animals living within a biome that has a range of annual precipitation that includes 30 inches but does not exceed a maximum temperature of 80°F. Based on the characteristics of biomes, he decided to study the animals living within a _____

Which choice most effectively uses data from the table to complete the text?

Ⓐ temperate forest.

Ⓑ tropical forest.

Ⓒ grassland.

Ⓓ boreal forest.

CONTINUE ➡

13 ☐ Mark for Review

Properties of Five Unknown Elements

Element	Boiling point (K)	Heat Capacity (J/g·k)	Electron affinity (kJ/mol)	First ionization energy (eV)
A	2,835	0.38	118.4	7.726
B	2,435	0.235	125.6	7.576
C	3,003	0.44	112	7.639
D	2,022	0.13	35.1	7.417
E	717.8	0.71	200	10.36

Unknown elements can be identified as metals or nonmetals based on a variety of characteristics. Metals are generally considered to have high boiling points (over 1,500 K) and low electron affinities (less than 150 kJ/mol), while nonmetals have low boiling points (less than 1,000 K) and very high electron affinities. A science student collected information about five unknown elements in the table above and stated that four of the elements are metals and one element is a nonmetal.

Which choice best describes data from the table that support the student's assertion?

(A) Four of the five elements have boiling points above 1,500 K, and all except for element E have electron affinities of less than 150 kJ/mol.

(B) Element E has a low boiling point of 717.8 K and a high first ionization energy of 10.36 eV.

(C) Four of the five elements have a first ionization energy around 7 eV, and all except element D have a heat capacity above 0.2 J/g·K.

(D) All of the elements have a heat capacity from 0.13 and 0.44 J/g·K, and only element E has an electron affinity greater than 150 kJ/mol.

14 ☐ Mark for Review

An art student is studying *chiaroscuro*, one of the specific painting styles used in the Renaissance period that features contrasting light and dark artistic elements within an art piece. While attending a local art museum to view its exhibit of Renaissance chiaroscuro paintings, the student notices the inclusion of a modern art portrait depicting Leonardo da Vinci, a famous Renaissance artist and inventor. However, the portrait does not contain elements of chiaroscuro and, thus, the student believes that the work was included as a way to attract new visitors.

Which statement, if true, would most directly support the student's claim?

(A) New museum visitors rarely visit the second floor of the museum, which contains exhibits from the Renaissance, Baroque, and Neoclassical art periods.

(B) The Renaissance exhibit also included other modern art portraits of Impressionist and Expressionist artists.

(C) The portrait of Leonardo da Vinci was placed at the entrance to the Renaissance exhibit.

(D) The exhibit's curators displayed the modern portrait of Leonardo da Vinci because of its appeal to people who don't normally visit art museums.

CONTINUE

15   ☐ Mark for Review

Studies on the effects of bilingualism on cognitive development have shown an array of benefits, such as improved memory recall, cognitive processing, and executive function. A team of researchers decided to compare the task-switching abilities of different bilinguals (Spanish-English, Chinese-English, and French-English speakers) to English monolinguals. All bilingual groups demonstrated a significantly shorter time spent on task-switching tests than did the English monolinguals. Thus, the researchers claim that bilinguals can switch between tasks at a faster rate due to their routine use of language-switching.

Which finding, if true, would most strongly support the researchers' claim?

(A) Bilinguals who speak both languages every day are faster at task-switching than are bilinguals who speak one of the languages less frequently.

(B) Both bilinguals and English monolinguals take a long time to complete cognitive processing tasks.

(C) English monolinguals have better memory recall than bilinguals do.

(D) Bilingual students tend to be academic achievers, and academic achievers are known to be faster at task-switching than the general population is.

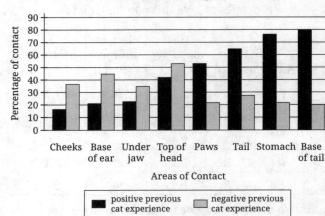

Effects of Previous Cat Experience on Areas of Contact and Percentage of Contact

Cats are generally known to be sensitive to human interactions and prefer certain contact areas, such as the cheeks, base of ear, and under the jaw, while disliking contact on the stomach or the base of the tail. A team of researchers investigated the effect of previous cat experience, either in the form of pet ownership or random interactions with cats, and whether this made participants more likely to exhibit good cat handling techniques according to the cats' preferred contact areas. Participants were asked to spend five minutes in a pen with a cat on three different occasions. The percentage of contact and areas contacted during this time were observed and plotted in the graph above. The researchers claimed that previous positive cat experience was not predictive of good cat handling techniques; in fact, participants with previous negative cat experience demonstrated better cat handling techniques.

CONTINUE ➤

16 ☐ Mark for Review

Which choice best describes data in the graph that support the researchers' claim?

- Ⓐ Participants with previous positive cat experiences had lower percentages of contact in areas disliked by cats than did participants with previous negative cat experiences.

- Ⓑ Participants with previous negative cat experiences had greater percentages of contact in areas preferred by cats than did participants with previous positive cat experiences.

- Ⓒ Participants with previous positive cat experiences had similar percentages of contact for the cats' cheeks, base of ear, and under jaw areas.

- Ⓓ Participants with previous negative cat experiences had more contact with cats' top of head than paws.

17 ☐ Mark for Review

Japanese producer and writer Hayao Miyazaki is renowned for the movie products of Studio Ghibli. Although the studio's films are presented through animation, the stories remain relevant to both children and adults. Drawing from Japanese elements, Miyazaki crafts poignant stories about humans and the environment as told through the eyes of children. For example, in *Princess Mononoke*, the nature spirits, referred to as *shishigami*, fight to preserve their forest against human industrialization. Miyazaki showcases the importance of protecting the environment for civilization to thrive, not through destruction but through communing with nature.

Which choice best describes Miyazaki's approach to film, as presented in the text?

- Ⓐ He is inspired by nature spirits when writing his films.

- Ⓑ He incorporates Japanese elements into his animated films.

- Ⓒ He showcases Japanese and Western influences equally in his films.

- Ⓓ He believes that films about environmental preservation will encourage people to commune with nature.

CONTINUE →

---

18 ☐ Mark for Review

In response to attacks by herbivorous insects, thale cress plants _____ with their neighbors by releasing volatile compounds called jasmonates. When nearby plants detect jasmonates in contact with their leaves, they bolster their defenses against herbivory by increasing the production of chemical insect repellents.

Which choice completes the text so that it conforms to the conventions of Standard English?

Ⓐ communicating

Ⓑ communicate

Ⓒ to communicate

Ⓓ having communicated

19 ☐ Mark for Review

Farmers throughout the islands of Polynesia _____ sweet potato as a staple crop since before the arrival of European explorers. Surprisingly, the plant is now known to have been domesticated in the Americas, leading some scientists to propose theories of pre-Columbian voyages from Polynesia to the west coast of South America; other researchers suggest travel by Indigenous Americans in the opposite direction.

Which choice completes the text so that it conforms to the conventions of Standard English?

Ⓐ having grown

Ⓑ to grow

Ⓒ growing

Ⓓ have grown

20 ☐ Mark for Review

In 1972, Jamaican American musician Clive Campbell, performing as DJ Kool Herc, first mixed extended percussion sections, or "breaks," into samples of older records. After this, breaks _____ one of the defining elements of the musical structure of hip hop.

Which choice completes the text so that it conforms to the conventions of Standard English?

Ⓐ became

Ⓑ become

Ⓒ had become

Ⓓ will become

21 ☐ Mark for Review

When German climatologist Alfred Wegener first published his hypothesis of continental drift in 1912, he was unable to come up with a plausible mechanism to explain how the continents could _____ it was not until the discovery of seafloor spreading at mid-ocean ridges that his idea became widely accepted.

Which choice completes the text so that it conforms to the conventions of Standard English?

Ⓐ move,

Ⓑ move

Ⓒ move and

Ⓓ move, and

CONTINUE ➡

22 ☐ Mark for Review

Since the European robin (*Erithacus rubecula*), like many other species of birds, is required to migrate seasonally to survive, it _____ between its summer and winter ranges by using a protein called cryptochrome in its eyes to sense the planet's magnetic field.

Which choice completes the text so that it conforms to the conventions of Standard English?

Ⓐ would navigate

Ⓑ navigates

Ⓒ navigated

Ⓓ had navigated

23 ☐ Mark for Review

Science commentator Anjana Ahuja wrote that a total solar eclipse is "the greatest show on Earth." This spectacular sight happens relatively rarely because of the eccentricity of the Moon's orbit. A total solar eclipse (visible only from a narrow strip of the Earth's surface during each event) is _____ the Moon appears large enough to completely obscure the solar disc.

Which choice completes the text so that it conforms to the conventions of Standard English?

Ⓐ observed wherever

Ⓑ observed, wherever

Ⓒ observed; wherever

Ⓓ observed. Wherever

24 ☐ Mark for Review

Canadian Cree/Métis poet and artist Gregory Scofield initially was ashamed of his Métis background and longed to be purely Cree. _____ Scofield learned to appreciate the Métis aspects of his identity after participating in a yearly Métis festival celebrating the culture.

Which choice completes the text with the most logical transition?

Ⓐ Additionally,

Ⓑ In fact,

Ⓒ Nevertheless,

Ⓓ Besides,

25 ☐ Mark for Review

The dulcimer is a three- or four-stringed instrument with diatonic fretting. While ancient versions have been found dating back to the early 1800s within Scotch and Irish communities in the Appalachian Mountains, there is very little archaeological or written evidence linking this instrument to the actual countries of Scotland or Ireland. _____ the history of the instrument is largely up for debate.

Which choice completes the text with the most logical transition?

Ⓐ Still,

Ⓑ However,

Ⓒ Furthermore,

Ⓓ Therefore,

CONTINUE ➡

26 ☐ Mark for Review

While researching a topic, a student has taken the following notes:

- Eric Gansworth is a Haudenosaunee author who writes about contemporary Native American life and culture.
- He published his young adult poetic memoir *Apple: Skin to the Core* in 2020.
- *Apple: Skin to the Core* discusses Gansworth's childhood on a Tuscarora reservation.
- Gansworth was an enrolled citizen of the Onondaga Nation but was raised within the Tuscarora Nation.

The student wants to describe *Apple: Skin to the Core* to an audience unfamiliar with Eric Gansworth. Which choice most effectively uses relevant information from the notes to accomplish this goal?

(A) Eric Gansworth's *Apple: Skin to the Core* discusses being raised within the Tuscarora Nation.

(B) Gansworth's 2020 book *Apple: Skin to the Core*, which discusses growing up on a Tuscarora reservation, focuses on contemporary Native American life and culture.

(C) *Apple: Skin to the Core*, a 2020 book by Haudenosaunee author Eric Gansworth, discusses Gansworth's childhood as an enrolled citizen of the Onondaga Nation being raised on a Tuscarora reservation.

(D) Haudenosaunee author Eric Gansworth published *Apple: Skin to the Core* in 2020.

27 ☐ Mark for Review

While researching a topic, a student has taken the following notes:

- When clothes develop holes or rips, they can be repaired with hand sewing.
- The running stitch is the most basic stitch and can be used to join two pieces of fabric.
- For areas of garments that are subject to greater pulling, the running stitch is not always ideal because it is relatively weak.
- Backstitch, which is a variation of the running stitch that has no gaps because it goes back over previous stitches, can be used to repair clothes.
- This stitch is strong and flexible.

The student wants to explain an advantage of backstitch. Which choice most effectively uses relevant information from the notes to accomplish this goal?

(A) Two methods for repairing clothes, the running stitch and backstitch, differ in their strength.

(B) To repair clothes that have holes or rips, both the basic running stitch and backstitch, a variation with no gaps, can be used.

(C) Going back over previous stitches produces stronger and more flexible repairs than does the running stitch, which is relatively weak.

(D) In repairing clothing that has holes or rips, the running stitch is not always ideal.

STOP
If you finish before time is called, you may check your work on this module only.
Do not turn to any other module in the test.

Test 2—Reading and Writing
Module 2—Harder

Turn to Section 1 of your answer sheet to answer the questions in this section.

---

1 ☐ Mark for Review

According to ecologists, bumblebees are particularly _____ the effects of climate change. When bumblebees are under stress during the early developmental stages of their life cycle, their wings grow to be asymmetrical, and scientists have observed that there has been an increase in imbalanced wings which coincided with the escalated temperatures caused by climate change.

Which choice completes the text with the most logical and precise word or phrase?

(A) unaffected by

(B) incongruent with

(C) independent of

(D) susceptible to

---

2 ☐ Mark for Review

Recent measurements of the mass of a certain subatomic particle, the W boson, were higher than would ordinarily be predicted by the Standard Model of particle physics. While these findings won't necessarily require that scientists _____ the Standard Model, the new data might indicate that some modifications to our understanding of the nature of these particles are warranted.

Which choice completes the text with the most logical and precise word or phrase?

(A) overhaul

(B) withhold

(C) embrace

(D) misapprehend

CONTINUE

---

3 ⚑ Mark for Review

Archimedes of Syracuse, an ancient Greek scientist active in the third century BCE, is predominantly renowned for a method for measuring volume using water displacement. However, in 1906, a parchment containing Archimedes's writings was discovered which revealed that he was also a pioneering mathematician who had _____ calculus, describing concepts thought to have been first developed in the 1500s.

Which choice completes the text with the most logical and precise word or phrase?

Ⓐ exemplified

Ⓑ verified

Ⓒ anticipated

Ⓓ translated

---

4 ⚑ Mark for Review

The Permian-Triassic extinction eliminated 90 percent of Earth's life and so was thought to have had a devastating effect on the remaining ecosystems. However, some scientists posit that the plants left over weren't as _____ as assumed; analysis of the reptile Palacrodon's fossilized teeth reveals that it had a diet of vegetation, indicating that plants at this time period were surprisingly resilient.

Which choice completes the text with the most logical and precise word or phrase?

Ⓐ assailable

Ⓑ determinate

Ⓒ objectionable

Ⓓ liminal

---

5 ⚑ Mark for Review

John Ball, a revolutionary priest active in the years following the Black Death during the late 14th century, quickly gained notoriety for _____ both religious and secular authorities: this condemnation was aimed at tearing down the class system in place at the time and establishing a new, egalitarian society.

Which choice completes the text with the most logical and precise word or phrase?

Ⓐ proselytizing

Ⓑ censuring

Ⓒ envisaging

Ⓓ declaring

CONTINUE ➡

6 ☐ Mark for Review

The following text is adapted from Hubert Crackanthorpe's 1896 short story "Anthony Garstin's Courtship."

A stampede of huddled sheep, wildly scampering over the slaty shingle, emerged from the leaden mist that muffled the fell-top, and a shrill shepherd's whistle broke the damp stillness of the air. And presently a man's figure appeared, following the sheep down the hillside. He halted a moment to whistle curtly to his two dogs, who, laying back their ears, chased the sheep at top speed beyond the brow; then, his hands deep in his pockets, he strode vigorously forward. A streak of white smoke from a toiling train was creeping silently across the distance: the great, grey, desolate undulations of treeless country showed no other sign of life.

Which choice best describes the function of the underlined sentence in the text as a whole?

(A) It emphasizes the man's solitude and the stillness of his environment.

(B) It suggests that the man longs to travel away from his dull home.

(C) It provides a description of what the man sees on his daily walk.

(D) It illustrates the vastness of the surroundings compared to the train's destination.

7 ☐ Mark for Review

The following text is adapted from Mary Johnston's 1915 novel *The Fortunes of Garin*. Garin, a young man bound to serve Lord Raimbaut, has been given an opportunity to leave and assist a church leader.

Garin sought his inn and his horse. He was in Roche-de-Frêne upon Raimbaut's business, but that over, he had leave to ride to Castel-Noir and spend three days with his brother. The merry-making in the town tempted, but the way was long and he must go. A chain of five girls crossed his path, laughing, making dancing steps, their robes kilted high, red and yellow flowers in their hair. "What a beautiful young man!" said their eyes. "Stay—stay!" Garin wanted to stay— but he was not without judgment and he went.

Which choice best describes the function of the underlined sentence in the text as a whole?

(A) It exemplifies a circumstance that is established in the previous sentence.

(B) It foreshadows an emotion that a character experiences in the following sentence.

(C) It provides a visual description of several characters in the scene.

(D) It hints at the urgency a character feels about the task before him.

CONTINUE ➡

8 ☐ Mark for Review

The following text is adapted from Charles Dickens's 1859 historical novel *A Tale of Two Cities*.

There were a king with a large jaw and a queen with a plain face, on the throne of England; there were a king with a large jaw and a queen with a fair face, on the throne of France. In both countries it was clearer than crystal to the lords of the State preserves of loaves and fishes, that things in general were settled for ever.

Which choice best states the main purpose of the text?

(A) To compare and contrast the conditions of two competing nations

(B) To establish that the ruling classes enjoyed an apparent stability in their respective nations

(C) To assert that the kings of each nation were similar to each other but the queens were strikingly distinct

(D) To criticize the upper classes for hoarding food and withholding resources from the lower classes

9 ☐ Mark for Review

Text 1

While both normal cells and cancer cells use the sugar glucose as an energy source, normal cells use mitochondria to process the glucose, whereas cancer cells, in need of a larger amount of energy, utilize a different, faster process. Thus, cancer cells process a sizable amount of glucose, which is unsurprising, but the mystery that has puzzled oncologists concerns the large amount of glucose that is excreted as waste—if cancer cells have such a high need for glucose, why are they processing the sugar so inefficiently?

Text 2

Dr. Gary Patti and colleagues have studied the mechanisms by which glucose is absorbed by cancer cells and compared them to the processes utilized by normal cells. Patti discovered that cancer cells have an upper limit for the amount of glucose that can be processed efficiently, as has long been observed in normal cells.

Based on the texts, how would Patti and colleagues (Text 2) most likely respond to the "mystery" discussed in Text 1?

(A) By proposing that further research into mitochondria is necessary in order to understand this issue

(B) By asserting that though normal cells and cancer cells process glucose differently, they both have a maximum threshold for the amount of glucose that can be efficiently converted into energy

(C) By arguing that not nearly as much glucose is required by cancer cells as was previously assumed

(D) By suggesting that, contrary to what was originally presumed, cancer cells are actually using the same mitochondrial processes that normal cells are

CONTINUE ➡

10 ⚑ Mark for Review

Personality is typically measured by five traits: extraversion, emotional stability, agreeableness, conscientiousness, and openness to experience. Psychologist Jean M. Twenge and colleagues have hypothesized that sociocultural environment—the evolving attitudes, behavior, and values in society—affects an individual's personality in addition to genetics and family environment, two factors that are more studied and thus better understood. Twenge purports to have found support for this relationship between sociocultural environment and personality. She looked at high school students and compared their birth cohorts (all people born the same year as a given individual) with their scores on the Eysenck Personality Inventory and Eysenck Personality Questionnaire, two scales by which an individual's level of extraversion can be measured.

Which finding from the researchers' study, if true, would most strongly support Twenge's hypothesis?

- Ⓐ Female participants scored significantly higher than did their male counterparts in both emotional stability and openness to experience.

- Ⓑ High school students from 1990 scored higher in extraversion than did high school students from 1970.

- Ⓒ Those who grew up in households above a certain income level scored significantly higher in agreeableness than those from a lower socioeconomic bracket.

- Ⓓ Participants from the older birth cohort used a greater number of words when describing their personalities than did those from the younger birth cohort.

11 ⚑ Mark for Review

Mexican Maya author Marisol Ceh Moo writes in both Spanish and Yucatec (one of the 33 Mayan languages). She gained notoriety upon publication of her debut novel *Teya, the Heart of a Woman*, the first novel written by a woman in the Yucatec language. Traditionally, Maya authors primarily write short stories, songs, and poems. They typically focus on retelling myths or writing about subjects such as Mayan culture and Indigenous peoples. Instead, Ceh Moo sets her story in contemporary times and depicts the life, career, and assassination of a young leader of a group of communist revolutionaries.

Which choice best describes Ceh Moo's approach to literature, as presented in the text?

- Ⓐ She is influenced by the myths of Maya culture but gives them a modern spin by setting her stories in the present day.

- Ⓑ She pays tribute to her Maya heritage while simultaneously defying the expectations that come from working in a Mayan language.

- Ⓒ She takes inspiration from both her Maya and Mexican heritages equally.

- Ⓓ She uses her work to criticize both colonialist powers and the traditionalists of her own culture.

CONTINUE ➡

Effects of Enhancement Measures on Flowers and Wild Bees

Enhancement measure	Mean flower abundance (number of individuals per species)	Mean flower species richness (number of different species)	Mean wild bee abundance (number of individuals per species)	Mean wild bee species richness (number of different species)
Control	82.4	2.6	0.6	0.5
Flower strip	302.1	6.2	6.7	3.1
Hedge	177.5	2.4	2.1	1.3
Improved hedge	249.7	4.2	3.1	1.6

Knowing that wild bees play an essential role in the cultivation of crops via pollination while noting that such bees are often scarce because of insufficient pollen, ecologists Vivien von Königslöw, Felix Fornoff, and Alexandra-Maria Klein studied the impact of three different additions to a landscape: perennial flower strips, hedges, and improved hedges that included a layer of sown herb. While all of the attempted methods for attracting more bees were successful to varying degrees when compared with a control group of regular ground vegetation, the researchers concluded that flower strips were most effective, observing that _____

Which choice most effectively uses data from the table to support the research team's conclusion?

(A) when hedges were enhanced with a layer of sown herb, the number of flower species was greater than that yielded by regular hedges.

(B) flower strips attracted significantly more wild bees than did the control group, suggesting that bees are more attracted to flowers than to the ground vegetation.

(C) for each metric of abundance and species richness that was measured, the flower strip yielded the greatest numbers.

(D) the control group actually had a more diverse array of flower species than did the improved hedges.

CONTINUE ➡

Effect of Physically Active Lessons on Academic Success

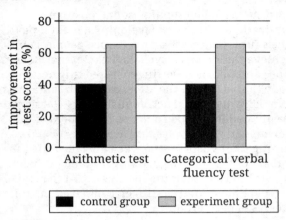

It has been suggested that the inclusion of physically active lessons with the regular mathematical curriculum can aid in academic success. To investigate this hypothesis, psychologist Daniele Magistro and colleagues looked at two groups of students: an experimental group that received physically active mathematics lessons and a control group that received the usual mathematics curriculum. At the end of a two-year period, both groups of students were subjected to a battery of tests of their cognitive function, including an arithmetic test and a categorical verbal fluency test (which tested their ability to describe mathematical calculations in words). Magistro and his colleagues recommended that physically active lessons be henceforth included in the mathematics curriculum.

---

13 ☐ Mark for Review

Which choice best describes data from the graph that support Magistro and colleagues' recommendation?

Ⓐ The students in the control group performed worse in verbal fluency at the end of the study than they did at the start.

Ⓑ The experimental group improved to a higher degree on the categorical verbal fluency test than on the arithmetic test.

Ⓒ While both groups increased their arithmetic and verbal fluency skills, the experimental group's increases were significantly greater than those of the control group.

Ⓓ Both the control group and the experimental group showed an improvement on the arithmetic test of at least 40%.

CONTINUE

14 ☐ Mark for Review

The Seagull is an 1895 play by Anton Chekhov. In the play, the character of Konstantin Treplev is an ambitious playwright and the son of a famous actress. Yearning to create an innovative style of theater, Treplev is heavily critical of the art form's established tropes, as is evident when he _____

Which choice most effectively uses a quotation from *The Seagull* to illustrate the claim?

(A) says of the stage, "Just like a real theater! See, there we have the curtain, the foreground, the background, and all."

(B) says of his craft, "Writing is a pleasure to me, and so is reading the proofs, but no sooner does a book leave the press than it becomes odious to me; it is not what I meant it to be; I made a mistake to write it at all; I am provoked and discouraged."

(C) introduces his play to the audience, "O, ye time-honored, ancient mists that drive at night across the surface of this lake, blind you our eyes with sleep, and show us in our dreams that which will be in twice ten thousand years!"

(D) says of other productions, "when playwrights give us under a thousand different guises the same, same, same old stuff, then I must needs run from it, as Maupassant ran from the Eiffel Tower that was about to crush him by its vulgarity."

15 ☐ Mark for Review

According to conventional wisdom, positive visualization—the act of developing a mental picture of one's future success—can enhance people's ability to achieve their goals. Psychologists Heather Barry Kappes and Gabriele Oettingen tested this notion with a study that looked at the effect that such fantasies had on participants' actual accomplishments. Participants were divided into two groups: the members of the experimental group were told to actively visualize attaining their goals for the week ahead, while the members of the control group were given no specific strategy for accomplishing their goals. At the end of the week, Kappes and Oettingen compared the relative successes of each group.

Which finding from Kappes and Oettingen's study, if true, would most directly weaken the claim made by people who favor the conventional view of positive visualization?

(A) The members of the control group accomplished fewer goals than did those in the experimental group, but the members of the control group reported greater feelings of pride in their accomplishments.

(B) Participants who were practicing positive visualization accomplished a slightly higher number of their goals than did those who utilized a different technique.

(C) Even though the participants in the control group were told they could select any strategy they wanted for achieving their goals, the vast majority of them elected to use positive visualization.

(D) Compared to the participants who were engaged in the practice of positive visualization, those who were not told to visualize attaining goals reported higher numbers of goals accomplished by the end of the week.

CONTINUE ➡

Self-Reported Intensity of Nightmares

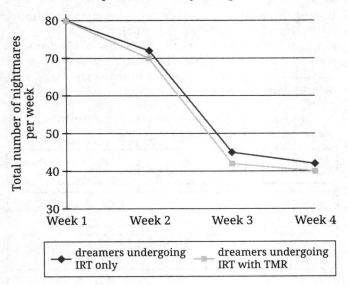

dreamers undergoing IRT only

dreamers undergoing IRT with TMR

The primary treatment for chronic nightmares is Imagery Rehearsal Therapy (IRT), by which the dreamer, after waking from a nightmare, talks through a reimagining of the dream to give it a positive ending. A supplemental intervention, Targeted Memory Reactivation (TMR), recruits the use of musical notes. With TMR, a dreamer already undergoing IRT is made to hear a certain piano chord when discussing the new positive ending of the dream. Then, that same piano chord is played during the person's next sleep. It is claimed that IRT is made even more effective when utilizing TMR. A graduate student tested this claim by observing the effects of each treatment on 50 participants over a four-week period and was surprised to observe that _____

16 ◻ Mark for Review

Which choice most effectively uses data from the graph to complete the statement?

(A) the maximum number of nightmares for participants of both groups occurred during the first week of the study.

(B) participants who underwent IRT along with TMR experienced only a slightly greater decrease in nightmares than did those undergoing IRT without TMR.

(C) at week 2, participants who underwent IRT with TMR reported having fewer nightmares than those who underwent IRT without TMR.

(D) although the participants of both forms of treatment experienced reduced nightmare intensity throughout the course of the study, the rate at which their nightmares decreased tapered off toward the end of the study.

CONTINUE →

17 ☐ Mark for Review

A team of psychologists led by Stefan Stieger, Hannah M. Graf, and Stella P. Riegler investigated the hypothesis that social media use is positively correlated with a lower body self-image, termed appearance satisfaction. The researchers recorded the participants' social media engagement and utilized a physical analogue scale (PAS) to measure appearance satisfaction. Participants angled their forearms to signify their sense of appearance satisfaction. A horizontal forearm at 0° indicated the lowest scale value, whereas 90° indicated the highest. Participants used social media to engage with a variety of accounts: some accounts belonged to known people such as friends and family, while other accounts belonged to users unknown to the participants. Social media engagement with known targets resulted in a reduction of appearance satisfaction of 12.4°, while for unknown targets there was a 5.9° reduction, which suggests that _____

Which choice most logically completes the text?

(A) people experience lower appearance satisfaction when they engage with content from strangers compared with that from friends.

(B) the physical analogue scale is more effective when measuring social media engagement with known targets than with unknown targets.

(C) there is some evidence for a correlation between social media use and lower appearance satisfaction, but it is not significant.

(D) social media engagement with content by people whom one knows personally is correlated with lower appearance satisfaction.

18 ☐ Mark for Review

During the West African Ebola virus epidemic in the 2010s, Yoshihiro Kawaoka and Alhaji N'jai—both affiliated with the University of Wisconsin–Madison—studied the virus and then eliminated the VP30 gene that allows the virus to attach to human cells _____ a potential Ebola vaccine.

Which choice completes the text so that it conforms to the conventions of Standard English?

(A) and creating

(B) created

(C) creating

(D) to create

19 ☐ Mark for Review

The watering of cultivated crops is sometimes based on a system known as irrigation scheduling, in which farmers use certain factors about the land and weather—specifically, the soil quality and projected _____ determine when and how much water is needed.

Which choice completes the text so that it conforms to the conventions of Standard English?

(A) rainfall, to

(B) rainfall—to

(C) rainfall: to

(D) rainfall to

CONTINUE

20 ☐ Mark for Review

On February 4, 1961, comedian Lenny Bruce was unsure whether anyone would show up for his performance at Carnegie Hall because of a massive blizzard. The audience was _____ flocking to the theater despite two feet of snow and a ban on driving to see the show that would become the well-known recording *The Carnegie Hall Concert*.

Which choice completes the text so that it conforms to the conventions of Standard English?

Ⓐ determined; however,

Ⓑ determined, however,

Ⓒ determined, however;

Ⓓ determined, however

21 ☐ Mark for Review

A recent study by a team of researchers at the University of Washington discovered a surprising source of atmosphere- and climate-changing _____ passive degassing, a process that occurs when volcanoes are not active but are leaking sulfur into the atmosphere to the extent that, according to the new research, it is a greater amount of sulfur than the amounts released during eruptions or by another common source of sulfur, marine phytoplankton.

Which choice completes the text so that it conforms to the conventions of Standard English?

Ⓐ gases. Volcanoes'

Ⓑ gases; volcanoes'

Ⓒ gases: volcanoes'

Ⓓ gases volcanoes'

22 ☐ Mark for Review

In 1995, animal behaviorist Temple Grandin wrote *Thinking in Pictures* about her life with autism and her pattern of visual thinking. A 2006 edition of the book added two more patterns of _____ some autistic people may be music and math thinkers, others verbal logic thinkers. Grandin continued to write about patterns of thinking in her 2013 book *The Autistic Brain: Thinking Across the Spectrum*.

Which choice completes the text so that it conforms to the conventions of Standard English?

Ⓐ thinking though

Ⓑ thinking, though

Ⓒ thinking,

Ⓓ thinking:

23 ☐ Mark for Review

Although it has become much dimmer than it was originally, the Centennial Light in California, known as the world's longest-lasting light bulb, began operating in the late 1890s. There were a few time periods when it briefly went out due to power failures and other technological challenges. _____ the bulb was connected to an uninterruptible power supply to determine how long it could actually burn.

Which choice completes the text with the most logical transition?

Ⓐ Similarly,

Ⓑ Consequently,

Ⓒ Additionally,

Ⓓ By contrast,

CONTINUE →

24 ☐ Mark for Review

While researching a topic, a student has taken the following notes:

- One of the world's oldest law schools was the law school of Berytus in Beirut, Lebanon.
- The exact date of its founding is unknown, but it was active during the time of the Roman Empire.
- Students at the law school went through four or five years of study focused on Roman law to become jurists, or legal scholars.
- Time in class included lectures, analyses of cases, reading and revision of classical legal texts, and discussions.
- Famous instructors included a group of seven revered law scholars known as the "ecumenical masters."

The student wants to explain how the law school of Berytus prepared jurists. Which choice most effectively uses relevant information from the notes to accomplish this goal?

Ⓐ The law school of Berytus taught students Roman law for multiple years in classes that included lectures and analyses.

Ⓑ A group of seven revered law scholars known as the "ecumenical masters" taught at the law school of Berytus.

Ⓒ Active during the time of the Roman Empire, the law school of Berytus prepared students to become jurists.

Ⓓ The law school of Berytus trained students to become jurists, or legal scholars, of Roman law.

25 ☐ Mark for Review

While researching a topic, a student has taken the following notes:

- In 1929, astronautics theorist Herman Potočnik described a geosynchronous orbit, or an Earth-centered orbit with an orbital period that is the same length of time as the Earth's rotation.
- Satellites with a geosynchronous orbit have an altitude of 35,786 km.
- Currently, there are 5,465 satellites in orbit around Earth, with 565 in geosynchronous orbit.
- 4,700 satellites are at low orbit with an altitude below 2,000 km and an orbital period less than 128 minutes.
- 140 satellites are at medium orbit with an altitude between 2,000 and 35,786 km and an orbital period greater than 2 hours but less than 24 hours.

The student wants to emphasize how high satellites in geosynchronous orbit are relative to those in low and medium orbits. Which choice most effectively uses the relevant information from the notes to accomplish this goal?

Ⓐ While most satellites are at low orbit, satellites at geosynchronous orbit have an altitude of 35,786 km.

Ⓑ Of the 5,465 satellites in orbit around the Earth, 4,700 of them are at low orbit with an altitude below 2,000 km and 565 are at a geosynchronous orbit.

Ⓒ Herman Potočnik described a geosynchronous orbit, which has a period the same length as Earth's rotation, while other orbits used by satellites have shorter periods.

Ⓓ Satellites in geosynchronous orbit have an altitude of 35,786 km, which is a higher altitude than that of satellites in both low and medium orbits.

CONTINUE ➡

26 🔖 Mark for Review

While researching a topic, a student has taken the following notes:

- Some animals use bright colors, such as red or yellow, to attract mates, while other animals use the same colors to warn predators.

- Researchers were curious whether there was an explanation for why animals evolved colors for one goal or the other.

- The researchers found that animals whose ancestors were active during the day use colors to attract mates.

- They also found that animals whose ancestors were active during the night use colors to warn predators.

- Warning predators with colors is known as aposematism.

The student wants to emphasize a similarity between the two ways animals use colors. Which choice most effectively uses relevant information from the notes to accomplish this goal?

Ⓐ As well as using bright colors to attract mates, animals use colors such as red or yellow to warn predators.

Ⓑ Animals can use bright colors for two different goals, one of which is known as aposematism.

Ⓒ The two different goals of animals' bright colors are determined by the time of day the animals' ancestors were active.

Ⓓ Animals evolved to use bright colors in two different ways: to attract mates or to warn predators.

27 🔖 Mark for Review

While researching a topic, a student has taken the following notes:

- Some species of fireflies, such as *Photinus carolinus*, seem to synchronize their flashes, even in large groups.

- A team of researchers from the University of Pittsburgh wanted to mimic the flashes by utilizing a model from neuroscience which describes brain cells' behavior.

- The model, called an elliptic burster, was used to simulate the flashes of firefly groups, ranging from one individual to a large swarm.

- The model was able to mimic flashes consistent with real-life observations of firefly swarms.

- The model could be used to make predictions about how the pattern of firefly flashes may be altered due to environmental changes or human impacts.

The student wants to present the study and its methodology. Which choice most effectively uses relevant information from the notes to accomplish this goal?

Ⓐ Researchers at the University of Pittsburgh found that the elliptic burster model could simulate firefly flashes consistent with real-life observations.

Ⓑ University of Pittsburgh researchers studied the synchronicity of the flashes of *Photinus carolinus*, a species of fireflies.

Ⓒ Hoping to mimic the synchronous flashes of fireflies, researchers at the University of Pittsburgh used an elliptic burster to mimic real-life observations of fireflies' flashes.

Ⓓ A study found that the pattern of fireflies flashing could be simulated using a model from neuroscience that describes brain cells' behavior.

STOP
**If you finish before time is called, you may check your work on this module only.
Do not turn to any other module in the test.**

Test 2—Math
Module 1

The questions in this section address a number of important math skills.
Use of a calculator is permitted for all questions.

NOTES

Unless otherwise indicated:

- All variables and expressions represent real numbers.
- Figures provided are drawn to scale.
- All figures lie in a plane.
- The domain of a given function f is the set of all real numbers x for which $f(x)$ is a real number.

REFERENCE

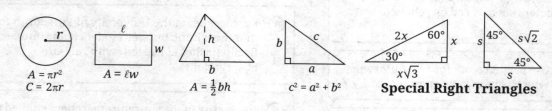

$A = \pi r^2$
$C = 2\pi r$

$A = \ell w$

$A = \frac{1}{2}bh$

$c^2 = a^2 + b^2$

Special Right Triangles

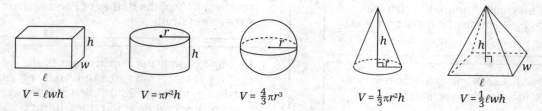

$V = \ell wh$

$V = \pi r^2 h$

$V = \frac{4}{3}\pi r^3$

$V = \frac{1}{3}\pi r^2 h$

$V = \frac{1}{3}\ell wh$

The number of degrees of arc in a circle is 360.
The number of radians of arc in a circle is 2π.
The sum of the measures in degrees of the angles of a triangle is 180.

CONTINUE

‒ ‒

For multiple-choice questions, solve each problem, choose the correct answer from the choices provided, and then fill in the circle with the answer letter. Enter only one answer for each question. You will not get credit for questions with more than one answer entered or for questions with no answers entered.

For student-produced response questions, solve each problem and write your answer in the test book as described below.

- Enter your answer into the box provided.
- If you find **more than one correct answer**, enter only one answer.
- Your answer can be up to 5 characters for a **positive** answer and up to 6 characters (including the negative sign) for a **negative** answer.
- If your answer is a **fraction** that is too long (over 5 characters for positive, 6 characters for negative), write the decimal equivalent.
- If your answer is a **decimal** that is too long (over 5 characters for positive, 6 characters for negative), truncate it or round at the fourth digit.
- If your answer is a **mixed number** (such as $3\frac{1}{2}$), write it as an improper fraction (7/2) or its decimal equivalent (3.5).
- Don't enter **symbols** such as a percent sign, comma, or dollar sign in your answer.

CONTINUE ➔

1 ☐ Mark for Review

A social media account posts at a constant rate. The relationship between the number of posts, p, and the number of days, d, is given by the equation $p = 45d$. How many posts does the account make during a 3-day period?

(A) 45

(B) 48

(C) 90

(D) 135

2 ☐ Mark for Review

Which of the following equations represents a line in the xy-plane if the line passes through the point $(0, 10)$ and has a slope of -3?

(A) $y = -3x - 10$

(B) $y = -3x + 10$

(C) $y = 3x - 10$

(D) $y = 3x + 10$

3 ☐ Mark for Review

What is the value of $\frac{x}{12}$ if $\frac{12}{x} = \frac{1}{7}$?

[____]

4 ☐ Mark for Review

Triangles MNO and XYZ are similar right triangles. Angles N and Y each have a measure of $90°$, and angle O corresponds to angle Z. If angle X has a measure of $23°$, what is the measure of angle M?

(A) $23°$

(B) $67°$

(C) $90°$

(D) $157°$

5 ☐ Mark for Review

If a, g, and n are positive numbers, which of the following expressions is equivalent to $(a^2 g^{-4} n)(a^3 g^{-2} n)$?

(A) $a^{-1} g^{-2} n^2$

(B) $a^5 g^{-12} n$

(C) $a^5 g^{-6} n^2$

(D) $a^6 g^8 n$

CONTINUE ➡

6 ☐ Mark for Review

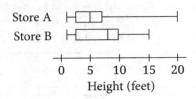

Store A

Store B

Height (feet)

The box plots represent the height, in feet, of ladders available at two hardware stores. Which of the following is a true statement based on the box plots?

(A) The mean height of the ladders at store A is greater than the mean height of the ladders at store B.

(B) The mean height of the ladders at store B is greater than the mean height of the ladders at store A.

(C) The median height of the ladders at store A is greater than the median height of the ladders at store B.

(D) The median height of the ladders at store B is greater than the median height of the ladders at store A.

7 ☐ Mark for Review

$$y = x^2 + 6$$
$$y = 150$$

When the given equations are graphed in the xy-plane, they intersect at the point (x, y). Which of the following is a possible value of x?

(A) 5

(B) 6

(C) 12

(D) 25

8 ☐ Mark for Review

Based on a random sample of adults, it is estimated that the proportion of adults who have insomnia is 0.35. The margin of error associated with the sample is 0.07. Which of the following is the most appropriate conclusion about the proportion of adults with insomnia in the population based on this estimate and margin of error?

(A) It is likely that the proportion is less than 0.28.

(B) It is likely that the proportion is greater than 0.42.

(C) It is likely that the proportion is between 0.28 and 0.42.

(D) It is likely that the proportion is exactly 0.35.

9 ☐ Mark for Review

$$y = 10x - 20$$
$$2y = 10x - 20$$

Two equations are given. At how many points do their graphs intersect in the xy-plane?

(A) Zero

(B) Exactly one

(C) Exactly two

(D) Infinitely many

CONTINUE

10 ☐ Mark for Review

The graph of the linear function g in the xy-plane passes through the points $(-3, 39)$ and $(0, 3)$. If $y = g(x)$, which of the following equations defines g?

Ⓐ $g(x) = -12x + 3$

Ⓑ $g(x) = -6x + 3$

Ⓒ $g(x) = 3x + 36$

Ⓓ $g(x) = 39x + 42$

11 ☐ Mark for Review

What is the value of k if $ab = 27$ and $2abk = 27$?

12 ☐ Mark for Review

The amount of money d, in dollars, that Sarah has saved from babysitting is modeled by the function $d(w) = 150 + 50w$, where w is the number of weeks since she started babysitting. What is the predicted amount of money, in dollars, that Sarah saved every week?

Ⓐ 3

Ⓑ 50

Ⓒ 150

Ⓓ 200

13 ☐ Mark for Review

The population of a certain town decreases by 150 people every 5 years. The population of the town is best described by what kind of function?

Ⓐ Decreasing linear

Ⓑ Decreasing exponential

Ⓒ Increasing linear

Ⓓ Increasing exponential

14 ☐ Mark for Review

$$x - 9y = -30$$
$$x - 27y = -12$$

If (x, y) is the solution to the given system of equations, what is the value of x?

15 ☐ Mark for Review

The equation $y = x^2 + 16x - 39$ relates the variables x and y. If (a, b) is the minimum of this equation, what is the value of a?

CONTINUE

16 ☐ Mark for Review

The function g is defined by $g(x) = 12 - 2x$. In the xy-plane, the x-intercept of the graph of $y = g(x)$ is at $(m, 0)$, and the y-intercept is at $(0, n)$. What is the value of $m - n$?

Ⓐ −18

Ⓑ −6

Ⓒ 12

Ⓓ 18

17 ☐ Mark for Review

A scale model of a square park has an area that is $\frac{1}{4,096}$ of the area of the actual park. If the side length of the actual park is x times the side length of the scale model, what is the value of x?

[____]

18 ☐ Mark for Review

The scatterplot shows the water remaining in a series of cups that initially held the same volume of water and were left sitting in the sun for several hours. A line of best fit is also shown.

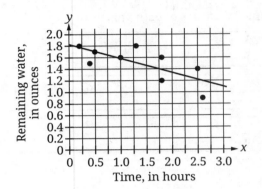

Which of the following is closest to the water remaining in a cup, in ounces, predicted by the line of best fit when 1.25 hours have elapsed?

Ⓐ 1.2

Ⓑ 1.5

Ⓒ 1.7

Ⓓ 1.8

CONTINUE

19 ⬜ Mark for Review

An angle is made of two smaller angles, A and B.

If Angle A measures 150 degrees, and the measure of Angle B is $\frac{1}{3}$ the measure of Angle A, what is the combined measure of both angles, in <u>radians</u>?

Ⓐ $\frac{5\pi}{18}$

Ⓑ $\frac{5\pi}{6}$

Ⓒ $\frac{9\pi}{10}$

Ⓓ $\frac{10\pi}{9}$

20 ⬜ Mark for Review

A sample of a certain radioactive element is tested and found to have 16,000 radioactive units. Two hours later, it is tested again and found to have 4,000 radioactive units. The formula $R = S(0.25)^{pt}$, where R is the number of radioactive units remaining t hours after the first test, and p and S are constants, models this situation. What is the value of p?

Ⓐ $\frac{1}{4,000}$

Ⓑ $\frac{1}{120}$

Ⓒ $\frac{1}{2}$

Ⓓ 2

CONTINUE ➡

21 🔖 Mark for Review

$$1 = \frac{\sqrt{7x + 65}}{\sqrt{(x+3)^2}}$$

What is the greatest solution to the given equation?

> ☐

22 🔖 Mark for Review

If c is a constant less than 26, which of the following are solutions to the equation $(x + 3c)(80 + x) = 80 + x$?

    I. -80
   II. $-3c$
  III. $1 - 3c$

(A)   I only

(B)   III only

(C)   I and II only

(D)   I and III only

YIELD

Once you've finished (or run out of time for) this section, use the answer key to determine how many questions you got right. If you got fewer than 14 questions right, move on to Module 2—Easier, otherwise move on to Module 2—Harder.

Test 2—Math
Module 2—Easier

The questions in this section address a number of important math skills.
Use of a calculator is permitted for all questions.

NOTES

Unless otherwise indicated:

- All variables and expressions represent real numbers.
- Figures provided are drawn to scale.
- All figures lie in a plane.
- The domain of a given function f is the set of all real numbers x for which $f(x)$ is a real number.

REFERENCE

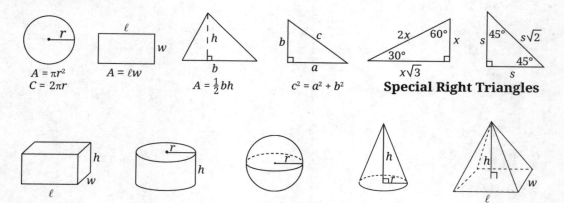

$A = \pi r^2$
$C = 2\pi r$

$A = \ell w$

$A = \frac{1}{2}bh$

$c^2 = a^2 + b^2$

Special Right Triangles

$V = \ell wh$

$V = \pi r^2 h$

$V = \frac{4}{3}\pi r^3$

$V = \frac{1}{3}\pi r^2 h$

$V = \frac{1}{3}\ell wh$

The number of degrees of arc in a circle is 360.
The number of radians of arc in a circle is 2π.
The sum of the measures in degrees of the angles of a triangle is 180.

CONTINUE

_____

For multiple-choice questions, solve each problem, choose the correct answer from the choices provided, and then fill in the circle with the answer letter. Enter only one answer for each question. You will not get credit for questions with more than one answer entered or for questions with no answers entered.

For student-produced response questions, solve each problem and write your answer in the test book as described below.

- Enter your answer into the box provided.
- If you find **more than one correct answer**, enter only one answer.
- Your answer can be up to 5 characters for a **positive** answer and up to 6 characters (including the negative sign) for a **negative** answer.
- If your answer is a **fraction** that is too long (over 5 characters for positive, 6 characters for negative), write the decimal equivalent.
- If your answer is a **decimal** that is too long (over 5 characters for positive, 6 characters for negative), truncate it or round at the fourth digit.
- If your answer is a **mixed number** (such as $3\frac{1}{2}$), write it as an improper fraction (7/2) or its decimal equivalent (3.5).
- Don't enter **symbols** such as a percent sign, comma, or dollar sign in your answer.

CONTINUE →

---

1 Mark for Review

What is 60% of 300?

Ⓐ 30

Ⓑ 120

Ⓒ 180

Ⓓ 240

2 Mark for Review

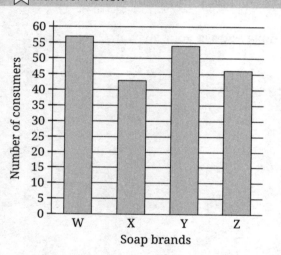

The bar graph shows the results of a market research survey that asked consumers to choose their favorite brand of soap. How many consumers chose Brand Y?

Ⓐ 43

Ⓑ 46

Ⓒ 54

Ⓓ 57

3 Mark for Review

If $2b - 12 = 144$, what is the value of b?

4 Mark for Review

A street artist takes 5 minutes to draw one portrait. At this rate, how many portraits would the artist draw in 35 minutes?

5 Mark for Review

$$h(x) = 3x - 2$$

The function h is defined by the given equation. If $h(x) = 10$, what is the value of x?

CONTINUE ➔

6 ⬚ Mark for Review

The function f is defined by $f(x) = x^2 - 15$. If $f(x) = 49$, what is the value of x?

Ⓐ 7

Ⓑ 8

Ⓒ 15

Ⓓ 32

7 ⬚ Mark for Review

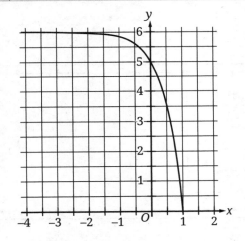

What is the y-intercept of the graph shown?

Ⓐ (0, 5)

Ⓑ (0, 6)

Ⓒ (5, 0)

Ⓓ (6, 0)

8 ⬚ Mark for Review

Dalisha is given a stipend of $3,600 to pay her student housing rent of $450 per month. If $m \le 8$, which equation represents the amount remaining in the stipend, s, in dollars, after m months?

Ⓐ $s = 450m - 3{,}600$

Ⓑ $s = 450 - 3{,}600m$

Ⓒ $s = 3{,}600m - 450$

Ⓓ $s = 3{,}600 - 450m$

9 ⬚ Mark for Review

$$\frac{3}{6-3y} + \frac{1}{y-4}$$

Which of the following expressions is equivalent to the given expression, when y is not equal to 2 or 4?

Ⓐ $-\dfrac{6}{(y-4)(6-3y)}$

Ⓑ $\dfrac{6}{(y-4)(6-3y)}$

Ⓒ $\dfrac{4}{2y+2}$

Ⓓ $\dfrac{18}{(y-4)(6-3y)}$

CONTINUE ➡

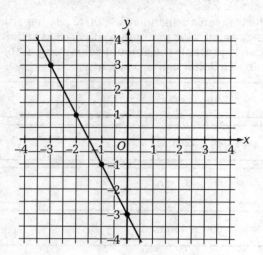

10 ☐ Mark for Review

A linear relationship between x and y is shown in the graph. Which of the following tables contains values of x and their corresponding values of y?

(A)

x	y
-3	-3
-2	-2
-1	-1
0	0

(B)

x	y
-3	3
-2	1
-1	-1
0	-3

(C)

x	y
-3	-3
-2	-1
-1	-1
0	3

(D)

x	y
-3	3
-2	2
-1	1
0	-3

CONTINUE ➡

11 ☐ Mark for Review

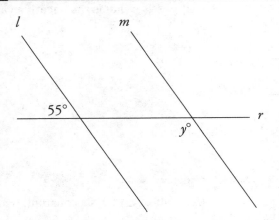

Note: Figure not drawn to scale.

In the figure shown, if line *l* is parallel to line *m*, what is the value of *y*?

12 ☐ Mark for Review

If a circle has a radius of 4 meters, what is the circumference, in meters, of the circle?

Ⓐ 2π

Ⓑ 4π

Ⓒ 8π

Ⓓ 16π

13 ☐ Mark for Review

Distinct positive numbers *a*, *b*, and *c* are related by the equation $9a - 2b = c$. Which of the following equations correctly expresses *a* in terms of *b* and *c*?

Ⓐ $a = \dfrac{2b + c}{9}$

Ⓑ $a = \dfrac{2b}{9} + c$

Ⓒ $a = 2b + \dfrac{c}{9}$

Ⓓ $a = 9(2b + c)$

14 ☐ Mark for Review

Which of the following systems of inequalities, when graphed in the *xy*-plane, includes the point $(2, -5)$ as a solution?

Ⓐ $x \leq 0$
$y \leq 0$

Ⓑ $x \leq 0$
$y \geq 0$

Ⓒ $x \geq 0$
$y \leq 0$

Ⓓ $x \geq 0$
$y \geq 0$

CONTINUE

15 ☐ Mark for Review

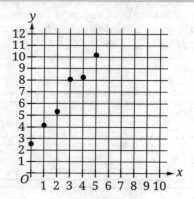

Which of the following linear equations best models the relationship between x and y shown in the scatterplot?

(A) $y = -1.5x - 2.6$

(B) $y = -1.5x + 2.6$

(C) $y = 1.5x - 2.6$

(D) $y = 1.5x + 2.6$

16 ☐ Mark for Review

The population of a certain species of fish is decreasing at a rate of 4 percent each year. Assuming the decline continues at the same rate, there will be approximately 804,944 fish of this species remaining 5 years from now. Which of the following equations could be used to find p, the current population of this species of fish?

(A) $p = 804,944(0.96)^5$

(B) $804,944 = p(0.96)^5$

(C) $p = 804,944(1.04)^5$

(D) $804,944 = p(1.04)^5$

17 ☐ Mark for Review

If $3|a + 2| - 5|a + 2| = -24$, what is the negative value of a?

18 ☐ Mark for Review

If $ax^7(8x + 7) = 56x^8 + 49x^7$, and a is a constant, what is the value of a?

19 ☐ Mark for Review

The expression $\pi(3r)(r)^2$ can represent the volume, in cubic feet, of a cylindrical barrel. If r is the radius, in feet, of the barrel, which term represents the height, in feet, of the barrel?

(A) r

(B) 3

(C) $3r$

(D) r^2

CONTINUE →

20 ☐ Mark for Review

p	q
-2	-10
1	8
4	20

The table shows values of p and their corresponding values of q. Which of the following inequalities could represent the relationship between p and q?

Ⓐ $q < 6p + 3$

Ⓑ $q > 6p + 3$

Ⓒ $q < 3p + 6$

Ⓓ $q > 3p + 6$

21 ☐ Mark for Review

$$g(x) = (x - 2)(x - 4)(x + 3)$$
$$h(x) = g(x + 3)$$

Functions g and h are defined by the given equations. The graph of $y = h(x)$ has x-intercepts at $(m, 0)$, $(n, 0)$, and $(p, 0)$. If m, n, and p are distinct constants, what is the value of mnp?

Ⓐ -21

Ⓑ -8

Ⓒ 0

Ⓓ 6

22 ☐ Mark for Review

A square with a diagonal length of 8 centimeters (cm) has a circle inscribed in it. What is the area, in cm^2, of the circle?

Ⓐ 4π

Ⓑ 8π

Ⓒ 16π

Ⓓ 32π

STOP
**If you finish before time is called, you may check your work on this module only.
Do not turn to any other module.**

Test 2—Math
Module 2—Harder

DIRECTIONS

The questions in this section address a number of important math skills.
Use of a calculator is permitted for all questions.

NOTES

Unless otherwise indicated:

- All variables and expressions represent real numbers.
- Figures provided are drawn to scale.
- All figures lie in a plane.
- The domain of a given function f is the set of all real numbers x for which $f(x)$ is a real number.

REFERENCE

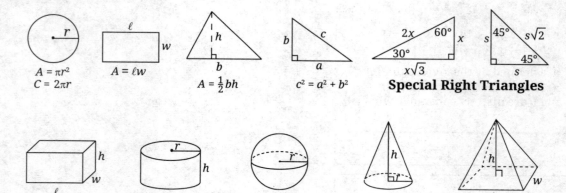

$A = \pi r^2$
$C = 2\pi r$

$A = \ell w$

$A = \frac{1}{2}bh$

$c^2 = a^2 + b^2$

Special Right Triangles

$V = \ell wh$

$V = \pi r^2 h$

$V = \frac{4}{3}\pi r^3$

$V = \frac{1}{3}\pi r^2 h$

$V = \frac{1}{3}\ell wh$

The number of degrees of arc in a circle is 360.
The number of radians of arc in a circle is 2π.
The sum of the measures in degrees of the angles of a triangle is 180.

CONTINUE ➡

For multiple-choice questions, solve each problem, choose the correct answer from the choices provided, and then fill in the circle with the answer letter. Enter only one answer for each question. You will not get credit for questions with more than one answer entered or for questions with no answers entered.

For student-produced response questions, solve each problem and write your answer in the test book as described below.

- Enter your answer into the box provided.
- If you find **more than one correct answer**, enter only one answer.
- Your answer can be up to 5 characters for a **positive** answer and up to 6 characters (including the negative sign) for a **negative** answer.
- If your answer is a **fraction** that is too long (over 5 characters for positive, 6 characters for negative), write the decimal equivalent.
- If your answer is a **decimal** that is too long (over 5 characters for positive, 6 characters for negative), truncate it or round at the fourth digit.
- If your answer is a **mixed number** (such as $3\frac{1}{2}$), write it as an improper fraction (7/2) or its decimal equivalent (3.5).
- Don't enter **symbols** such as a percent sign, comma, or dollar sign in your answer.

CONTINUE →

1 🔖 Mark for Review

If $y - 7 = x$, which table gives three values of x and their corresponding values of y?

Ⓐ

x	y
4	3
5	2
6	1

Ⓑ

x	y
4	11
5	12
6	13

Ⓒ

x	y
4	11
5	2
6	13

Ⓓ

x	y
4	13
5	12
6	11

2 🔖 Mark for Review

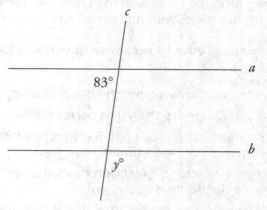

Note: Figure not drawn to scale.

In the figure shown, line c intersects parallel lines a and b. What is the value of y?

Ⓐ 7

Ⓑ 83

Ⓒ 97

Ⓓ 173

3 🔖 Mark for Review

The number 24 is what percentage of 80?

Ⓐ 24%

Ⓑ 30%

Ⓒ 56%

Ⓓ 70%

CONTINUE ➡

4 ⬜ Mark for Review

The function f is defined by $f(x) = 3x + 12$. For what value of x is $f(x) = 27$?

5 ⬜ Mark for Review

The function g is defined by $g(x) = 120(x)^0$, when $x \neq 0$. What is the value of $g\left(\dfrac{1}{3}\right)$?

Ⓐ 0

Ⓑ 40

Ⓒ 120

Ⓓ 360

6 ⬜ Mark for Review

In right triangle LMN, angle N is a right angle, and the value of $\tan(L)$ is $\dfrac{\sqrt{7}}{3}$. What is the value of $\sin(M)$?

Ⓐ $\dfrac{\sqrt{7}}{7}$

Ⓑ $\dfrac{\sqrt{7}}{4}$

Ⓒ $\dfrac{3}{4}$

Ⓓ $\dfrac{3\sqrt{7}}{7}$

7 ⬜ Mark for Review

$$g(x) = (-11)(5)^x - 17$$

The function g is defined by the given equation. Which of the following is the y-intercept when $y = g(x)$ is graphed in the xy-plane?

Ⓐ $(0, -11)$

Ⓑ $(0, 5)$

Ⓒ $(0, -17)$

Ⓓ $(0, -28)$

8 ⬜ Mark for Review

$$\frac{3}{6 - 3y} + \frac{1}{y - 4}$$

Which of the following expressions is equivalent to the given expression?

Ⓐ $-\dfrac{6}{(y-4)(6-3y)}$

Ⓑ $\dfrac{6}{(y-4)(6-3y)}$

Ⓒ $\dfrac{4}{2y+2}$

Ⓓ $\dfrac{18}{(y-4)(6-3y)}$

CONTINUE ➤

---

9 ☐ Mark for Review

The function q is defined by $q(x) = (x - 9)(x + 2)(x + 9)$. When the graph of $y = q(x)$ is translated down 10 units in the xy-plane, the graph of $y = r(x)$ is the result. What is the value of $r(0)$?

---

10 ☐ Mark for Review

If a rectangular prism has a height of 10 feet, a length of 12 feet, and a volume of 6,000 cubic feet, what is the surface area, in square feet, of the prism?

---

11 ☐ Mark for Review

For the function f, when the value of x increases by 1, the value of $f(x)$ increases by 28%. Which of the following equations defines f if $f(0) = 11$?

Ⓐ $f(x) = 0.72(11)^x$

Ⓑ $f(x) = 1.28(11)^x$

Ⓒ $f(x) = 11(0.72)^x$

Ⓓ $f(x) = 11(1.28)^x$

---

12 ☐ Mark for Review

Which of the following tables gives three values of x and their corresponding values of y that are all solutions to the inequality $y > 4x - 5$?

Ⓐ

x	y
2	0
4	8
6	16

Ⓑ

x	y
2	6
4	14
6	22

Ⓒ

x	y
2	6
4	14
6	19

Ⓓ

x	y
2	3
4	11
6	19

CONTINUE ▶

13 🔖 Mark for Review

Which of the following expressions is (are) a factor of $5x^2 - 61x + 66$?

   I. $x - 11$
  II. $5x - 6$

Ⓐ I only

Ⓑ II only

Ⓒ I and II

Ⓓ Neither I nor II

14 🔖 Mark for Review

$$4 - 5y = 7x + 5y$$
$$7x - 4 = ky$$

The given system of equations has infinitely many solutions. What is the value of the constant k?

Ⓐ −10

Ⓑ −5

Ⓒ 5

Ⓓ 10

15 🔖 Mark for Review

If $3|a + 2| - 5|a + 2| = -24$, what is the negative value of a?

16 🔖 Mark for Review

A vendor sells vases for \$6.50 and bowls for \$12.30. The maximum combined number of vases and bowls she can sell during one weekend is 750. If, during that weekend, she sells only vases and bowls and earns at least \$7,780, what is the maximum number of vases she could sell?

17 🔖 Mark for Review

For a certain chemistry experiment, the number of moles of product increases each minute by $r\%$ of the number of moles the preceding minute. The function $g(x) = 78,500(1.52)^{\frac{x}{60}}$ models the number of moles of product created x seconds after the start of the experiment. What is the value of r?

Ⓐ 48

Ⓑ 52

Ⓒ 60

Ⓓ 554

CONTINUE

18 ▢ Mark for Review

The function g is defined by the equation $g(x) = -3(5)^x$. Which of the following equations defines the function h if $h(x) = g(x + 3)$?

(A) $h(x) = -27(125)^x$

(B) $h(x) = -9(15)^x$

(C) $h(x) = -9(5)^x$

(D) $h(x) = -375(5)^x$

19 ▢ Mark for Review

One solution to the equation $x^2 + 4x - 14 = 0$ can be written as $-2 - \sqrt{c}$. What is the value of the constant c?

(A) 18

(B) 23

(C) 36

(D) 72

CONTINUE ➡

20 Mark for Review

The equation $7x(7x + 6) = -c$ has exactly two real solutions. If c is an integer constant, what is the greatest possible value of c?

```
┌─────────┐
│         │
│ ─────── │
└─────────┘
```

21 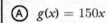 Mark for Review

A band member earns $500 for the first four concerts performed during a given month plus a flat rate for each additional concert that month. The band member earned a total of $900 for playing 6 concerts in a month. Which function g gives the total earnings, in dollars, for x concerts, where $x \geq 4$?

Ⓐ $g(x) = 150x$

Ⓑ $g(x) = 150x + 500$

Ⓒ $g(x) = 200x - 300$

Ⓓ $g(x) = 200x + 500$

22 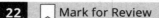 Mark for Review

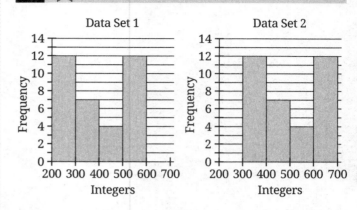

The histograms summarize two data sets, each with 35 integers. For each histogram, the intervals each represent the frequency of integers greater than or equal to the number at the left of the bar and less than the number at the right of the bar. For example, the first interval represents the frequency of integers greater than or equal to 200 and less than 300. What is the greatest possible difference between the means of the two data sets?

Ⓐ 1

Ⓑ 35

Ⓒ 100

Ⓓ 199

STOP

**If you finish before time is called, you may check your work on this module only.
Do not turn to any other module.**

Chapter 4
Practice Test 2:
Answers and
Explanations

PRACTICE TEST 2: ANSWER KEY

Reading and Writing				Math		
Module 1	Module 2 (Easier)	Module 2 (Harder)		Module 1	Module 2 (Easier)	Module 2 (Harder)
1. C	1. D	1. D		1. D	1. C	1. B
2. D	2. A	2. A		2. B	2. C	2. C
3. C	3. C	3. C		3. 7	3. 78	3. B
4. B	4. B	4. A		4. A	4. 7	4. 5
5. B	5. C	5. B		5. C	5. 4	5. C
6. A	6. A	6. A		6. D	6. B	6. C
7. B	7. D	7. A		7. C	7. A	7. D
8. D	8. A	8. B		8. C	8. D	8. A
9. D	9. C	9. B		9. B	9. A	9. −172
10. C	10. B	10. B		10. A	10. B	10. 2440
11. D	11. C	11. B		11. $\frac{1}{2}$ or .5	11. 125	11. D
12. B	12. D	12. C		12. B	12. C	12. B
13. A	13. A	13. C		13. A	13. A	13. C
14. C	14. D	14. D		14. −39	14. C	14. A
15. B	15. A	15. D		15. −8	15. D	15. −14
16. B	16. B	16. B		16. B	16. B	16. 249
17. D	17. B	17. D		17. 64	17. −14	17. B
18. B	18. B	18. D		18. B	18. 7	18. D
19. A	19. D	19. B		19. D	19. C	19. A
20. A	20. A	20. B		20. C	20. A	20. 8
21. A	21. D	21. C		21. 8	21. D	21. C
22. D	22. B	22. D		22. D	22. B	22. D
23. A	23. A	23. B				
24. B	24. C	24. A				
25. D	25. D	25. D				
26. A	26. C	26. C				
27. C	27. C	27. C				

PRACTICE TEST 2—READING AND WRITING EXPLANATIONS

Module 1

1. **C**   This is a Vocabulary question, as it asks for *the most logical and precise word or phrase*. Read the text and highlight what can help to fill in the blank, which describes how Earhart didn't *consider* her *feat*. The beginning of the sentence draws a contrast by saying *Even though no woman pilot had accomplished this*, so Earhart must not have considered it "impossible." Write "impossible" in the annotation box and use process of elimination.

    -   (A) is wrong because *definitive* means "certain."

    -   (B) is wrong because *enigmatic* means "mysterious."

    -   (C) is correct because *impracticable* means "impossible."

    -   (D) is wrong because *appropriate* doesn't match with "impossible."

2. **D**   This is a Vocabulary question, as it asks for *the most logical and precise word or phrase*. Read the text and highlight what can help to fill in the blank, which describes how the *music* relates to *looping and phrasing techniques* with certain elements. The second sentence states that Richter weaves *synthesizer sounds with samples*, which elaborates on the aspects of his compositions mentioned in the previous sentence. Therefore, the blank should be something like "made of." Write "made of" in the annotation box and use process of elimination.

    -   (A) is wrong because *portrayed by* means "modeled by."

    -   (B) is wrong because the music isn't *coupled with* those elements; it's made from them.

    -   (C) is wrong because *denoted* means "named."

    -   (D) is correct because *constructed from* matches with "made of."

3. **C**   This is a Vocabulary question, as it asks for *the most logical and precise word or phrase*. Read the text and highlight what can help to fill in the blank, which describes the *hydrocarbons*. The part with the blank is followed by a colon, which indicates that the second part of the sentence will elaborate on the first. It defines the blank as *chemically created without having any association with living organisms*, so write "not associated with living things" in the annotation box and use process of elimination.

    -   (A) and (D) are wrong because *flexible* and *alterable* mean "able to change."

    -   (B) is wrong because *genuine* means "sincere."

    -   (C) is correct because *inorganic* matches with "not associated with living things."

4. **B**   This is a Vocabulary question, as it asks for *the most logical and precise word or phrase*. Read the text and highlight what can help to fill in the blank, which describes how Beethoven's *musical output* related to *his deteriorating hearing*. The part with the blank is followed by a colon, which indicates that the second part of the sentence will elaborate on the first. It states that almost all of his symphonies and choral works were written after he started losing his hearing. Therefore, it would seem that his output was *not substantially* "harmed by" his hearing loss. Write "harmed by" in the annotation box and use process of elimination.

- (A) is wrong because while "limited by" could work, *limited to* means "excluding others."

- (B) is correct because *inhibited by* matches with "harmed by."

- (C) and (D) are wrong because they are both positive, and a negative word is needed here.

5. **B**   This is a Vocabulary question, as it asks what a word *most nearly means*. Read the text and highlight what can help to understand the underlined word. The blank is followed by *knew all about a vessel*. The second sentence says that Mrs. Budd *knew something* about *boats*, which is what *a vessel* refers to. Therefore, she "believed" she knew about boats. Write "believed" in the annotation box and use process of elimination.

- (A) is wrong because *formulated* means "created."

- (B) is correct because *imagined* matches with "believed."

- (C) is wrong because *conceded* means "gave in."

- (D) is wrong because *characterized* means "described."

6. **A**   This is a Purpose question, as it asks for the *overall structure*. Read the text and highlight what can help to understand the structure. The narrator describes fear of thinking about his death and concludes by stating that he would rather be *A living mouse than dead as a man dies*, so write "fear of death, would rather be alive" in the annotation box and use process of elimination.

- (A) is correct because it matches the annotation.

- (B) is wrong because the text never says that the fears *are intensifying*.

- (C) is wrong because there is no *transformation* of beliefs.

- (D) is wrong because the speaker doesn't criticize anyone else.

7. **B**   This is a Retrieval question, as it says *According to the text*. Read the text and highlight what it says about how Horowitz determined the dogs' *level of interest*. The second sentence states that her determination of interest was *based on the amount of time dogs spent sniffing* certain odors. Eliminate any answer that isn't supported by the text.

- (A) is wrong because the study included another substance besides the dogs' *own urine*.

- (B) is correct because it matches the reason given in the text.

- (C) is wrong because *the urine of other dogs* wasn't included in the study.

- (D) is wrong because *facial reactions* weren't mentioned.

8. **D** This is a Retrieval question, as it says *According to the text*. Read the text and highlight what it says about *why* biologists are *concerned about the Great Barrier Reef*. The second sentence says *marine biologists are concerned that reef coverage has declined significantly*. Eliminate any answer that isn't supported by the text.

- (A) is wrong because accommodating *new reefs* isn't mentioned.

- (B) is wrong because the text says that *fertilizers* are harmful, not beneficial, to reefs.

- (C) is wrong because *generating new reefs* isn't mentioned.

- (D) is correct because if the reef coverage has declined, then its size was once larger.

9. **D** This is a Main Idea question, as it asks for the *main idea*. Read and highlight the main phrases or lines that the other sentences seem to support. The text introduces Escoffier and states that *his first cookbook* made him *a legend*. The text goes on to explain the aspects of the book that made it influential, so write "Escoffier's cookbook was important" in the annotation box and use process of elimination.

- (A) is wrong because the text doesn't mention readers creating *their own recipes*.

- (B) is wrong because the text doesn't say that the cookbook wasn't considered to be influential until later.

- (C) is wrong because it only refers to information in the first sentence, not the *main idea*.

- (D) is correct because it matches the annotation.

10. **C** This is a Claims question, as it asks for a *quotation* that *illustrates the claim*. Read the text and highlight the claim, which is that *Dick Horner* is *a good-hearted boy whose adventurous nature can cause him trouble*. Eliminate answers that don't *illustrate* this idea.

- (A), (B), and (D) are wrong because they don't state that Horner's *adventurous nature* is the source of his trouble.

- (C) is correct because it mentions his *wild spirits* and *some new mischief*, and the idea that he *promised to turn over a new leaf* and *would be sorry* matches with *good-hearted*.

11. **D** This is a Conclusions question, as it asks for the choice that *most logically completes the text*. Read the text and highlight the main ideas. The text describes hula's *spiritual and meaningful* background and states that *commercialized hula dancers have been applauded by millions of tourists*. Then the text provides a contrast, stating that *audience members must have a strong familiarity with the history* in order to *recognize the full significance*. Eliminate any answer that states a conclusion that isn't supported by the text.

- (A) is wrong because *other forms of dance* aren't mentioned.

- (B) is wrong because the author doesn't compare hula to other *dance forms*.

- (C) is wrong because *other forms of artistic expression* aren't mentioned.

- (D) is correct because the text suggests that *tourists* may not *recognize the full significance* of hula, whereas *natives*, who may be aware of the *spiritual and meaningful* history of the dance, may understand it more.

12. **B** This is a Conclusions question, as it asks for the choice that *most logically completes the text*. Read the text and highlight the main ideas. The text states that *Many art historians* think that an aspect of two statues *proves that they were cast* in *the Early Classical Period*. Then the text offers a contrast, stating that someone else thinks the statues could have been made later, when *artists consciously imitated Early Classical style*. Eliminate any answer that states a conclusion that isn't supported by the text.

- (A) is wrong because the text does explain how the statues could have been made in a different time period.

- (B) is correct because it's consistent with the alternative view provided in the text, which questions the first time period proposed.

- (C) is wrong because the text doesn't provide enough information to know what was true about *later statues* in general.

- (D) is wrong because *proves* is too strong; the alternate theory calls into question the previous viewpoint but doesn't necessarily prove it wrong.

13. **A** This is a Conclusions question, as it asks for the choice that *most logically completes the text*. Read the text and highlight the main ideas. The text introduces *dissertations* and identifies a problem with them, which is that *citations are necessary* but *too many direct quotes* can make the dissertation *difficult to read*. Therefore, *paraphrasing* instead of using *direct quotes* could make a dissertation easier to read. Eliminate any answer that states a conclusion that isn't supported by the text.

- (A) is correct because it shows how *paraphrasing* could solve the problem stated in the text.

- (B) is wrong because popularity *among non-scientists* isn't related to the text.

- (C) is wrong because *the consensus views of most renowned psychologists* aren't related to the text.

- (D) is wrong because the text states that *citations are necessary*; it's *too many direct quotes* that are the problem.

14. **C** In this Rules question, punctuation is changing in the answer choices. The first part of the sentence says *An American tennis player considered one of the greatest ever*, which is an introductory phrase that is not essential to the sentence's meaning. It should therefore be followed by a comma to separate it from the rest of the sentence. Eliminate answers that do not have a comma.

- (A), (B), and (D) are wrong because they don't use a comma.

- (C) is correct because it uses a comma after the introductory phrase.

15. **B**   In this Rules question, punctuation is changing in the answer choices. Look for independent clauses. The first part of the sentence says *A photographer and member of the Swinomish and Tulalip tribes, Matika Wilbur started traveling throughout all 50 US states in 2012 to complete Project 562*, which is an independent clause. The second part of the sentence says *a multi-year photography project dedicated to documenting contemporary Indigenous life in the more than 562 federally recognized tribes in the US*, which is not an independent clause. Eliminate any option that doesn't correctly connect the independent clause to the describing phrase that follows.

- (A) is wrong because the sentence needs a comma to separate the independent clause and the describing phrase.

- (B) is correct because it correctly connects the independent clause and the describing phrase.

- (C) and (D) are wrong because the word *and* suggests two things, but the last part is a description of *Project 562*, not a separate thing.

16. **B**   In this Rules question, punctuation is changing in the answer choices. Look for independent clauses. The first part of the sentence says *Paul Baran's invention of packet switching allowed for a more efficient and cost-effective way to transmit data and forms the basis of the modern internet*, which is an independent clause. The second part says *before packet switching's invention, networks transmitted data by relying on circuit switching*, which is also an independent clause. Eliminate any answer that can't correctly connect two independent clauses.

- (A) is wrong because a coordinating conjunction (*and*) without a comma can't connect two independent clauses.

- (B) is correct because the period makes each independent clause its own sentence, which is fine.

- (C) is wrong because a comma without a coordinating conjunction can't connect two independent clauses.

- (D) is wrong because some type of punctuation is needed in order to connect two independent clauses.

17. **D**   In this Rules question, the subjects of the answers are changing, which suggests it may be testing modifiers. Look for and highlight a modifying phrase: *while studying bones at a 16th-century historical site*. Whoever is *studying bones* needs to come immediately after the comma. Eliminate any answer that doesn't start with someone who can study something.

- (A) and (C) are wrong because a *discovery* can't study something.

- (B) is wrong because a *horse tooth* can't study something.

- (D) is correct because an *archaeologist* can study something.

18. **B** In this Rules question, the subjects of the answers are changing, which suggests it may be testing modifiers. Look for and highlight a modifying phrase: *Listed as one of Time magazine's top ten medical breakthroughs in 2011*. Whatever is *Listed as* a *breakthrough* needs to come immediately after the comma. Eliminate any answer that doesn't start with something that is a *medical breakthrough*.

- (A) is wrong because an *organ* itself isn't a *medical breakthrough*.

- (B) is correct because the *development* of *organs* is a *medical breakthrough*.

- (C) is wrong because a *team* isn't a *medical breakthrough*.

- (D) is wrong because a doctor isn't a *medical breakthrough*.

19. **A** In this Rules question, verbs are changing in the answer choices, so it's testing consistency with verbs. Find and highlight the subject, *DustBuster*, which is singular, so a singular verb is needed. Write an annotation saying "singular." Eliminate any answer that is not singular.

- (A) is correct because it's singular.

- (B), (C), and (D) are wrong because they are plural.

20. **A** In this Rules question, punctuation is changing in the answer choices. Look for independent clauses. The first part of the sentence says *Thomas Herbert Elliot Jackson earned his living as a soldier and a coffee farmer, but he was also keenly interested in lepidopterology, the study of moths and butterflies*, which is an independent clause. The second part of the sentence says *amassing the largest collection of native African butterflies and donating his specimens to museums around the world*, which is not an independent clause. Eliminate any option that doesn't correctly connect an independent clause to a describing phrase.

- (A) is correct because a comma can be used between the independent clause and the describing phrase.

- (B) is wrong because there should be a comma between the independent clause and the describing phrase, as there is a shift in ideas.

- (C) and (D) are wrong because both a period and a semicolon connect two independent clauses, and the second part of the sentence isn't an independent clause.

21. **A** This is a Transitions question, so highlight ideas that relate to each other. The preceding sentence says *The tidal flats…are listed as Wetland Protected Areas under the Wetlands Conservation Act*, and this sentence says *these sites still face a wide variety of threats from humans*. These ideas disagree, so an opposite-direction transition is needed. Make an annotation that says "disagree." Eliminate any answer that doesn't match.

- (A) is correct because *However* is an opposite-direction transition.

- (B), (C), and (D) are wrong because they are same-direction transitions.

22. **D** This is a Transitions question, so highlight ideas that relate to each other. The preceding sentence describes what happened with *James Soong*, and this sentence states that *Shui-bian Chen* won the election instead of Soong. These ideas disagree, so an opposite-direction transition is needed. Make an annotation that says "disagree." Eliminate any answer that doesn't match.

- (A), (B), and (C) are wrong because they are all same-direction transitions.

- (D) is correct because *Afterward* suggests a change in time, which can function as an opposite-direction transition.

23. **A** This is a Transitions question, so highlight ideas that relate to each other. The first sentence describes Leigh's intentions behind her art. The second sentence gives an example of Leigh's art, and this sentence provides a second example. These ideas agree, so a same-direction transition is needed. Make an annotation that says "agree." Eliminate any answer that doesn't match.

- (A) is correct because *Similarly* is same-direction and shows that this sentence is a second example of Leigh's work.

- (B) is wrong because this sentence isn't an example of a claim from the sentence right before it.

- (C) is wrong because it is an opposite-direction transition.

- (D) is wrong because this sentence isn't a conclusion based on previously stated evidence.

24. **B** This is a Rhetorical Synthesis question, so highlight the goal(s) stated in the question: *explain an advantage of the format of Mystery House*. Eliminate any answer that doesn't fulfill this purpose.

- (A) and (D) are wrong because the *format* is mentioned but no *advantage* of it is stated.

- (B) is correct because it shows how the game's *format* was different from *other games at the time*, giving it an advantage.

- (C) is wrong because it doesn't mention the *format*.

25. **D** This is a Rhetorical Synthesis question, so highlight the goal(s) stated in the question: *emphasize the significance of Evans's research*. Eliminate any answer that doesn't fulfill this purpose.

- (A), (B), and (C) are wrong because they don't say why the discovery is significant.

- (D) is correct because *vital to the public's wider acceptance of pasteurization and reduction in brucellosis infections* shows how the discovery is significant.

26. **A** This is a Rhetorical Synthesis question, so highlight the goal(s) stated in the question: *contrast the superconductivity of mercury wire with that of cuprates*. Eliminate any answer that doesn't fulfill this purpose.

- (A) is correct because it contrasts the different temperatures at which each material becomes a superconductor.

- (B) is wrong because it doesn't specifically say at what temperature *mercury wire* becomes a superconductor, so it doesn't *contrast* their *superconductivity*.

- (C) is wrong because it doesn't mention *mercury wire*.

- (D) is wrong because it doesn't contrast the two materials' *superconductivity*.

27. **C** This is a Rhetorical Synthesis question, so highlight the goal(s) stated in the question: *present the significance of the Kefauver-Harris Amendment to an audience unfamiliar with the medication thalidomide*. Eliminate any answer that doesn't *present the significance* in a way that assumes the audience is *unfamiliar with the medication thalidomide*.

- (A) and (B) are wrong because they don't describe *thalidomide* but the audience is *unfamiliar* with it.

- (C) is correct because it describes the *significance of the Kefauver-Harris Amendment* and describes *thalidomide* since the audience is *unfamiliar* with it.

- (D) is wrong because it doesn't describe the *significance of the Kefauver-Harris Amendment*.

Module 2 – Easier

1. **D** This is a Vocabulary question, as it asks for *the most logical and precise word or phrase*. Read the text and highlight what can help to fill in the blank, which describes what *Environmental analysts* need to do *through the use of life-cycle assessments*. The part after the colon describes how *life-cycle assessments* are used to *find out the environmental impact of a product*, so write "finding out" in the annotation box and use process of elimination.

- (A), (B), and (C) are wrong because they don't match with "finding out."

- (D) is correct because *determining* matches with "finding out."

2. **A** This is a Vocabulary question, as it asks for *the most logical and precise word or phrase*. Read the text and highlight what can help to fill in the blank, which describes how *Paa Joe* remains as he produces his art. The text describes Joe as *carefully drawing up* designs, honoring people's requests, memorializing *the life of the individual*, and believing that *his designs* will *carry a piece of life in this world to the afterlife*. All of these details suggest that Joe is "considerate," so write that in the annotation box and use process of elimination.

- (A) is correct because *compassionate* matches with "considerate."

- (B) and (D) are wrong because they are negative words, and the text describes Joe using positive language.

- (C) is wrong because *assertive* means "confident."

3.   **C**   This is a Vocabulary question, as it asks for *the most logical and precise word or phrase*. Read the text and highlight what can help to fill in the blank, which refers to *ways to prevent the disease* that were lacking *In the early 2000s*. The second sentence provides a contrast with *However* and states that in 2007 a gel was invented that could *lower the risk*. This contrast suggests that "successful" ways *to prevent the disease* were lacking prior to 2007, so write "successful" in the annotation box and use process of elimination.

- (A) and (B) are wrong because they are both negative words, but "successful" is positive.

- (C) is correct because *effective* matches with "successful."

- (D) is wrong because *charismatic* means "charming and likeable."

4.   **B**   This is a Vocabulary question, as it asks for *the most logical and precise word or phrase*. Read the text and highlight what can help to fill in the blank, which describes the *attempts for change*. The text states that the actions included *nonviolent sit-ins, boycotts, and marches*, so write "nonviolent" in the annotation box and use process of elimination.

- (A) is wrong because *indifferent* means "not having an opinion."

- (B) is correct because *peaceful* matches with "nonviolent."

- (C) is wrong because *essential* doesn't match with "nonviolent."

- (D) is wrong because *bland* means "dull."

5.   **C**   This is a Vocabulary question, as it asks for *the most logical and precise word or phrase*. Read the text and highlight what can help to fill in the blank, which describes how *Washington* did *not* respond to Bushnell's *appeal*. The first sentence states that Bushnell *unsuccessfully requested increased security for her mission several times*, and the last part of the text says that after *Washington was not able* to do something, she pleaded to a specific person *for support but was ignored*. All of this suggests that Washington was not able to "fulfill" *her appeal* for *increased security*, so write "fulfill" in the annotation box and use process of elimination.

- (A) is wrong because *certify* means "confirm," but Bushnell was looking for *increased security*, so certifying the request would only suggest confirming that she had made it, not responding to it.

- (B) is wrong because *mistake* is a negative word, and a positive word is needed here.

- (C) is correct because approving her appeal would suggest providing the requested security.

- (D) is wrong because *demonstrate* doesn't match with "fulfill."

6. **A** This is a Vocabulary question, as it asks for *the most logical and precise word or phrase*. Read the text and highlight what can help to fill in the blank, which describes how Heyer did or did not *engage in all forms of publicity for her publications*. There is a contrast with *Despite being a best-selling writer*, which suggests that Heyer may not have engaged in publicity. Furthermore, the second sentence says *She so believed that her private life was irrelevant to the success of her novels*, which also indicates that she didn't like publicity, so write "didn't want" in the annotation box and use process of elimination.

    - (A) is correct because *refused* matches with "didn't want."

    - (B), (C), and (D) are wrong because they are all positive words, but "didn't want" is negative.

7. **D** This is a Purpose question, as it asks for the *main purpose*. Read the text and highlight what can help to understand the overall purpose. The text introduces *Dr. Donald Hopkins* and states that he was hired *to help implement a program to eradicate smallpox in Sierra Leone*. Then it explains how he used *mass distribution of the smallpox vaccine* to reduce the incidence of disease, so write "tell how Hopkins helped with smallpox" in the annotation box and use process of elimination.

    - (A) and (C) are wrong because they don't mention *Hopkins*.

    - (B) is wrong because the text doesn't state that this encapsulates Hopkins' whole *career*.

    - (D) is correct because it matches the annotation.

8. **A** This is a Purpose question, as it asks for the *main purpose*. Read the text and highlight what can help to understand the overall purpose. The poem states that the speaker has *no wealth to give* to someone but states, *You have my heart*. Then the speaker vows to always think of this person and asks whether this thought is mutual, so write "leaving but will always think of the person" in the annotation box and use process of elimination.

    - (A) is correct because it matches the annotation.

    - (B) is wrong because the text never says *why* the speaker loves the other person.

    - (C) is wrong because the text never says *when he will be back*.

    - (D) is wrong because no instructions are given.

9. **C** This is a Dual Texts question, as it has two texts. The question asks what *the researchers in Text 2* would say about *the scientists' initial belief in Text 1*. Start by understanding the *initial belief* in Text 1. Text 1 describes the famine resulting from damage to the potato crop and states that *scientists originally believed the disease was caused by the US-1 strain of the bacteria*. Next, look for a similar idea in Text 2 to see how its author feels about this view. Text 2 describes research on potato plants from the famine and states that the researchers *found that US-1 was not the cause of the catastrophe*. The text goes on to state that *although the US-1 strain is a common cause of crop loss, a formerly undiscovered strain* caused the famine. Therefore, the researchers in Text 2 would "say the claim makes sense but is wrong." Write that in the annotation box and use process of elimination.

- (A) is wrong because the mistaken viewpoint is about *US-1*, not *HERB-1*.

- (B) is wrong because *only affects potato crops* is never stated.

- (C) is correct because it matches the annotation.

- (D) is wrong because Text 2 acknowledges that *US-1* is *a common cause of crop loss*, so the researchers do understand *why the scientists would think that US-1 caused the famine*.

10. **B** This is a Retrieval question, as it says *Based on the text*. Read the text and highlight what it says about *the speaker* being *like the sun*. The text mentions the other person needing the speaker *through and through, as flowers need the sun*. Eliminate any answer that isn't supported by the text.

- (A) is wrong because the speaker is not described as shining.

- (B) is correct because it matches the highlighted text.

- (C) is wrong because the sun is not described as being *completely alone*.

- (D) is wrong because *the world* is described as *asleep*, but neither the speaker nor the sun is.

11. **C** This is a Claims question, as it asks for a *quotation* to *illustrate the claim*. Read the text and highlight the claim, which is that *the main character* is *eager to help bring peace to the restless spirit*, a *young girl* whom he *suspects* is haunting his orchard. Eliminate answers that don't *illustrate* this idea.

- (A) and (B) are wrong because they mention the character's suspicion but not his desire to *help bring peace* to the spirit.

- (C) is correct because *that I may help your sorrowing heart to rest* supports *eager to help bring peace* from the claim.

- (D) is wrong because it doesn't clearly mention anything about the *spirit* or helping it.

12. **D** This is a Charts question, as it asks for *data from the table*. The graph charts several biomes, their maximum temperatures, and their annual precipitation ranges. Read the text and highlight the specifications mentioned, which are *a range of annual precipitation that includes 30 inches* and *does not exceed a maximum temperature of 80°F*. Start with the temperature maximum, which leaves only boreal forest and tropical forest. Then, of those two, boreal forest is the one that includes 30 inches in its precipitation range.

- (A), (B), and (C) are wrong because they don't meet both specifications from the text.

- (D) is correct because it meets both specifications.

13.   **A**   This is a Charts question, as it asks for *data from the table*. The graph charts several elements, their boiling points, heat capacities, electron affinities, and first ionization energies. Highlight the *assertion* in the text, which is that *four of the elements are metals and one element is a nonmetal*. The text associates *boiling points* and *electron affinities* with being a metal or a nonmetal, so eliminate any answers that refer to other characteristics, are inconsistent with the table, or don't support the assertion.

- (A) is correct because *boiling points above 1,500 K* would mean that four are metals, and the same four having *electron affinities of less than 150 kJ/mol* further matches with the description of metals, which is consistent with the student's assertion.

- (B) is wrong because it only mentions one element, but the claim relates to all five.

- (C) is wrong because *first ionization energy* and *heat capacity* aren't stated in relation to whether elements are metals or nonmetals.

- (D) is wrong because *heat capacity* isn't stated in relation to determining whether an element is a metal or a nonmetal.

14.   **D**   This is a Claims question, as it asks for an answer that would *support the student's claim*. Read the text and highlight the claim, which is that *the work was included as a way to attract new visitors*. Eliminate answers that don't *support* this idea.

- (A) is wrong because it contradicts the claim by suggesting that *new visitors* wouldn't be interested in this type of exhibit.

- (B) and (C) are wrong because they don't relate to *new visitors*.

- (D) is correct because *appeal to people who don't normally visit art museums* matches with *attract new visitors*.

15.   **A**   This is a Claims question, as it asks for an answer that would *support the researchers' claim*. Read the text and highlight the claim, which is that *bilinguals can switch between tasks at a faster rate due to their routine use of language-switching*. Eliminate answers that don't *support* this idea.

- (A) is correct because it supports the idea that there is a link between speaking two languages and task-switching.

- (B) is wrong because it's not consistent with the *faster rate* for bilinguals in the claim.

- (C) is wrong because it doesn't relate to the claim about task-switching.

- (D) is wrong because it weakens the claim by providing an alternate cause for bilinguals' faster rate of task-switching.

16.   **B**   This is a Charts question, as it asks for *data in the graph*. The graph charts the percentage of cat contact in different spots for people with previous positive cat experience and those with previous negative cat experience. Highlight the *claim* in the text, which is that *previous positive cat experience was*

not predictive of good cat handling techniques; in fact, participants with previous negative cat experience demonstrated better cat handling techniques. Read more of the text to identify the link between good and bad cat handling techniques and the contact areas: cats *prefer certain contact areas, such as the cheeks, base of ear, and under the jaw, while disliking contact on the stomach or the base of the tail.* Eliminate any answer that doesn't *support* the claim or is inconsistent with the data on the graph.

- (A) is wrong because it contradicts the claim, as *lower percentages of contact in areas disliked by cats* would be in line with good cat handling techniques, which the claim said was associated with those who had *previous negative cat experience.*

- (B) is correct because it is consistent with the claim and supported by the graph.

- (C) is wrong because *similar percentages of contact* isn't consistent with the contrast stated in the claim.

- (D) is wrong because it doesn't relate to a difference between those with positive experience and those with negative experience.

17. **B** This is a Conclusions question, as it asks for something *presented in the text.* Highlight what the text says about *Miyazaki's approach to film*: the films use *animation* but *remain relevant to both children and adults,* they draw from *Japanese elements,* and they include *poignant stories about humans and the environment as told through the eyes of children.* The text also states that Miyazaki *showcases the importance of protecting the environment* through *communing with nature.* Eliminate any answer that states a conclusion that isn't supported by the text.

- (A) is wrong because *nature spirits* are mentioned in relation to one movie, not his approach as a whole.

- (B) is correct because it's fully supported by the text.

- (C) is wrong because *Western influences* aren't mentioned as playing an equal role to *Japanese elements.*

- (D) is wrong because the text never states what Miyazaki believes his films *will encourage* people to do.

18. **B** In this Rules question, verb forms are changing in the answer choices, so it's testing sentence structure. The subject of the sentence is *thale cress plants,* and there is no main verb, so the answer must provide the main verb. Eliminate any answer that isn't in the correct form to be the main verb.

- (A) and (D) are wrong because an *-ing* verb can't be the main verb in a sentence.

- (B) is correct because it's in the right form to be the main verb.

- (C) is wrong because a "to" verb can't be the main verb in a sentence.

19. **D**   In this Rules question, verb forms are changing in the answer choices, so it's testing sentence structure. The subject of the sentence is *Farmers*, and there is no main verb, so the answer must provide the main verb. Eliminate any answer that isn't in the correct form to be the main verb.

- (A) and (C) are wrong because an *-ing* verb can't be the main verb in a sentence.

- (B) is wrong because a "to" verb can't be the main verb in a sentence.

- (D) is correct because it's in the right form to be the main verb.

20. **A**   In this Rules question, verbs are changing in the answer choices, so it's testing consistency with verbs. Find and highlight the subject, *breaks*, which is plural, so a plural verb is needed. All of the answers work with a plural subject, so look for a clue regarding tense. The previous sentence describes something that happened in the past, *In 1972*, and this sentence describes what happened *After this*, but still in the past, as the sentence is explaining a *defining element* of hip hop today. Highlight these phrases and write an annotation that says "past." Eliminate any answer not in past tense.

- (A) is correct because it's in past tense.

- (B) is wrong because it's in present tense.

- (C) is wrong because *had become* suggests that this event happened prior to another event, but it happened after the events of the previous sentence.

- (D) is wrong because it's in future tense.

21. **D**   In this Rules question, punctuation is changing in the answer choices. Look for independent clauses. The first part of the sentence says *he was unable to come up with a plausible mechanism to explain how the continents could move*, which is an independent clause. The second part says *it was not until the discovery of the seafloor spreading at mid-ocean ridges that his idea became widely accepted*, which is also an independent clause. Eliminate any answer that can't correctly connect two independent clauses.

- (A) is wrong because a comma without a coordinating conjunction can't connect two independent clauses.

- (B) is wrong because some type of punctuation is needed in order to connect two independent clauses.

- (C) is wrong because a coordinating conjunction (*and*) without a comma can't connect two independent clauses.

- (D) is correct because it connects the independent clauses with a comma + a coordinating conjunction (*and*), which is acceptable.

22. **B**   In this Rules question, verbs are changing in the answer choices, so it's testing consistency with verbs. Find and highlight the subject, *it*, which is singular, so a singular verb is needed. All of the answers work with a singular subject, so look for a clue regarding tense. The sentence uses a present

tense verb: *is*. Highlight this verb, which is in present tense, so write an annotation that says "present." Eliminate any answer not in present tense.

- (A) is wrong because it's not in present tense.

- (B) is correct because it's in present tense.

- (C) and (D) are wrong because they're in past tense.

23.   **A**   In this Rules question, punctuation is changing in the answer choices. The first part of the sentence says *A total solar eclipse…is observed*, which is an independent clause. The second part says *wherever the Moon appears large enough to completely obscure the solar disc*, which is a describing phrase that is not an independent clause. Eliminate any answer that doesn't correctly connect the independent clause to the describing phrase that follows.

- (A) is correct because no punctuation should be used here.

- (B) is wrong because the comma suggests that the second part of the sentence is not essential to the sentence's meaning, but the phrase is essential in order to specify where the eclipse is observed.

- (C) is wrong because a semicolon links two independent clauses, and the second part isn't independent.

- (D) is wrong because the second part is not an independent clause, so it can't stand on its own.

24.   **C**   This is a Transitions question, so highlight ideas that relate to each other. The preceding sentence says *Canadian Cree/Métis poet and artist Gregory Scofield initially was ashamed*, and this sentence says *Scofield learned to appreciate the Métis aspects of his identity*. These ideas disagree, so an opposite-direction transition is needed. Make an annotation that says "disagree." Eliminate any answer that doesn't match.

- (A), (B), and (D) are wrong because they are same-direction transitions.

- (C) is correct because *Nevertheless* is an opposite-direction transition.

25.   **D**   This is a Transitions question, so highlight ideas that relate to each other. The preceding sentence says *there is very little archaeological or written evidence linking this instrument to the actual countries of Scotland or Ireland*, and this sentence says *the history of the instrument is largely up for debate*. These ideas agree, so a same-direction transition is needed. Make an annotation that says "agree." Eliminate any answer that doesn't match.

- (A) and (B) are wrong because they are opposite-direction transitions.

- (C) is wrong because this sentence isn't an additional point.

- (D) is correct because this sentence offers a conclusion based on the evidence in the previous sentence.

26. **C** This is a Rhetorical Synthesis question, so highlight the goal(s) stated in the question: *describe Apple: Skin to the Core to an audience unfamiliar with Eric Gansworth*. Eliminate any answer that doesn't describe the book in a way that assumes the audience is *unfamiliar with Eric Gansworth*.

- (A) and (B) are wrong because they don't provide information about Gansworth, and the audience is unfamiliar, so he should be described.

- (C) is correct because it describes the book and introduces Gansworth since the audience is unfamiliar with him.

- (D) is wrong because it doesn't *describe* the book.

27. **C** This is a Rhetorical Synthesis question, so highlight the goal(s) stated in the question: *explain an advantage of backstitch*. Eliminate any answer that doesn't fulfill this purpose.

- (A) and (B) are wrong because they don't describe *an advantage of backstitch*.

- (C) is correct because it describes *an advantage of backstitch*.

- (D) is wrong because it doesn't mention the technique of *backstitch*.

Module 2 – Harder

1. **D** This is a Vocabulary question, as it asks for *the most logical and precise word or phrase*. Read the text and highlight what can help to fill in the blank, which describes the relationship between *bumblebees* and *the effects of climate change*. The following sentence explains how the bees' *imbalanced wings* have *coincided with the escalated temperatures caused by climate change*, so the bees must be affected by it. Write "affected by" in the annotation box and use process of elimination.

- (A) and (C) are wrong because they're the opposite of the annotation.

- (B) is wrong because *incongruent with* means "not matching up with."

- (D) is correct because *susceptible to* matches with "affected by."

2. **A** This is a Vocabulary question, as it asks for *the most logical and precise word or phrase*. Read the text and highlight what can help to fill in the blank, which refers to what scientists *won't necessarily* have to do to *the Standard Model* as a result of the *findings*. The previous sentence states that *Recent measurements* were different from what *would ordinarily be predicted by the Standard Model*. Then there is a contrast word (*While*), and after the blank the text says that *the new data might indicate that some modifications...are warranted*. So, scientists won't necessarily have to "get rid of" the Standard Model, but some changes might be needed. Write "get rid of" in the annotation box and use process of elimination.

- (A) is correct because *overhaul* matches with "get rid of."

- (B) is wrong because *withhold* means "not provide."

- (C) is wrong because it's the opposite of the annotation.

- (D) is wrong because *misapprehend* means "misunderstand."

3.   **C**   This is a Vocabulary question, as it asks for *the most logical and precise word or phrase*. Read the text and highlight what can help to fill in the blank, which refers to the link between Archimedes and *calculus*. The text states that Archimedes, who was *active in the third century BCE* and is also described as *pioneering*, had described *concepts thought to have been first developed in the 1500s*. This is referring to *calculus*, so Archimedes worked with calculus before it was thought to have been developed. Write "invented" or "worked with before" in the annotation box and use process of elimination.

- (A) is wrong because *exemplified* means "was an example of."

- (B) is wrong because *verified* means "confirmed to be true," but the text suggests that Archimedes might have originated the ideas, not confirmed them.

- (C) is correct because *anticipated* means "saw before it happened," which matches the annotation.

- (D) is wrong because *translated* doesn't match the annotation.

4.   **A**   This is a Vocabulary question, as it asks for *the most logical and precise word or phrase*. Read the text and highlight what can help to fill in the blank, which refers to an aspect of the *plants left over* that was *assumed*. The previous sentence says that the extinction *was thought to have had a devastating effect on the remaining ecosystems*. This sentence begins with a contrast (*However*), and the second part of the sentence suggests that the plants were still surviving. Therefore, they weren't as "destroyed" as it was assumed. Write "destroyed" in the annotation box and use process of elimination.

- (A) is correct because *assailable* means "vulnerable" or "able to be destroyed," and the idea that the plants weren't as vulnerable as they were assumed to be is consistent with the text.

- (B) is wrong because *determinate* means "having defined limits."

- (C) is wrong because *objectionable* means "controversial."

- (D) is wrong because *liminal* means "in an intermediate stage."

5.   **B**   This is a Vocabulary question, as it asks for *the most logical and precise word or phrase*. Read the text and highlight what can help to fill in the blank, which describes what Ball *gained notoriety* for doing to *religious and secular authorities*. The part with the blank is followed by a colon, indicating that the second part of the sentence will explain the first. It begins with *this condemnation*, so the blank must mean "condemning." Write "condemning" in the annotation box and use process of elimination.

- (A) is wrong because *proselytizing* means "trying to convert."

- (B) is correct because *censuring* means "condemning."

- (C) is wrong because *envisaging* means "visualizing."

- (D) is wrong because *declaring* isn't a negative word like "condemning."

6. **A** This is a Purpose question, as it asks for the *function* of a sentence. Read the text and highlight what can help to understand the function of the underlined sentence. The text describes how the *man* instructs his *two dogs* to herd the sheep. The setting is described in terms of *the damp stillness of the air* and *the hillside*. Then the underlined sentence expands on the description of the setting and uses the phrases *creeping silently across the distance, desolate, treeless country*, and *no other sign of life*. Write "show how isolated the man's environment is" in the annotation box and use process of elimination.

     - (A) is correct because it matches the annotation.

     - (B) is wrong because no information is given on what the man *longs* to do.

     - (C) is wrong because the text does not state that the man makes a *daily walk*.

     - (D) is wrong because no comparison is made to *the train's destination*.

7. **A** This is a Purpose question, as it asks for the *function* of a sentence. Read the text and highlight what can help to understand the function of the underlined sentence. The text details Garin's actions on his *business* and then states that *The merry-making in the town tempted, but the way was long and he must go*. Then the underlined sentence gives an example of the *merry-making* that Garin had to refuse to join, as the text goes on to say that he *wanted to stay* but decided to leave. Write "example of merry-making" in the annotation box and use process of elimination.

     - (A) is correct because it matches the annotation.

     - (B) is wrong because no *emotion* of Garin's is foreshadowed in this sentence.

     - (C) is wrong because, while it does visually describe the girls, they are not really part of the text's *scene* (they only cross his path), and this statement does not match with the *function* of the sentence; it's used to give an example of the merrymaking, not to describe characters.

     - (D) is wrong because the underlined sentence doesn't give any information about Garin or his *urgency*.

8. **B** This is a Purpose question, as it asks for the *main purpose*. Read the text and highlight what can help to understand the overall purpose. The text describes the king and queen of *England* and the king and queen of *France* and then says that *In both countries* it was clear *that things in general were settled for ever*, so write "describe settled ruling situation in England and France" in the annotation box and use process of elimination.

     - (A) is wrong because there is no *contrast* between the *conditions* of the two countries.

     - (B) is correct because it matches the annotation.

- (C) is wrong because the similarity and difference stated are not part of the *main purpose* of the text.

- (D) is wrong because the text doesn't mention *hoarding food* or *withholding resources*.

9. **B** This is a Dual Texts question, as it has two texts. The question asks how *Patti and colleagues* in Text 2 would respond to *the "mystery" discussed in Text 1*. Start by understanding the *"mystery"* in Text 1. Text 1 states that the *mystery…concerns the large amount of glucose that is excreted as waste* from cancer cells. Next, look for a similar idea in Text 2 to see how *Patti and colleagues* feel about this mystery. Text 2 states that *Patti discovered that cancer cells have an upper limit for the amount of glucose that can be processed efficiently, as has long been observed in normal cells.* Therefore, Patti and colleagues in Text 2 would say exactly that, so use process of elimination with this highlighted portion.

- (A) is wrong because *further research* is not mentioned in Text 2.

- (B) is correct because it matches the highlighting in Text 2.

- (C) is wrong because the amount of glucose that *is required by cancer cells* isn't mentioned in Text 2; it's the amount that is absorbed and processed.

- (D) is wrong because Text 2 doesn't mention *mitochondrial processes*.

10. **B** This is a Claims question, as it asks for the choice that would *support Twenge's hypothesis*. Read the text and highlight the hypothesis, which is that *sociocultural environment…affects an individual's personality in addition to genetics and family environment.* Eliminate answers that don't *support* this idea.

- (A) is wrong because gender isn't related to *sociocultural environment*, as defined by the text.

- (B) is correct because students in the 1970s versus those in the 1990s would have grown up within different sociocultural environments and, according to the hypothesis, would therefore have different personality traits.

- (C) is wrong because *income level* isn't related to *sociocultural environment*, as defined by the text.

- (D) is wrong because the *number of words* people used to describe their personalities doesn't have a clear link to anything in the text.

11. **B** This is a Conclusions question, as it asks for something *presented in the text*. Highlight what the text says about *Ceh Moo's approach to literature*: she wrote *the first novel written by a woman in the Yucatec language*, which is untraditional because *Maya authors primarily write* works other than novels. The text goes on to describe another way Ceh Moo's story is different from traditional ones. Eliminate any answer that states a conclusion that isn't supported by the text.

- (A) is wrong because the text doesn't say that Ceh Moo takes the *myths* and sets them in the present day.

- (B) is correct because it's fully supported by the text.

- (C) is wrong because the text doesn't say that these influences are equal.

- (D) is wrong because the text never states that Ceh Moo's work criticizes anything.

12. **C**   This is a Charts question, as it asks for *data from the table*. The table charts the mean flower abundance and species richness as well as mean wild bee abundance and species richness for four environments. Highlight the *conclusion* in the text, which is that *flower strips were most effective*. The text defines success in terms of *attracting more bees*, so higher values in the table correlate with effectiveness. Eliminate any answers that are inconsistent with the table or don't support the conclusion.

- (A) and (D) are wrong because they don't mention *flower strips*, which were the enhancement measure in the conclusion.

- (B) is wrong because it only compares flower strips to the *control group*, which doesn't support the conclusion that the flower strips were *most effective* among the interventions.

- (C) is correct because it compares the flower strips to everything else in the table, supporting the fact that they were *most effective*.

13. **C**   This is a Charts question, as it asks for *data from the graph*. The graph charts the percentage improvement in test scores for two test types for a control group and an experimental group. Highlight the *recommendation* in the text, which is that *physically active lessons* should be *included in the mathematics curriculum*. The text states that the experimental group *received physically active mathematics lessons*, so to support the recommendation, the experimental group would need to have more improvements than the control group. Eliminate any answers that are inconsistent with the graph or don't support the recommendation.

- (A) is wrong because both groups improved their scores.

- (B) is wrong because it doesn't compare the experimental group to the control group, so the effect of the lessons isn't evident.

- (C) is correct because it suggests that the physically active lessons had benefits.

- (D) is wrong because it doesn't show the benefit of the physically active lessons.

14. **D**   This is a Claims question, as it asks for a *quotation* that *illustrates the claim*. Read the text and highlight the claim, which is that *Treplev is heavily critical of the art form's* (theater's) *established tropes*. Eliminate answers that don't *illustrate* this idea.

- (A) and (C) are wrong because they don't contain anything critical.

- (B) is wrong because it doesn't mention the theater.

- (D) is correct because *other productions* and *playwrights* refer to the theater, and *the same, same, same old stuff* and *must needs run from it* suggest the speaker's disdain for the *established tropes*.

15.   **D**   This is a Claims question, as it asks for something that would *weaken the claim.* Highlight the *claim made by people who favor the conventional view of positive visualization*, which is that positive visualization *can enhance people's ability to achieve their goals.* Eliminate answers that don't *weaken* this idea.

  - (A) is wrong because if *members of the control group accomplished fewer goals*, this would support, not weaken, the claim that positive visualization helps people achieve their goals.

  - (B) is wrong because accomplishing even *a slightly higher number of their goals* would support the claim that positive visualization is effective, and the task here is to *weaken* the claim.

  - (C) is wrong because no result is given for the effect of positive visualization on accomplishing goals.

  - (D) is correct because it contradicts the claim by stating that those who were not told to use positive visualization actually accomplished more goals.

16.   **B**   This is a Charts question, as it asks for *data from the graph.* The graph charts the number of nightmares over four weeks for dreamers undergoing two types of interventions. Highlight the *claim* in the text, which is that *IRT is made even more effective when utilizing TMR.* Then, the sentence states that the graduate student *was surprised to observe* something, so the blank must refer to something that goes against the claim. Eliminate any answers that are inconsistent with the graph or don't go against the claim.

  - (A) and (D) are wrong because they don't relate to whether TMR is effective.

  - (B) is correct because if the decrease was only *slightly greater* for the group with TMR, this would somewhat weaken the idea that TMR makes the treatment *more effective* and could therefore be a surprising result.

  - (C) is wrong because this result is consistent with the claim, so it wouldn't be surprising.

17.   **D**   This is a Conclusions question, as it asks for the choice that *most logically completes the text.* Read the text and highlight the main ideas. The text describes an experiment in which people *used social media* to engage with accounts belonging to people they knew as well as *users unknown to the participants.* The text contrasts the reduction in appearance satisfaction for known and unknown targets, stating that there was a greater reduction for known targets. Therefore, unknown targets caused a lesser reduction in appearance satisfaction. Eliminate any answer that states a conclusion that isn't supported by the text.

  - (A) is wrong because it states the opposite of what the last sentence indicates.

  - (B) is wrong because no conclusion can be drawn about the effectiveness of the *scale* that was used.

  - (C) is wrong because there is no evidence from the text to say whether the correlation is *significant* or not.

- (D) is correct because it matches the relationship described in the last sentence.

18.　**D**　In this Rules question, verb forms are changing in the answer choices, so it's testing sentence structure. The phrase after the second dash describes how the two scientists created an *Ebola vaccine*. Eliminate any answer that does not make the phrase clear and correct.

- (A) is wrong because it makes the creation of the vaccine an item in a list, but there is no other *-ing* verb to form the list.

- (B) is wrong because there is no clear subject for the verb *created*.

- (C) is wrong because it's not clear who or what is *creating* the vaccine.

- (D) is correct because it states that the gene was *eliminated...to create a potential Ebola vaccine*, which provides a clear and correct meaning.

19.　**B**　In this Rules question, punctuation is changing in the answer choices. The main meaning of the sentence is *The watering of cultivated crops is sometimes based on a system known as irrigation scheduling, in which farmers use certain factors about the land and weather...to determine when and how much water is needed.* The phrase *specifically, the soil quality and projected rainfall* is a describing phrase that has a dash before it, so it must have a dash after it to show that it is not essential to the sentence's meaning. Eliminate answers that do not have a dash after the describing phrase.

- (A), (C), and (D) are wrong because they don't use a dash.

- (B) is correct because it uses a dash after the non-essential information.

20.　**B**　In this Rules question, punctuation with a transition is changing in the answer choices. Look for independent clauses. The first part of the sentence says *The audience was determined*. The part after *however* doesn't have a subject, so it's not an independent clause. Eliminate any answer that doesn't correctly link the independent clause to the phrase after it.

- (A) and (C) are wrong because a semicolon links two independent clauses, but the second part isn't an independent clause.

- (B) is correct because it puts commas before and after *however*, which is a word that isn't essential to the meaning of the sentence.

- (D) is wrong because the word *however* needs commas before and after to show that it's non-essential.

21.　**C**　In this Rules question, punctuation is changing in the answer choices. Look for independent clauses. The first part of the sentence says *A recent study by a team of researchers at the University of Washington discovered a surprising source of atmosphere- and climate-changing gases*, which is an independent clause. The second part of the sentence is not an independent clause and explains what the source of the gases was. Eliminate any option that doesn't correctly connect the independent clause to the explanation of the source.

- (A) is wrong because the period makes *volcanoes' passive degassing…* its own sentence, which doesn't work because it's not an independent clause.

- (B) is wrong because a semicolon links two independent clauses, but the second part isn't an independent clause.

- (C) is correct because a colon is used when the second part of the sentence elaborates on the first.

- (D) is wrong because some punctuation is needed between the independent clause and the explanation of the source.

22. **D** In this Rules question, punctuation is changing in the answer choices. Look for independent clauses. The first part of the sentence says *A 2006 edition of the book added two more patterns of thinking*, which is an independent clause. The second part of the sentence says *some autistic people may be music and math thinkers, others verbal logic thinkers*, which is an independent clause that states the new *patterns of thinking*. Eliminate any option that doesn't correctly connect the independent clause to new *patterns of thinking*.

- (A) and (B) are wrong because the second part is the *new patterns of* thinking, not a contrast from the first part of the sentence as *though* implies.

- (C) is wrong because a comma alone can't separate two independent clauses.

- (D) is correct because a colon is used when the second part of the sentence elaborates on the first.

23. **B** This is a Transitions question, so highlight ideas that relate to each other. The preceding sentence says *There were a few time periods when it briefly went out due to power failures and other technological challenges*, and this sentence says *the bulb was connected to an uninterruptible power supply to determine how long it could actually burn*. These ideas agree, so a same-direction transition is needed. Make an annotation that says "agree." Eliminate any answer that doesn't match.

- (A) is wrong because this sentence doesn't provide a different idea that has something in common with the previous sentence.

- (B) is correct because *Consequently* is same-direction, and the *uninterruptible power supply* is a consequence of the *power failures and other technological challenges*.

- (C) is wrong because this sentence isn't an additional point.

- (D) is wrong because it is an opposite-direction transition.

24. **A** This is a Rhetorical Synthesis question, so highlight the goal(s) stated in the question: *explain how the law school of Berytus prepared jurists*. Eliminate any answer that doesn't fulfill this purpose.

- (A) is correct because it shows the techniques used by Berytus (*classes that included lectures and analyses*).

- (B), (C), and (D) are wrong because they don't include any information about the techniques.

25. **D** This is a Rhetorical Synthesis question, so highlight the goal(s) stated in the question: *emphasize how high satellites in geosynchronous orbit are relative to those in low and medium orbits*. Eliminate any answer that doesn't fulfill this purpose.

- (A) is wrong because it doesn't include the altitudes of satellites in *low and medium orbits*.

- (B) is wrong because it doesn't include the altitude of satellites in *geosynchronous orbit*.

- (C) is wrong because it doesn't give any information about the altitudes of satellites in any orbit.

- (D) is correct because it includes the altitude of satellites in *geosynchronous orbit* and compares this altitude to satellites in *low and medium orbits*.

26. **C** This is a Rhetorical Synthesis question, so highlight the goal(s) stated in the question: *emphasize a similarity between the two ways animals use colors*. Eliminate any answer that doesn't fulfill this purpose.

- (A), (B), and (D) are wrong because they describe the *two ways animals use colors* but don't include a *similarity*.

- (C) is correct because it includes a *similarity* between the *two ways animals use colors*—they are both *determined by the time of day the animals' ancestors were active*.

27. **C** This is a Rhetorical Synthesis question, so highlight the goal(s) stated in the question: *present the study and its methodology*. Eliminate any answer that doesn't fulfill this purpose.

- (A) is wrong because it includes the results of the study but does not *present* what the study was actually doing.

- (B) is wrong because it includes information about the goal of the study but not the *methodology*.

- (C) is correct because it introduces the purpose of the study and describes the *methodology* (what the researchers did).

- (D) is wrong because it doesn't *introduce* the study, such as by presenting its purpose.

PRACTICE TEST 2—MATH EXPLANATIONS

Module 1

1. **D** The question asks for a value given a specific situation. The question states that the equation $p = 45d$ represents the *relationship between the number of posts, p, and the number of days, d.* Since the question asks for the number of posts during a 3-day period, plug in 3 for d to get $p = 45(3)$. Simplify the right side of the equation to get $p = 135$. The correct answer is (D).

2. **B** The question asks for the equation that represents a line. Translate the information in bite-sized pieces and eliminate after each piece. The answer choices are all in slope-intercept form, $y = mx + b$, in which m is the slope and b is the y-intercept. One piece of information says that the line *has a slope of –3*, so $m = -3$. Eliminate (C) and (D) because they have the wrong slope. The y-intercept is the point where the graph crosses the y-axis, which happens when $x = 0$. Thus, the point $(0, 10)$ is the y-intercept, and b in slope-intercept form is 10. Eliminate (A) because it has the wrong y-intercept. The correct answer is (B).

3. **7** The question asks for the value of an expression based on an equation. When an SAT question asks for the value of an expression, there is usually a straightforward way to solve for the expression without needing to completely isolate the variable. Since $\dfrac{12}{x}$ is the reciprocal of $\dfrac{x}{12}$, take the reciprocal of both sides of the equation. The reciprocal of $\dfrac{1}{7}$ is $\dfrac{7}{1}$, or 7, so the equation becomes $\dfrac{12}{x} = 7$. The correct answer is 7.

4. **A** The question asks for the value of the measure of an angle on a geometric figure. Start by drawing two triangles on the scratch paper. Similar triangles have the same angle measures and proportional side lengths, so draw two triangles that look alike but are different sizes. Be sure to match up the corresponding angles that are given in the question. Next, label the figure with the given information. Label angles N and Y as 90° or with the right-angle symbol, and label angle X as 23°. The drawing should look something like this:

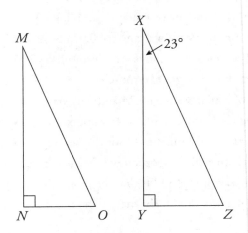

The question asks for the measure of angle M, which corresponds to angle X. Thus, angle M also measures 23°. The correct answer is (A).

5. **C** The question asks for an equivalent form of an expression. Although there are variables in the answer choices, plugging in on this question would be difficult given all the exponents. Instead, use bite-sized pieces and process of elimination to tackle this question. Start with the a terms. When dealing with exponents, write down MADSPM to remember the exponent rules. The MA part of the acronym indicates that Multiplying matching bases means to Add the exponents. Add the exponents on the a terms to get $(a^2)(a^3) = a^5$. Eliminate (A) and (D) because they have the wrong exponent on a. Compare the remaining answers. One difference is the exponent on the g terms. Add the exponents on the g terms to get $(g^{-4})(g^{-2}) = g^{-6}$. Eliminate (B) because it has the wrong exponent on g. The correct answer is (C).

6. **D** The question asks which statement must be true given data in two box plots. Check each answer and eliminate the ones that are false. A box plot can be used to determine the median, range, and interquartile range of a data set, but it cannot be used to determine the mean. Eliminate (A) and (B) because it is not possible to compare the means. Compare the remaining answer choices, (C) and (D), which compare the medians of the two data sets. In a box plot, the median is the value at the vertical line inside the box. The line representing the median for store A is at 5 feet, and the line representing the median for store B is at approximately 8 feet. Eliminate (C) because the median of store A is less than the median of store B, not greater than. The correct answer is (D).

7. **C** The question asks for the value of the x-coordinate of the solution to a system of equations. One method is to enter both equations into the built-in calculator, and then scroll and zoom as needed to find the points of intersection. The graph shows two points of intersection, (–12, 150) and (12, 150), so the x-coordinate is either –12 or 12. Only 12 is an answer choice, so choose (C).

To solve the system for the x-coordinate algebraically, substitute 150 for y in the first equation to get $150 = x^2 + 6$. Subtract 6 from both sides of the equation to get $144 = x^2$. Both 12^2 and $(-12)^2$ equal 144, so x can equal 12 or –12.

Using either of these methods, the correct answer is (C).

8. **C** The question asks about the most appropriate conclusion based on a survey and a margin of error. A margin of error expresses the amount of random sampling error in a survey's results. The margin of error is 0.07, meaning that results within a range of 0.07 above and 0.07 below the estimate are reasonable. Since the estimated proportion of adults with insomnia is 0.35, subtract the margin of error to get $0.35 - 0.07 = 0.28$, and add the margin of error to get $0.35 + 0.07 = 0.42$. The most appropriate conclusion is that a proportion of adults between 0.28 and 0.42 have insomnia. Eliminate (A) because it only addresses the lower range of plausible results. In addition, it is unlikely that the proportion will be less than the lower end of the range. Eliminate (B) for the same reasons: it only addresses the upper end of the range, and it is unlikely that the proportion will be greater than the upper end of the range. Choice (C) matches the range and says it is plausible that the proportion is within that range, so keep (C). Eliminate (D) because it does not account for the margin of error. The correct answer is (C).

9. **B** The question asks for the number of points of intersection in a system of equations. One method is to use the built-in calculator. Enter both equations into the calculator, and then scroll and zoom as needed to see where, if at all, they intersect. The lines intersect once at $(2, 0)$, so there is exactly one solution, and (B) is correct.

To solve algebraically, multiply the entire first equation by 2 to get $2y = 20x - 40$. Now that both equations are equal to $2y$, set them equal to each other to get $20x - 40 = 10x - 20$. Subtract $10x$ from both sides of the equation to get $10x - 40 = -20$, and then add 40 to both sides of the equation to get $10x = 20$. Divide both sides of the equation by 10 to get $x = 2$. Plug $x = 2$ into the first equation to get $y = 10(2) - 20$, which becomes $y = 20 - 20$, and then $y = 0$. There is one point of intersection at $(2, 0)$, so (B) is correct.

Using either of these methods, the correct answer is (B).

10. **A** The question asks for the equation that defines a function. In function notation, the number inside the parentheses is the x-value that goes into the function, or the input, and the value that comes out of the function is the y-value, or the output. The question provides two pairs of input and output values, so plug those into the answer choices and eliminate answers that don't work with both points. Start by plugging $x = -3$ and $g(x) = 39$ into the answer choices. Choice (A) becomes $39 = -12(-3) + 3$, or $39 = 36 + 3$, and then $39 = 39$. This is true, so try the second pair of values in (A). Plug $x = 0$ and $g(x) = 3$ into the equation in (A) to get $3 = -12(0) + 3$, or $3 = 0 + 3$, and then $3 = 3$. This is also true. Since both points work in the function defined by (A), it is the correct equation. The correct answer is (A).

11. $\dfrac{1}{2}$ **or .5**

The question asks for the value of a constant in a system of equations. Both expressions are equal to 27, so set them equal to each other to get $ab = 2abk$. Divide both sides of the equation by ab to get $1 = 2k$, and then divide both sides of the equation by 2 to get $\dfrac{1}{2} = k$. The answer can also be entered in the fill-in box in decimal form as .5. The correct answer is $\dfrac{1}{2}$ or .5.

12. **B** The question asks for a value based on a function. The question states that d represents the amount in dollars saved and w represents the number of weeks, and it asks for the amount of money saved every week. Plug in two values for w to see what happens to the amount of money saved. Plug in $w = 1$ to get $d(1) = 150 + 50(1)$, which becomes $d(1) = 150 + 50$, and then $d(1) = 200$. Sarah's amount saved after one week is $200. Next, plug in $w = 2$ to get $d(2) = 150 + 50(2)$, which becomes $d(2) = 150 + 100$, and then $d(2) = 250$. Sarah's amount saved after two weeks is $250. After one additional week, the amount saved increased by $250 - $200 = 50, so the amount increases by $50 every week. The correct answer is (B).

13. **A** The question asks for a description of a function that models a specific situation. Compare the answer choices. Two choices say the function is increasing, and two say it is decreasing. The question states that *the population of a certain town decreases*, so eliminate (C) and (D) because they describe an in-

creasing function. The difference between (A) and (B) is whether the function is linear or exponential. Determine this by plugging in an initial value for the population, such as 1,000. After 5 years, the population is 1,000 – 150 = 850. After another 5 years, the population is 850 – 150 = 700. The population decreased by the same amount each year, so the relationship between population and time is linear. Eliminate (B) because it describes an exponential function. The correct answer is (A).

14. **–39** The question asks for the value of the x-coordinate of the solution to a system of equations. The most efficient method is to enter both equations into the built-in calculator, and then scroll and zoom as needed to find the point of intersection. The lines intersect at (–39, –1), so the x-coordinate is –39.

To solve the system for the x-coordinate algebraically, find a way to make the y-coordinates disappear when stacking and adding the equations. Compare the y-terms: one coefficient, –27, is 3 times the other one, –9. Multiply the entire first equation by –3 to get the same coefficient with opposite signs on the y-terms. The first equation becomes $-3x + 27y = 90$. Now stack and add the two equations.

$$\begin{array}{rr} -3x + 27y = & 90 \\ + x - 27y = & -12 \\ \hline -2x = & 78 \end{array}$$

Divide both sides of the resulting equation by –2 to get $x = -39$.

Using either of these methods, the correct answer is –39.

15. **–8** The question asks for the value of the x-coordinate when a quadratic function reaches its minimum. A parabola reaches its minimum or maximum at its vertex, so find the x-coordinate of the vertex. One method is to enter the equation into the built-in calculator, and then scroll and zoom as needed to find the vertex. The vertex is at (–8, –103), so the value of the x-coordinate is –8.

To solve algebraically, find the value of h, which is the x-coordinate of the vertex (h, k). When a quadratic is in standard form, which is $ax^2 + bx + c$, the x-coordinate of the vertex can be found using the formula $h = -\dfrac{b}{2a}$. In this quadratic, $a = 1$ and $b = 16$, so the formula becomes $h = -\dfrac{16}{2(1)}$. Solve to get $h = -\dfrac{16}{2}$, or $h = -8$.

Using either of these methods, the correct answer is –8.

16. **B** The question asks for the difference between two values based on the graph of a function. One method is to use the built-in calculator. Enter the equation of the line, and then scroll and zoom as needed to find the intercepts, which are indicated by gray dots. The x-intercept is at (6, 0), and the y-intercept is at (0, 12). Thus, $m = 6$, $n = 12$, and $m - n = 6 - 12$, or $m - n = -6$, which matches (B).

To solve algebraically, plug the given points into the equation of the line. Plug in $x = m$ and $g(x) = 0$ to get $0 = 12 - 2m$. Add $2m$ to both sides of the equation to get $2m = 12$, and then divide both sides of the equation by 2 to get $m = 6$. Next, plug in $x = 0$ and $g(x) = n$ to get $n = 12 - 2(0)$. Simplify to get $n = 12 - 0$, or $n = 12$. Plug $m = 6$ and $n = 12$ into $m - n$ to get $6 - 12 = -6$, which makes (B) correct.

Using either of these methods, the correct answer is (B).

17. **64** The question asks for a value given a proportional relationship between two geometric figures. Start by drawing two squares of different sizes, and then label the figure with the given information. The question only gives information about a relationship, not specific values, so plug in. Pick a small value for the area of the scale model, such as 4. The question states that the scale model *has an area that is* $\frac{1}{4,096}$ *of the area of the actual park*, so the area of the actual park is $4,096(4) = 16,384$. To find the side lengths of both squares, write out the formula for the area of a square, which is $A = s^2$. Plug in the area of the scale model to get $4 = s^2$. Take the positive square root of both sides of the equation to get $2 = s$. Label this on the smaller square. Plug the area of the actual park into the area formula to get $16,384 = s^2$. Take the positive square root of both sides of the equation to get $128 = s$. Label this on the larger square. To find the value of x, divide the side length of the actual park by the side length of the scale model to get $\frac{128}{2} = 64$. The side length of the actual park is 64 times the side length of the scale model, or $x = 64$. The correct answer is 64.

18. **B** The question asks for a value on a scatterplot. Find 1.25 on the x-axis: it is halfway between the labeled vertical line for 1 and the labeled vertical line for 1.5. Move up from there to the line of best fit, using the mouse pointer or scratch paper as a ruler if necessary. From there, move left to the y-axis to see that the value is between the labeled horizontal line for 1.4 and the labeled horizontal line for 1.6. Eliminate (A), (C), and (D) because those values are not between 1.4 and 1.6. The correct answer is (B).

19. **D** The question asks for the measure of an angle in radians. Start by finding the measure of angle B in degrees. The question states that *angle A measures 150 degrees, and the measure of angle B is* $\frac{1}{3}$ *the measure of angle A*, so take one-third of 150 to find that the measure of angle B is $\frac{1}{3}(150) = 50°$. The combined measure of both angles is $150 + 50 = 200°$. Either write down a conversion between radians and degrees from memory or open the reference sheet, which states that the number of degrees of arc in a circle is 360 and that the number of radians of arc in a circle is 2π. Thus, $360° = 2\pi$

radians. Set up a proportion, being sure to match up units. The proportion is $\dfrac{360°}{2\pi \text{ radians}} =$ $\dfrac{200°}{x \text{ radians}}$. Cross-multiply to get $(2\pi)(200) = (360)(x)$. Simplify to get $400\pi = 360x$, and then divide both sides of the equation by 360 to get $\dfrac{400\pi}{360} = x$. Reduce the fraction by dividing both the numerator and the denominator by 40 to get $\dfrac{10\pi}{9} = x$. The correct answer is (D).

20. **C** The question asks for the value of a constant based on an equation. The question refers to exponential growth, so write down the growth and decay formula. The formula is *final amount = (original amount)*$(1 \pm rate)^{number\ of\ changes}$. The question states that *a sample of a certain radioactive element is tested and found to have 16,000 radioactive units*, so the *original amount*, or S, is 16,000. The question also states that *it is tested again and found to have 4,000 radioactive units*, so the *final amount*, or R, is 4,000. Finally, the question states that *t* is the number of remaining hours after the first test and that the second test was *two hours later*, so t = 2. Plug these values into the equation to get $4{,}000 = 16{,}000(0.25)^{2p}$. Divide both sides of the equation by 16,000 to get $\dfrac{1}{4} = (0.25)^{2p}$. Since $\dfrac{1}{4} = 0.25$, both sides of the equation have the same base, so the exponents must be equal. The value on the left side of the equation does not have an exponent written, so it has an implied exponent of 1. Thus, 1 = 2p. Divide both sides of this equation by 2 to get $\dfrac{1}{2} = p$. The correct answer is (C).

21. **8** The question asks for a solution to an equation. One approach is to enter the equation into the built-in add a comma after "calculator" then scroll and zoom as needed to find the solutions. The graph shows solutions at –7 and 8. Since the question asks for the greatest solution, the answer is 8.

To solve algebraically, start by multiplying both sides of the equation by the denominator to get rid of the fraction. The equation becomes $\sqrt{(x + 3)^2} = \sqrt{7x + 65}$. Then, square both sides of the equation to remove the square root signs. The equation becomes $(x + 3)^2 = 7x + 65$. Expand the left side of the equation using FOIL to get $x^2 + 6x + 9 = 7x + 65$. Put the quadratic into standard form by setting one side equal to 0. Subtract 7x and 65 from both sides of the equation, which becomes $x^2 - x - 56 = 0$. Find two numbers that multiply to –56 and add to –1. These are –8 and 7. Thus, the quadratic factors into $(x - 8)(x + 7) = 0$. To find the values of x, set each factor equal to 0 to get two equations: x – 8 = 0 and x + 7 = 0. Add 8 to both sides of the first equation to get x = 8. Subtract 7 from both sides of the second equation to get x = –7. The greatest solution is 8.

Using either of these methods, the correct answer is 8.

22. **D**   The question asks for solutions to an equation. A solution to an equation is a value of x that makes the equation true, so test each statement by substituting the value in it for x. Half of the answer choices contain statement (III), so start there. Plug $x = 1 - 3c$ into the equation to get $[(1 - 3c) + 3c]$ $[80 + (1 - 3c)] = [80 + (1 - 3c)]$. Simplify both sides of the equation to get $(1)(81 - 3c) = (81 - 3c)$, which becomes $81 - 3c = 81 - 3c$. This is true, so $1 - 3c$ is a solution to the equation, and statement (III) is true. Eliminate (A) and (C) because they do not include statement (III).

Compare the remaining answer choices. The difference between (B) and (D) is statement (I), so try it next. Plug $x = -80$ into the equation to get $(-80 + 3c)[80 + (-80)] = [80 + (-80)]$. Simplify both sides of the equation to get $(-80 + 3c)(0) = 0$, which becomes $0 = 0$. Thus, -80 is a solution to the equation, and statement (I) is true. Eliminate (B) because it does not contain statement (I). The correct answer is (D).

Module 2 – Easier

1. **C**   The question asks for a percent of a number. Translate the English to math in bite-sized pieces. Translate *what* as a variable, such as x. Translate *is* as equals. *Percent* means out of 100, so translate 60% as $\frac{60}{100}$. Translate *of* as times. The translated equation is $x = \frac{60}{100}(300)$. Solve by hand or with a calculator to get $x = 180$. The correct answer is (C).

2. **C**   The question asks for a value on a graph. First, check the units on each axis of the bar graph. Soap brands are on the x-axis, so find Brand Y on the x-axis. Look at the top of the bar for Brand Y, and then look left to the y-axis, using the mouse pointer or the edge of the scratch paper as a ruler. The y-axis shows the number of consumers, and the top of the bar for Brand Y comes almost all the way up to 55. Thus, the number of consumers who chose Brand Y must be a little less than 55. Eliminate (A) and (B) because 43 and 46 are too small. Eliminate (D) because 57 is greater than 55. The correct answer is (C).

3. **78**   The question asks for the solution to an equation. To solve for b, isolate the variable. First, add 12 to both sides of the equation to get $2b = 156$. Next, divide both sides of the equation by 2 to get $b = 78$. The correct answer is 78.

4. **7**   The question asks for a value given a rate. Begin by reading the question to find information about the rate. The question states that *a street artist takes 5 minutes to draw one portrait*. Set up a proportion to determine how many portraits can be drawn in 35 minutes at this rate. The proportion is $\frac{5 \text{ minutes}}{1 \text{ portrait}} = \frac{35 \text{ minutes}}{x \text{ portraits}}$. Cross-multiply to get $(1)(35) = (5)(x)$, which becomes $35 = 5x$. Divide both sides of the equation by 5 to get $7 = x$. The correct answer is 7.

5. **4** The question asks for a value given a function. In function notation, the number inside the parentheses is the x-value that goes into the function, or the input, and the value that comes out of the function is the y-value, or the output. The question provides an output value of 10, so substitute 10 for $h(x)$ and solve for the input value, x. The equation becomes $10 = 3x - 2$. Add 2 to both sides of the equation to get $12 = 3x$, and then divide both sides of the equation by 3 to get $4 = x$. The correct answer is 4.

6. **B** The question asks for a value given a function. In function notation, the number inside the parentheses is the x-value that goes into the function, or the input, and the value that comes out of the function is the y-value, or the output. The question provides an output value of 49, and the answers have numbers that could represent the x-value, so plug in the answers. Start with one of the middle numbers and try (B), 8. Plug 8 into the function for x to get $49 = 8^2 - 15$, which becomes $49 = 64 - 15$, or $49 = 49$. This is true, so stop here. The correct answer is (B).

7. **A** The question asks for the y-intercept of a graph. This is the point at which $x = 0$. Eliminate (C) and (D) because they do not have an x-value of 0. Find $x = 0$ on the graph and move straight up to see that the graph crosses the y-axis at $y = 5$. Points on a graph are represented as ordered pairs in the form (x, y), with the x-value first and the y-value second, so the point at the y-intercept is $(0, 5)$. The correct answer is (A).

8. **D** The question asks for an equation that models a specific situation. Translate the English to math in bite-sized pieces, and eliminate after each piece. One piece of information says that *Dalisha is given a stipend of $3,600*. Since the stipend is only given once, 3,600 should not be multiplied by another value. Eliminate (B) and (C) because they multiply 3,600 by another value. The question also states that the stipend is used to *pay her student housing rent of $450 per month,* so the monthly rent must be subtracted from the initial stipend. Eliminate (A) because it subtracts the stipend from the monthly rent. The correct answer is (D).

9. **A** The question asks for an equivalent form of an expression. There are variables in the answer choices, so plug in. Make $y = 5$ because it will make the denominator of the second fraction equal 1. The expression becomes $\dfrac{3}{6 - 3(5)} + \dfrac{1}{5 - 4}$. Simplify to get $\dfrac{3}{6 - 15} + \dfrac{1}{1}$, and then $\dfrac{3}{-9} + 1$. Use a common denominator of 9 and make $1 = \dfrac{9}{9}$ to get $-\dfrac{3}{9} + \dfrac{9}{9} = \dfrac{6}{9}$, which reduces to $\dfrac{2}{3}$. This is the target value; write it down and circle it. Now plug $y = 5$ into the answer choices, and eliminate any that do not match the target value. Choice (A) becomes $-\dfrac{6}{(5 - 4)[6 - 3(5)]}$. Simplify to get $-\dfrac{6}{(1)(6 - 15)}$, then $-\dfrac{6}{-9}$, and finally $\dfrac{2}{3}$. This matches the target value, so keep (A), but check the remaining answers just in case. Choice (B) is the same fraction as (A), but it doesn't have the negative sign, so it will equal $-\dfrac{2}{3}$.

This does not match the target value, so eliminate (B). Choice (C) becomes $\dfrac{4}{2(5)+2}$. Simplify to get

$\dfrac{4}{10+2}$, then $\dfrac{4}{12}$, and finally $\dfrac{1}{3}$. Eliminate (C). Choice (D) has the same denominator as (A) with a

different numerator, so it cannot equal the same value; eliminate (D). The correct answer is (A).

10.   **B**   The question asks for correct values on a graph. When given a graph and asked for the table of values, check one point at a time and eliminate answers that contain a point that is not on the graph. Two of the answers contain the point $(-3, -3)$, and two contain the point $(-3, 3)$. On the graph, when $x = -3$, $y = 3$. Eliminate (A) and (C) because they have the wrong y-value for this point. Compare the remaining answer choices to see that they have different y-values for an x-value of -2. On the graph, when $x = -2$, $y = 1$. Eliminate (D) because it has the wrong y-value for this point. The correct answer is (B).

11.   **125**   The question asks for the value of an angle on a figure. The figure is already drawn and labeled, but redraw it on the scratch paper if that makes it easier to see what's going on. When a line intersects two parallel lines, two kinds of angles are created: big and small. All of the small angles are equal to each other, all of the big angles are equal to each other, and any small angle plus any big angle = 180°. The angle marked $y°$ is a big angle, and the angle marked 55° is a small angle. Thus, $y + 55 = 180$. Subtract 55 from both sides of the equation to get $y = 125$. The correct answer is 125.

12.   **C**   The question asks for a measurement of a geometric figure. Start by drawing a circle on the scratch paper. Next, label the figure with information from the question: label the radius as 4. The drawing should look something like this:

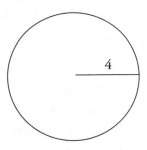

Next, write down the formula for the circumference of a circle, either from memory or after looking it up on the reference sheet. The formula is $C = 2\pi r$. Plug in the value of the radius, 4, to get $C = 2\pi(4)$, which becomes $C = 8\pi$. The correct answer is (C).

13.   **A**   The question asks for an equation in terms of a specific variable. The question asks about the relationship among variables and there are variables in the answer choices, so one option is to plug in. However, that might get messy with three variables. All of the answer choices have a by itself, so the other option is to solve for a. To isolate a, add $2b$ to both sides of the equation to get $9a = 2b + c$. Divide both sides of the equation by 9 to get $a = \dfrac{2b+c}{9}$. The correct answer is (A).

14. **C** The question asks for the system of inequalities that contains a specific point. Use the point given in the question and plug $x = 2$ and $y = -5$ into the answer choices to see which one works. Choice (A) becomes $2 \leq 0$ and $-5 \leq 0$. Only the second inequality is true, so eliminate (A). Since $y \leq 0$ is true, the correct answer should include it. Eliminate (B) and (D) because they have $y \geq 0$ instead. Since $2 \geq 0$, the first inequality is also true in (C), so (C) is correct.

It is also possible to answer this question using the built-in calculator. First, enter the point given in the question into an entry field. Next, enter each pair of inequalities from the answer choices one at a time to see which system contains the point $(2, -5)$. Only the graph of the system in (C) includes this point in the shaded area representing the overlapping solutions, so (C) is correct.

Using either of these methods, the correct answer is (C).

15. **D** The question asks for an equation that represents a graph. One method is to use the built-in calculator. Enter each of the equations in the answer choices into the graphing calculator and see which line looks most like the line of best fit of the scatterplot given. The graph of the equation in (D) matches where the line of best fit would be, so (D) is correct.

Another method is to translate the information into bite-sized pieces and eliminate after each piece. The equations in the answer choices are all in slope-intercept form, $y = mx + b$, in which m is the slope and b is the y-intercept. The y-intercept is the point where $x = 0$, which is between 2 and 3 on this graph. Eliminate (A) and (C) because they have negative y-intercepts. Compare the remaining answer choices. The difference between (B) and (D) is the sign of the slope. If the line of best fit were graphed, it would ascend from left to right, so it would have a positive slope. Eliminate (B) because it has a negative slope.

Using either of these methods, the correct answer is (D).

16. **B** The question asks for an equation that represents a specific situation. The population of fish is decreasing by a certain percent over time, so this question is about exponential decay. Write down the growth and decay formula, which is *final amount* = (*original amount*)$(1 \pm rate)^{number\ of\ changes}$. The question states that the number of fish 5 years from now will be 804,944. Eliminate (A) and (C) because they do not have 804,944 as the final amount on the left side of the equation. Since this situation involves a decrease, the original amount must be multiplied by $(1 - rate)$, so the value in parentheses should be less than 1. Eliminate (D), which has a value in parentheses greater than 1. The only remaining answer is (B), and it matches the decay formula because the original amount is multiplied by $(1 - 0.04) = (0.96)$. The correct answer is (B).

17. **−14** The question asks for a solution to an equation with absolute values. One method is to enter the equation into the built-in calculator, replacing a with x in order to see a graph of the equation. The values of x are shown by vertical lines; scroll and zoom as needed to see that these cross the x-axis at −14 and 10. The question asks for the negative solution, which is −14.

To solve algebraically, recall that, with an absolute value, the value inside the absolute value bars can be either positive or negative, so this equation has two possible solutions. To start solving for a, treat the absolute value as a term and combine the absolute value terms on the left side of the equation to get $-2|a + 2| = -24$. Next, divide both sides of the equation by -2 to get $|a + 2| = 12$. The value in the absolute values bars could equal 12 or -12, so set $a + 2$ equal to each. When $a + 2 = 12$, subtract 2 from both sides of the equation to get $a = 10$. When $a + 2 = -12$, subtract 2 from both sides of the equation to get $a = -14$. The question asks for the negative value, which is -14.

Using either of these methods, the correct answer is -14.

18. **7**   The question asks for the value of a constant. To avoid the chance of distributing incorrectly with exponents, plug in for x and solve for a. Keep the math simple and make $x = 2$. The first expression becomes $a(2)^7[8(2) + 7]$. Simplify to get $a(128)(16 + 7)$, then $a(128)(23)$, and finally $2,944a$. The second expression becomes $56(2)^8 + 49(2)^7$. Simplify to get $56(256) + 49(128)$, then $14,336 + 6,272$, and finally $20,608$. The two expressions are equivalent, so set them equal to each other: $2,944a = 20,608$. Divide both sides of the equation by $2,944$ to get $a = 7$.

It is also possible to answer this question using the built-in calculator. Enter each side of the equation into a separate entry field, and then click on the slider for a. Move the slider left and right until the graphs are exactly the same. The happens when $a = 7$.

Using either of these methods, the correct answer is 7.

19. **C**   The question asks for an expression based on a geometric figure. One method is to recognize that the expression $\pi(3r)(r)^2$ looks like the right side of the formula for the volume of a cylinder, $V = \pi r^2 h$. The question states that r is the radius, and π is a constant, so the other term, $3r$, must be the height, making (C) correct.

Another method is to draw a cylinder on the scratch paper, and then label the figure with the given information. No specific values are given, so plug in. Make $r = 2$, and plug it into the expression given in the question to get $\pi[(3)(2)](2)^2$, or $\pi(6)(4)$, or 24π. This is the volume of the cylinder. Next, write down the formula for the volume of a cylinder, either from memory or after looking it up on the reference sheet. The formula is $V = \pi r^2 h$. Substitute the volume of 24π and the radius of 2 to get $24\pi = \pi(2)^2 h$. Simplify to get $24\pi = 4\pi h$, and then divide both sides of the equation by 4π to get $6 = h$. This is the target value; write it down and circle it. Now plug $r = 2$ into each answer choice and eliminate any that do not match the target value of 6. Choice (A) becomes 2. This does not match the target value, so eliminate (A). Choice (B), 3, does not equal 6; eliminate (B). Choice (C) becomes $3(2) = 6$; keep (C). Choice (D) becomes $(2)^2 = 4$; eliminate (D), leaving (C) as the correct answer.

Using either of these methods, the correct answer is (C).

20. **A**   The question asks for the inequality that represents the values shown in a table. When given a table of values and asked for an inequality, plug values from the table into the inequalities and eliminate ones that don't work. Plugging in 1 is likely to make more than one answer work, and negative numbers can be tricky, so start with the third pair of values in the table. Plug $p = 4$ and $q = 20$ into each inequality in the answer choices. Choice (A) becomes $20 < 6(4) + 3$. Simplify to get $20 < 24 + 3$,

and then 20 < 27. This is true, so keep (A), but check the remaining answers with this pair of values. Choice (B) becomes 20 > 6(4) + 3. Simplify to get 20 > 24 + 3, and then 20 > 27. This is not true, so eliminate (B). Choice (C) becomes 20 < 3(4) + 6. Simplify to get 20 < 12 + 6, and then 20 < 18; eliminate (C). Choice (D) becomes 20 > 3(4) + 6. Simplify to get 20 > 12 + 6, and then 20 > 18; keep (D). Since there are two answers left, try another pair of values. Plug $p = -2$ and $q = -10$ into the remaining answer choices. Choice (A) becomes $-10 < 6(-2) + 3$. Simplify to get $-10 < -12 + 3$, and then $-10 < -9$; keep (A). Choice (D) becomes $-10 > 3(-2) + 6$. Simplify to get $-10 > -6 + 6$, and then $-10 > 0$; eliminate (D). The correct answer is (A).

21. **D**   The question asks for the product of constants given a function. In function notation, the number inside the parentheses is the x-value that goes into the function, or the input, and the value that comes out of the function is the y-value, or the output. One method is to use the built-in calculator. Enter the equations for both functions into separate entry fields. Either use the color-coding or click on the entry field with the $h(x)$ equation to see that the parabola on the left is the graph of $h(x)$. Scroll and zoom as needed to find the values of the x-intercepts, which are represented by gray dots. The x-intercepts of $h(x)$ are $(-6, 0)$, $(-1, 0)$, and $(1, 0)$. This means that m, n, and p are -6, -1, and 1. It is impossible to know which letter has which value, but that won't matter when they are multiplied together. Therefore, $mnp = (-6)(-1)(1) = 6$, and (D) is correct.

It is also possible to solve using knowledge of the transformation of graphs. The x-intercepts of a quadratic are the values that give an output of 0. Function g is already factored, so set each factor equal to 0 and solve to find all of the x-intercepts. The x-intercepts of $g(x)$ are $(2, 0)$, $(4, 0)$ and $(-3, 0)$. When graphs are translated, or shifted, adding inside the parentheses shifts the graph to the left. Thus, $x + 3$ shifts the graph three units to the left, which shifts the x-intercepts to $(-1, 0)$, $(1, 0)$, and $(-6, 0)$. The x-coordinates of the x-intercepts of function h are -1, 1, and -6, and $mnp = (-1)(1)(-6) = 6$, making (D) correct.

Using either of these methods, the correct answer is (D).

22. **B**   The question asks for a value based on a geometric figure. Start by drawing a circle inscribed in a square. *Inscribed* means it takes up as much space as possible without going outside of the boundaries of the outer shape, so the circle touches each side of the square at one point. Draw the diagonal of the square, as well. When two geometric figures overlap, look for something they have in common. In this case, the diameter of the circle is equal in length to a side of the square. Add this to the drawing, which should look something like this:

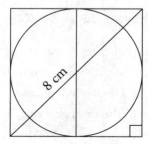

When a square is divided in half by a diagonal, two identical isosceles right triangles, or 45:45:90 triangles, are created. It may help to draw a second figure for one of the 45:45:90 triangles. Write down the ratio of the sides of a 45:45:90 triangle, either from memory or after looking it up on the reference sheet. The ratio is $s : s : s\sqrt{2}$. The diagonal of the square is the hypotenuse of each triangle, so $s\sqrt{2} = 8$. Divide both sides of the equation by $\sqrt{2}$ to get $s = \dfrac{8}{\sqrt{2}}$. Rationalize the denominator by multiplying the fraction by $\dfrac{\sqrt{2}}{\sqrt{2}}$ to get $\left(\dfrac{8}{\sqrt{2}}\right)\left(\dfrac{\sqrt{2}}{\sqrt{2}}\right) = 4\sqrt{2}$. Label the legs of the triangle as $4\sqrt{2}$. The legs of the 45:45:90 triangle are also sides of the square, so each side of the square has length $4\sqrt{2}$.

Since the side of the square has the same length as the diameter of the circle, the diameter of the circle is also $4\sqrt{2}$; label this on the figure. The radius of a circle is half the diameter, so the radius is $\dfrac{4\sqrt{2}}{2}$, or $2\sqrt{2}$. Write down the formula for the area of a circle, either from memory or after looking it up on the reference sheet. The area of a circle is $A = \pi r^2$, so the area of this circle is $A = \pi \left(2\sqrt{2}\right)^2$, which becomes $A = 8\pi$. The correct answer is (B).

Module 2 – Harder

1. **B** The question asks for the table that contains values that are solutions to an equation. When given an equation and asked for a table of values, plug values from the table into the equation to see which ones work. All of the tables include an x-value of 4, so start there. Plug $x = 4$ into the equation to get $y - 7 = 4$. Add 7 to both sides of the equation to get $y = 11$. Eliminate (A) and (D) because they have different y-values when $x = 4$. Now try another value from the table. Plug $x = 5$ into the equation to get $y - 7 = 5$. Add 7 to both sides of the equation to get $x = 12$. Eliminate (C) because it has a different y-value when $x = 5$. The correct answer is (B).

2. **C** The question asks for the value of an angle on a figure. The figure is already drawn and labeled, but redraw it on the scratch paper if that makes it easier to see what's going on. When a line intersects two parallel lines, two kinds of angles are created: big and small. All of the small angles have measures that are equal to each other, all of the big angles have measures that are equal to each other, and the measure of any small angle plus the measure of any big angle equals 180°. The angle labeled $y°$ is a big angle, and the angle labeled 83° is a small angle. Thus, $y + 83 = 180$. Subtract 83 from both sides of the equation to get $y = 97$. The correct answer is (C).

3. **B** The question asks for a percent based on the information provided. Translate the English to math in bite-sized pieces. Translate *is* as equals. Translate *what* as a variable, such as x. *Percent* means out of 100, so translate *what percentage* as $\frac{x}{100}$. Translate *of* as times. The equation becomes $24 = \frac{x}{100}(80)$. Simplify the right side of the equation to get $24 = \frac{8x}{10}$. Multiply both sides of the equation by 10 to get $240 = 8x$, and then divide both sides of the equation by 8 to get $30 = x$. The correct answer is (B).

4. **5** The question asks for a value given a function. In function notation, the number inside the parentheses is the x-value that goes into the function, or the input, and the value that comes out of the function is the y-value, or the output. The question provides an output value of 27, so plug in 27 for $f(x)$. The equation becomes $27 = 3x + 12$. Subtract 12 from both sides of the equation to get $15 = 3x$. Divide both sides of the equation by 3 to get $5 = x$. The correct answer is 5.

5. **C** The question asks for the value of a function. In function notation, the number inside the parentheses is the x-value that goes into the function, or the input, and the value that comes out of the function is the y-value, or the output. The question gives an input value of $\frac{1}{3}$, so plug that into the function to get $g\left(\frac{1}{3}\right) = 120\left(\frac{1}{3}\right)^0$. Either solve with a calculator or recall that any value raised to the power of zero is 1 to get $g\left(\frac{1}{3}\right) = 120(1)$, or $g\left(\frac{1}{3}\right) = 120$. The correct answer is (C).

6. **C** The question asks for the value of a trigonometric function. Begin by drawing a triangle and labeling the vertices, being certain to put the longest side opposite the right angle N. The drawing should look something like this:

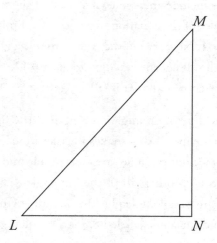

Next, write out SOHCAHTOA to remember the trig functions. The TOA part defines the tangent as $\frac{opposite}{adjacent}$, and the question states that $\tan(L) = \frac{\sqrt{7}}{3}$. Label the side opposite angle L as $\sqrt{7}$, and label the side adjacent to angle L as 3. The drawing now looks like this:

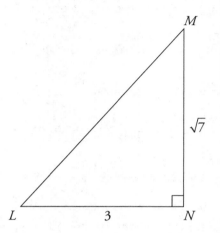

Use the Pythagorean Theorem, $a^2 + b^2 = c^2$, to solve for the length of the hypotenuse. Plug in the known side lengths to get $3^2 + \left(\sqrt{7}\right)^2 = c^2$. Square the terms on the left side of the equation to get $9 + 7 = c^2$, or $16 = c^2$. Take the positive square root of both sides of the equation to get $4 = c$. Label the hypotenuse as 4. The SOH part of SOHCAHTOA defines the sine as $\frac{opposite}{hypotenuse}$. The side opposite angle M is 3, and the hypotenuse is 4. Therefore, $\sin(M) = \frac{3}{4}$. The correct answer is (C).

7. **D** The question asks for the y-intercept of the graph of a function. The most efficient method is to enter the equation into the built-in calculator, and then scroll and zoom as needed to find the y-intercept. Click on the gray dot to see that the coordinates are $(0, -28)$, which is (D).

To solve mathematically, plug $x = 0$ into the function. The function becomes $g(0) = (-11)(5)^0 - 17$. Either use a calculator or remember that any number raised to the power of zero equals 1. The function becomes $g(0) = (-11)(1) - 17$, then $g(0) = (-11) - 17$, and finally $g(0) = -28$. Thus, the y-intercept is $(0, -28)$, and (D) is correct.

Using either of these methods, the correct answer is (D).

8. **A** The question asks for an equivalent form of an expression. There are variables in the answer choices, so plug in. Make $y = 5$ because it will make the denominator of the second fraction equal 1. The expression becomes $\frac{3}{6 - 3(5)} + \frac{1}{5 - 4}$. Simplify to get $\frac{3}{6 - 15} + \frac{1}{1}$, and then $\frac{3}{-9} + 1$. Use a common denominator of 9 and make $1 = \frac{9}{9}$ to get $-\frac{3}{9} + \frac{9}{9} = \frac{6}{9}$, which reduces to $\frac{2}{3}$. This is the target value;

write it down and circle it. Now plug $y = 5$ into the answer choices, and eliminate any that do not

match the target value. Choice (A) becomes $-\dfrac{6}{(5-4)[6-3(5)]}$. Simplify to get $-\dfrac{6}{(1)(6-15)}$, then

$-\dfrac{6}{-9}$, and finally $\dfrac{2}{3}$. This matches the target value, so keep (A), but check the remaining answers just

in case. Choice (B) is the same fraction as (A), but it doesn't have the negative sign, so it will equal $-\dfrac{2}{3}$.

This does not match the target value, so eliminate (B). Choice (C) becomes $\dfrac{4}{2(5)+2}$. Simplify to get

$\dfrac{4}{10+2}$, then $\dfrac{4}{12}$, and finally $\dfrac{1}{3}$. Eliminate (C). Choice (D) has the same denominator as (A) with a

different numerator, so it cannot equal the same value; eliminate (D). The correct answer is (A).

9. **−172** The question asks for the value of a function. In function notation, the number inside the parentheses is the x-value that goes into the function, or the input, and the value that comes out of the function is the y-value, or the output. Together, they represent points on the graph of the function. The question provides an input value, so plug $x = 0$ into function q to get $q(0) = (0-9)(0+2)(0+9)$, which becomes $q(0) = (-9)(2)(9)$, and then $q(0) = -162$. The question states that the graph of function r is the result of translating the graph of function q down 10 units. This means decreasing the value of y by 10. Because $f(x) = y$, this is the same as subtracting 10 from the value of $r(0)$, which becomes $r(0) = -162 - 10$, or $r(0) = -172$.

Another method is to enter the equation for function q into the built-in calculator. Scroll and zoom as needed to find the point at $(0, -162)$, and then count down ten to the point at $(0, -172)$.

Using either of these methods. the correct answer is −172.

10. **2440** The question asks for the surface area of a geometric figure. Draw a rectangular prism as best as possible, and then write down the relevant formulas. Write down the formula for the volume of a rectangular prism, either from memory or after looking it up on the reference sheet. The formula is $V = lwh$. Plug in the values for the volume, height, and length given in the question to get $6{,}000 = 12(w)(10)$ or $6{,}000 = 120w$. Divide both sides of the equation by 120 to get $w = 50$.

The surface area of a geometric figure is the sum of the areas of its sides. A rectangular prism has 2 sides with an area of length × width, 2 sides with an area of length × height, and 2 sides with an area of width × height, so the formula for the surface area of a rectangular prism is $SA = 2(lw + lh + wh)$. Plug the length of 12, width of 50, and height of 10 into the surface area formula to get $SA = 2[(12)(50) + (12)(10) + (50)(10)]$. Simplify to get $SA = 2(600 + 120 + 500)$, which becomes $SA = 2(1{,}220)$, and then $SA = 2{,}440$. Leave out the comma when entering the answer in the fill-in box. The correct answer is 2440.

11. **D**   The question asks for a function that represents a specific situation. The value of the function is increasing by a certain percent as x increases, so this question is about exponential growth. Write down the exponential growth and decay formula, which is *final amount* = (*original amount*)$(1 \pm rate)^{number\ of\ changes}$. In this case, $f(x)$ is the final amount. The original amount is the value when $x = 0$, so the original amount is 11. Eliminate (A) and (B) because they do not have 11 as the original amount in front of the parentheses. Since this situation involves an increase, the original amount must be multiplied by $(1 + rate)$. The rate is given as 28%, which translates to 0.28, so the value in parentheses should be $1 + 0.28 = 1.28$. Eliminate (C) because it does not have this value in the parentheses. The only remaining answer is (D), and it matches the growth formula, so (D) is correct.

Without this formula, it is still possible to answer this question. Plug in two values of x to see how the function changes over time. When $x = 0$, $f(x) = 11$, so plug these numbers into the answer choices. Any number raised to the power of zero equals 1, so only (C) and (D) work with these values. When x increases by 1, $f(x)$ increases by 28%. Thus, $f(1) = 11 + \left(\dfrac{28}{100}\right)(11)$, which becomes $f(1) = 11 + 3.08$, and then $f(1) = 14.08$. Plug $x = 1$ and $f(1) = 14.08$ into the remaining answers. Choice (C) becomes $14.08 = 11(0.72)^1$, or $14.08 = 7.92$. This is not true, so eliminate (C), Choice (D) becomes $14.08 = 11(1.28)^1$, or $14.08 = 14.08$. Only (D) worked with both pairs of values, so it is correct.

Using either of these methods, the correct answer is (D).

12. **B**   The question asks for the table that contains values that are solutions to an inequality. When given an inequality and asked for a table of values, plug values from the table into the inequality and eliminate tables with values that don't work. All of the tables include an x-value of 2, so start there. Plug $x = 2$ into the inequality to get $y > 4(2) - 5$, which becomes $y > 8 - 5$, and then $y > 3$. Eliminate (A) and (D) because their y-values when $x = 2$ are not greater than 3. Compare the remaining answer choices. Choices (B) and (C) have different y-values when $x = 6$, so plug $x = 6$ into the inequality to get $y > 4(6) - 5$, which becomes $y > 24 - 5$, and then $y > 19$. Eliminate (C) because 19 is not greater than 19. The correct answer is (B).

13. **C**   The question asks which binomials are factors of a quadratic. One method is to use the built-in calculator. Enter the expression into an entry field, and then scroll and zoom as needed to see that the solutions are (1.2, 0) and (11, 0). A solution can be found by setting a factor equal to 0, so set the factors in the statements equal to 0 and solve for the solutions. Start with statement (I). When $x - 11 = 0$, $x = 11$. This is one of the solutions, so statement (I) is a factor the expression. Eliminate (B) and (D) because they do not include statement (I) as a factor. When $5x - 6 = 0$, add 6 to both sides of the equation to get $5x = 6$, and then divide both sides of the equation by 5 to get $x = \dfrac{6}{5}$, or $x = 1.2$. Thus,

statement (II) is also factor of the expression. Eliminate (A) because it does not include statement (II), leaving (C) as correct.

Another method is to work with each possible factor one at a time. A solution can be found by setting a factor equal to 0. When $x - 11 = 0$, $x = 11$. Plug $x = 11$ into the expression to get $5(11)^2 - 61(11) + 66$, which becomes $5(121) - 671 + 66$, then $605 - 605$, and finally 0. Thus, 11 is a solution to the expression and statement (I) is a factor. Eliminate (B) and (D) because they do not include statement (I) as a factor. When $5x - 6 = 0$, add 6 to both sides of the equation to get $5x = 6$, and then divide both sides of the equation by 5 to get $x = \dfrac{6}{5}$, or $x = 1.2$. Plug $x = 1.2$ into the expression to get $5(1.2)^2 - 61(1.2) + 66$, which becomes $5(1.44) - 73.2 + 66$, then $7.2 - 7.2$, and finally 0. Thus, 1.2 is a solution to the expression and statement (II) is a factor. Eliminate (A) because it does not include statement (II), leaving (C) as correct.

Using either of these methods, the correct answer is (C).

14.   **A**   The question asks for the value of a constant in a system of equations. When a system of linear equations has infinitely many solutions, the two equations are equivalent and graph the same line. One method is to use the built-in calculator. Enter each equation into a separate entry field, and then click on the slider for k. Move the slider left and right until the two lines are exactly the same. This happens when $k = -10$, so (A) is correct.

To solve for k algebraically, rewrite the two equations so they have the same terms in the same order. For the first equation, add $5y$ to both sides of the equation to get $4 = 7x + 10y$. Subtract 4 from both sides of the equation to get $0 = 7x + 10y - 4$. For the second equation, subtract ky from both sides of the equation to get $7x - ky - 4 = 0$. Both equations are now equal to 0, so set them equal to each other to get $7x + 10y - 4 = 7x - ky - 4$. Subtract $7x$ from both sides of the equation and add 4 to both sides of the equation to get $10y = -ky$. Divide both sides of the equation by $-y$ to get $-10 = k$. Rearranging the two equations into another familiar form—such as slope-intercept form or standard form—would also result in $k = -10$, making (A) correct.

Using either of these methods, the correct answer is (A).

15.   **−14**   The question asks for a solution to an equation with absolute values. One method is to enter the equation into the built-in calculator, replacing a with x in order to see a graph of the equation. The values of x are shown by vertical lines; scroll and zoom as needed to see that these cross the x-axis at −14 and 10. The question asks for the negative solution, which is −14.

To solve algebraically, recall that, with an absolute value, the value inside the absolute value bars can be either positive or negative, so this equation has two possible solutions. To start solving for a, treat the absolute value as a term and combine the absolute value terms on the left side of the equation to get $-2|a + 2| = -24$. Next, divide both sides of the equation by -2 to get $|a + 2| = 12$. The value in the absolute values bars could equal 12 or -12, so set $a + 2$ equal to each. When $a + 2 = 12$, subtract 2 from both sides of the equation to get $a = 10$. When $a + 2 = -12$, subtract 2 from both sides of the equation to get $a = -14$. The question asks for the negative value, which is -14.

Using either of these methods, the correct answer is -14.

16. **249** The question asks for a maximum value given a specific situation. Translate the English to math in bite-sized pieces. The number of vases can be represented by v and the number of bowls by b. One piece of information states that *the maximum combined number of vases and bowls she can sell during one weekend is 750*, so the combined total is no more than 750. Represent this with the inequality $v + b \leq 750$. Another piece of information states that *a vendor sells vases for $6.50 and bowls for $12.30*. Multiply the amount earned per vase by the number of vases to get $6.50v$, and multiply the amount earned per bowl by the number of bowls to get $12.30b$. The question states that the *she sells only vases and bowls and earns at least $7,780*, so the total amount earned is greater than or equal to $7,780. Represent this with the inequality $6.50v + 12.30b \geq 7,780$. Now there are two inequalities with two variables:

$$v + b \leq 750$$
$$6.50v + 12.30b \geq 7,780$$

The question asks for the number of vases, which is v, so find a way to make the b-terms disappear. Multiply the entire first inequality by -12.30, remembering to flip the inequality sign, to get $-12.30v - 12.30b \geq -9,225$. Now the two inequalities have the same b-value with opposite signs, so add the two inequalities.

$$
\begin{array}{r}
-12.30v - 12.30b \geq -9,225 \\
+\ 6.50v + 12.30b \geq \ \ 7,780 \\
\hline
-5.8v \qquad\qquad\quad \geq -1,445
\end{array}
$$

Divide both sides of the resulting inequality by -5.8, remembering again to flip the inequality sign, to get $v \leq 249.14$. The number of vases must be an integer less than or equal to 249.14, so round down to 249. The correct answer is 249.

17. **B** The question asks for the value of a percent increase given a function that represents a specific situation. The value of the function is increasing by a certain percent, so this question is about exponential growth. Write down the growth and decay formula, which is *final amount* = (*original amount*)$(1 \pm rate)^{number\ of\ changes}$. The *number of changes* is given in seconds, but the question asks about the increase each <u>minute</u>, so convert seconds to minutes. One minute is equivalent to 60 seconds, so plug 60 into the function to see the amount after 1 minute: $g(60) = 78,500(1.52)^{\frac{60}{60}}$, which becomes $g(60) = 78,500(1.52)^1$. The value of the number of moles of product is increasing

once, so 1.52 = 1 + *rate*. Subtract 1 from both sides of this equation to get *rate* = 0.52. The question asks for the rate as a percentage, so multiply 0.52 by 100 to get 52%. The correct answer is (B).

18. **D** The question asks for the equation that defines a function. One method is to use the built-in calculator. Enter the equation for each function into a separate entry field. Click on the circular icon next to function *g* to hide it and focus on the graph of function *h*. Next, enter each answer choice equation until one of them matches the graph of function *h*. Only the graph of the equation in (D) matches, so (D) is correct.

There are variables in the answer choices, so another option is to plug in. Make $x = 2$ to keep the math easy. Since $h(x) = g(x + 3)$, $h(2) = g(2 + 3)$, or $h(2) = g(5)$. Plug $x = 5$ into the *g* function to get $g(5) = -3(5)^5$, which becomes $g(5) = -3(3,125)$, and then $g(5) = -9,375$. Since $h(2) = g(5)$, $h(2)$ also equals $-9,375$. This is the target value; write it down and circle it. Now plug $x = 2$ into the answer choices and eliminate any that do not match the target value. Choice (A) becomes $h(2) = -27(125)^2$, or $h(2) = -27(15,625)$, and then $h(2) = -421,875$. This does not match the target value, so eliminate (A). Choice (B) becomes $h(2) = -9(15)^2$, or $h(2) = -9(225)$, and then $h(2) = -2,025$; eliminate (B). Choice (C) becomes $h(2) = -9(5)^2$, or $h(2) = -9(25)$, and then $h(2) = -225$; eliminate (C). The remaining answer must be correct, and (D) becomes $h(2) = -375(5)^2$, or $h(2) = -375(25)$, and then $h(2) = -9,375$. This matches the target value, so (D) is correct.

Using either of these methods, the correct answer is (D).

19. **A** The question asks for the value of a constant in the solution to a quadratic. The question asks for a specific value and the answers contain numbers in order, so plug in the answers. First, enter the quadratic into the built-in calculator, and then scroll and zoom as needed to find the solutions. Either enter the equation the way it is to see vertical lines at the solutions or leave out "= 0" to see a parabola. Either way, the coordinates of the solutions are (–6.243, 0) and (2.243, 0). Next, plug in each answer choice for *c* until one of them makes $-2 - \sqrt{c}$ equal one of the solutions. Start with one of the middle answers and try (B), 23. Enter $-2 - \sqrt{23}$ into the calculator to get approximately –6.796. This is approximately 0.5 away from one of the solutions, so eliminate (B). A smaller value for *c* will make the result larger, so try (A) next. Enter $-2 - \sqrt{18}$ into the calculator to get approximately –6.243. This is one of the solutions, so stop here. The correct answer is (A).

20. **8** The question asks for the value of a constant in a quadratic. One method is to use the built-in calculator. Enter the equation as written. The slider for *c* does not appear, so add *c* to both sides of the equation to get $7x(7x + 6) + c = 0$. Delete "= 0" and the slider appears. When $c = 1$, the parabola intersects the *x*-axis twice, meaning there are two solutions. Move the slider left and right to see that, when $c = 9$, there is only one solution. The question states that *c* is an integer constant, so the greatest possible value of *c* when the equation has exactly two real solutions is 8.

To determine algebraically when a quadratic equation has two real solutions, use the discriminant. The discriminant is the part of the quadratic formula under the square root sign and is written as

$D = b^2 - 4ac$. When the discriminant is positive, the quadratic has exactly two real solutions; when the discriminant is 0, the quadratic has exactly one real solution; and when the discriminant is negative, the quadratic has no real solutions. Thus, the discriminant of this quadratic must equal a positive number. First, put the quadratic in standard form, which is $ax^2 + bx + c = 0$, by distributing $7x$ on the left side of the equation to get $49x^2 + 42x = -c$. Add c to both sides of the equation to get $49x^2 + 42x + c = 0$. Now that the quadratic is in standard form, $a = 49$, $b = 42$, and $c = c$. Plug these into the discriminant formula to get $D = (42)^2 - 4(49)(c)$, or $D = 1,764 - 196c$. Since there are exactly two real solutions, $1,764 - 196c > 0$. Add $196c$ to both sides of the inequality to get $1,764 > 196c$, and then divide both sides of the inequality by 196 to get $9 > c$. The greatest integer that is smaller than 9 is 8.

Using either of these methods, the correct answer is 8.

21.   **C**   The question asks for the function that represents a certain situation. In function notation, the number inside the parentheses is the x-value that goes into the function, or the input, and the value that comes out of the function is the y-value, or the output. The question gives an input value of 6 and an output value of $900. Plug these into the functions in the answer choices, and eliminate any that do not work. Choice (A) becomes $900 = 150(6)$, or $900 = 900$. Keep (A), but check the remaining answers just in case. Choice (B) becomes $900 = 150(6) + 500$, or $900 = 1,400$. This is not true, so eliminate (B). Choice (C) becomes $900 = 200(6) - 300$, or $900 = 900$; keep (C). Choice (D) becomes $900 = 200(6) + 500$, or $900 = 1,700$; eliminate (D).

Two answers worked with the first pair of values, so plug in a different value for x. The question states that the band member earns $500 for 4 concerts, so plug these input and output values into the remaining answers. Choice (A) becomes $500 = 150(4)$, or $500 = 600$; eliminate (A). Choice (C) becomes $500 = 200(4) - 300$, or $500 = 500$; keep (C). The correct answer is (C).

22.   **D**   The question asks for the greatest possible difference in the mean, or average, of two data sets. For averages, use the formula $T = AN$, in which T is the *Total*, A is the *Average*, and N is the *Number of things*. Each of the data sets has 35 integers, so the number of things for each is 35. Because the number of things is equal, a larger total will lead to a larger average. Data set 1 contains integers between 200 and 600, so it is likely to have a smaller total and average, while data set 2 contains integers between 300 and 700, so it is likely to have a larger total and average. Thus, to find the greatest possible difference between the mean of data set 1 and the mean of data set 2, find the smallest possible mean for data set 1 and the largest possible mean for data set 2.

Start with finding the smallest possible mean of data set 1. This means the total should be as small as possible. Since the intervals can include the smallest number in the intervals, data set 1 could contain 12 values of 200, 7 values of 300, 4 values of 400, and 12 values of 500. Multiply and then add these numbers: $(12)(200) + (7)(300) + (4)(400) + (12)(500) = 2,400 + 2,100 + 1,600 + 6,000 = 12,100$. The average formula for data set 1 becomes $12,100 = (A)(35)$. Divide both sides of the equation by 35 to get $\dfrac{12,100}{35} = A$. To find the largest possible mean of data set 2, make the total as large as possible. Since the intervals do not include the largest number in the intervals, select the integer that is one less than the upper boundary of the interval. Data set 2 could contain 12 values of 399, 7 values of 499, 4 values of 599, and 12 values of 699. Multiply and then add these numbers to get $12(399) + 7(499) + 4(599) + 12(699) = 4,788 + 3,493 + 2,396 + 8,388 = 19,065$. The average formula for data set 2 becomes $19,065 = (A)(35)$. Divide both sides of the equation by 35 to get $\dfrac{19,065}{35} = A$. Finally, find the difference of the two averages: $\dfrac{19,065}{35} - \dfrac{12,100}{35} = \dfrac{6,965}{35}$, which is 199. The correct answer is (D).

Chapter 5
Practice Test 3

HOW TO EMULATE THE DIGITAL SAT ON PAPER

Practice Tests 5 and 6 are available in your online student tools in a digital, adaptive environment. The four tests in this physical book are printed on paper, but otherwise emulate the digital test in every way: test style, difficulty, and content. Please use the checklist below to ensure that you are able to emulate the adaptive nature of the test and get the preparation that you need for test day. Feel free to use the versions of Module 2 that you do not take during your test as additional practice.

- [ ] Take Reading and Writing (RW) Module 1, allowing yourself 32 minutes to complete it.

- [ ] Go to the answer key on page 298 and determine the number of questions you got correct in RW Module 1.

- [ ] If you get fewer than 15 questions correct, take RW Module 2 – Easier, which starts on page 248. If you get 15 or more questions correct, take RW Module 2 – Harder, which starts on page 259.

- [ ] Whichever RW Module 2 you take, start immediately and allow yourself 32 minutes to complete it.

- [ ] Take a 10-minute break between RW Module 2 and Math Module 1.

- [ ] Take Math Module 1, allowing yourself 35 minutes to complete it.

- [ ] Go to the answer key on page 298 and determine the number of questions you got correct in Math Module 1.

- [ ] If you get fewer than 14 questions correct, take Math Module 2 – Easier, which starts on page 280. If you get 14 or more questions correct, take Math Module 2 – Harder, which starts on page 288.

- [ ] Whichever Math Module you take, start it immediately and allow yourself 35 minutes to complete it.

- [ ] After you finish the test, check your answers to RW Module 2 and Math Module 2.

- [ ] Only after you complete the entire test should you read the explanations for the questions, which start on page 299.

Test 3—Reading and Writing
Module 1

Turn to Section 1 of your answer sheet to answer the questions in this section.

DIRECTIONS

The questions in this section address a number of important reading and writing skills. Each question includes one or more passages, which may include a table or graph. Read each passage and question carefully, and then choose the best answer to the question based on the passage(s).

All questions in the section are multiple-choice with four answer choices. Each question has a single best answer. Fill in the circle with the answer letter for the answer you think is best.

---

1 ☐ Mark for Review

The intergenerational Bulgarian female choir group Bistritsa Babi has been working to preserve customary songs and dances from the Shopluk region of the country since 1939. Through these _____ performances, members of Bistritsa Babi hope to keep this centuries-old ritual of expression alive. In 2005, the group was added to the UNESCO List of Intangible Cultural Heritage for Eastern Europe.

Which choice completes the text with the most logical and precise word or phrase?

(A) traditional

(B) obscure

(C) discreet

(D) eccentric

2 ☐ Mark for Review

Located in the old city of Marrakesh, Jemaa el-Fnaa, the main square, is a marketplace and vibrant hub for residents and visitors alike. During the day, snake charmers and stalls selling beverages fill the square, while at night the _____ center is filled with throngs of people coming to hear storytellers tell traditional fables, watch the performances of magicians, and browse multiple booths offering herbal medicines. As the night goes on, dozens of food vendors set up their stalls to feed the crowds.

Which choice completes the text with the most logical and precise word or phrase?

(A) formal

(B) bustling

(C) unpredictable

(D) deserted

CONTINUE

3 ☐ Mark for Review

When developing the procedure for LASIK eye surgery, inventor Gholam A. Peyman faced many obstacles in trying to create a way to use lasers on the delicate tissues within the eye without causing pain or scarring. Through many experiments, he was able to gather that using a flap of tissue instead of performing surgery on the surface of the cornea could greatly reduce the incidence of _____ of the procedure. Peyman was able to secure patents in the US for his ideas and furthered his research to help the field of ophthalmology.

Which choice completes the text with the most logical and precise word or phrase?

Ⓐ characteristics

Ⓑ prospects

Ⓒ efficacy

Ⓓ repercussions

4 ☐ Mark for Review

The process of rainwater harvesting includes gathering and reserving rainwater instead of allowing it to trickle away. When it rains, water is collected from an awning or roof and _____ in a large vessel like a well or reservoir where it can drain back to the ground water source for things like domestic and livestock use.

Which choice completes the text with the most logical and precise word or phrase?

Ⓐ aggregated

Ⓑ dissipated

Ⓒ percolated

Ⓓ collaborated

5 ☐ Mark for Review

In 2012, thousands of scientists working at the Large Hadron Collider in Switzerland were finally able to _____ the existence of the long-predicted Higgs boson particle, first theorized as necessary in order to explain the mass of a fundamental particle by Peter Higgs and François Englert in 1964. These scientists confirmed a pattern of decay products that could be explained only by the Higgs boson particle.

Which choice completes the text with the most logical and precise word or phrase?

Ⓐ corroborate

Ⓑ exonerate

Ⓒ contextualize

Ⓓ postulate

6 ☐ Mark for Review

A highly influential leader of the US civil rights movement, Martin Luther King Jr. _____ his commitment to nonviolent resistance by organizing and directing numerous peaceful protests and sit-ins across the United States in the 1960s: his actions revealed his unwavering dedication to advancing the cause of civil rights without resorting to violence.

Which choice completes the text with the most logical and precise word or phrase?

Ⓐ characterized

Ⓑ evinced

Ⓒ elided

Ⓓ gauged

CONTINUE ➡

7 ☐ Mark for Review

An experiment headed by University of Wisconsin psychologist Sohad Murrar provides compelling evidence that individuals feel more inclusive toward other groups when they are informed that pro-diversity attitudes and behaviors are extremely popular among their peers. Students were presented with either a neutrally messaged poster or a poster that displayed fellow students of diverse ethnic backgrounds, a statement about valuing diversity, and statistics indicating their fellow students' strong support for the statement. The study found that students were more likely to embrace inclusive statements and reject racist statements even weeks after they were exposed to the pro-diversity poster.

Which choice best describes the function of the underlined sentence in the text as a whole?

Ⓐ To analyze the implications of the results of the experiment

Ⓑ To demonstrate the difficulty of assessing individuals' views on inclusivity and racism

Ⓒ To highlight a specific instance in which the findings of the experiment were confirmed

Ⓓ To describe certain aspects of the design and methodology of the experiment

8 ☐ Mark for Review

The following text is adapted from Alphonse Daudet's short story "The Siege of Berlin." The narrator is a doctor, coming to the aid of a grandfather who has fallen unconscious.

He had a fine face, magnificent teeth, a thick head of curly white hair, and though eighty years old did not look more than sixty. Near him his granddaughter knelt weeping. There was a strong family resemblance between them. Seeing them side by side, you thought of two beautiful Greek medals struck from the same matrix, but one old and worn and the other bright and clear-cut with all the brilliancy and smoothness of a first impression. I found the child's grief very touching.

According to the text, what is true about the granddaughter and grandfather?

Ⓐ They look alike.

Ⓑ They are of Greek heritage.

Ⓒ They look younger than their ages.

Ⓓ They are lying side-by-side.

CONTINUE

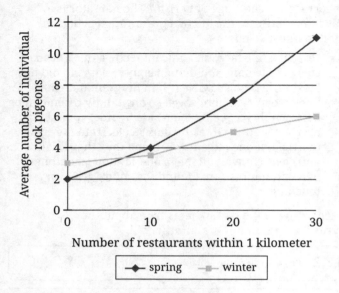

Restaurant Distribution and Average
Rock Pigeon Abundance

Urbanization invariably results in a decrease in overall species diversity and abundance, though certain species seem to preternaturally thrive in city environments. *Columba livia*, the rock pigeon, is thought to be well-suited to survival in urbanized environments because of the anthropogenic food sources supplied in the form of refuse from restaurants. Thus, researchers Jeffrey A. Brown, Susannah B. Lerman, and colleagues hypothesized that the number of nearby restaurants might be a predictor of the abundance of rock pigeons in the area. They visited 57 sites during spring and winter for three years and logged the number of restaurants and the number of rock pigeons in the vicinity. Looking at the lines of best fit for the scatterplot of the compiled data, the researchers concluded that there is indeed a relationship between proximity to restaurants and abundance of rock pigeons and that this relationship was especially strong in the spring, noting that _____

9 ⌷ Mark for Review

Which choice most effectively uses data from the graph to complete the statement?

(A) around ten rock pigeons were observed at a site with three restaurants within one kilometer, while around thirty rock pigeons were observed at a site with six restaurants within one kilometer.

(B) around three rock pigeons were observed at a site with ten restaurants within one kilometer, while around six rock pigeons were observed at a site with thirty restaurants within one kilometer.

(C) fewer than five rock pigeons were observed at a site with ten restaurants within one kilometer, while more than ten rock pigeons were observed at a site with thirty restaurants within one kilometer.

(D) fewer than ten rock pigeons were observed at a site with five restaurants within one kilometer, while more than thirty rock pigeons were observed at a site with ten restaurants within one kilometer.

CONTINUE

10 ☐ Mark for Review

Chandra Wickramasinghe, director of the University of Buckingham's Centre for Astrobiology, is an influential proponent of the controversial theory of panspermia, which suggests that life on Earth originated from microorganisms that were carried to our planet by comets or other celestial bodies. Wickramasinghe has argued for panspermia using several sources of scientific data including the detection of living microorganisms at extremely high altitudes in Earth's atmosphere and the confirmation of complex organic molecules in interstellar dust and comets.

Which choice best describes the main idea of the text?

(A) Wickramasinghe's theory of panspermia is far too controversial to be accepted by other astrobiologists.

(B) Wickramasinghe has presented evidence that life on Earth may in fact come from somewhere beyond Earth.

(C) The preponderance of available scientific data strongly supports Wickramasinghe's theory of panspermia.

(D) If microorganisms can survive at extremely high altitudes in Earth's atmosphere, then they can also survive space travel.

11 ☐ Mark for Review

C. difficile is a bacterium that causes an inflammation of the colon that can be life-threatening. The metabolic processes by which *C. difficile* takes advantage of a host's inflammatory process to increase toxin production are not well understood. Previously, higher levels of sorbitol (a sugar alcohol) were found to be released by the immune system during inflammation from toxin production. Thus, a team of researchers decided to investigate sorbitol metabolism in *C. difficile* and its effect on toxin production in mice. In the study, mice with *C. difficile* that ingested sorbitol were found to have lower levels of toxin production than mice that did not ingest sorbitol. One possible explanation is that metabolizing sorbitol prevents *C. difficile* from producing toxins.

Which finding, if true, would most directly strengthen the potential explanation?

(A) *C. difficile* lacks the enzyme that metabolizes sorbitol and thus reduces its production of toxins when sorbitol is ingested.

(B) *C. difficile* metabolizes sorbitol at a faster rate than it does other naturally occurring sugar alcohols.

(C) Low levels of sorbitol reduce inflammation in mice and prevent toxin production.

(D) Mice naturally produce sorbitol in their intestines and do not contract *C. difficile*.

CONTINUE ➡

12 ☐ Mark for Review

Scholars generally agree that amputations were dangerous and deadly prior to 10,000 years ago due to a lack of proper surgical tools and techniques. The earliest evidence of a successful limb-removal surgery was a 7,000-year-old skeleton found in France that had an amputation above the elbow. Recently, archaeologists uncovered a 31,000-year-old skeleton with an amputated leg in Indonesia. Analysis of the early stone age skeleton shows that the amputation occurred when the man was just a child and lacked any evidence of infection. Thus, _____

Which choice most logically completes the text?

(A) early stone age people must have had doctors who performed these successful amputations.

(B) life as an amputee must have been difficult for early stone age people without access to post-operational care.

(C) there is insufficient evidence to support that most amputations performed prior to 10,000 years ago were deadly.

(D) early stone age people prior to 10,000 years ago may have been more advanced than was previously acknowledged.

13 ☐ Mark for Review

In game theory, the prisoner's dilemma is a thought experiment in which two people who are isolated from each other each have the choice to betray the other. An individual who betrays the other person will experience a personal benefit; however, if both players choose to betray each other then they will both experience a worse punishment than if neither betrays the other. Game theorists generally agree that the choice to cooperate (that is, refusing to betray the other person) is irrational, as it defies one's self-interest; therefore, these game theorists suggest that _____

Which choice most logically completes the text?

(A) it is more rational for one to betray the other participant.

(B) both individuals should cooperate, as their punishment will be reduced.

(C) people always act in their own self-interest, as it is the rational choice.

(D) the thought experiment likely has limited relevance in everyday life.

14 ☐ Mark for Review

Karni Mata Temple is a Hindu temple located in the town of Deshnoke in India. The temple is dedicated to Karni Mata and is an important pilgrimage site. Numerous rats, known as *kābā* and considered holy, live in Karni Mata Temple, earning the temple _____ nickname, "Temple of Rats."

Which choice completes the text so that it conforms to the conventions of Standard English?

(A) it's

(B) its

(C) their

(D) they're

CONTINUE ➤

15 ▢ Mark for Review

In addition to her research into the effects of hormones, ultraviolet light, and chemotherapy agents on cell _____ Jewel Plummer Cobb served as dean at Connecticut College and Rutgers University and as president of California State University, Fullerton, where she led many projects expanding the school's facilities.

Which choice completes the text so that it conforms to the conventions of Standard English?

Ⓐ division: biologist

Ⓑ division. Biologist

Ⓒ division biologist

Ⓓ division, biologist

16 ▢ Mark for Review

Poetra Asantewa is a performer from Ghana who combines three elements to create her _____ lyrics incorporating social issues, vocalization evoking different emotions, and rhythms using soulful elements.

Which choice completes the text so that it conforms to the conventions of Standard English?

Ⓐ pieces

Ⓑ pieces,

Ⓒ pieces:

Ⓓ pieces;

17 ▢ Mark for Review

Compared to other Ukrainian scientists and mathematicians, _____ she has worked with differential equations, partial differential equations, and integrable systems in Dnipro, Cyprus, and Kyiv.

Which choice completes the text so that it conforms to the conventions of Standard English?

Ⓐ there is a wide range of fields and Ukrainian cities that Olena Vaneeva has worked in:

Ⓑ many Ukrainian cities and fields have been home to Olena Vaneeva:

Ⓒ the range of fields and Ukrainian cities that Olena Vaneeva has worked in is very wide:

Ⓓ Olena Vaneeva has worked in a wide range of fields and Ukrainian cities:

18 ▢ Mark for Review

Astronaut William Anders was a member of the Apollo 8 mission, the first human spaceflight to reach the Moon and orbit it. During the mission, Anders took a photo of Earth rising above the lunar surface, an _____ was later named *Earthrise.*

Which choice completes the text so that it conforms to the conventions of Standard English?

Ⓐ image, that

Ⓑ image

Ⓒ image that

Ⓓ image,

CONTINUE ➡

19 ☐ Mark for Review

French philosopher Denis Diderot was the chief editor of the *Encyclopédie*, which was completed by 1772. Motivated by the principles of the Enlightenment, the writers of the *Encyclopédie* _____ to compile all of the world's knowledge in a single resource available to the ordinary person.

Which choice completes the text so that it conforms to the conventions of Standard English?

(A) attempted

(B) are attempting

(C) will attempt

(D) attempt

20 ☐ Mark for Review

As one of the most prominent French astrophysicists, Françoise Combes has contributed to research about how galaxies form and _____ she has studied the composition of galaxies and how they interact with one another.

Which choice completes the text so that it conforms to the conventions of Standard English?

(A) evolve; additionally,

(B) evolve additionally

(C) evolve, additionally,

(D) evolve, additionally;

21 ☐ Mark for Review

American avant-garde jazz composer and guitarist Mary Halvorson's musical discography includes *Dragon's Head*, an album created with bassist John Hébert and drummer Ches _____ a solo album; and *Away with You*, which featured pedal steel player Susan Alcorn, cellist Tomeka Reid, and saxophonist Ingrid Laubrock.

Which choice completes the text so that it conforms to the conventions of Standard English?

(A) Smith; *Meltframe*,

(B) Smith; *Meltframe*

(C) Smith, *Meltframe*,

(D) Smith, *Meltframe*:

22 ☐ Mark for Review

Mice were studied in an experiment focused on the relationship between room temperature and cancer growth. Cooler room temperatures were found to stimulate fat cells that eradicate the sugar molecules that sustain cancer cells. _____ the cancer cells started to die off in the mice exposed to cooler room temperatures.

Which choice completes the text with the most logical transition?

(A) Consequently,

(B) For example,

(C) However,

(D) In comparison,

CONTINUE ▶

23 ☐ Mark for Review

While researching a topic, a student has taken the following notes:

- Satyajit Ray was an Indian filmmaker.
- He is well-known for *The Apu Trilogy*.
- The first film in the trilogy, *Pather Panchali*, is about the childhood of a small Bengali boy named Apu.
- The second film, *Aparajito*, depicts Apu in his adolescence and his relationship to both his mother and their home.
- In *Apur Sansar*, the third film, adult Apu marries Aparna and has a son, Kajal.

The student wants to emphasize how Apu changed throughout the trilogy. Which choice most effectively uses relevant information from the notes to accomplish this goal?

- (A) Apu went from being a child in *Pather Panchali* to an adult with his own family in *Apur Sansar*.

- (B) Satyajit Ray, an Indian filmmaker, made *The Apu Trilogy* about a boy named Apu.

- (C) The three films of *The Apu Trilogy* are *Pather Panchali*, *Aparajito*, and *Apur Sansar*.

- (D) The character Apu grew up in Bengal and eventually marries and has a son.

24 ☐ Mark for Review

While researching a topic, a student has taken the following notes:

- Haenyeo are female divers on Jeju Island, a Korean province.
- Haenyeo earn money by harvesting mollusks and shellfish, such as abalone, sea urchins, and oysters.
- They dive without the use of oxygen masks and tanks.
- They can hold their breath for over three minutes.
- They can dive up to 30 meters below the surface of the water.
- Jellyfish, sharks, and poor weather are different dangers they face while diving.

The student wants to emphasize the abilities of haenyeo. Which choice most effectively uses relevant information from the notes to accomplish this goal?

- (A) Haenyeo are female divers on Jeju Island who harvest shellfish.

- (B) While diving, haenyeo contend with jellyfish, sharks, and poor weather.

- (C) Haenyeo earn money by selling abalone, sea urchins, and oysters, which they harvest by diving without oxygen masks and tanks.

- (D) Haenyeo can dive 30 meters below the surface and hold their breath for over three minutes.

CONTINUE ➡

25 ☐ Mark for Review

While researching a topic, a student has taken the following notes:

- Heliconian Hall was built in 1876 as the Olivet Congregational Church.
- Heliconian Hall is in the Yorkville neighborhood of Toronto.
- The Heliconian Club purchased and renamed Heliconian Hall in 1923.
- The Heliconian Club's membership includes women professional artists.
- Heliconian Hall hosts music, art, dance, drama, and literature events.

The student wants to describe the history of Heliconian Hall to an audience familiar with the Heliconian Club. Which choice most effectively uses relevant information from the notes to accomplish this goal?

- (A) Heliconian Hall was purchased in 1923 by the Heliconian Club, an organization which includes women professional artists.

- (B) Heliconian Hall, located in the Yorkville neighborhood of Toronto, hosts music, art, dance, drama, and literature events.

- (C) Heliconian Hall, formerly known as the Olivet Congregational Church, is in the Yorkville neighborhood of Toronto.

- (D) Heliconian Hall, built as the Olivet Congregational Church in 1876, was purchased and renamed by the Heliconian Club in 1923.

26 ☐ Mark for Review

While researching a topic, a student has taken the following notes:

- Evan Adams is an Indigenous Canadian actor.
- He is well-known for his role as Thomas in the film *Smoke Signals*.
- The film was released in 1998.
- It is about two friends, Thomas and Victor, and their complicated relationships with Victor's father, Arnold.
- Adams is also known for his role as Seymour in *The Business of Fancydancing* (2002).

The student wants to introduce Evan Adams and his role in *Smoke Signals* to a new audience. Which choice most effectively uses relevant information from the notes to accomplish this goal?

- (A) Evan Adams, an Indigenous Canadian actor, has starred as Thomas in *Smoke Signals* and Seymour in *The Business of Fancydancing*.

- (B) *Smoke Signals*, released in 1998, explores the complicated relationships of friends Thomas and Victor.

- (C) Evan Adams starred in the film *Smoke Signals* before he starred in *The Business of Fancydancing*.

- (D) Indigenous Canadian actor Evan Adams starred as Thomas in the 1998 film *Smoke Signals*, which depicts two friends, Thomas and Victor, and their complicated relationships with Victor's father, Arnold.

CONTINUE ➡

27 ☐ Mark for Review

While researching a topic, a student has taken the following notes:

- Marie Byrd Land is an unclaimed region of Antarctica.
- Construction of Byrd Station in Marie Byrd Land was begun in 1956 by the US.
- Byrd Station was abandoned in 1972.
- John Carpenter used Byrd Station as a model for an Antarctic station in crisis for his movie *The Thing*.
- James Rollins used Byrd Station as a model for an Antarctic station in crisis for his novel *The 6th Extinction*.

The student wants to highlight a similarity between fictional depictions of a real-world location. Which choice most effectively uses relevant information from the notes to accomplish this goal?

(A) Both John Carpenter's movie *The Thing* and James Rollins's novel *The 6th Extinction* used Byrd Station as a model for an Antarctic station in crisis.

(B) In 1956, the US began construction of Byrd Station in Marie Byrd Land, an unclaimed region of Antarctica.

(C) Abandoned in 1972, Byrd Station was the model for an Antarctic station in crisis in John Carpenter's *The Thing*.

(D) John Carpenter used Byrd station as a model for an Antarctic station in crisis for his movie *The Thing*; however, James Rollins used Byrd Station as a model for an Antarctic station in crisis for his novel *The 6th Extinction*.

YIELD
Once you've finished (or run out of time for) this section, use the answer key to determine how many questions you got right. If you got fewer than 14 questions right, move on to Module 2—Easier, otherwise move on to Module 2—Harder.

Test 3—Reading and Writing
Module 2—Easier

Turn to Section 1 of your answer sheet to answer the questions in this section.

---

1 ☐ Mark for Review

During World War II, hundreds of scientists, including many prominent physicists such as Robert Oppenheimer, _____ the Manhattan Project, pooling their efforts and expertise in order to develop the first bombs that successfully exploited the tremendous power of nuclear energy.

Which choice completes the text with the most logical and precise word or phrase?

Ⓐ collaborated on

Ⓑ invested with

Ⓒ plotted against

Ⓓ learned from

---

2 ☐ Mark for Review

Advising farmers on how to prevent the disruption of soil due to plowing, experts in agriculture have recommended the method of no-till farming. This _____ allows for soil to remain settled while seeds are planted, unlike traditional practices in which the soil is disturbed in order for new crops to be grown, thus making sowing easier to manage. Through no-till farming, agriculturalists are able to grow new batches with very little labor or equipment required.

Which choice completes the text with the most logical and precise word or phrase?

Ⓐ intention

Ⓑ agenda

Ⓒ distraction

Ⓓ technique

CONTINUE

3 ☐ Mark for Review

Ethologists and beekeepers use the phrase "waggle dance" to describe the movement a bee makes in order to communicate with other bees in the colony about the location of resources. This silent _____ of information among the bees allows them to pass on knowledge of how close or far away a source is and what direction it is in. The source being broadcasted can be a site for possible nesting or an opportunity for sustenance.

Which choice completes the text with the most logical and precise word or phrase?

(A) transmission

(B) confidence

(C) prolongation

(D) devastation

4 ☐ Mark for Review

Chronic hepatitis B (CHB) can _____ affect Asians Americans and Pacific Islanders (AAPIs), who are not affected by most other major hepatitis strains. While everyone should be screened for hepatitis viruses, AAPIs are strongly encouraged to get tested and treated for chronic hepatitis B.

Which choice completes the text with the most logical or precise word or phrase?

(A) disproportionately

(B) exclusively

(C) essentially

(D) initially

5 ☐ Mark for Review

There are countless stories of people whose hair turns white overnight from fright in a condition called canities subita, also known as Marie Antoinette syndrome. Scientists _____ this as historical fiction and explain that visible hair is dead material that can be changed by undergoing a chemical drying process, but not by experiencing a great shock.

Which choice completes the text with the most logical or precise word or phrase?

(A) trivialize

(B) illustrate

(C) dismiss

(D) promote

CONTINUE ➡

6 ☐ Mark for Review

The following text is adapted from Honoré de Balzac's 1829 novel *The Chouans*. Marie, an aristocrat, is tidying a room and speaking to Francine, her maid.

She began to arrange the silk and muslin curtains which draped the window, making them intercept the light and produce in the room a voluptuous chiaro-scuro.

"Francine," she said, "take away those knick-knacks on the mantelpiece; leave only the clock and the two Dresden vases. I'll fill those vases myself with the flowers Corentin brought me. Take out the chairs, I want only this sofa and a fauteuil. Then sweep the carpet, so as to <u>bring out</u> the colors, and put wax candles in the sconces and on the mantel."

As used in the text, what does the word "bring out" most nearly mean?

- Ⓐ Distribute

- Ⓑ Transport

- Ⓒ Introduce

- Ⓓ Emphasize

7 ☐ Mark for Review

The following text is adapted from Jane Austin's 1811 novel *Sense and Sensibility*. Elinor Dashwood is in her cottage speaking with her Uncle Edward and her younger sister Marianne.

"I have frequently detected myself in such kind of mistakes," said Elinor, "in a total misapprehension of character in some point or other: fancying people so much more gay or grave, or ingenious or stupid than they really are, and I can hardly tell why or in what the deception originated. Sometimes one is guided by what they say of themselves, and very frequently by what other people say of them, without giving oneself time to deliberate and judge."

Which choice best describes the overall structure of the text?

- Ⓐ The speaker describes how someone can be deceived by the impressions of others and then promises to be more careful in the future.

- Ⓑ The speaker relates her misgivings of the character of another individual and then rationalizes her mistaken perception.

- Ⓒ The speaker considers the duplicity of human nature and then issues a warning about the misconceptions of personal opinion.

- Ⓓ The speaker describes a type of error and then reveals the sources of information that lead to such errors.

CONTINUE ➡

8 ☐ Mark for Review

In order to combat the effects of human life on the planet's climate, many environmental and governmental establishments lay the foundation for forests in localities that previously did not have woodland areas, also known as afforestation. To begin the operation, potential sites are first surveyed in order to select regions with the best factors in terms of aspects such as vegetation, amount of human activity, weather, and soil quality. Once a site has been selected, the land must then be developed for planting. After the land has been prepared, trees can be planted with different methods of seeding, depending on the site and soil present.

Which choice best describes the overall structure of the text?

(A) It presents a solution to a widespread issue, then elaborates on why the issue should be solved.

(B) It defines a strategy, then lists the reasons why the strategy is useful.

(C) It examines an effective practice, then argues that the practice has negative consequences.

(D) It introduces a process, then explains the steps taken in executing that process.

9 ☐ Mark for Review

Text 1

A recent series of psychological studies that included subjects from different parts of the world looked at the effects that nostalgia, the feeling and experience of thinking about one's own past, has on psychological well-being. The results of the studies demonstrated a relationship between nostalgia and authenticity, one's sense of being aligned with one's true self. A greater sense of authenticity was found to correlate with greater measurements of all aspects of psychological well-being.

Text 2

While there has been some demonstration that nostalgia is associated with mental health benefits, it is important to remember that there are different types of nostalgia and that some can be highly destructive. A recent study performed by psychologists David B. Newman, Arthur A. Stone, and Norbert Schwarz found that conscious acts of extreme nostalgia have positive effects, while smaller and momentary, more unconscious nostalgic experiences can result in negative mental health effects, such as neuroticism.

Based on the texts, what would Newman, Stone, and Schwarz (Text 2) say about the results of the studies discussed in Text 1?

(A) They are completely consistent with the results of other studies on the subject.

(B) They are from studies that fail to differentiate between different types of nostalgia and so provide an incomplete picture of nostalgia's impact on mental health.

(C) They provide empirical evidence for a hypothesis long untested but assumed to be true.

(D) They suggest a possible new direction for future research but provide no definitive resolutions.

CONTINUE ➤

Impact of Package Label on Consumer Choices

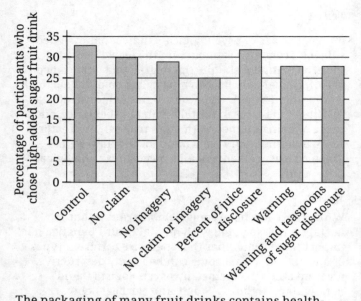

The packaging of many fruit drinks contains health-related claims and imagery that can sometimes be misleading to parents who purchase such drinks for their children. To assess the impact of the front of packaging on consumers' purchasing decisions, nutrition researchers Aviva A. Musicus, Christina A. Roberto, and Alyssa J. Moran conducted a study wherein participants were shown fruit drinks with high amounts of sugar added with seven different conditions of packaging: with claim and imagery (control), no claim, no imagery, no claim or imagery, disclosure of percentage of juice, a warning, and disclosure of amount of added sugar in teaspoons. At the end of the study, the researchers concluded that the presence of warnings and absence of claims and imagery may reduce likelihood of purchase, whereas disclosure of percentage of juice may have very little impact.

10 🔖 Mark for Review

Which choice most effectively uses data from the graph to support the researchers' conclusion?

(A) The percentage of participants who selected the high-added sugar fruit drink was highest when a warning was placed on the front of the packaging.

(B) The percentage of participants who selected the high-added sugar fruit drink when the percentage of juice was disclosed on the front of the packaging was comparable to the percentage who selected the drink in the control group.

(C) The absence of the claim had the same impact as did the absence of imagery from the front of the packaging.

(D) When the front of packaging disclosed the amount of added sugar in teaspoons, participants were more likely to select a low-added sugar fruit drink than a high-added sugar fruit drink.

CONTINUE ➡

11 ☐ Mark for Review

"The Emerald Eyes" is an 1861 short story by Gustavo Adolfo Bécquer, originally written in Spanish. In the story, the protagonist, Fernando, is continually drawn to a Poplar fountain in an attempt to learn the identity of a mysterious woman with emerald eyes. Fernando's friend Iñigo is worried and tries to warn him to stay away from the fountain when he says, _____

Which quotation from a translation of the "The Emerald Eyes" most effectively illustrates the claim?

(A) "Do you not see that [the stag] is going toward the fountain of the Poplars, and if he lives to reach it we must give him up for lost?"

(B) "I exposed myself to death under his horse's hoofs to hold him back."

(C) "You do not go to the mountains now preceded by the clamorous pack of hounds, nor does the blare of your horns awake the echoes."

(D) "I conjure you by that which you love most on earth not to return to the fountain of the Poplars."

12 ☐ Mark for Review

Anthony Doerr won a Pulitzer Prize, among other literary awards, for his work in fiction novels, and his short stories have been anthologized in collections of American literature. In an essay about Doerr's works, a student claims that Doerr uses children as his protagonists in order to create a story from an unbiased and hopeful perspective of humanity.

Which quotation from a literary critic best supports the student's claim?

(A) "Doerr's novels are influenced by the themes present in fables, thus presenting an ordeal through which the protagonist learns a lesson about life."

(B) "Doerr prefers to have the protagonist's story told through the eyes of a child who seeks to learn more about the world."

(C) "Doerr's novels often contain multiple story arcs or perspectives culminating in a universal truth."

(D) "Doerr's protagonists are often children who see the world with an open mind and contribute towards the betterment of humanity."

CONTINUE →

---

13 ⬜ Mark for Review

Ratings of Mood and Need Satisfaction after Social Inclusion and Exclusion

	Human exclusion	Human inclusion	Computer exclusion	Computer inclusion
Need satisfaction scale, reflexive stage	3.13	5.88	3.29	5.94
Mood, reflexive stage	3.29	5.50	3.43	4.59
Need satisfaction scale, reflective stage	3.38	5.03	3.81	5.38
Mood, reflective stage	3.46	4.71	4.43	4.09

Social exclusion can have a detrimental impact on an individual's mental and emotional state. Psychologists Melissa Jauch, Selma Carolin Rudert, and Rainer Greifendeder hypothesized that individuals would experience equivalent effects of social exclusion regardless of whether the source of exclusion was human or computer. The researchers conducted a study in which subjects played a word riddle game. The subjects were grouped with other players who were computer-generated, though some subjects were told that they were playing with other humans. Throughout the game, the other players would either include the subjects or exclude them from participating. After the game, researchers measured the subjects' need satisfaction (a psychological metric of the degree to which an individual's basic needs are met) and mood on a scale of 1 to 9 immediately after the game (the reflexive stage) as well as after some time had passed (the reflective stage).

Which choice most effectively uses data from the table to support the researchers' hypothesis?

(A) At the reflexive stage, subjects' ratings in both mood and need satisfaction when excluded by a human were comparable to the corresponding ratings when excluded by a computer.

(B) Subjects reported higher mood and need satisfaction ratings when included than they did when excluded.

(C) When included by a human or a computer, subjects exhibited lower need satisfaction at the reflective stage than they did at the reflexive stage.

(D) Subjects experienced the highest mood rating when they believed they were socially included by a human.

CONTINUE ➡

14 ☐ Mark for Review

It is commonly accepted that the Cretaceous–Paleogene extinction event some 66 million years ago was caused by an asteroid impact, believed to correspond to an impact crater in Chicxulub, Mexico, that dates to the same time and is the second-largest impact structure on Earth. Geologist Uisdean Nicholson discovered an undersea impact crater while reviewing seismic survey data and conducted a study that demonstrated that this crater also formed around 66 million years ago. Nicholson claims that the rock whose impact caused the formation of the undersea crater could have broken off from a parent asteroid that also caused the Chicxulub impact.

Which finding, if true, would most directly support Nicholson's claim?

Ⓐ The undersea impact would have caused major earthquakes and tsunamis, leading to significant damage to the planet.

Ⓑ Some evidence points to a gradual Cretaceous–Paleogene extinction rather than a sudden one caused by an asteroid.

Ⓒ Many species of marine animals, in addition to land animals, went extinct during the Cretaceous–Paleogene extinction.

Ⓓ The undersea impact crater contains some of the same minerals not normally found on Earth that were also found at the Chicxulub impact site.

15 ☐ Mark for Review

In a study of neuronal sleeping patterns, researchers tracked the electrical waves (using EEG) and blood flow patterns (using fMRI) in participants while they slept. Researchers hypothesized that a correlation between electrical wave activity and blood flow patterns could indicate which regions of the brain, if any, fell asleep or awoke first. Like with previous studies, the researchers found that the thalamus, a region located near the center of the brain, had decreased blood flow patterns in association with increased electrical sleep waves in the early minutes of sleep activity. This suggests that _____

Which choice most logically completes the text?

Ⓐ the thalamus is one of the first brain regions to fall asleep.

Ⓑ increased blood flow patterns in association with decreased electrical sleep waves indicate a brain region that is asleep.

Ⓒ the thalamus is the last brain region to fall asleep.

Ⓓ humans may use only one hemisphere of the brain while asleep.

CONTINUE

16 ▢ Mark for Review

In order to avoid physical damage, a formula is used to calculate the maximum gross weight for a commercial vehicle traveling over a bridge. The Federal Bridge Gross Weight Formula takes into account not only the weight of the vehicle but also its number of axles (shafts for wheels) and the spacing between axles, given that a shorter vehicle with its weight concentrated in a smaller area could cause more damage than could a longer vehicle of the same weight whose mass is more dispersed. This suggests that, when comparing a two-axle vehicle to a 4-axle vehicle, _____

Which choice most logically completes the text?

(A) the four-axle vehicle likely has a lower weight limit on a given bridge than does the two-axle vehicle.

(B) the vehicles likely have the same weight limit on a given bridge.

(C) the two-axle vehicle is unlikely to surpass the bridge's weight limit, as it is smaller.

(D) the two-axle vehicle likely has a lower weight limit on a given bridge than does the four-axle vehicle.

17 ▢ Mark for Review

A recent study looked at whether students who took photos of PowerPoint slides during lessons remembered the content. When students took a photo of the slides, they were able to better remember the information on those slides compared to slides _____ did not photograph.

Which choice completes the text so that it conforms to the conventions of Standard English?

(A) they

(B) one

(C) it

(D) we

18 ▢ Mark for Review

Soft drinks have become very popular in recent years, but consuming too many is associated with many diseases and intellectual deterioration. Scientists wanted to explore another question related to this topic: _____

Which choice completes the text so that it conforms to the conventions of Standard English?

(A) does the consumption of soft drinks cause changes in mammal behavior?

(B) does the consumption of soft drinks cause changes in mammal behavior.

(C) the consumption of soft drinks causes changes in mammal behavior?

(D) the consumption of soft drinks causes changes in mammal behavior.

19 ▢ Mark for Review

Heat islands are urban areas that, due to a high number of buildings and limited greenery, have a higher temperature compared to outlying areas. There are several strategies and technologies to counteract the higher temperatures of heat islands. For example, green roofs, which are rooftops covered in vegetation, reduce the temperatures of _____ cool pavements, which are made with materials that reflect solar energy, can lower the temperatures above the pavement surface and the surrounding air.

Which choice completes the text so that it conforms to the conventions of Standard English?

(A) roofs, while

(B) roofs; while

(C) roofs. While

(D) roofs: while

CONTINUE ➡

20 ☐ Mark for Review

With a focus on public health, Abla Mehio Sibai is currently working at a university in Lebanon. She primarily focuses on the process of aging, especially in the context of different demographics, and _____ to research on noncontagious illnesses.

Which choice completes the text so that it conforms to the conventions of Standard English?

Ⓐ contribute

Ⓑ contributes

Ⓒ are contributing

Ⓓ have contributed

21 ☐ Mark for Review

Bribery is recognized as a problem in India by local and international organizations. In response to this problem, 5th Pillar, a non-governmental organization, printed a zero-rupee _____ imitation banknote that resembles real money and is covered in anti-corruption slogans.

Which choice completes the text so that it conforms to the conventions of Standard English?

Ⓐ note. An

Ⓑ note, an

Ⓒ note an

Ⓓ note; an

22 ☐ Mark for Review

Scientists wanted to learn how verbal statements can alter someone's visual interpretation of a situation. Participants were shown an image of 100 colored dots alongside a written hint and asked to identify the dominant color. When the hint accurately identified the dominant color, participants self-identified as more confident and _____ quicker response times.

Which choice completes the text so that it conforms to the conventions of Standard English?

Ⓐ exhibit

Ⓑ exhibits

Ⓒ exhibiting

Ⓓ exhibited

23 ☐ Mark for Review

Quantum computers rely on entangled building blocks to perform computational calculations. Scientists are attempting to find a new source for these building _____ photons, or small quanta of light, emitted by an atom.

Which choice completes the text so that it conforms to the conventions of Standard English?

Ⓐ blocks, such as:

Ⓑ blocks

Ⓒ blocks,

Ⓓ blocks:

CONTINUE →

24 ▢ Mark for Review

Suzan Shown Harjo initially worked to write poems and produce news shows advocating for equal rights for Native Americans. _____ she moved to Washington, D.C., and served as Congressional Liaison for Indian Affairs for President Jimmy Carter while continuing to produce powerful pieces.

Which choice completes the text with the most logical transition?

(A) As a rule,

(B) Despite this,

(C) Conversely,

(D) After some time,

25 ▢ Mark for Review

Scientists studied how electrical stimulation to the brain affected honeybees' ability to steer while flying. They were able to determine the parameters for honeybee flight and develop strategies to manipulate it. _____ scientists hope to use a similar technique to control the flight of miniature drones that will perform a variety of tasks for the military and other industries.

Which choice completes the text with the most logical transition?

(A) In contrast,

(B) Eventually,

(C) On one hand,

(D) Specifically,

26 ▢ Mark for Review

In order to study an abrupt increase in global mean lower stratosphere temperatures, scientists used a time-specific analysis of wildfires in Australia. They determined that the wildfires are the source of this abrupt increase in temperature. _____ reducing the number of wildfires in Australia may help return the temperature to a normal value.

Which choice completes the text with the most logical transition?

(A) On the other hand,

(B) Meanwhile,

(C) Instead,

(D) Therefore,

27 ▢ Mark for Review

Ed Yost designed the first modern hot air balloon with an in-flight heating system after working with General Mills on the company's research balloons. The first piloted hot air balloon was designed in France, but it heated the air on the ground and came with a large risk of explosion. _____ Yost's balloon design involved heating the fuel in the air and was much safer.

Which choice completes the text with the most logical transition?

(A) Ultimately,

(B) On the other hand,

(C) Otherwise,

(D) Despite this fact,

STOP

If you finish before time is called, you may check your work on this module only. Do not turn to any other module.

Test 3—Reading and Writing
Module 2—Harder

Turn to Section 1 of your answer sheet to answer the questions in this section.

---

1 ☐ Mark for Review

As an educator, artistic creator, and supporter of Māori culture, Cliff Whiting spent a significant portion of his career advocating for the inclusion of Māori arts in the schools of New Zealand. While mentoring students and artists within these communities, Whiting was encouraged to broaden his contributions and work on the renovation of historic buildings. By way of this, he became one of the chief officials on the _____ of Māori buildings in New Zealand. Whiting's ability to create a close-knit relationship with local communities aided his success in these preservation projects.

Which choice completes the text with the most logical and precise word or phrase?

- (A) repossession
- (B) rehabilitation
- (C) reciprocation
- (D) reindustrialization

2 ☐ Mark for Review

Used to test the resistance to corrosion of surface coatings and materials, the salt spray test is a common method employed to aid in quality testing of metallic, ceramic, stone, and polymer products. The _____ process is brief, low-cost, and highly methodized, allowing for producers to easily spot differences in quality and adjust their manufacturing accordingly.

Which choice completes the text with the most logical and precise word or phrase?

- (A) rudimentary
- (B) pervasive
- (C) erroneous
- (D) intermittent

CONTINUE →

3 ☐ Mark for Review

Dr. Jane Goodall has worked tirelessly to _____ the effects of climate change on chimpanzees in Tanzania: her research has shown that government commitments to reforestation efforts can help lessen the negative impacts of warming temperatures on chimpanzee populations in Tanzania as well as in other African countries.

Which choice completes the text with the most logical and precise word or phrase?

- Ⓐ insulate
- Ⓑ downplay
- Ⓒ tolerate
- Ⓓ mitigate

4 ☐ Mark for Review

In 1968, surrealistic artist William Nelson Copley and his friend and fellow artist Dimitri Petrov founded an innovative artists' magazine known as S.M.S., in which contributors enjoyed complete freedom to create artistic works that Copley and Petrov would then reproduce with _____ fidelity, sparing no expense in producing a biweekly folio of painstakingly replicated art facsimiles.

Which choice completes the text with the most logical and precise word or phrase?

- Ⓐ evenhanded
- Ⓑ prudent
- Ⓒ scrupulous
- Ⓓ complacent

5 ☐ Mark for Review

The following text is adapted from L. Frank Baum's 1911 novel *The Sea Fairies*. Mayre Griffiths, nicknamed Trot, is a little girl. Cap'n Bill Weedles is a retired sailor with a wooden leg.

Trot liked Cap'n Bill and had a great deal of confidence in his wisdom, and a great admiration for his ability to make tops and whistles and toys with that marvelous jackknife of his. In the village were many boys and girls of her own age, but she never had as much fun playing with them as she had wandering by the sea accompanied by the old sailor and listening to his fascinating stories.

Which choice best describes the function of the underlined sentence in the text as a whole?

- Ⓐ It reiterates Trot's fascination with Cap'n Bill's impressive creative talents.
- Ⓑ Its comparison conveys the depth of Trot's regard and affection for Cap'n Bill.
- Ⓒ It contrasts the carefree pleasures of youth with the weighty responsibilities of adulthood.
- Ⓓ It reveals the subtle differences between Trot's assessment of Cap'n Bill and his assessment of her.

CONTINUE

6 ☐ Mark for Review

The following text is adapted from Fyodor Dostoevsky's 1864 novella *Notes from the Underground*. The narrator is an unnamed Russian man employed as a civil servant.

I could never stand more than three months of dreaming at a time without feeling an irresistible desire to plunge into society. To plunge into society meant to visit my superior at the office .... I was overcome by a sort of paralysis; but this was pleasant and good for me. On returning home I deferred for a time my desire to embrace all humankind.

Which choice best states the main purpose of the text?

(A) To convey the man's apprehension about his employment and his relationship with his employer

(B) To foreshadow the man's imminent termination from his job for daydreaming

(C) To suggest that the man's social engagement with a colleague prolonged his isolation from society

(D) To advocate the social benefits of working with others in an office environment

7 ☐ Mark for Review

The following text is from Alexander S. Pushkin's 1834 short story "The Queen of Spades." A man named Tomsky is sharing with friends a story about his grandmother.

"On returning home, my grandmother removed the patches from her face, took off her hoops, informed my grandfather of her loss at the gaming-table, and ordered him to pay the money. My deceased grandfather, as far as I remember, was a sort of house-steward to my grandmother. He dreaded her like fire; but, on hearing of such a heavy loss, he almost went out of his mind; he calculated the various sums she had lost, and pointed out to her that in six months she had spent half a million francs, that neither their Moscow nor Saratov estates were in Paris, and finally refused point blank to pay the debt."

Which choice best states the function of the underlined sentence in the text as a whole?

(A) It explains the previous dynamic between the narrator's grandparents.

(B) It provides background information on the narrator's relationship with his grandfather.

(C) It reveals why the grandmother lost money at the gaming-table.

(D) It establishes the memories of the narrator in his house.

CONTINUE

8 🔖 Mark for Review

Nuclear energy, a power source expected to grow in the coming decades, relies upon an element that is considered a finite resource on land: uranium. However, vast amounts of uranium exist in low concentrations in seawater. The time, effort, and cost needed to extract uranium from seawater has long been prohibitive, but a team of researchers from the Indian Institute of Science Education and Research has created a metal-organic framework that was able to pull 96.3% of uranium from seawater samples in two hours, representing a significant improvement from previous methods. Nevertheless, the new method has not yet been tested in a real-world marine setting, and it's expected that even with the improvements it is not likely to result in a net energy gain.

Which choice best describes the overall structure of the text?

(A) It presents a scientific challenge, then describes a failed attempt to address that challenge.

(B) It evaluates the effectiveness of a method of energy production, then addresses a potential criticism of the method.

(C) It explains the significance of a technological advancement, then qualifies its current usability.

(D) It establishes the problems associated with obtaining a resource, then cautions against reliance on that resource.

9 🔖 Mark for Review

Text 1

There have been many theories put forward to explain the decline of the Ancient Maya societies. One such theory points to various primary sources that indicate an escalation in infighting among rival factions in the society that coincided with increasing droughts. Thus, some anthropologists have proposed that climate change put a strain on the social, political, and economic institutions and played a crucial role in the demise of those institutions.

Text 2

There has been much debate surrounding the role that the changing climate played in the dissolution of Ancient Maya political systems. While it is often correctly pointed out that drought conditions of the time were correlated with the fall of the social order and the rise of civil unrest, it was more specifically the increasing unpredictability of precipitation patterns that had the strongest impact on the health of Maya society.

Based on the texts, how would the author of Text 2 most likely respond to the claims of the author of Text 1?

(A) By disagreeing with the premise that droughts corresponded to social unrest

(B) By asserting that if Maya society leaders were increasingly unable to predict the weather, it would logically follow that the population would increasingly mistrust the political institutions

(C) By conceding that water resources played a vital role in the decline of Maya societies but noting that the relevant factor was the society's inability to predict rainfall rather than strictly the lack of rainfall

(D) By arguing that if weather patterns had remained stable, Maya civilization would not have declined

CONTINUE ➡

10 ☐ Mark for Review

Characteristics of Common pH Indicators

pH indicator	pH range	Acid form color	Base form color
thymol blue	1.2–2.8	red	yellow
p-Nitrophenol	5.0–7.0	colorless	yellow
alizarin yellow	10.0–12.0	yellow	lilac
Nile blue	10.1–11.1	blue	red
nitramine	11.0–13.0	colorless	orange-brown

A student in chemistry class is studying acid-base titrations. For her experiment, she needs to use a pH indicator that has a colorless acid form and a pH range above a pH of 10. Based on the characteristics of common pH indicators, she selected _____.

Which choice most effectively uses data from the table to complete the text?

- (A) thymol blue.

- (B) p-Nitrophenol.

- (C) alizarin yellow.

- (D) nitramine.

11 ☐ Mark for Review

"Remembrance" is a 1906 poem by Walter de la Mare. In the poem, the author describes a sense of profound emptiness: _____

Which quotation from "Remembrance" most effectively illustrates the claim?

- (A) "The sky was like a waterdrop / In shadow of a thorn."

- (B) "Lightning along its margin ran; / A rumour of the sea."

- (C) "Lofty and few the elms, the stars / In the vast boughs most bright."

- (D) "Not wonder, worship, not even peace / Seemed in my heart to be."

CONTINUE

Concentration of Circulating Leukocytes Before and After Administration of Probiotics

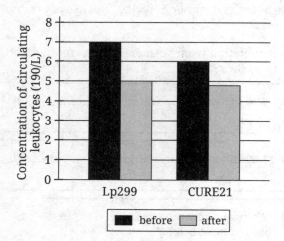

During inflammation, the body's immune system response to infection or tissue damage, leukocytes (also known as white blood cells) are released into the bloodstream. While inflammation can be normal and healthy, it can be harmful when the process lasts too long or occurs in healthy cell tissue, so the development of anti-inflammatory therapies is in demand. One such therapy under consideration is the use of certain bacteria called probiotics. To learn more about the systemic impact of these bacteria, medical researchers Christina Stene, Andrada Röme, and colleagues gave test subjects a daily dose of one of two probiotic strains, *Lactiplantibacillus plantarum* 299 (Lp299) and *Bifidobacterium infantis* CURE21 (CURE21). The researchers compared the concentration of leukocytes in the subjects' bloodstreams at the start and end of a six-week period and concluded that both Lp299 and CURE21 have anti-inflammatory properties, citing that

---

12 ☐ Mark for Review

Which choice best describes data from the graph to support the researchers' conclusion?

Ⓐ there was a larger number of leukocytes in the test subjects' bloodstreams before the treatment with either Lp299 or CURE21 than there was after the treatment.

Ⓑ subjects treated with Lp299 experienced a larger decrease in leukocytes than did those treated with CURE21.

Ⓒ those who were given the CURE21 treatment had a smaller number of leukocytes in their bloodstream at the start of study than did those who were given Lp299.

Ⓓ at the end of the study, the group of subjects that received Lp299 exhibited a number of leukocytes in their bloodstream comparable to that of the group that received CURE21.

CONTINUE

13 ☐ Mark for Review

Traumatic brain injury (TBI) can have short-term symptoms as well as long-term consequences. Researchers continue to investigate methods that can improve detection and treatment of TBI. GFAP and UCH-L1 are two protein biomarkers that have been associated with severe TBI and subsequent death. In a study, researchers analyzed blood samples from over 1,000 patients on the same day as their injuries. They found that patients with GFAP values greater than the top 20th percentile were at 23 times greater risk of death in the next six months, while patients with UCH-L1 values greater than the top 20th percentile were at 63 times greater risk of death in the next six months. According to the researchers, this suggests that the level of these biomarkers can detect TBI and indicate its severity.

Which finding, if true, would most directly weaken the underlined claim?

Ⓐ Follow-up visits of patients with low GFAP and UCH-L1 showed that over 50% had improved symptoms.

Ⓑ Patients with high UCH-L1 levels but low GFAP levels showed severe TBI symptoms within six months after injury.

Ⓒ GFAP and UCH-L1 occur in high levels immediately following an injury but significantly decrease after a few days, before many people seek treatment for a potential TBI.

Ⓓ Follow-up visits of patients with high GFAP and UCH-L1 levels showed that 70% had died within six months after injury.

14 ☐ Mark for Review

Prometheus Bound is a circa 460 BCE Greek tragedy written by Aeschylus, translated in 1921 by E. D. A. Morshead. The play follows the punishment of Prometheus for defying Zeus and providing humanity with the gift of fire. In the play, Prometheus questions the justice of his punishment and denounces Zeus as a cruel ruler, as when he says, _____

Which quotation from a translation of *Prometheus Bound* most effectively illustrates the claim?

Ⓐ "O Earth, the Mighty Mother, and thou Sun, / Whose orbed light surveyeth all – attest, / What ills I suffer from the gods, a god!"

Ⓑ "Such and so shameful is the chain / Which Heaven's new tyrant doth ordain / To bind me helpless here."

Ⓒ "Ay, stern is Zeus, and Justice stands, / Wrenched to his purpose, in his hands –"

Ⓓ "Such the aid / I gave the lord of heaven – my meed for which / He paid me thus, a penal recompense!"

CONTINUE ➔

15 ☐ Mark for Review

Mindfulness has been found to be useful in minimizing stress or pain as well as improving empathy. A team of researchers in Toronto was interested in testing whether short-term exposure to mindfulness treatment resulted in greater empathy and helpfulness toward a stranger. To do so, the researchers had participants in an experimental group undergo two sessions of mindfulness therapy while participants in a control group listened to a lecture on empathy and helping strangers. Then the participants watched an interview detailing a stranger's story and were evaluated on their levels of empathy and commitment to helping the stranger. Participants in the experimental group were found to have increased levels of empathy toward the stranger, while participants in the control group did not. However, both groups had similar levels of commitment to help the stranger, which suggests that _____

Which choice most logically completes the text?

- Ⓐ though mindfulness improved levels of empathy in the experimental group, there remained a greater lack of willingness to help the stranger than there was in the control group.

- Ⓑ participants in both experimental and control groups were willing to volunteer help to the stranger.

- Ⓒ short-term mindfulness can improve empathy, but more mindfulness therapy sessions are needed to change behavior.

- Ⓓ an increase in empathy does not necessarily result in an increased willingness to volunteer help.

16 ☐ Mark for Review

A large silicified sandstone block in Kent, England, dubbed the Coffin Stone, was long believed to be part of a now-destroyed chambered long barrow, a style of monument consisting of a long mound with linear ditches on each side. It was believed that the chambered long barrow would have been constructed in the fourth millennium BCE by a pastoralist community, given that such barrows are associated with agricultural traditions and were constructed during the Early Neolithic period. In the 2000s, however, archaeologists found no evidence of a chambered long barrow at the location of the Coffin Stone and determined that the stone had been placed at its current location in the 15th or 16th century. Therefore, the archaeologists concluded that _____

Which choice most logically completes the text?

- Ⓐ pastoral communities from the Early Neolithic period did not construct chambered long barrows.

- Ⓑ the Coffin Stone is not associated with a chambered long barrow.

- Ⓒ the Coffin Stone must have been part of a chambered long barrow elsewhere before it was moved.

- Ⓓ the chambered long barrow that included the Coffin Stone was destroyed in the 15th or 16th century.

CONTINUE →

17 ☐ Mark for Review

Most individuals in America don't walk as much as is _____ when a group of individuals was given step-trackers, researchers found that these individuals took more steps.

Which choice completes the text so that it conforms to the conventions of Standard English?

Ⓐ recommended

Ⓑ recommended,

Ⓒ recommended, but

Ⓓ recommended but

18 ☐ Mark for Review

Learning and practicing new skills over a long period of time can cause the brain to _____ for individuals who become blind, areas of the brain that are normally responsible for vision may change and become involved in other important processes, such as touch.

Which choice completes the text so that it conforms to the conventions of Standard English?

Ⓐ change

Ⓑ change,

Ⓒ change;

Ⓓ change and

19 ☐ Mark for Review

Swedish inventor Ninni Kronberg is known for her work on creating powdered milk. She developed processes for milk serum and longer-lasting powdered milk. Sweden used powdered milk produced using Kronberg's methods as part of _____ emergency food supply during World War II.

Which choice completes the text so that it conforms to the conventions of Standard English?

Ⓐ its

Ⓑ her

Ⓒ their

Ⓓ one's

20 ☐ Mark for Review

Chemical engineer Kristi Anseth works with a number of multidisciplinary teams on projects such as developing hydrogel materials to help promote tissue _____ a particularly important area of research because some tissues such as cartilage cannot regrow, unlike other tissues such as bone or muscle.

Which choice completes the text so that it conforms to the conventions of Standard English?

Ⓐ regeneration; and

Ⓑ regeneration,

Ⓒ regeneration

Ⓓ regeneration and

CONTINUE

21 ☐ Mark for Review

The jet streams are fast flowing air currents in the upper atmosphere which occur due to the Earth's rotation and can shift location over time. The movements of the northern polar jet stream _____ important for airlines looking to save time and fuel on eastbound flights.

Which choice completes the text so that it conforms to the conventions of Standard English?

- (A) has been
- (B) was
- (C) are
- (D) is

22 ☐ Mark for Review

Meiro Koizumi creates videos that explore the relationship between an individual and his or her role in a situation of _____ his videos might portray a commonplace situation converted into a site of tension or conflict and allow the viewer to process how he or she would respond in the situation.

Which choice completes the text so that it conforms to the conventions of Standard English?

- (A) conflict, for example;
- (B) conflict; for example,
- (C) conflict, for example,
- (D) conflict for example

23 ☐ Mark for Review

Quantum physicist Jacquiline Romero is working to develop a new quantum alphabet, in which a single photon can encode more information than the two binary options used in classical computing. Romero is not solely focused on _____ emphasizing that it is possible to be a parent and have a successful science career.

Which choice completes the text so that it conforms to the conventions of Standard English?

- (A) research; however,
- (B) research, however,
- (C) research, however
- (D) research, however;

24 ☐ Mark for Review

Barefoot running decreases the risk of ankle sprains, plantar fasciitis, and chronic leg injuries. _____ running in shoes decreases the risk of puncture wounds, thermal injuries, and bruising.

Which choice completes the text with the most logical transition?

- (A) Therefore,
- (B) In contrast,
- (C) Similarly,
- (D) Additionally,

CONTINUE →

25 ☐ Mark for Review

During the War of 1812, dispatch runners traveling between Montreal and present-day Mackinaw City, Michigan, faced difficulties with their long greatcoats in deep snow drifts. _____ a shorter jacket, the Mackinaw jacket, was developed.

Which choice completes the text with the most logical transition?

(A) Hence,

(B) Similarly,

(C) However,

(D) Furthermore,

26 ☐ Mark for Review

While researching a topic, a student has taken the following notes:

- Cargo bikes are bikes that feature built-in boxes to carry goods or people.
- Boxes can be as large as 6 square feet and carry up to 450 pounds.
- A large grocery load typically weighs around 100 pounds.
- Some cargo bikes use electric motors to assist in pedaling.
- Other cargo bikes rely solely on the rider for propulsion.

The student wants to explain the usefulness of cargo bikes for grocery shopping to an audience unfamiliar with cargo bikes. Which choice most effectively uses relevant information from the notes to accomplish this goal?

(A) Some cargo bikes use electric motors to assist in pedaling, yet other cargo bikes lack electric motors and rely on the rider's pedaling alone.

(B) A cargo bike can carry the 100-pound weight of a typical large grocery load.

(C) The built-in box of a cargo bike, intended for goods or people, can be as large as 6 square feet and carry up to 450 pounds.

(D) A cargo bike, which is a bike that features a built-in box to carry goods or people, can have a carrying capacity of up to 450 pounds, which is more than sufficient to handle the typical large grocery load of 100 pounds.

CONTINUE

_____

27 ☐ Mark for Review

While researching a topic, a student has taken the following notes:

- *Te lapa* is a Polynesian term for flashing light on or under the surface of the ocean.

- Polynesian sailors use te lapa to navigate by following the light towards an island.

- It is unknown what causes te lapa.

- Many phenomena have been ruled out as the causes of te lapa.

- Kent State professor Richard Feinberg has expressed skepticism about the usefulness of te lapa for navigation.

The student wants to highlight a dispute about te lapa to an audience familiar with the phenomenon. Which choice most effectively uses relevant information from the notes to accomplish this goal?

(A) While it is unknown what causes te lapa, many phenomena have been ruled out as the causes of te lapa.

(B) Te lapa, flashing light on or under the surface of the ocean, is used by Polynesian sailors to navigate by following the light towards an island.

(C) Polynesian sailors use te lapa to navigate by following the light towards an island, but Kent State professor Richard Feinberg has expressed skepticism about the usefulness of te lapa for that purpose.

(D) Kent State professor Richard Feinberg has expressed skepticism about the usefulness of te lapa—flashing lights on or under the surface of the ocean—for navigation.

STOP
**If you finish before time is called, you may check your work on this module only.
Do not turn to any other module in the test.**

THIS PAGE LEFT INTENTIONALLY BLANK.

Test 3—Math
Module 1

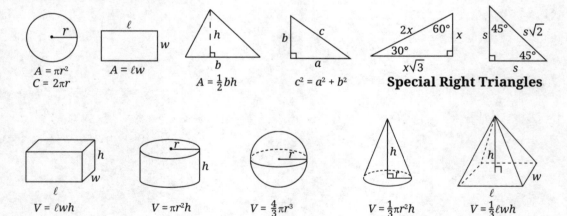
CONTINUE

For multiple-choice questions, solve each problem, choose the correct answer from the choices provided, and then fill in the circle with the answer letter. Enter only one answer for each question. You will not get credit for questions with more than one answer entered or for questions with no answers entered.

For student-produced response questions, solve each problem and write your answer in the test book as described below.

- Enter your answer into the box provided.
- If you find **more than one correct answer**, enter only one answer.
- Your answer can be up to 5 characters for a **positive** answer and up to 6 characters (including the negative sign) for a **negative** answer.
- If your answer is a **fraction** that is too long (over 5 characters for positive, 6 characters for negative), write the decimal equivalent.
- If your answer is a **decimal** that is too long (over 5 characters for positive, 6 characters for negative), truncate it or round at the fourth digit.
- If your answer is a **mixed number** (such as $3\frac{1}{2}$), write it as an improper fraction (7/2) or its decimal equivalent (3.5).
- Don't enter **symbols** such as a percent sign, comma, or dollar sign in your answer.

CONTINUE ➡

1 ☐ Mark for Review

If $4s = 28$, what is the value of $8s + 13$?

Ⓐ 7

Ⓑ 56

Ⓒ 69

Ⓓ 84

2 ☐ Mark for Review

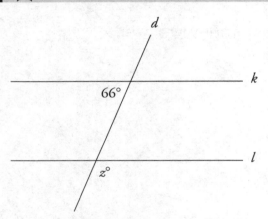

Note: Figure not drawn to scale.

In the figure, line k is parallel to line l. What is the value of z?

Ⓐ 24

Ⓑ 66

Ⓒ 106

Ⓓ 114

3 ☐ Mark for Review

Infant	Height	Infant	Height
A	25	G	22
B	22	H	26
C	23	I	30
D	27	J	21
E	24	K	27
F	30	L	25

The table shows the heights, in inches, of 12 infants at a daycare. According to the table, what is the mean height, in inches, of these infants?

4 ☐ Mark for Review

During a certain week, Jan worked j hours each day for 3 days, and Noah worked n hours each day for 5 days. Which of the following represents the total combined number of hours worked that week by Jan and Noah?

Ⓐ $3j + 5n$

Ⓑ $5j + 3n$

Ⓒ $8jn$

Ⓓ $15jn$

CONTINUE

5 ☐ Mark for Review

Which of the following is equivalent to $b^{\frac{3}{4}}$ for all values of b?

Ⓐ $\sqrt[4]{b^{\frac{1}{3}}}$

Ⓑ $\sqrt[4]{3b}$

Ⓒ $\sqrt[4]{b^3}$

Ⓓ $\sqrt[3]{b^4}$

6 ☐ Mark for Review

| Species | Eye color | | Total |
	Yellow	Brown	
Grey wolf	16	2	18
Coyote	7	5	12
Total	23	7	30

The table shows the distribution by species and eye color for the 30 canids living in a nature conservancy. If one canid is selected at random, what is the probability that it will be either a grey wolf with yellow eyes or a coyote with brown eyes?

Ⓐ $\frac{11}{30}$

Ⓑ $\frac{17}{30}$

Ⓒ $\frac{21}{30}$

Ⓓ $\frac{23}{30}$

7 ☐ Mark for Review

A random sample of 75 students in a first-year medical school class of 265 students was surveyed to determine the distribution of blood types among the students. Based on the survey, it is estimated that 39% of the students have O-positive blood type, with an associated margin of error of 6%. Based on these results, what is a plausible number of students out of the entire first-year class who have O-positive blood type?

Ⓐ 16

Ⓑ 39

Ⓒ 74

Ⓓ 100

8 ☐ Mark for Review

$$w = 3{,}150 + 450l$$

A marine biologist uses the given equation to estimate the weight, w, of a mature great white shark, in pounds, in terms of the shark's fork length, l, in feet. Based on the equation, what is the estimated weight increase, in pounds, for each foot of growth in fork length in a great white shark?

Ⓐ 450

Ⓑ 1,350

Ⓒ 2,700

Ⓓ 3,150

CONTINUE

9 ☐ Mark for Review

$$|2x - 6| + 6 = 74$$

For the given equation, which of the following is a possible value of x?

Ⓐ −37

Ⓑ −31

Ⓒ 31

Ⓓ 34

10 ☐ Mark for Review

At the end of each year, an item loses 6% of the value that it had at the beginning of the year. What type of function best represents this scenario?

Ⓐ Decreasing exponential

Ⓑ Decreasing linear

Ⓒ Increasing exponential

Ⓓ Increasing linear

11 ☐ Mark for Review

The function f is defined by $f(x) = \frac{5}{3}x + k$, where k is a constant. If $f(90) = 120$, what is the value of $f(-30)$?

Ⓐ −120

Ⓑ −80

Ⓒ −30

Ⓓ −20

12 ☐ Mark for Review

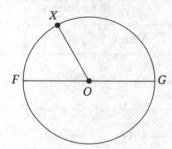

The circle shown has center O, and $\overline{FG}$ is a diameter. If the length of arc FXG is 14π, what is the length of line segment $\overline{XO}$?

Ⓐ 7

Ⓑ 14

Ⓒ 28

Ⓓ 56

CONTINUE

---

13 ☐ Mark for Review

$$x + y = -10$$
$$2x + y = -33$$

What is the value of y in the system of equations shown?

[____]

14 ☐ Mark for Review

A bank account contains \$5,400 today. The account earns interest annually at a rate of 7%. The bank uses the equation $A = 5,400(r)^y$ to determine the amount of money in the account, A, after y years if no other deposits or withdrawals are made. To the nearest whole dollar, how much money will be in the account four years from now?

(A) \$4,039

(B) \$5,778

(C) \$6,912

(D) \$7,078

15 ☐ Mark for Review

$$G = \frac{ab}{d^2}$$

The given equation relates a, b, d, and G, which are distinct constants. Which of the following equations correctly expresses d^2 in terms of a, b, and G?

(A) $d^2 = \dfrac{Gb}{a}$

(B) $d^2 = \dfrac{Ga}{b}$

(C) $d^2 = \dfrac{ab}{G}$

(D) $d^2 = \dfrac{G}{ab}$

16 ☐ Mark for Review

In the xy-plane, the line determined by the points $(c, 3)$ and $(27, c)$ intersects the origin. Which of the following could be the value of c?

(A) 0

(B) 3

(C) 6

(D) 9

CONTINUE ➡

17 ☐ Mark for Review

A certain cone has a height of 15 centimeters (cm) and a volume of 80π cm^3. What is the diameter, in cm, of this cone?

Ⓐ 4

Ⓑ 8

Ⓒ 16

Ⓓ 32

18 ☐ Mark for Review

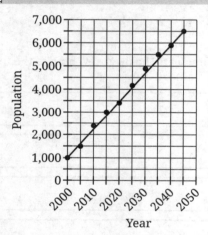

The scatterplot shows the population of town T starting in 2000 and projected through 2045. According to the line of best fit, which of the following best approximates the year in which the population of town T is projected to reach 5,000?

Ⓐ 2027

Ⓑ 2032

Ⓒ 2038

Ⓓ 2043

19 ☐ Mark for Review

In triangle DEF, angle D is a right angle. If $\sin(E) = \frac{21}{29}$, what is the value of $\sin(F)$?

20 ☐ Mark for Review

If $x = 3\sqrt{5}$ and $5x = \sqrt{5y}$, what is the value of y?

CONTINUE ➤

---

21 ☐ Mark for Review

At 9:00 A.M. on Monday, a trash can with a capacity of 20 cubic feet contains 8 cubic feet of garbage. Each day after Monday, 3 cubic feet of garbage are added to the trash can. If no garbage is removed and d represents the number of days after Monday, which of the following inequalities describes the set of days for which the trash can is full or overflowing?

Ⓐ $8 + 3d \geq 20$

Ⓑ $12 \geq 3d$

Ⓒ $20 - 3 \leq d$

Ⓓ $20 \leq 3d$

22 ☐ Mark for Review

The equation of a parabola is written in the standard form $y = ax^2 + bx + c$, where a, b, and c are constants. When graphed in the xy-plane, the parabola reaches its maximum at $(-3, 8)$. Which of the following could be equivalent to $a + b + c$?

Ⓐ -8

Ⓑ 8

Ⓒ 16

Ⓓ 24

YIELD

Once you've finished (or run out of time for) this section, use the answer key to determine how many questions you got right. If you got fewer than 14 questions right, move on to Module 2—Easier, otherwise move on to Module 2—Harder.

Test 3—Math
Module 2—Easier

The questions in this section address a number of important math skills.
Use of a calculator is permitted for all questions.

NOTES

Unless otherwise indicated:

- All variables and expressions represent real numbers.
- Figures provided are drawn to scale.
- All figures lie in a plane.
- The domain of a given function f is the set of all real numbers x for which $f(x)$ is a real number.

REFERENCE

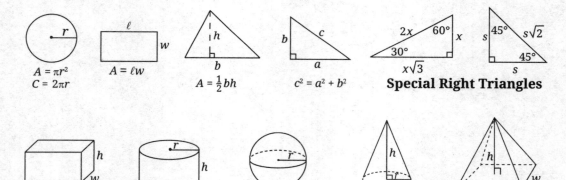

$A = \pi r^2$
$C = 2\pi r$

$A = \ell w$

$A = \frac{1}{2}bh$

$c^2 = a^2 + b^2$

Special Right Triangles

$V = \ell w h$

$V = \pi r^2 h$

$V = \frac{4}{3}\pi r^3$

$V = \frac{1}{3}\pi r^2 h$

$V = \frac{1}{3}\ell w h$

The number of degrees of arc in a circle is 360.
The number of radians of arc in a circle is 2π.
The sum of the measures in degrees of the angles of a triangle is 180.

CONTINUE

For multiple-choice questions, solve each problem, choose the correct answer from the choices provided, and then fill in the circle with the answer letter. Enter only one answer for each question. You will not get credit for questions with more than one answer entered or for questions with no answers entered.

For student-produced response questions, solve each problem and write your answer in the test book as described below.

- Enter your answer into the box provided.
- If you find **more than one correct answer**, enter only one answer.
- Your answer can be up to 5 characters for a **positive** answer and up to 6 characters (including the negative sign) for a **negative** answer.
- If your answer is a **fraction** that is too long (over 5 characters for positive, 6 characters for negative), write the decimal equivalent.
- If your answer is a **decimal** that is too long (over 5 characters for positive, 6 characters for negative), truncate it or round at the fourth digit.
- If your answer is a **mixed number** (such as $3\frac{1}{2}$), write it as an improper fraction (7/2) or its decimal equivalent (3.5).
- Don't enter **symbols** such as a percent sign, comma, or dollar sign in your answer.

CONTINUE →

1 ☐ Mark for Review

What is 90% of 1,000?

Ⓐ 90

Ⓑ 100

Ⓒ 900

Ⓓ 910

2 ☐ Mark for Review

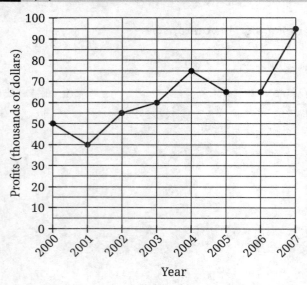

The line graph shows the annual profits of a particular clothing store from 2000 to 2007. According to the graph, in which year was the store's profit the least?

Ⓐ 2000

Ⓑ 2001

Ⓒ 2004

Ⓓ 2007

3 ☐ Mark for Review

If $y^2 = 36$ and $y < 0$, what is the value of y?

4 ☐ Mark for Review

A contractor creates a mosaic floor pattern in which there are 9 blue tiles for every 80 tiles in total. At this rate, how many blue tiles will there be in a floor pattern of 4,800 tiles?

5 ☐ Mark for Review

When 6 times a number a is subtracted from 15, the result is the number b. Which of the following equations represents the relationship between a and b?

Ⓐ $\frac{15}{6a} = b$

Ⓑ $6a - 15 = b$

Ⓒ $15 - 6a = b$

Ⓓ $90a = b$

CONTINUE ➤

6 ☐ Mark for Review

The function g is defined by the equation $g(x) = 4x - 7$. What is the value of $g(x)$ when $x = -3$?

(A) -19

(B) -1

(C) 1

(D) 5

7 ☐ Mark for Review

The circumference of a circle is 56π. What is the radius of the circle?

8 ☐ Mark for Review

The number of members of a club in April was three times the number of members of the club in February. If the club had 27 members in April and m members in February, which of the following equations is true?

(A) $\frac{m}{3} = 27$

(B) $m + 27 = 3$

(C) $3m = 27$

(D) $27m = 3$

9 ☐ Mark for Review

If $4x = 20$, what is the value of $12x - 4$?

10 ☐ Mark for Review

$$g(x) = 2x^2 - 16$$

The function g is defined by the given equation. What is the value of $g(2)$?

(A) -12

(B) -8

(C) 0

(D) 3

11 ☐ Mark for Review

A ride-sharing service uses the function $g(x) = 2.40 + 0.30x$ to calculate the total charge, in dollars, for a ride that is x miles long. How long, in miles, was a ride that had a total charge of $3.60?

(A) 2

(B) 3

(C) 4

(D) 12

CONTINUE

12 ☐ Mark for Review

Which expression is equivalent to $(4x^2 + 3x - 2) - (3x^2 - 8x + 9)$?

Ⓐ $x^2 - 5x - 11$

Ⓑ $x^2 + 11x - 11$

Ⓒ $x^2 + 11x + 7$

Ⓓ $7x^2 + 11x - 11$

13 ☐ Mark for Review

x	1	2	3	4	5
$g(x)$	−3	1	5	9	13

The table shows selected values of the linear function g. Which of the following best defines g?

Ⓐ $g(x) = x - 1$

Ⓑ $g(x) = 2x - 4$

Ⓒ $g(x) = 3x - 5$

Ⓓ $g(x) = 4x - 7$

14 ☐ Mark for Review

$$4x - 1 \leq y$$
$$2 > x + y$$

Which of the following ordered pairs (x, y) satisfies the given system of inequalities?

Ⓐ $(-3, -1)$

Ⓑ $(2, -5)$

Ⓒ $(3, 1)$

Ⓓ $(4, -1)$

15 ☐ Mark for Review

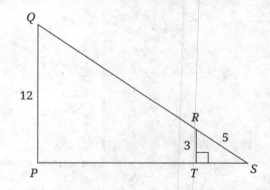

In the figure, $\overline{PQ}$ is parallel to $\overline{RT}$. What is the length of $\overline{PS}$?

CONTINUE

16 ⬜ Mark for Review

The population of a small town is currently 800. It is estimated that the population of the town will decrease by 14% per year for the next five years. This estimate is modeled by the equation $P = 800(k)^x$, where P is the population of the town after x years. What value should be used for k in this model?

17 ⬜ Mark for Review

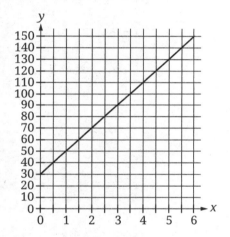

The graph shows the relationship between x and y. Which of the following could be the equation of the graph?

Ⓐ $y = 25x$

Ⓑ $y = x + 30$

Ⓒ $y = 10x + 30$

Ⓓ $y = 20x + 30$

18 ⬜ Mark for Review

$$g(x) = \sqrt{4x^2 + 28}$$

The function g is defined by the given equation. For what value of x does $g(x) = 8$?

Ⓐ 3

Ⓑ 4

Ⓒ 5

Ⓓ 6

19 ⬜ Mark for Review

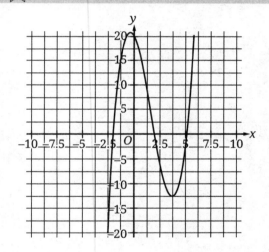

The function f is graphed in the xy-plane, where $y = f(x)$. Which of the following could be the equation of $f(x)$?

Ⓐ $f(x) = (x - 5)(x - 2)^2$

Ⓑ $f(x) = (x - 5)(x - 2)(x + 2)$

Ⓒ $f(x) = (x - 2)(x + 2)(x + 5)$

Ⓓ $f(x) = (x + 5)(x + 2)^2$

CONTINUE ▶

20 ☐ Mark for Review

When three numbers are added together, the result is 665. The largest number is four-thirds the sum of the other two numbers. What is the value of the largest number?

Ⓐ 95

Ⓑ 245

Ⓒ 350

Ⓓ 380

21 ☐ Mark for Review

$$y = x^2 + 2x + k$$
$$y = 2x$$

If the given system of equations has exactly one real solution, which of the following is the value of k?

Ⓐ −4

Ⓑ 0

Ⓒ 2

Ⓓ 4

CONTINUE

22 ☐ Mark for Review

$$LM = 180$$
$$MN = 385$$
$$NL = 425$$

Triangles LMN and PQR are similar right triangles, where L corresponds to P and M corresponds to Q. The side lengths of triangle LMN are shown. What is the value of $\cos R$?

Ⓐ $\frac{36}{85}$

Ⓑ $\frac{36}{77}$

Ⓒ $\frac{77}{85}$

Ⓓ $\frac{85}{36}$

STOP
**If you finish before time is called, you may check your work on this module only.
Do not turn to any other module.**

Test 3—Math
Module 2—Harder

CONTINUE

For multiple-choice questions, solve each problem, choose the correct answer from the choices provided, and then fill in the circle with the answer letter. Enter only one answer for each question. You will not get credit for questions with more than one answer entered or for questions with no answers entered.

For student-produced response questions, solve each problem and write your answer in the test book as described below.

- Enter your answer into the box provided.
- If you find **more than one correct answer**, enter only one answer.
- Your answer can be up to 5 characters for a **positive** answer and up to 6 characters (including the negative sign) for a **negative** answer.
- If your answer is a **fraction** that is too long (over 5 characters for positive, 6 characters for negative), write the decimal equivalent.
- If your answer is a **decimal** that is too long (over 5 characters for positive, 6 characters for negative), truncate it or round at the fourth digit.
- If your answer is a **mixed number** (such as $3\frac{1}{2}$), write it as an improper fraction (7/2) or its decimal equivalent (3.5).
- Don't enter **symbols** such as a percent sign, comma, or dollar sign in your answer.

CONTINUE ➡

---

1 ☐ Mark for Review

The expression $5a^3 - 3a^3 + 6a^2$ is equivalent to which of the following expressions?

Ⓐ $2a^3 + 6a^2$

Ⓑ $5a^3 + 3a^2$

Ⓒ $6a^2 - 15a^6$

Ⓓ $8a^2$

2 ☐ Mark for Review

x	$g(x)$
2	–4
3	–2
4	0
5	2

The table shows four values of x and their corresponding values of $g(x)$ for function g. Which equation defines function g?

Ⓐ $g(x) = x - 6$

Ⓑ $g(x) = 2x - 8$

Ⓒ $g(x) = 3x - 12$

Ⓓ $g(x) = 4x - 12$

3 ☐ Mark for Review

Yesterday, Tiki cycled 13 fewer miles than Irina. If the two of them cycled a total of 51 miles yesterday, how many miles did Irina cycle?

Ⓐ 19

Ⓑ 32

Ⓒ 38

Ⓓ 64

4 ☐ Mark for Review

$$8x - 5y = 27$$
$$5x + 10y = 30$$

The solution set of the given system of equations is (x, y). What is the value of y?

5 ☐ Mark for Review

$$g(x) = 2x^2 - kx + 14$$

Function g is defined by the given equation. If the graph of function g in the xy-plane contains the point $(4, -2)$, what is the value of k?

CONTINUE

6 ☐ Mark for Review

The total rainfall, in inches, for a certain county from 2010 to 2020 can be modeled by the equation $y = -0.14x + 7.8$, where x is the number of years since 2010 and y is the total annual rainfall. Which of the following is the best interpretation of the number -0.14 in this context?

Ⓐ The total annual rainfall in 2010

Ⓑ The total annual rainfall in 2020

Ⓒ The difference between the total rainfall in 2010 and the total rainfall in 2020

Ⓓ The decrease in average rainfall per year from 2010 to 2020

7 ☐ Mark for Review

$$3y < 7$$
$$x < 3y + 4$$

If the point (x, y) is a solution to the given system of inequalities, what is the greatest possible integer value of x?

☐

8 ☐ Mark for Review

$$-3x + 4y = 5$$

In the xy-plane, the graph of which of the following equations is perpendicular to the graph of the given equation?

Ⓐ $3x + 6y = 5$

Ⓑ $3x + 8y = 2$

Ⓒ $4x + 3y = 5$

Ⓓ $4x + 6y = 5$

9 ☐ Mark for Review

Banerji currently owns 6,500 baseball cards. He is gradually selling his collection and estimates that the number of cards he owns will decrease by 20 percent every 6 months. Which of the following functions best models Banerji's estimate of the number of baseball cards, B, he will own m months from now?

Ⓐ $B(m) = 6,500(0.2)^{\frac{m}{6}}$

Ⓑ $B(m) = 6,500(0.2)^{6m}$

Ⓒ $B(m) = 6,500(0.8)^{\frac{m}{6}}$

Ⓓ $B(m) = 6,500(0.8)^{6m}$

CONTINUE →

10 ⚑ Mark for Review

The volume of a cube is $v = \frac{1}{8}c^3$, where c is a positive constant. Which of the following gives the surface area of the cube?

Ⓐ $6\left(\frac{c}{2}\right)^2$

Ⓑ $6\left(\frac{c^2}{2}\right)$

Ⓒ $6c^2$

Ⓓ $12c^2$

11 ⚑ Mark for Review

$$y = (x - 7)(3x + 4)$$
$$x = 3y - 1$$

At how many points do the graphs of the given equations intersect in the xy-plane?

Ⓐ Exactly one

Ⓑ Exactly two

Ⓒ Infinitely many

Ⓓ Zero

12 ⚑ Mark for Review

Jessica owns a store that sells only laptops and tablets. Last week, her store sold 90 laptops and 210 tablets. This week, the sales, in number of units, of laptops increased by 50 percent, and the sales, in number of units, of tablets increased by 30 percent. By what percentage did total sales, in units, in Jessica's store increase?

Ⓐ 20 percent

Ⓑ 25 percent

Ⓒ 36 percent

Ⓓ 80 percent

13 ⚑ Mark for Review

$$-2(5 - 9x) = 6(3x + 4)$$

The given equation has how many solutions?

Ⓐ Exactly one

Ⓑ Exactly two

Ⓒ Infinitely many

Ⓓ Zero

CONTINUE ➡

14 Mark for Review

The mean weight of 6 people in an elevator is 160.5 pounds. If the person with the lowest weight gets off, the mean weight of the remaining 5 people becomes 168 pounds. What is the weight, in pounds, of the person with the lowest weight?

15 Mark for Review

$$4x^2 - 5x = k$$

In the given equation, k is a constant. If the equation has two real solutions, which of the following could be the value of k?

(A) -4

(B) -3

(C) -2

(D) -1

16 Mark for Review

$$x^2 = y$$
$$6x + 9 = -3(2y - 3)$$

If (x, y) is a solution to the given system of equations and $x < 0$, what is the value of xy?

(A) -3

(B) -2

(C) -1

(D) 1

17 Mark for Review

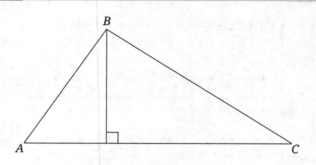

In triangle ABC, $\sin(A) = \cos(C)$. If angle A measures $6m - 9$ degrees and angle C measures $8m - 6$ degrees, what is the value of m?

(A) 5.4

(B) 7.5

(C) 10.5

(D) 13.5

CONTINUE

---

18 ☐ Mark for Review

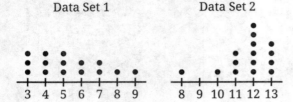

Data Set 1   Data Set 2

The dot plots represent 15 values in data set 1 and 15 values in data set 2. Which of the following statements about the standard deviations and ranges of the two data sets is true?

(A) The standard deviation of data set 1 is less than the standard deviation of data set 2, and the range of data set 1 is greater than the range of data set 2.

(B) The standard deviation of data set 1 is less than the standard deviation of data set 2, and the range of data set 1 is equal to the range of data set 2.

(C) The standard deviation of data set 1 is greater than the standard deviation of data set 2, and the range of data set 1 is equal to the range of data set 2.

(D) The standard deviation of data set 1 is greater than the standard deviation of data set 2, and the range of data set 1 is greater than the range of data set 2.

19 ☐ Mark for Review

$$\frac{1}{2}x + ay = 16$$

$$4y = 48 - bx$$

In the given system of equations, a and b are constants. If there are infinitely many solutions to this system, what is the value of $a + b$?

20 ☐ Mark for Review

In the equation $43x^2 + (43d + e)x + de = 0$, d and e are positive constants. If the sum of the solutions to the given equation is $k(43d + e)$, where k is a constant, what is the value of k?

(A) $-\frac{1}{45}$

(B) $-\frac{1}{43}$

(C) 43

(D) 45

CONTINUE →

21 ☐ Mark for Review

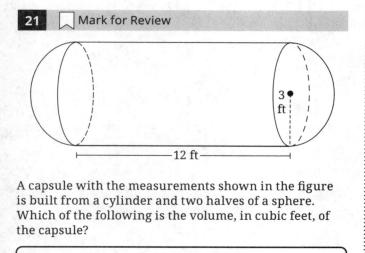

A capsule with the measurements shown in the figure is built from a cylinder and two halves of a sphere. Which of the following is the volume, in cubic feet, of the capsule?

(A) 108π

(B) 126π

(C) 144π

(D) 180π

22 ☐ Mark for Review

In the xy-plane, the graph of $4x^2 + 20x + 4y^2 - 12y = 110$ is a circle. What is the radius of the circle?

[____]

STOP

**If you finish before time is called, you may check your work on this module only.
Do not turn to any other module.**

Chapter 6
Practice Test 3:
Answers and
Explanations

PRACTICE TEST 3: ANSWER KEY

Reading and Writing		
Module 1	Module 2 (Easier)	Module 2 (Harder)
1. A	1. A	1. B
2. B	2. D	2. B
3. D	3. A	3. D
4. A	4. A	4. C
5. A	5. C	5. B
6. B	6. D	6. C
7. D	7. D	7. A
8. A	8. D	8. C
9. C	9. B	9. C
10. B	10. B	10. D
11. A	11. D	11. D
12. D	12. D	12. A
13. A	13. A	13. C
14. B	14. D	14. B
15. D	15. A	15. D
16. C	16. D	16. B
17. D	17. A	17. C
18. C	18. A	18. C
19. A	19. A	19. A
20. A	20. B	20. B
21. A	21. B	21. C
22. A	22. D	22. B
23. A	23. D	23. B
24. D	24. D	24. B
25. D	25. B	25. A
26. D	26. D	26. D
27. A	27. B	27. C

Math		
Module 1	Module 2 (Easier)	Module 2 (Harder)
1. C	1. C	1. A
2. D	2. B	2. B
3. 25.16 or 25.17	3. −6	3. B
4. A	4. 540	4. 1
5. C	5. C	5. 12
6. C	6. A	6. D
7. D	7. 28	7. 10
8. A	8. C	8. C
9. B	9. 56	9. C
10. A	10. B	10. A
11. B	11. C	11. B
12. B	12. B	12. C
13. 13	13. D	13. D
14. D	14. A	14. 123
15. C	15. 16	15. D
16. D	16. 0.86 or .86	16. C
17. B	17. D	17. B
18. B	18. A	18. D
19. $\frac{20}{29}$	19. B	19. $\frac{17}{6}$ or 2.833
20. 225	20. D	20. B
21. A	21. B	21. C
22. A	22. C	22. 6

PRACTICE TEST 3—READING AND WRITING EXPLANATIONS

Module 1

1. **A** This is a Vocabulary question, as it asks for *the most logical and precise word or phrase*. Read the text and highlight what can help to fill in the blank, which describes the *performances*. The text describes the group as *working to preserve customary songs and dances* and mentions the *centuries-old ritual*. Write "customary" in the annotation box and use process of elimination.

   • (A) is correct because it matches with "customary."

   • (B) is wrong because *obscure* means "little-known."

   • (C) is wrong because *discreet* means "not publicly shown."

   • (D) is wrong because *eccentric* means "unusual."

2. **B** This is a Vocabulary question, as it asks for *the most logical and precise word or phrase*. Read the text and highlight what can help to fill in the blank, which describes the *center*. The text says that it is *filled with throngs of people* and later mentions *crowds*, so write "crowded" in the annotation box and use process of elimination.

   • (A) is wrong because *formal* means "done ceremoniously."

   • (B) is correct because *bustling* matches with "crowded."

   • (C) is wrong because *unpredictable* doesn't match with "crowded."

   • (D) is wrong because *deserted* is the opposite of "crowded."

3. **D** This is a Vocabulary question, as it asks for *the most logical and precise word or phrase*. Read the text and highlight what can help to fill in the blank, which refers to something that can happen during *the procedure*. The text states that Peyman's research allowed him to *reduce the incidence* of something, and considering the positive tone of the text, he accomplished something good. Therefore, he must have reduced the incidence of "bad things happening." Write that in the annotation box and use process of elimination.

   • (A) is wrong because *characteristics* doesn't match with "bad things happening."

   • (B) and (C) are wrong because they are positive words.

   • (D) is correct because *repercussions* matches with "bad things happening."

4. **A**   This is a Vocabulary question, as it asks for *the most logical and precise word or phrase*. Read the text and highlight what can help to fill in the blank, which refers to what rainwater does *in a large vessel*. The text describes *gathering and reserving water*, so the vessel must "gather" the water. Write "gathered" in the annotation box and use process of elimination.

    - (A) is correct because *aggregated* means "collected together."

    - (B) is wrong because *dissipated* means "went away," which is the opposite.

    - (C) is wrong because *percolated* means "filtered through."

    - (D) is wrong because *collaborated* means "worked as a team."

5. **A**   This is a Vocabulary question, as it asks for the most logical and precise word or phrase. Read the text and highlight what can help to fill in the blank, which refers to what *scientists* were *finally able to* do with respect to *the existence of the long-predicted Higgs boson particle*. The final sentence says *These scientists confirmed* something that *could be explained only by the Higgs boson particle*, so write "confirm" in the annotation box and use process of elimination.

    - (A) is correct because it matches with "confirm."

    - (B) is wrong because *exonerate* means "free from blame."

    - (C) is wrong because *contextualize* means "give background information."

    - (D) is wrong because *postulate* means "theorize."

6. **B**   This is a Vocabulary question, as it asks for *the most logical and precise word or phrase*. Read the text and highlight what can help to fill in the blank, which refers to what King did to *his commitment to nonviolent resistance*. The first part of the sentence is followed by a colon, which suggests that the second part will expand on the first. It states that *his actions revealed his unwavering dedication to advancing the cause...without resorting to violence*, which suggests that he was committed to nonviolent resistance and showed it through his actions. Write "showed" in the annotation box and use process of elimination.

    - (A) is wrong because he didn't *characterize* his commitment through his actions.

    - (B) is correct because *evinced* means "showed clearly."

    - (C) is wrong because *elided* means "passed over."

    - (D) is wrong because *gauged* means "assessed."

7. **D** This is a Purpose question, as it asks for the *function* of a sentence. Read the text and highlight what can help to understand the function of the underlined sentence. The text introduces an *experiment* and states the *evidence* provided by the experiment. Then, in the underlined sentence, the text explains what was done in the experiment. Write "describe the experiment" in the annotation box and use process of elimination.

- (A) is wrong because the *results* are given in other sentences, not the underlined one.

- (B) is wrong because this sentence doesn't mention any *difficulty*.

- (C) is wrong because the sentence gives an overall explanation of the study, not *a specific instance*.

- (D) is correct because it matches the annotation.

8. **A** This is a Retrieval question, as it says *According to the text*. Read the text and highlight what it says about the *granddaughter and grandfather*. The third sentence says *There was a strong family resemblance between them*, and the text goes on to describe how they were *struck from the same matrix* but differ because of their ages. Eliminate any answer that isn't supported by the text.

- (A) is correct because it matches with *strong family resemblance between them*.

- (B) is wrong because the text says that they would make one think of *beautiful Greek medals struck from the same matrix*, not that they are *of Greek heritage*.

- (C) is wrong because neither is described as looking *younger*.

- (D) is wrong because the text states that the granddaughter *knelt* near the grandfather.

9. **C** This is a Charts question, as it asks for *data from the graph*. The graph charts the number of pigeons in both spring and winter, based on the number of restaurants nearby. Highlight the conclusion in the text, which is that *there is indeed a relationship between proximity to restaurants and abundance of rock pigeons* and *this relationship was especially strong in the spring*. Look at the line for spring and eliminate any answers that are inconsistent with the graph or don't support the conclusion.

- (A) is wrong because *three restaurants* doesn't correspond with *ten rock pigeons*.

- (B) is wrong because these numbers are consistent with the winter line, but the conclusion is about *spring*.

- (C) is correct because the information is consistent with the graph and the conclusion.

- (D) is wrong because *more than thirty rock pigeons* weren't observed anywhere.

10.   **B**   This is a Main Idea question, as it asks for the *main idea*. Read and highlight the main phrases or lines that the other sentences seem to support. The text introduces Wickramasinghe's viewpoint, that *life on Earth originated from microorganisms that were carried to our planet by comets or other celestial bodies*. Then, it mentions the *sources of scientific data* that Wickramasinghe uses to support this view. Write "CW thinks life came from space" in the annotation box and use process of elimination.

- (A) is wrong because the text describes the theory as *controversial* but doesn't go so far as to say that it can't be *accepted by other astrobiologists*.

- (B) is correct because it matches the annotation.

- (C) is wrong because the text describes the theory as *controversial* and does not state that the *preponderance* (majority) of data *strongly supports* the theory.

- (D) is wrong because the main idea is about Wickramasinghe's theory, not specifics about *microorganisms*.

11.   **A**   This is a Claims question, as it asks for an answer that would *strengthen the potential explanation*. Read the text and highlight the *potential explanation*, which is that *metabolizing sorbitol prevents C. difficile from producing toxins*. Read more of the text to understand what this is explaining. The third sentence says that *higher levels of sorbitol…were found to be released* as a result of *C. difficile* inflammation. Then the text describes a study in which *mice that ingested sorbitol were found to have lower levels of toxin production than mice that did not ingest sorbitol*. Eliminate answers that don't *strengthen* the given explanation for this outcome.

- (A) is correct because it provides a reason that ingesting sorbitol would reduce the production of toxins.

- (B) and (D) are wrong because they don't mention *toxins*.

- (C) is wrong because giving sorbitol to the mice caused *lower levels of toxins*, so *Low levels of sorbitol* preventing toxin production contradicts the explanation.

12.   **D**   This is a Conclusions question, as it asks for the choice that *most logically completes the text*. Read the text and highlight the main ideas. The text states that *Scholars generally agree that amputations were dangerous and deadly prior to 10,000 years ago* and then states that the first known *successful limb-removal surgery* was 7,000 years ago. Then, the text describes a recent discovery of a *31,000-year-old skeleton* that had a successful amputation. Eliminate any answer that states a conclusion that isn't supported by the text.

- (A) is wrong because the text doesn't provide evidence suggesting that it must have been a *doctor* who did the amputation.

- (B) is wrong because there is no information on *life as an amputee* or *post-operational care*.

- (C) is wrong because the text offers no information about *most amputations*.

- (D) is correct because the text contrasts the viewpoint that *a lack of proper surgical tools and techniques* prevented successful amputations prior to 10,000 years ago with the fact that a successful one did occur long before that.

13. **A** This is a Conclusions question, as it asks for the choice that *most logically completes the text*. Read the text and highlight the main ideas. The text introduces *the prisoner's dilemma* and then describes possible outcomes. Then it explains that *Game theorists generally agree that the choice to cooperate…is irrational, as it defies one's self-interest*, suggesting that the choice to not cooperate (betray the other person) is rational. Eliminate any answer that states a conclusion that isn't supported by the text.

- (A) is correct because it logically follows from the information in the last sentence.

- (B) is wrong because, while this might provide a benefit to both people, the *game theorists* are focused on what is *rational*, which the text says refers to acting in *one's self-interest*.

- (C) is wrong because it's too strong; there is no evidence that people *always* act in their self-interest, even if the text says that this is *rational*.

- (D) is wrong because there is no information in the text regarding the *relevance* of the thought experiment to *everyday life*.

14. **B** In this Rules question, pronouns and apostrophes are changing in the answer choices, so it's testing consistency with pronouns. Find and highlight the phrase that the pronoun refers back to: *Karni Mata Temple*. This phrase is singular, so in order to be consistent, a singular pronoun is needed. Eliminate any answer that isn't consistent with *Karni Mata Temple* or is incorrectly punctuated.

- (A) is wrong because it means "it is."

- (B) is correct because it is singular and possessive.

- (C) and (D) are wrong because they are plural.

15. **D** In this Rules question, punctuation is changing in the answer choices. The first part of the sentence says *In addition to her research into the effects of hormones, ultraviolet light, and chemotherapy agents on cell division*, which is an introductory phrase that is not essential to the meaning of the sentence. It should therefore be followed by a comma to separate it from the rest of the sentence. Eliminate answers that do not have a comma.

- (A), (B), and (C) are wrong because they don't use a comma.

- (D) is correct because it uses a comma after the non-essential information.

16. **C** In this Rules question, punctuation is changing in the answer choices. Look for independent clauses. The first part of the sentence says *Poetra Asantewa is a performer from Ghana who combines three elements to create her pieces*, which is an independent clause. The second part of the sentence says *lyrics incorporating social issues, vocalization evoking different emotions, and rhythms using soulful elements*, which is a list of what she combines. Eliminate any option that doesn't correctly connect the independent clause to the list.

- (A) is wrong because some punctuation is needed to separate the independent clause from the list.

- (B) is wrong because the comma makes it look like *create her pieces* is part of the list, but it's not.

- (C) is correct because a colon is used when the second part explains the first, such as by providing a list of things.

- (D) is wrong because a semicolon can only connect two independent clauses, and the list isn't an independent clause.

17. **D** In this Rules question, the subjects of the answers are changing, which suggests it may be testing modifiers. Look for and highlight a modifying phrase: *Compared to other Ukrainian scientists and mathematicians*. Whoever is *Compared to* other scientists and mathematicians needs to come immediately after the comma. Eliminate any answer that doesn't start with someone who can be compared to scientists and mathematicians.

- (A) is wrong because *there is* can't be compared with scientists and mathematicians.

- (B) is wrong because *many Ukrainian cities* can't be compared with scientists and mathematicians.

- (C) is wrong because *the range of fields* can't be compared with scientists and mathematicians.

- (D) is correct because *Olena Vaneeva* can be compared with other scientists and mathematicians.

18. **C** In this Rules question, commas and the word *that* are changing in the answers, which suggests that the question is testing the construction of describing phrases. The first part of the sentence says *During the mission, Anders took a photo of Earth rising above the lunar surface*, which is an independent clause followed by a comma. Eliminate any answer that isn't consistent with the first part of the sentence.

- (A) is wrong because a phrase starting with *that* is essential to the meaning of the sentence and never follows a comma.

- (B) is wrong because it creates two independent clauses separated by a comma, which is never allowed.

- (C) is correct because it correctly forms a phrase to describe the *image*.

- (D) is wrong because it leaves the verb *was* with no subject.

19.   **A**   In this Rules question, verbs are changing in the answer choices, so it's testing consistency with verbs. Find and highlight the subject, *writers*, which is plural, so a plural verb is needed. All of the answers work with a plural subject, so look for a clue regarding tense. The previous sentence uses past tense verbs: *was* and *was completed*. Highlight those verbs, which are past tense, and write an annotation that says "past." Eliminate any answer not in past tense.

- (A) is correct because it's in past tense.

- (B) and (D) are wrong because they're in present tense.

- (C) is wrong because it's in future tense.

20.   **A**   In this Rules question, punctuation with a transition is changing in the answer choices. Look for independent clauses. The first part of the sentence says *Françoise Combes has contributed to research about how galaxies form and evolve*. There is an option to add *additionally* to this independent clause, but it's not adding on to a previous idea as nothing came before it. Eliminate options with *additionally* in the first part.

- (A) is correct because it puts *additionally* with the second independent clause and puts a semicolon between the independent clauses.

- (B) and (C) are wrong because the sentence contains two independent clauses, which need some punctuation other than commas to properly connect them.

- (D) is wrong because it puts *additionally* with the first independent clause.

21.   **A**   In this Rules question, commas and semicolons are changing in the answer choices. The sentence already contains a semicolon near the end, and the part after it is not an independent clause, which suggests that the sentence contains a list separated by semicolons. Use the third example to determine the structure of each item: Title, Comma, Description. Make an annotation of this pattern and eliminate any answer that doesn't follow it.

- (A) is correct because it follows the pattern of the third item.

- (B) is wrong because it doesn't have a comma after the title of the second album.

- (C) and (D) are wrong because they don't have a semicolon after the first item.

22.   **A**   This is a Transitions question, so highlight ideas that relate to each other. The preceding sentence says *Cooler room temperatures were found to stimulate fat cells that eradicate the sugar molecules that sustain cancer cells*, and this sentence says *the cancer cells started to die off in the mice exposed to cooler room temperatures*. These ideas agree, so a same-direction transition is needed. Make an annotation that says "agree." Eliminate any answer that doesn't match.

- (A) is correct because *Consequently* is same-direction and conveys that the events of the third sentence happened as a result of what was said in the second sentence.

- (B) is wrong because this sentence is not an example of the previous idea.

- (C) and (D) are wrong because they are opposite-direction transitions.

23. **A** This is a Rhetorical Synthesis question, so highlight the goal(s) stated in the question: *emphasize how Apu changed throughout the trilogy*. Eliminate any answer that doesn't fulfill this purpose.

- (A) is correct because it includes *how Apu changed* and specifies when those changes occurred within the *trilogy*.

- (B) and (C) are wrong because they don't mention a change.

- (D) is wrong because it doesn't explain how the changes occurred in relation to the *trilogy*.

24. **D** This is a Rhetorical Synthesis question, so highlight the goal(s) stated in the question: *emphasize the abilities of haenyeo*. Eliminate any answer that doesn't fulfill this purpose.

- (A) and (B) are wrong because they don't mention any specific abilities.

- (C) is wrong because it doesn't include specific details about the *abilities*.

- (D) is correct because it includes specific details about the *abilities*.

25. **D** This is a Rhetorical Synthesis question, so highlight the goal(s) stated in the question: *describe the history of Heliconian Hall to an audience familiar with the Heliconian Club*. Eliminate any answer that doesn't *describe the history* in a way that assumes the audience is *familiar with the Heliconian Club*.

- (A) is wrong because it explains the *Heliconian Club*, but the audience is already familiar with it.

- (B) and (C) are wrong because they don't *describe the history of Heliconian Hall*.

- (D) is correct because it describes the *history of Heliconian Hall* and doesn't explain the *Heliconian Club* since the audience is familiar with it.

26. **D** This is a Rhetorical Synthesis question, so highlight the goal(s) stated in the question: *introduce Evan Adams and his role in Smoke Signals to a new audience*. Eliminate any answer that doesn't *introduce Evan Adams* in a way that assumes the audience is not familiar with him.

- (A) is wrong because it doesn't focus on Adams's *role in Smoke Signals*.

- (B) is wrong because it doesn't *introduce Evan Adams*.

- (C) is wrong because it doesn't mention Adams's specific *role in Smoke Signals*.

- (D) is correct because it introduces *Evan Adams* and describes *his role in Smoke Signals*.

27. **A** This is a Rhetorical Synthesis question, so highlight the goal(s) stated in the question: *highlight a similarity between fictional depictions of a real-world location*. Eliminate any answer that doesn't fulfill this purpose.

- (A) is correct because it includes a *similarity*.

- (B) and (C) are wrong because they don't include a *similarity*.

- (D) is wrong because the similarity is set up as a contrast with the word *however*.

Module 2 – Easier

1. **A** This is a Vocabulary question, as it asks for *the most logical and precise word or phrase*. Read the text and highlight what can help to fill in the blank, which refers to what *hundreds of scientists* did with regards to *the Manhattan Project*. Right after this, the text says that they were *pooling their efforts and expertise*, so write "worked together on" in the annotation box and use process of elimination.

- (A) is correct because it matches with "worked together on."

- (B), (C), and (D) are wrong because they don't match with "worked together on."

2. **D** This is a Vocabulary question, as it asks for *the most logical and precise word or phrase*. Read the text and highlight what can help to fill in the blank, which refers to something previously mentioned (given the word *This*) that *allows for soil to remain settled while seeds are planted, unlike traditional practices*. Thus, the blank must be another *practice*, and specifically it's *the method of no-till farming*, mentioned in the first sentence. Write "method" in the annotation box and use process of elimination.

- (A) is wrong because *intention* means "goal."

- (B) is wrong because *agenda* means "plan."

- (C) is wrong because *distraction* doesn't match with "method."

- (D) is correct because *technique* matches with "method."

3. **A** This is a Vocabulary question, as it asks for *the most logical and precise word or phrase*. Read the text and highlight what can help to fill in the blank, which comes after the words *This silent*, so it refers to something that was previously mentioned. The first sentence refers to the *"waggle dance"* that allows bees to *communicate with other bees*. Given that the blank is followed by *of information*, the blank must be something like "communication." Write that in the annotation box and use process of elimination.

- (A) is correct because it matches with "communication."

- (B) is wrong because *confidence* doesn't match with "communication."

- (C) is wrong because *prolongation* means "lasting longer than planned."

- (D) is wrong because *devastation* means "destruction."

4. **A**   This is a Vocabulary question, as it asks for *the most logical and precise word or phrase*. Read the text and highlight what can help to fill in the blank, which refers to how chronic hepatitis B *affects Asian Americans and Pacific Islanders*. The second sentence draws a contrast between *everyone* needing to be screened for the disease and AAPIs being particularly encouraged to do so. This suggests that this group of people is overly affected by the disease compared to the general population. Write "overly" in the annotation box and use process of elimination.

- (A) is correct because *disproportionately* means "more or less than the general population."

- (B) is wrong because *exclusively* is too strong; the second sentence states that *everyone should be screened*, so it's not true that the disease only affects AAPIs.

- (C) is wrong because *essentially* means "at its essence."

- (D) is wrong because *initially* means "at the beginning."

5. **C**   This is a Vocabulary question, as it asks for *the most logical and precise word or phrase*. Read the text and highlight what can help to fill in the blank, which refers to how *Scientists* view *canities subita*. The second sentence indicates that scientists have an explanation that contradicts the *stories* from the first sentence, and the part after the blank says *as historical fiction*, which suggests that they think the stories are historical fiction. It is unclear whether the blank suggests a word like "describe" or a word like "reject," so use process of elimination to eliminate any answer that doesn't clearly indicate that the scientists don't believe the stories.

- (A) is wrong because *trivialize* means "portray as unimportant," which doesn't convey the scientists' skepticism.

- (B) is wrong because there is no evidence from the text that scientists are illustrating the condition.

- (C) is correct because *Scientists dismiss this as historical fiction* accurately conveys their viewpoint.

- (D) is wrong because there isn't evidence that scientists are promoting their point of view, just that they disagree with the *stories*.

6. **D**   This is a Vocabulary question, as it asks what a word *most nearly means*. Read the text and highlight what can help to understand the underlined word. Marie instructs Francine to *sweep the carpet* in order to *bring out the colors*, which is one of several instructions given to make the room look nicer. Write "make it look better" in the annotation box and use process of elimination.

- (A) and (B) are wrong because these words wouldn't suggest improving the look of the room.

- (C) is wrong because it would suggest that the carpet doesn't have any color prior to being swept, which isn't implied by the text.

- (D) is correct because emphasizing the colors would help the look of the room.

7. **D** This is a Purpose question, as it asks for the *overall structure*. Read the text and highlight what can help to understand the overall structure. In the text, Elinor mentions *mistakes* she has *frequently* made, thinking someone is a certain way but the person isn't that way. Then, in the last sentence, she says that this is caused by not *giving oneself time to deliberate and judge*, so write "Elinor's mistake and why people make it" in the annotation box and use process of elimination.

- (A) is wrong because Elinor never *promises to be more careful in the future*.

- (B) is wrong because the text isn't about a specific *individual*, and Elinor doesn't rationalize her *mistaken perception*.

- (C) is wrong because it's too strong; *duplicity* (deceitfulness) *of human nature* is much broader than the mistake Elinor mentions, and her assessment of the cause isn't a *warning*.

- (D) is correct because it matches the annotation.

8. **D** This is a Purpose question, as it asks for the *overall structure*. Read the text and highlight what can help to understand the overall structure. The text introduces *afforestation* and then describes the steps that go into that process, so write "how afforestation is done" in the annotation box and use process of elimination.

- (A) is wrong because it only relates to the first sentence, not the *overall structure*.

- (B) is wrong because the text lists the steps for the *strategy*, not the *reasons why the strategy is useful*.

- (C) is wrong because no *negative consequences* are mentioned.

- (D) is correct because it matches the annotation.

9. **B** This is a Dual Texts question, as it has two texts. The question asks what *Newman, Stone, and Schwarz (Text 2)* would *say about the results of the studies discussed in Text 1*. Start by understanding the *results of the studies* in Text 1. Text 1 states that *The results of the studies demonstrated a relationship between nostalgia and authenticity* and then says that this *was found to correlate with greater measurements of all aspects of psychological well-being*. Next, look for a similar idea in Text 2 to see how its author feels about this view. Text 2 begins by acknowledging that *nostalgia is associated with mental health benefits* but then draws a contrast by saying that *there are different types of nostalgia* and *some can be highly destructive*. Then, it describes a study that found that some *more unconscious nostalgic experiences can result in negative mental health effects*. Therefore, the psychologists in Text 2 would "say some kinds of nostalgia are bad." Write that in the annotation box and use process of elimination.

- (A) and (C) are wrong because they are only positive, but the texts express disagreement.

- (B) is correct because it matches the annotation.

- (D) is wrong because Text 2 never mentions *future research*.

10. **B** This is a Charts question, as it asks for *data from the graph*. The graph charts the percentage of participants who chose the sugary drink for a control package and for packaging with various changes. Highlight the conclusion in the text, which is that *the presence of warnings and absence of claims and imagery may reduce the likelihood of purchase, whereas disclosure of percentage of juice may have very little impact*. Eliminate any answers that are inconsistent with the graph or don't support the conclusion.

- (A) is wrong because the claim says that warnings *may reduce likelihood of purchase*, so this statement contradicts the claim.

- (B) is correct because comparing the percent disclosure to the control demonstrates the *little impact* that disclosure had.

- (C) is wrong because it doesn't state what the *impact* of these absences was, so it doesn't support the claim.

- (D) is wrong because the option to select a *low-added sugar fruit drink* isn't in the graph or text.

11. **D** This is a Claims question, as it asks for a *quotation* that *illustrates the claim*. Read the text and highlight the *claim*, which is that *Fernando's friend…is worried and tries to warn him to stay away from the fountain*. Eliminate answers that don't *illustrate* this idea.

- (A) is wrong because it doesn't relate to Fernando going to or staying away from the fountain.

- (B) and (C) are wrong because they don't mention the *fountain*.

- (D) is correct because it provides a warning *not to return to the fountain of the Poplars*.

12. **D** This is a Claims question, as it asks for a *quotation* that *supports the student's claim*. Read the text and highlight the *claim*, which is that *Doerr uses children as his protagonists in order to create a story from an unbiased and hopeful perspective of humanity*. Eliminate answers that don't *support* this idea.

- (A) and (C) are wrong because they don't mention *children*.

- (B) is wrong because *seeks to learn more about the world* doesn't match with *unbiased and hopeful perspective of humanity*.

- (D) is correct because it mentions *children*, the phrase *see the world with an open mind* matches with *unbiased*, and *betterment of humanity* matches with *hopeful perspective of humanity*.

13. **A** This is a Charts question, as it asks for *data from the table*. The graph charts the need satisfaction scale and mood in two stages with respect to human and computer inclusion and exclusion. Highlight the *hypothesis* in the text, which is that *individuals would experience equivalent effects of social exclusion regardless of whether the source of exclusion was human or computer*. Eliminate any answers that are inconsistent with the table or don't support the conclusion.

- (A) is correct because *comparable to* matches with *equivalent effects*, and like the hypothesis, it compares something between humans and computers.

- (B) and (D) are wrong because they don't draw a comparison between human and computer inclusion/exclusion.

- (C) is wrong because it contrasts the *reflective* and *reflexive* stages instead of comparing human and computer inclusion/exclusion.

14. **D** This is a Claims question, as it asks for an answer that would *support Nicholson's claim*. Read the text and highlight the *claim*, which is that *the rock whose impact caused the formation of the undersea crater could have broken off from a parent asteroid that also caused the Chicxulub impact*. Eliminate answers that don't *support* this claim.

- (A), (B), and (C) are wrong because they don't mention the *Chicxulub impact*.

- (D) is correct because if the two sites contain *some of the same minerals not normally found on Earth*, this would suggest that the asteroids that created those craters could have come from the same source.

15. **A** This is a Conclusions question, as it asks for the choice that *most logically completes the text*. Read the text and highlight the main ideas. The text states that *a correlation between* certain things *could indicate which regions of the brain...fell asleep or awoke first*. Then it states that in the experiment *the thalamus* had such a correlation, so it may have fallen asleep or awoken first. Eliminate any answer that states a conclusion that isn't supported by the text.

- (A) is correct because it matches with the correlation stated.

- (B) and (D) are wrong because the text is focused on which regions of the brain fall asleep or awaken first, not what happens during sleep.

- (C) is wrong because it's the opposite of what the text suggests.

16. **D** This is a Conclusions question, as it asks for the choice that *most logically completes the text*. Read the text and highlight the main ideas. The text states that the formula *takes into account not only the weight of the vehicle but also its number of axles*. Then it explains that *a shorter vehicle with its weight concentrated in a smaller area could cause more damage than could a longer vehicle of the same weight whose mass is dispersed*. The text then compares *a two-axle vehicle to a four-axle vehicle*. Eliminate any answer that states a conclusion that isn't supported by the text.

- (A) is wrong because it's the opposite of what the text indicates; a four-axle vehicle would likely be longer and have its weight more dispersed, so it could be heavier.

- (B) is wrong because the text draws a contrast between vehicles of different lengths, not a comparison.

- (C) is wrong because it doesn't relate to the four-axle vehicle.

- (D) is correct because it is consistent with the text, as the two-axle vehicle would likely be shorter and therefore need to have a lower weight, given what the text stated about shorter vehicles.

17.   **A**   In this Rules question, pronouns are changing in the answer choices, so it's testing consistency with pronouns. Find and highlight the word the pronoun refers back to, *students*, which is plural, so a plural pronoun is needed. Write an annotation saying "plural." Eliminate any answer that isn't plural or doesn't clearly refer back to *students*.

- (A) is correct because *they* is plural and is consistent with *students*.

- (B) and (C) are wrong because they are singular.

- (D) is wrong because *we* doesn't refer back to *students*.

18.   **A**   In this Rules question, periods and question marks are changing in the answer choices, so it's testing questions versus statements. The beginning of the sentence states that *Scientists wanted to explore another question related to this topic*, so the second part of the sentence should be a question. Eliminate answers that aren't correctly written as questions.

- (A) is correct because it's correctly written as a question.

- (B) and (D) are wrong because they are statements.

- (C) is wrong because it has a question mark but is written as a statement.

19.   **A**   In this Rules question, punctuation is changing in the answer choices. Look for independent clauses. The first part of the sentence says *For example, green roofs, which are rooftops covered in vegetation, reduce the temperatures of roofs*, which is an independent clause. The second part of the sentence says *while cool pavements, which are made with materials that reflect solar energy, can lower the temperatures above the pavement surface and the surrounding air*, which is a dependent clause. Eliminate any option that doesn't correctly connect an independent + a dependent clause.

- (A) is correct because independent + dependent can be connected with a comma.

- (B), (C), and (D) are wrong because independent + dependent cannot be connected with punctuation other than a comma.

20.   **B**   In this Rules question, verb forms are changing in the answer choices, so it's testing sentence structure. The subject of the sentence is *She*, and the main verb is *focuses*. The second part of the sentence follows *and* and describes a second thing that Sibai does, so the answer must be consistent with *focuses*. Eliminate any answer that isn't consistent with *focuses*.

- (A), (C), and (D) are wrong because they aren't consistent with *focuses*.

- (B) is correct because it's consistent with *focuses*.

21. **B** In this Rules question, punctuation is changing in the answer choices. The last part of the sentence says *an imitation banknote that resembles real money and is covered in anti-corruption slogans*, which is a describing phrase. Noun phrases beginning with "a" or "an" are always non-essential to the meaning of the sentence and should be set off with commas. Eliminate answers that do not have a comma.

   - (A) and (D) are wrong because the second part isn't an independent clause, and a semicolon or period can only be used when both clauses are independent.

   - (B) is correct because it uses a comma after the non-essential information.

   - (C) is wrong because a comma is needed for non-essential information.

22. **D** In this Rules question, verb forms are changing in the answer choices, so it's testing sentence structure. The subject of the sentence is *participants*, and the main verb is *self-identified*. The second part of the sentence follows *and* and describes a second thing that the participants did, so the answer must be consistent with *self-identified*. Eliminate any answer that isn't consistent with *self-identified*.

   - (A), (B), and (C) are wrong because they aren't consistent with *self-identified*.

   - (D) is correct because it's consistent with *self-identified*.

23. **D** In this Rules question, punctuation is changing in the answer choices. The first part of the sentence says *Scientists are attempting to find a new source for these building blocks*, which is an independent clause. The second part of the sentence is not an independent clause and tells what the *new source* is. Eliminate any answer that doesn't correctly connect the independent clause to the source.

   - (A) is wrong because adding *such as* to the first part makes it no longer independent, in which case it can't be followed by a colon.

   - (B) is wrong because some punctuation is needed to link the independent clause to the explanation of the source that follows.

   - (C) is wrong because it makes it sound like *building blocks*, *photons*, and *small quanta of light* are part of a list, which isn't the intended meaning.

   - (D) is correct because a colon is used when the second part of the sentence elaborates on the first.

24. **D** This is a Transitions question, so highlight ideas that relate to each other. The preceding sentence describes what Harjo *initially* did, and this sentence describes some other things she did. These ideas represent a time change, so a time-change transition is needed. Make an annotation that says "time change." Eliminate any answer that doesn't match.

   - (A) is wrong because this sentence doesn't indicate a rule.

   - (B) and (C) are wrong because they are opposite-direction transitions but this idea doesn't contrast with the one before.

   - (D) is correct because *After some time* matches with *initially* in the preceding sentence.

25. **B** This is a Transitions question, so highlight ideas that relate to each other. The preceding sentence says *They were able to determine the parameters for honeybee flight and develop strategies to manipulate it*, and this sentence says *scientists hope to use a similar technique to control the flight of miniature drones*. These ideas represent a time change, since there is a shift from what scientists found and what they hope to do, so a time-change transition is needed. Make an annotation that says "time change." Eliminate any answer that doesn't match.

- (A) and (C) are wrong because they are opposite-direction transitions but this sentence doesn't contrast with the one before.

- (B) is correct because *Eventually* matches the link between what scientists did do and what they *hope* to do.

- (D) is wrong because this sentence is not a more specific version of the preceding sentence.

26. **D** This is a Transitions question, so highlight ideas that relate to each other. The preceding sentence says *They determined that the wildfires are the source of this abrupt increase in temperature*, and this sentence says *reducing the number of wildfires in Australia may help return the temperature to a normal value*. These ideas agree, so a same-direction transition is needed. Make an annotation that says "agree." Eliminate any answer that doesn't match.

- (A) and (C) are wrong because they are opposite-direction transitions.

- (B) is wrong because this sentence doesn't indicate something that happened while the preceding sentence was occurring.

- (D) is correct because *Therefore* is same-direction and suggests a conclusion that can be drawn from the information in the previous sentence.

27. **B** This is a Transitions question, so highlight ideas that relate to each other. The preceding sentence says *The first piloted hot air balloon…heated the air on the ground and came with a large risk of explosion*, and this sentence says *Yost's balloon design involved heating the fuel in the air and was much safer*. These ideas disagree, so an opposite-direction transition is needed. Make an annotation that says "opposite." Eliminate any answer that doesn't match.

- (A) is wrong because it is a same-direction transition.

- (B) is correct because *On the other hand* is opposite-direction.

- (C) and (D) are wrong because they do not convey the comparison between *Yost's balloon* and the *first piloted hot air balloon*.

Module 2 – Harder

1. **B** This is a Vocabulary question, as it asks for *the most logical and precise word or phrase*. Read the text and highlight what can help to fill in the blank, which refers to what was to be done with the *buildings*. The previous sentence mentions *the renovation of historic buildings*, and the last sentence says *these preservation projects*, so write "renovation" in the annotation box and use process of elimination.

   - (A) is wrong because *repossession* means "taking back ownership."

   - (B) is correct because *rehabilitation* matches with "renovation."

   - (C) is wrong because *reciprocation* means "giving in return."

   - (D) is wrong because *reindustrialization* means "revitalizing industry," and there is no evidence that the buildings will be used for industrial purposes.

2. **B** This is a Vocabulary question, as it asks for *the most logical and precise word or phrase*. Read the text and highlight what can help to fill in the blank, which describes the *process* of *the salt spray test*. The text describes the test as *a common method*, so write "common" in the annotation box and use process of elimination.

   - (A) is wrong because *rudimentary* means "at a low level."

   - (B) is correct because *pervasive* matches with "common."

   - (C) is wrong because *erroneous* means "incorrect."

   - (D) is wrong because *intermittent* means "happening at intervals."

3. **D** This is a Vocabulary question, as it asks for *the most logical and precise word or phrase*. Read the text and highlight what can help to fill in the blank, which refers to what Goodall has tried to do to *the effects of climate change on chimpanzees*. The part after the colon describes a way to *help lessen the negative impacts of warming temperatures*, which is another way of saying *climate change*, so write "lessen" in the annotation box and use process of elimination.

   - (A) is wrong because *insulate* means "prevent outside exposure."

   - (B) is wrong because *downplay* means "act like something is not as bad as it is," which isn't what she is doing; the text suggests that the effects of climate change are *negative*, and she wants to do something about it.

   - (C) is wrong because it's the opposite of the clue in the sentence.

   - (D) is correct because *mitigate* means "make better."

4. **C**   This is a Vocabulary question, as it asks for *the most logical and precise word or phrase*. Read the text and highlight what can help to fill in the blank, which refers to the *fidelity* (accuracy) with which the artists would *reproduce* the *artistic works*. The last part of the sentence states that their magazine included *painstakingly replicated art facsimiles*, which means "exact copies." Therefore, the artists used "painstaking" fidelity when reproducing the works. Write "painstaking" in the annotation box and use process of elimination.

    - (A) is wrong because *evenhanded* means "fair."

    - (B) is wrong because *prudent* means "wise."

    - (C) is correct because *scrupulous* means "exact and precise."

    - (D) is wrong because *complacent* means "satisfied."

5. **B**   This is a Purpose question, as it asks for the *function* of a sentence. Read the text and highlight what can help to understand the function of the underlined sentence. The first sentence explains what Trot *liked* about Cap'n Bill, and the second sentence elaborates on this by comparing the fun she had with Cap'n Bill to the lesser enjoyment she experienced among the children. Write "she has more fun with Bill than with kids" in the annotation box and use process of elimination.

    - (A) is wrong because his *creative talents* aren't mentioned in this sentence.

    - (B) is correct because it matches the annotation.

    - (C) is wrong because it's too broad; the sentence is about Trot's feelings, not about *youth* and *adulthood* in general.

    - (D) is wrong because *his assessment of her* is not mentioned.

6. **C**   This is a Purpose question, as it asks for the *main purpose*. Read the text and highlight what can help to understand the overall purpose. The text begins by introducing the narrator's *desire to plunge into society* after some time and then states that he visited his *superior at the office*. Then it states that although the visit was *pleasant and good* for him, he *deferred* (put off) *for a time* his *desire to embrace all humankind*, so write "he goes to office and then doesn't want to see people for a while" in the annotation box and use process of elimination.

    - (A) is wrong because no *apprehension* (anxiety) *about his employment* is conveyed.

    - (B) is wrong because the text doesn't say that the man is about to be terminated.

    - (C) is correct because it matches the annotation.

    - (D) is wrong because the text is describing one man's experience and thoughts, not *social benefits* in general.

7. **A** This is a Purpose question, as it asks for the *function* of a sentence. Read the text and highlight what can help to understand the function of the underlined sentence. In the text, the speaker describes his grandmother ordering his grandfather to *pay the money*. Then, the underlined sentence describes the relationship between the grandparents, suggesting that the grandfather is somewhat subservient to the grandmother. The following sentences contrast this by explaining how he stood up to her and *refused...to pay the debt*. Write "relationship between grandparents" in the annotation box and use process of elimination.

    - (A) is correct because it matches the annotation; this is how the grandparents interacted before the grandfather's apparently unusual response.

    - (B) is wrong because the narrator himself isn't described in relation to the grandparents.

    - (C) is wrong because this sentence doesn't mention the loss of money.

    - (D) is wrong because nothing about *his house* is mentioned here.

8. **C** This is a Purpose question, as it asks for the *overall structure*. Read the text and highlight what can help to understand the overall structure of the text. The text states that nuclear energy *relies upon* uranium, a *finite resource on land* that exists in large quantities *in seawater*. Then it describes a technology that is a *significant improvement* in its ability to extract uranium from seawater. The last sentence begins with a contrast and explains some downsides to the new method. Write "new method to get uranium from seawater but has some downsides" in the annotation box and use process of elimination.

    - (A) is wrong because the technology isn't a *failed attempt*; it just isn't perfect yet.

    - (B) is wrong because while the last sentence could be called a *potential criticism*, the author does not *address this*; the author is the one stating it.

    - (C) is correct because it matches the annotation: *qualifies* means that it explains an exception, as the text describes some ways that the technology isn't perfect.

    - (D) is wrong because the text never *cautions against reliance* on uranium.

9. **C** This is a Dual Texts question, as it has two texts. The question asks how *the author of Text 2* would respond to *the claims of the author of Text 1*. Start by understanding the *claims of the author* in Text 1. Text 1 describes a theory that *an escalation in infighting* that *coincided with increasing droughts* caused *the decline of the Ancient Maya societies*. It goes on to say that *climate change* was behind *the demise* of the societies. Next, look for a similar idea in Text 2 to see how its author feels about this view. Text 2 acknowledges that the *drought conditions...were correlated with the fall of the social order and the rise of civil unrest* but contrasts this by stating that *it was more specifically the increasing unpredictability of precipitation patterns*. Therefore, the author of Text 2 would "say it's unpredictable precipitation patterns rather than drought." Write that in the annotation box and use process of elimination.

    - (A) is wrong because Text 2 states that *it is often correctly pointed out that drought conditions... were correlated* with the social unrest, so Text 2 doesn't disagree with this view.

- (B) is wrong because this statement isn't related to anything from Text 1.

- (C) is correct because it matches the annotation.

- (D) is wrong because Text 2 never says what *would have* happened.

10. **D** This is a Charts question, as it asks for *data from the table*. The table charts pH range, acid form color, and base form color for several pH indicators. The text provides two criteria: *colorless acid form and a pH range above a pH of 10*. The first criterion narrows it down to p-Nitrophenol and nitramine, and the second one leaves only nitramine.

- (A), (B), and (C) are wrong because they don't meet both criteria.

- (D) is correct because it meets both criteria.

11. **D** This is a Claims question, as it asks for a *quotation* that *illustrates the claim*. Read the text and highlight the *claim*, which is that *the author describes a sense of profound emptiness*. Eliminate answers that don't *illustrate* this idea.

- (A), (B), and (C) are wrong because they focus on nature and don't say anything related to *profound emptiness*.

- (D) is correct because it describes the author's feeling of nothing being in his heart, which matches with *profound emptiness*.

12. **A** This is a Charts question, as it asks for *data from the graph*. The graph charts the concentration of circulating leukocytes before and after people were given two probiotic strains. Highlight the conclusion in the text, which is that *both Lp299 and CURE21 have anti-inflammatory properties*. Read more of the text to understand the link between the conclusion and the graph: *leukocytes* are released during *inflammation*, so if these probiotics are *anti-inflammatory*, they should cause a reduction in leukocytes. Eliminate any answers that are inconsistent with the graph or don't support the conclusion.

- (A) is correct because it demonstrates a reduction in leukocytes and thus a reduction in inflammation.

- (B), (C), and (D) are wrong because the conclusion doesn't relate to a comparison between the two probiotics; the conclusion states that they're both effective.

13. **C** This is a Claims question, as it asks for an answer that would *weaken the underlined claim*. Read the text and highlight the *claim*, which is that *the level of these biomarkers can detect TBI and indicate its severity*. Read more of the text to understand the terms used here. The text introduces two biomarkers that have been associated with severe traumatic brain injury and then describes a study that showed a link between higher levels of these biomarkers and people's risk of death. Eliminate answers that don't *weaken* the claim.

- (A) is wrong because it strengthens the claim, as low levels of the biomarkers would correspond to people who were at lower risk of dying.

- (B) is wrong because the claim doesn't relate to a difference between the two biomarkers.

- (C) is correct because the claim states that the level of the biomarkers *can detect TBI*, but this answer suggests that people might have a TBI but have low levels of the biomarkers.

- (D) is wrong because it strengthens the claim, as the claim indicates that high levels of the biomarkers would correlate with greater likelihood of death.

14. **B** This is a Claims question, as it asks for a *quotation* that *illustrates the claim*. Read the text and highlight the *claim*, which is that *Prometheus questions the justice of his punishment and denounces Zeus as a cruel ruler*. Eliminate answers that don't *illustrate* this idea.

- (A) is wrong because it says *What ills I suffer from the gods* but doesn't question whether this punishment is just.

- (B) is correct because *tyrant* matches with *cruel ruler*, *bind me helpless here* matches with *punishment*, and stating that the punishment is *shameful* supports the idea of questioning the punishment.

- (C) is wrong because it doesn't say anything about *punishment*.

- (D) is wrong because it doesn't describe a *cruel ruler*.

15. **D** This is a Conclusions question, as it asks for the choice that *most logically completes the text*. Read the text and highlight the main ideas. The text describes a study testing the link between *short-term exposure to mindfulness treatment* and *empathy and helpfulness to a stranger*. The result was that those who had mindfulness therapy had *increased levels of empathy*, while those who didn't have the treatment *did not*; however, *both groups had similar levels of commitment to help the stranger*. Eliminate any answer that states a conclusion that isn't supported by the text.

- (A) is wrong because it contradicts the last sentence.

- (B) is wrong because the text never says whether people were *willing to volunteer help*; the groups had *similar levels of commitment*, but that level could be unwillingness.

- (C) is wrong because it's too strong; the results can't provide information on what is *needed to change behavior*.

- (D) is correct because the treatment group had greater empathy but not greater willingness to help compared to the control group.

16. **B** This is a Conclusions question, as it asks for the choice that *most logically completes the text*. Read the text and highlight the main ideas. The text states that the Coffin Stone *was long believed to be part of a now-destroyed chambered long barrow* and states that this structure would have been *constructed in the fourth millennium BCE by a pastoralist community*. Then it contrasts this by describing a finding that there was *no evidence of a chambered long barrow* and that *the stone had been placed at its current location in the 15th or 16th century*. Eliminate any answer that states a conclusion that isn't supported by the text.

- (A) is wrong because it contradicts the text, which says that these communities are associated with creating chambered long barrows.

- (B) is correct because the newer research suggests that the chambered long barrow theory isn't supported.

- (C) is wrong because there is no information in the text suggesting what the stone might have been *part of* before it was moved.

- (D) is wrong because the text doesn't indicate when the barrow would have been *destroyed*, if it ever existed.

17. **C** In this Rules question, punctuation is changing in the answer choices. Look for independent clauses. The first part of the sentence says *Most individuals in America don't walk as much as is recommended*, which is an independent clause. The second part says *when a group of individuals was given step-trackers, researchers found that these individuals took more steps*, which is also an independent clause. Eliminate any answer that can't correctly connect two independent clauses.

- (A) is wrong because some type of punctuation is needed in order to connect two independent clauses.

- (B) is wrong because a comma without a coordinating conjunction can't connect two independent clauses.

- (C) is correct because it connects the independent clauses with a comma plus a coordinating conjunction (*but*), which is acceptable.

- (D) is wrong because a coordinating conjunction (*but*) without a comma can't connect two independent clauses.

18. **C** In this Rules question, punctuation is changing in the answer choices. Look for independent clauses. The first part of the sentence says *Learning and practicing new skills over a long period of time can cause the brain to change*, which is an independent clause. The second part says *for individuals who become blind, areas of the brain that are normally responsible for vision may change and become involved in other important processes, such as touch*, which is also an independent clause. Eliminate any answer that can't correctly connect two independent clauses.

- (A) is wrong because some type of punctuation is needed in order to connect two independent clauses.

- (B) are wrong because a comma without a coordinating conjunction can't connect two independent clauses.

- (C) is correct because a semicolon can connect two independent clauses.

- (D) is wrong because a coordinating conjunction (*and*) without a comma can't connect two independent clauses.

19. **A** In this Rules question, pronouns are changing in the answer choices, so it's testing consistency with pronouns. Find and highlight the word the pronoun refers back to, *Sweden*, which is singular, so a singular pronoun is needed. Write an annotation saying "singular." Eliminate any answer that isn't singular or doesn't clearly refer back to *Sweden*.

- (A) is correct because *its* is singular and is consistent with *Sweden*.

- (B) is wrong because *her* refers to a person, not a country.

- (C) is wrong because it's plural.

- (D) is wrong because *one's* doesn't refer back to a specific thing.

20. **B** In this Rules question, punctuation is changing in the answer choices. Look for independent clauses. The first part of the sentence says *Chemical engineer Kristi Anseth works with a number of multidisciplinary teams on projects such as developing hydrogel materials to help promote tissue regeneration*, which is an independent clause. The second part of the sentence says *a particularly important area of research because some tissues such as cartilage cannot regrow, unlike other tissues such as bone or muscle*, which is not an independent clause. Eliminate any option that doesn't correctly connect the independent clause to the describing phrase that follows.

- (A) is wrong because a semicolon connects two independent clauses, but the second part of the sentence isn't an independent clause.

- (B) is correct because a comma can be used to connect the independent clause to the describing phrase.

- (C) is wrong because a comma is needed to separate the independent clause and the describing phrase.

- (D) is wrong because the second part is meant to describe the first, but the word *and* makes this unclear.

21. **C** In this Rules question, verbs are changing in the answer choices, so it's testing consistency with verbs. Find and highlight the subject, *movements*, which is plural, so a plural verb is needed. Write an annotation saying "plural." Eliminate any answer that is not plural.

- (A), (B), and (D) are wrong because they are singular.

- (C) is correct because it's plural.

22. **B** In this Rules question, punctuation with a transition is changing in the answer choices. Look for independent clauses. The first part of the sentence says *Meiro Koizumi creates videos that explore the relationship between an individual and his or her role in a situation of conflict*. There is an option to add *for example* to this independent clause, but it's not giving an example of a previous idea as nothing came before it. Eliminate options with *for example* in the first part.

- (A) is wrong because it puts *for example* with the first independent clause.

- (B) is correct because it puts *for example* with the second independent clause and puts a semi-colon between the independent clauses.

- (C) and (D) are wrong because the sentence contains two independent clauses, which must be connected with some type of punctuation other than commas.

23. **B** In this Rules question, punctuation is changing in the answer choices. Look for independent clauses. The first part of the sentence says *Romero is not solely focused on research*, which is an independent clause. The second part of the sentence says *emphasizing that it is possible to be a parent and have a successful science career*, which is not an independent clause. Eliminate any option that doesn't correctly connect the independent clause to the describing phrase that follows.

- (A) and (D) are wrong because a semicolon connects two independent clauses, but the second part is not an independent clause.

- (B) is correct because a comma should be used to connect the independent clause to the describing phrase.

- (C) is wrong because *however* is a non-essential word that needs to be surrounded by commas.

24. **B** This is a Transitions question, so highlight ideas that relate to each other. The first sentence says *Barefoot running decreases the risk of* several things, and this sentence says *running in shoes decreases the risk of* several other things. These ideas disagree, so an opposite-direction transition is needed. Make an annotation that says "disagree." Eliminate any answer that doesn't match.

- (A), (C), and (D) are wrong because they are all same-direction transitions.

- (B) is correct because it's an opposite-direction transition.

25. **A** This is a Transitions question, so highlight ideas that relate to each other. The first sentence says *dispatch runners…faced difficulties with their long greatcoats*, and this sentence says *a shorter jacket… was developed*. These ideas agree, so a same-direction transition is needed. Make an annotation that says "agree." Eliminate any answer that doesn't match.

- (A) is correct because *Hence* is same-direction and conveys that the shorter jacket was developed as a result of the difficulties with the longer jacket.

- (B) is wrong because the second sentence is not a second point that shares a similarity with the previous point.

- • (C) is wrong because it is opposite-direction.

- • (D) is wrong because this sentence doesn't provide an additional point.

26. **D** This is a Rhetorical Synthesis question, so highlight the goal(s) stated in the question: *explain the usefulness of cargo bikes for grocery shopping to an audience unfamiliar with cargo bikes*. Eliminate any answer that doesn't *explain the usefulness of cargo bikes for grocery shopping* in a way that assumes the audience is *unfamiliar with cargo bikes*.

  - • (A) is wrong because it doesn't *explain the usefulness of cargo bikes*.

  - • (B) and (C) are wrong because they don't explain what a cargo bike is, and the audience is *unfamiliar* with it.

  - • (D) is correct because it *explains the usefulness* of cargo bikes (*handle the typical large grocery load*) and describes what a cargo bike is.

27. **C** This is a Rhetorical Synthesis question, so highlight the goal(s) stated in the question: *highlight a dispute about te lapa to an audience familiar with the phenomenon*. Eliminate any answer that doesn't *highlight a dispute* in a way that assumes the audience is *familiar with* te lapa.

  - • (A) and (B) are wrong because they don't provide a *dispute*.

  - • (C) is correct because it highlights *a dispute* (Feinberg's skepticism) and doesn't explain te lapa since the audience is familiar with it.

  - • (D) is wrong because it explains te lapa, but the audience is already familiar with it.

PRACTICE TEST 3—MATH EXPLANATIONS

Module 1

1. **C**   The question asks for the value of an expression. The question states that $4s = 28$. Divide both sides of this equation by 4 to get $s = 7$. Plug $s = 7$ into the expression to get $8(7) + 13$, which becomes $56 + 13$, and then 69. The correct answer is (C).

2. **D**   The question asks for the value of an angle on a figure. The figure is already drawn and labeled, but redraw it on the scratch paper if that makes it easier to see what's going on. When a line intersects two parallel lines, two kinds of angles are created: big and small. All of the small angles are equal to each other, all of the big angles are equal to each other, and any small angle plus any big angle = 180°. The angle marked 66° is a small angle, and the angle marked $z°$ is a big angle. Thus, $66 + z = 180$. Subtract 66 from both sides of the equation to get $z = 114$. The correct answer is (D).

3.   **25.16 or 25.17**

The question asks for the mean, or average, of data shown in a table. For averages, use the formula $T = AN$, in which T is the *total*, A is the *average*, and N is the *number of things*. There are 12 infants at the daycare, so that is the *number of things*. Add up all of the heights in the table to get a *total* of 302. The formula becomes $302 = A(12)$. Divide both sides of the equation by 12 to get $25.1\overline{6}$.

It is also possible to calculate the mean of a list of numbers using the built-in calculator. Type the word *mean* followed by the list of heights from the table inside parentheses, and the calculated mean will appear in the lower right corner of the entry field. The calculator shows the mean as 25.1666666667.

When the answer is positive on a fill-in question, there is room in the fill-in box for five characters, including the decimal point. Either stop when there's no more room and enter 25.16, or round the last digit and enter 25.17.

Using either of these methods, the correct answer is 25.16 or 25.17.

4. **A**   The question asks for an expression that represents a specific situation. Translate the English to math in bite-sized pieces and eliminate after each piece. One piece of information says that Jan worked j hours a day for 3 days, so translate her total number of hours worked as $3j$. Eliminate (B), (C), and (D) because they do not include the term. Choice (A) also correctly translates the number of hours Noah worked as $5n$ and adds the two values to represent the total combined hours worked. The correct answer is (A).

5. **C**   The question asks for an equivalent expression. The expression includes a fractional exponent. With fractional exponents, the numerator is the power and the denominator is the root. To rewrite $b^{\frac{3}{4}}$, make 3 the power, or the exponent, and make 4 the root. The expression becomes $\sqrt[4]{b^3}$, so (B) is correct.

It is possible to get the question right without knowing how to work with fractional exponents. Plug in a value for b, use the built-in calculator to find the result, and then plug in the same value for b into the answer choices and eliminate any that do not equal the same result. The expression in (C) matches for any value of b, so (C) is correct.

Using either of these methods, the correct answer is (C).

6. **C**   The question asks for a probability based on data in a table. Probability is defined as $\frac{\text{\# of outcomes that fit requirements}}{\text{total \# of outcomes}}$. Read the table carefully to find the numbers to make the probability. There are 30 total canids in the nature conservancy, so that is the *total # of outcomes*. The question asks for the probability of selecting either a grey wolf with yellow eyes or a coyote with brown eyes, so look up both values. Find where the column for Yellow eyes and the row for Grey wolf meet: the value is 16. Find where the column for Brown eyes and the row for Coyote meet: the value is 5. The *# of outcomes that fit requirements* is 16 + 5 = 21. Therefore, the probability that a canid chosen at random is either a grey wolf with yellow eyes or a coyote with brown eyes is $\frac{21}{30}$. The correct answer is (C).

7. **D**   The question asks for a plausible value based on survey results and a margin of error. A margin of error expresses the amount of random sampling error in a survey's results. The question states that *39% of students in the survey have O-positive blood type*, so apply this percent to the number of students in the entire first-year class: $\frac{39}{100}(265) = 103.35$. Eliminate (A) and (B) because they are not close to this value and do not represent a plausible number of students in the first-year class who have O-positive blood type. Only (D) is close to 103.35, so it is likely correct. To check, calculate the range based on the margin of error. The margin of error is 6%, meaning that results within a range of 6% above and 6% below the estimate are reasonable. Since 100 is less than 103.35, start with the lower limit of the range. To find the lower limit, subtract 6% from the actual percent of 39% to get 33%. Take 33% of the number of students to get $\frac{33}{100}(265) = 87.45$. Since 100 is between 87.45 and 103.35, it is a plausible number of students in the first-year class with an O-positive blood type. The correct answer is (D).

8. **A**   The question asks for a change in value based on a function. Plug in two values for the fork length to see what happens to the weight. Start with a fork length of 2. Fork length is represented by l, so plug $l = 2$ into the function to get $w = 3{,}150 + 450(2)$, or $w = 3{,}150 + 900$, and then $w = 4{,}050$. The

question asks about the weight increase for each foot of growth of the fork length, so increase the fork length to 2 + 1 = 3. Plug $l = 3$ into the function to get $w = 3{,}150 + 450(3)$, or $w = 3{,}150 + 1{,}350$, and then $w = 4{,}500$. The weight increases by $4{,}500 - 4{,}050 = 450$. The correct answer is (A).

9. **B** The question asks for a solution to an equation with an absolute value. One method is to enter the equation into the built-in calculator. The values of x are shown by vertical lines; scroll and zoom as needed to see that these cross the x-axis at -31 and 37. Only -31 is an answer choice, so (B) is correct.

To solve algebraically, recall that, with an absolute value, the value inside the absolute value bars can be either positive or negative, so this equation has two possible solutions. To start solving for x, subtract 6 from both sides of the equation to get $|2x - 6| = 68$. The value in the absolute value bars could equal 68 or -68, so set $2x - 6$ equal to each. When $2x - 6 = 68$, add 6 to both sides of the equation to get $2x = 74$, and then divide both sides of the equation by 2 to get $x = 37$. When $2x - 6 = -68$, add 6 to both sides of the equation to get $2x = -62$, and then divide both sides of the equation by 2 to get $x = -31$, which is (B).

Using either of these methods, the correct answer is (B).

10. **A** The question asks for a description of a function that models a specific situation. Compare the answer choices. Two choices say the function is increasing, and two say it is decreasing. The question states that *an item loses 6% of the value*. Eliminate (C) and (D) because they describe an increasing function. The difference between (A) and (B) is whether the function is exponential or linear. Determine this by plugging in an initial value of the item. Plug in $100 to make it easy to work with percents. *Percent* means out of 100, so translate 6% as $\frac{6}{100}$. The value of the item decreases the first year by $\frac{6}{100}$ ($100) = $6. Subtract this from the original value to get $100 - $6 = $94. Now decrease the new value by 6% to get $94 - \frac{6}{100}$ ($94) = $94 - $5.64 = $88.36. The value decreased by $6 the first year and by $5.64 the second year. A linear function would change by the same amount every year, so eliminate (B). The correct answer is (A).

11. **B** The question asks for the value of a function. In function notation, the number inside the parentheses is the x-value that goes into the function, or the input, and the value that comes out of the function is the y-value, or the output. The question provides an input value and an output value, so plug $x = 90$ and $f(x) = 120$ into the function, and solve for k. The function becomes $120 = \frac{5}{3}(90) + k$. Simplify to get $120 = 150 + k$, and then subtract 150 from both sides of the equation to get $-30 = k$. The question gives a second input value of -30, so plug $x = -30$ and $k = -30$ into the function to get $f(-30) = \frac{5}{3}(-30) + (-30)$. Simplify to get $f(-30) = -50 - 30$, and then $f(-30) = -80$. The correct answer is (B).

12. **B** The question asks for the value of a length on a geometric figure. Redraw the figure on the scratch paper, and then label it with the information given. Label arc *FXG* as 14π. Since the line segment that defines arc *FXG* is a diameter of the circle, the arc is a semicircle, which makes its length half of the circumference. The circumference is thus $14\pi(2) = 28\pi$. Write down the formula for the circumference of a circle, either from memory or after looking it up on the reference sheet. The formula is $C = 2\pi r$. Plug in the length of the circumference to get $28\pi = 2\pi r$. Divide both sides of the equation by 2π to get $14 = r$. Since $\overline{XO}$ is a radius, its length is 14. The correct answer is (B).

13. **13** The question asks for the value of the *y*-coordinate of the solution to a system of equations. The most efficient method is to enter both equations into the built-in calculator, and then scroll and zoom as needed to find the point of intersection. The graph shows one point of intersection at $(-23, 13)$. The question asks for the *y*-coordinate, which is 13.

To solve the system for the *y*-coordinate algebraically, find a way to make the *x*-coordinates disappear when stacking and adding the equations. Compare the *x*-terms: the larger coefficient, 2, is 2 times the smaller one, 1. Multiply the entire first equation by -2 to get the same coefficient with opposite signs on the *x*-terms. The first equation becomes $-2x - 2y = 20$. Now stack and add the two equations.

$$\begin{aligned} -2x - 2y &= 20 \\ + 2x + y &= -33 \\ \hline -y &= -13 \end{aligned}$$

Divide both sides of the resulting equation by -1 to get $y = 13$.

Using either of these methods, the correct answer is 13.

14. **D** The question asks for a value based on an equation that describes a specific situation. The value of the account is increasing by a certain percent over time, so this question is about exponential growth. Write down the growth and decay formula, which is *final amount = (original amount)*$(1 \pm rate)^{number\ of\ changes}$. The question states that the *original amount* is \$5,400. The amount increases by 7%, so the *rate* is 0.07, and the value in parentheses is $1 + 0.07$, or 1.07. The account earns annual interest, so the *number of changes* is the number of years, which is *y*. The question asks for the amount four years from now, so plug in 4 for *y*. The equation becomes *final amount = *$\$5,400(1.07)^4$. Solve with a calculator to get *final amount* $\approx \$7,078.30$. The correct answer is (D).

15. **C** The question asks for an equation in terms of a specific variable. The question asks about the relationship among variables and there are variables in the answer choices, so one option is to plug in. However, that might get messy with four variables. All of the answer choices have d^2 by itself, so the other option is to solve for d^2. To isolate d^2, multiply both sides of the equation by d^2 to get $d^2G = ab$. Divide both sides of the equation by *G* to get $d^2 = \dfrac{ab}{G}$. The correct answer is (C).

16.   **D**   The question asks for a constant in two points on a line. The question states that the line intersects the origin, which is (0, 0), as well as the points $(c, 3)$ and $(27, c)$. Any two points are sufficient to determine the slope of a line, so find the slope using two pairs of points. Find the slope by using the formula $slope = \dfrac{y_2 - y_1}{x_2 - x_1}$. Start with the points $(c, 3)$ and (0, 0). The slope formula becomes $slope = \dfrac{3 - 0}{c - 0}$, or $\dfrac{3}{c}$. Use the points $(27, c)$ and (0, 0) to get $slope = \dfrac{c - 0}{27 - 0}$, or $\dfrac{c}{27}$. Set the two slopes equal to get $\dfrac{3}{c} = \dfrac{c}{27}$. Cross-multiply to get $(c)(c) = (3)(27)$, or $c^2 = 81$. The answer choices are all positive, so take the positive square root of both sides of the equation to get $c = 9$. The correct answer is (D).

17.   **B**   The question asks for the value of a length on a geometric figure. Draw a cone as best as possible, and then write down the formula for the volume of a cone, either from memory or after looking it up on the reference sheet. The formula is $V = \dfrac{1}{3}\pi r^2 h$. Plug in the given values to get $80\pi = \dfrac{1}{3}\pi r^2(15)$. Simplify the right side of the equation to get $80\pi = 5\pi r^2$. Divide both sides of the equation by 5π to get $16 = r^2$, and then take the positive square root of both sides of the equation to get $4 = r$. Read carefully: the question asks for the diameter, which is twice the length of the radius. The diameter is $2(4) = 8$. The correct answer is (B).

18.   **B**   The question asks for a value on a scatterplot. First, check the units on each axis. Population is on the y-axis, so find 5,000 on that axis. Move right from there to the line of best fit, using the mouse pointer or edge of the scratch paper if necessary. From there, move down to the x-axis to see that the value is between the labeled vertical line for 2030 and the unlabeled vertical line for 2035. Eliminate (A), (C), and (D) because those values are not between 2030 and 2035. The correct answer is (B).

19. $\dfrac{20}{29}$ The question asks for the value of a trigonometric function. Begin by drawing a right triangle and labeling the vertices, being certain to put the longest side opposite right angle D. The drawing should look something like this:

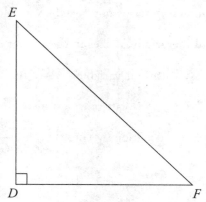

Next, write out SOHCAHTOA to remember the trig functions. The SOH part defines the sine as $\frac{opposite}{hypotenuse}$, and the question states that $\sin(E) = \frac{21}{29}$. Label the side opposite angle E as 21, and label the hypotenuse as 29. The drawing now looks like this:

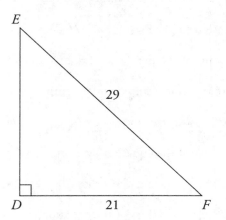

Use the Pythagorean Theorem, $a^2 + b^2 = c^2$, to solve for the length of the remaining side. Plug in the known side lengths to get $a^2 + 21^2 = 29^2$, which becomes $a^2 + 441 = 841$. Subtract 441 from both sides of the equation to get $a^2 = 400$, and then take the positive square root of both sides of the equation to get $a = 20$. Label this on the figure. Use SOHCAHTOA again: the side opposite F is 20, and the hypotenuse is 29, so $\sin(F) = \frac{opposite}{hypotenuse} = \frac{20}{29}$. The correct answer is $\frac{20}{29}$.

20. **225** The question asks for a value given two equations with square roots. One method is to use the built-in calculator. Enter each equation into a separate entry field; type "sqrt" and the calculator will insert the square root symbol. Next, scroll and zoom as needed to see that the two graphs intersect at the point (6.708, 225). The question asks for the value of y, which is 225.

To solve algebraically, substitute $3\sqrt{5}$ for x in the second equation to get $5(3\sqrt{5}) = \sqrt{5y}$. Distribute the 5 on the left side of the equation to get $15\sqrt{5} = \sqrt{5y}$. Square both sides of the equation to get $(225)(5) = 5y$, or $1,125 = 5y$. Divide both sides of the equation by 5 to get $225 = y$.

Using either of these methods, the correct answer is 225.

21. **A** The question asks for an inequality that represents a specific situation. Translate the information in bite-sized pieces and eliminate after each piece. One piece of information says that *each day after Monday, 3 cubic feet of garbage are added*. Therefore, after d days, $3d$ cubic feet have been added. Eliminate (C) because it does not include the term $3d$. Another piece of information says that, on Monday, the trash can *contains 8 cubic feet of garbage*. The 3 cubic feet per day are added to this, so the amount of garbage in the trash can after d days is $8 + 3d$. Eliminate (B) and (D) because they

do not include the initial 8 cubic feet. Choice (A) also includes ≥ 20, which correctly represents when the amount of trash in the trash can is at or above the maximum capacity of 20 cubic feet. The correct answer is (A).

22. **A** The question asks for the sum of three constants in a quadratic equation. Plug the point given in the question into the equation to get $8 = a(-3)^2 + b(-3) + c$. Simplify to get $8 = 9a - 3b + c$. The point $(-3, 8)$ is the maximum of the parabola, and a parabola reaches its minimum or maximum value at its vertex. When a quadratic is in standard form, which is $ax^2 + bx + c$, the x-coordinate of the vertex can be found using the formula $h = -\dfrac{b}{2a}$. Since $h = -3$, this formula becomes $-3 = -\dfrac{b}{2a}$. Multiply both sides of the equation by $-2a$ to get $6a = b$. Substitute $6a$ for b in the first equation to get $8 = 9a - 3(6a) + c$, which becomes $8 = 9a - 18a + c$. Combine the a-terms to get $8 = -9a + c$, and then add $9a$ to both sides of the equation to get $9a + 8 = c$.

Now all three terms can be written in terms of a: $a = a$, $b = 6a$, and $c = 9a + 8$. Thus, $a + b + c = a + 6a + 9a + 8$, which becomes $a + b + c = 16a + 8$. Since the parabola has a maximum, it opens downward, which means that a is negative. Set $16a + 8$ equal to each answer choice, and eliminate any that do not result in a negative value of a. Choice (A) becomes $16a + 8 = -8$. Subtract 8 from both sides of the equation to get $16a = -16$, and then divide both sides of the equation by 16 to get $a = -1$. This is negative, so keep (A). Choice (B) becomes $16a + 8 = 8$. Subtract 8 from both sides of the equation to get $16a = 0$, and then divide both sides of the equation by 16 to get $a = 0$. A larger value will make a positive, so stop here. The correct answer is (A).

Module 2 – Easier

1. **C** The question asks for a percentage of a number. One method is to use the built-in calculator. The calculator automatically adds "of" after the percent sign, so enter "90%" and then "1,000" into an entry field. The result in the lower right corner of the entry field is 900, so (C) is correct.

Another method is to translate the English to math in bite-sized pieces. Translate *what* as a variable, such as x. Translate *is* as equals. *Percent* means out of 100, so translate 90% as $\dfrac{90}{100}$. Translate *of* as times. The translated equation is $x = \dfrac{90}{100}(1,000)$. Solve by hand or with a calculator to get $x = 900$, which is (C).

Using either of these methods, the correct answer is (C).

2. **B** The question asks for a value on a graph. First, check the units on each axis of the line graph. Profits are on the y-axis, so find the point at which the line is lowest, which indicates the least profit. Year is on the x-axis, so move down from the lowest point on the line to the x-axis, using the mouse pointer or edge of the scratch paper if necessary. The year is 2001, so that is when the store's profit was the least. The correct answer is (B).

3. **−6** The question asks for the solution to an equation. One method is to enter the equation into the built-in calculator. The values of y are shown by horizontal lines at $y = 6$ and $y = -6$. The question states that $y < 0$, so -6 is correct.

   To solve for y algebraically, take the square root of both sides of the equation to get $y = \pm 6$. The question states that $y < 0$, so -6 is correct.

   Using either of these methods, the correct answer is -6.

4. **540** The question asks for a value given a ratio. Begin by reading the question to find information about the ratio. The question states that the mosaic floor pattern has *9 blue tiles for every 80 tiles in total*. Set up a proportion to determine how many blue tiles will be in a floor with 4,800 tiles if the ratio of blue tiles to total tiles stays the same. The proportion is $\frac{9 \text{ blue tiles}}{80 \text{ total tiles}} = \frac{x \text{ blue tiles}}{4,800 \text{ total tiles}}$. Cross-multiply to get $(80)(x) = (9)(4,800)$, which becomes $80x = 43,200$. Divide both sides of the equation by 80 to get $x = 540$. The correct answer is 540.

5. **C** The question asks for an equation that represents a relationship among values. Translate the English to math in bite-sized pieces and eliminate after each piece. Translate *6 times a number a* as $6a$. Eliminate (D) because it does not have this piece. Translate *is subtracted from 15* as $15 -$. Eliminate (A) and (B) because they do not have this piece. The correct answer is (C).

6. **A** The question asks for the value of a function. In function notation, the number inside the parentheses is the x-value that goes into the function, or the input, and the value that comes out of the function is the y-value, or the output. The question gives an input value of -3, so plug that into the function to get $g(-3) = 4(-3) - 7$, which becomes $g(-3) = -12 - 7$, and then $g(-3) = -19$. The correct answer is (A).

7. **28** The question asks for a measurement of a geometric figure. Write down the formula for the circumference of a circle, either from memory or after looking it up on the reference sheet. The formula is $C = 2\pi r$. Plug in the value given for the circumference to get $56\pi = 2\pi r$. Divide both sides of the equation by 2π to get $28 = r$. The correct answer is 28.

8. **C** The question asks for an equation that represents a specific situation. Translate the English to math in bite-sized pieces and eliminate after each piece. The question states that m is the number of members of the club in February, so translate *three times the number of members of the club in February* as $3m$. Eliminate (A), (B), and (D) because they do not have this term. Choice (C) also correctly translates *was* as = and sets $3m$ equal to the number of members of the club in April, which is 27. The correct answer is (C).

9. **56**   The question asks for the value of an expression based on an equation. When an SAT question asks for the value of an expression, there is usually a straightforward way to solve for the expression without needing to completely isolate the variable. Multiply both sides of the equation by 3 to get $12x = 60$. Subtract 4 from both sides of the equation to get $12x - 4 = 56$. The correct answer is 56.

10. **B**   The question asks for the value of a function. In function notation, the number inside the parentheses is the x-value that goes into the function, or the input, and the value that comes out of the function is the y-value, or the output. The question provides an input value, so plug $x = 2$ into function g to get $g(2) = 2(2)^2 - 16$, which becomes $g(2) = 2(4) - 16$. Continue solving to get $g(2) = 8 - 16$, and then $g(2) = -8$. The correct answer is (B).

11. **C**   The question asks for a value given a specific situation. Since the question asks for a specific value and the answers contain numbers in increasing order, plug in the answers. Rewrite the answers on the scratch paper and label them "miles." Next, start with one of the middle numbers and try (B), 3. The question states that the base fee is $2.40, and that *there is an additional charge of $0.30 per mile*. The additional charge for a 3-mile trip is ($0.30)(3) = $0.90. Add this to the base fee to get $2.40 + $0.90 = $3.30. This is not $3.60, so eliminate (B). The result was too small, so also eliminate (A), and try (C), 4, next. The additional charge for a 4-mile trip is ($0.30)(4) = $1.20. Add this to the base fee to get $2.40 + $1.20 = $3.60. This matches the information in the question, so stop here. The correct answer is (C).

12. **B**   The question asks for an equivalent form of an expression. Use bite-sized pieces and process of elimination to tackle this question. Start by combining the terms that have x^2 to get $4x^2 - 3x^2 = x^2$. Eliminate (D) because it does not include this term. Next, combine the terms that have x to get $3x - (-8x) = 3x + 8x = 11x$. Eliminate (A) because it does not include this term. Finally, combine the integer terms to get $-2 - 9 = -11$. Eliminate (C) because it does not include this term. The correct answer is (B).

13. **D**   The question asks for the equation that defines a function. In function notation, the number inside the parentheses is the x-value that goes into the function, or the input, and the value that comes out of the function is the y-value, or the output. The table provides several pairs of input and output values, so plug those into the answer choices and eliminate answers that don't work. Plugging in 1 often makes more than one answer work, so start with the third point, and plug $x = 3$ and $g(x) = 5$ into each answer choice. Choice (A) becomes $5 = 3 - 1$, or $5 = 2$. This is not true, so eliminate (A). Choice (B) becomes $5 = 2(3) - 4$, or $5 = 2$; eliminate (B). Choice (C) becomes $5 = 3(3) - 5$, or $5 = 4$; eliminate (C). Choice (D) becomes $5 = 4(3) - 7$, or $5 = 5$; keep (D). The correct answer is (D).

14. **A**   The question asks for a point that satisfies a system of inequalities. One method is to enter both inequalities into the built-in calculator, and then see which point in the answer choices is in the shaded area that represents the solution to the system. Only $(-3, -1)$ is in that shaded area, so (A) is correct.

Another approach is to plug in the answers. Rewrite the answer choices on the scratch paper and label them "(x, y)." Start with one of the answers in the middle and try (C). Plug $x = 3$ and $y = 1$ into the first inequality to get $4(3) - 1 \le 1$, which becomes $12 - 1 \le 1$, and then $11 \le 1$. This is not true, so eliminate (C). The left side of the first inequality should be smaller, so try (A). Plug $x = -3$ and $y = -1$ into the first inequality to get $4(-3) - 1 \leq -1$, which becomes $-12 - 1 \leq -1$, and then $-13 \leq -1$. This is true, so plug the same values into the second inequality to get $2 > -3 + (-1)$, which becomes $2 > -4$. This is also true, so the point $(-3, -1)$ satisfies the system of inequalities, and (A) is correct.

Using either of these methods, the correct answer is (A).

15. **16** The question asks for a measurement on a geometric figure. Start by redrawing the figure on the scratch paper. Since $\overline{PQ}$ is parallel to $\overline{RT}$, angle P is also a right angle; label this on the figure. The two triangles share angle S, so they are similar triangles. This means the sides are proportional. Sides $\overline{RT}$ and $\overline{PQ}$ are opposite the same angle, so they are proportional. Sides $\overline{PS}$ and $\overline{TS}$ are proportional for the same reason, so find the length of side $\overline{TS}$. Either recognize one of the Pythagorean Triples or use the Pythagorean Theorem to get $TS = 4$; label this on the figure, which now looks like this.

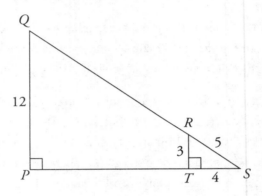

Now set up a proportion: $\dfrac{RT}{PQ} = \dfrac{TS}{PS}$. Plug in the known values to get $\dfrac{3}{12} = \dfrac{4}{PS}$. Cross-multiply to get $(12)(4) = 3(PS)$, which becomes $48 = 3(PS)$. Divide both sides of the equation by 3 to get $16 = PS$. The correct answer is 16.

16. **0.86** The question asks for the value of a constant given a function that represents a specific situation. The value of the function is decreasing by a certain percent, so this question is about exponential decay. Write down the growth and decay formula, which is *final amount = (original amount)*$(1 \pm rate)^{number\ of\ changes}$. The constant k is in parentheses, so it represents $1 \pm rate$. The question states that the population *will decline by 14 percent per year*, so the *rate* is 14%. Convert this to a decimal to get 0.14. The population is declining, so the value in parentheses, or k, is $1 - 0.14 = 0.86$. The correct answer is 0.86.

17. **D** The question asks for the equation that represents a graph. One method is to use the built-in calculator. Enter each answer choice equation until one of them matches the graph shown in the question. Only the graph of the equation in (D) matches, so (D) is correct.

Another method is to plug in points from the graph and eliminate equations that don't work. Since 0 and 1 are likely to make more than one answer work, start with the point at $(2, 70)$. Plug in $x = 2$ and $y = 70$, and eliminate answers that don't work. Choice (A) becomes $70 = 25(2)$, or $70 = 50$. This is not true, so eliminate (A). Choice (B) becomes 70 = 2 + 30, or 70 = 32; eliminate (B). Choice (C) becomes 70 = 10(2) + 30, or 70 = 50; eliminate (C). Choice (D) becomes 70 = 20(2) + 30, or 70 = 70. Only (D) worked with this point, so it is correct.

Using either of these methods, the correct answer is (D).

18. **A** The question asks for a value given a function. In function notation, the number inside the parentheses is the *x*-value that goes into the function, or the input, and the value that comes out of the function is the *y*-value, or the output. The question provides an output value of 8, and the answers have numbers that could represent the *x*-value, so plug in the answers. Start with one of the middle numbers and try (B), 4. Plug $x = 4$ into the function to get $g(4) = \sqrt{4(4)^2 + 28}$, which becomes $g(4) = \sqrt{4(16) + 28}$. Continue solving to get $g(4) = \sqrt{64 + 28}$, and then $g(4) = \sqrt{92}$. Use a calculator to get $g(4) \approx 9.59$. This does not match the output value of 8, so eliminate (B). The result was too large, so also eliminate (C) and (D). The correct answer is (A).

19. **B** The question asks for an equation that represents a graph. One method is to use the built-in calculator. Enter each of the equations in the answer choices and see which one looks most like the graph in the question. Only the graph of the equation in (B) looks like the graph in the question, so (B) is correct.

Another option is to use knowledge of the graphs of higher-degree polynomials. There are three *x*-intercepts on the graph, at (–2, 0), (2, 0), and (5, 0). These are three distinct values, so there should be three distinct factors. Eliminate (A) and (D) because they square one of the factors, which would result in a double root where the graph touches $y = 0$ and then curves away. To check (B) and (C), plug in a point from the graph. Both equations have $(x - 2)$ and $(x + 2)$ as factors, so avoid those and start with the point (5, 0). Plug $x = 5$ and $f(x) = 0$ into the remaining answers. Choice (B) becomes 0 = (5 – 5)(5 – 2)(5 + 2), then 0 = (0)(3)(7), and finally 0 = 0. This is true, so keep (B). Choice (C) becomes 0 = (5 – 2)(5 + 2)(5 + 5), then 0 = (3)(7)(10), and finally 0 = 210. This is not true, so eliminate (C). It is also possible to plug in points from the graph and eliminate answers without knowing about double roots.

Using either of these methods, the correct answer is (B).

20. **D** The question asks for a number given relationships among three numbers. Since the question asks for a specific value and the answers contain numbers in increasing order, plug in the answers. Rewrite the answer choices on the scratch paper and label them as "largest #." Next, start with a number in the middle and try (B), 245. The question states that when *three numbers are added together, the result is 665*. If the largest number is 245, the sum of the other two numbers is 665 – 245 = 420. The question also states that the *largest number is four-thirds the sum of the other two numbers*. If the sum of the other two numbers is 420, the largest number is $\frac{4}{3}(420) = 560$. There are two different values for the largest number, 245 and 560, so eliminate (B). The two values were not close to each other, and (A) is too small to be the

largest number, so try (D), 380, next. If the largest number is 380, the sum of the other two numbers is 665 – 380 = 285. If the sum of the other two numbers is 285, the largest number is $\frac{4}{3}(285) = 380$. The two results for the largest number match, so 380 is the correct value. The correct answer is (D).

21. **B** The question asks for the value of a constant in a quadratic with exactly one real solution. One method is to enter both equations into the built-in calculator, and then select the slider for k. Either use the slider or enter each answer choice in the "k =" equation. Only when $k = 0$ does the graph of the system have exactly one real solution, so $k = 0$, and the answer is (B).

To solve algebraically, use the discriminant. The discriminant is the part of the quadratic formula under the square root sign and is written as $D = b^2 - 4ac$. When the discriminant is positive, the quadratic has exactly two real solutions; when the discriminant is 0, the quadratic has exactly one real solution; and when the discriminant is negative, the quadratic has no real solutions. Thus, the discriminant of this quadratic must equal 0. First, substitute $2x$ for y in the first equation to get $2x = x^2 + 2x + k$. Next, put the quadratic in standard form, which is $ax^2 + bx + c = 0$, by subtracting $2x$ from both sides of the equation to get $0 = x^2 + k$. Now that the quadratic is in standard form, $a = 1$, $b = 0$, and $c = k$. Plug these into the discriminant formula to get $D = (0)^2 - 4(1)(k)$, or $D = -4k$. Since there is exactly one real solution, $-4k = 0$. Divide both sides of the equation by –4 to get $0 = k$.

Using either of these methods, the correct answer is (B).

22. **C** The question asks for the value of a trigonometric function. Start by drawing two right triangles that are similar to each other, meaning they have the same proportions but are different sizes. Be certain to match up the corresponding angles that are given in the question, and put the longest side opposite the right angle. Next, label the figures with the information given and label the side lengths of triangle LMN. The drawing should look something like this:

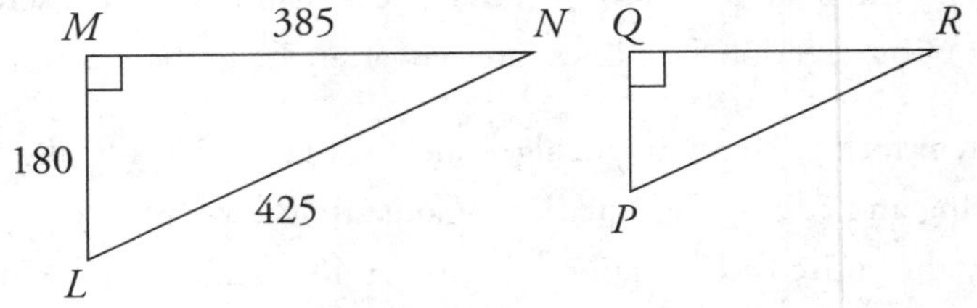

Trig functions are proportions, and angle R corresponds to angle N, so $\cos(R) = \cos(N)$. Use SOHCAH-TOA to remember the trig functions. The CAH part of the acronym defines the cosine as $\frac{adjacent}{hypotenuse}$. The side adjacent to angle N is 385, and the hypotenuse is 425, so $\cos(N) = \frac{385}{425}$. Thus, $\cos(R)$ is also $\frac{385}{425}$. Reduce the fraction by dividing the numerator and denominator by 5 to get $\cos(R) = \frac{77}{85}$. It is also possible to use a calculator to find the decimal form of $\frac{385}{425}$ and the decimal form of each answer choice and see which answer matches. The correct answer is (C).

Module 2 – Harder

1. **A** The question asks for an equivalent form of an expression. Use bite-sized pieces and process of elimination to tackle this question. Start by combining the terms that have a^3. Subtract the coefficients to get $5a^3 - 3a^3 = 2a^3$. Eliminate (B), (C), and (D) because they do not include this term. Choice (A) also correctly leaves $6a^2$ by itself because no other terms have an exponent of 2. The correct answer is (A).

2. **B** The question asks for the equation that defines a function. In function notation, the number inside the parentheses is the x-value that goes into the function, or the input, and the value that comes out of the function is the y-value, or the output. The table provides several pairs of input and output values, so plug those into the answer choices and eliminate answers that don't work. Pairs of values that include 0 often make more than one answer work, and negative numbers can be tricky to work with, so start with the fourth pair of values. Plug $x = 5$ and $g(x) = 2$ into each answer choice. Choice (A) becomes $2 = 5 - 6$, or $2 = -1$. This is not true, so eliminate (A). Choice (B) becomes $2 = 2(5) - 8$, or $2 = 2$. This is true, so keep (B), but check the remaining answers with this pair of values. Choice (C) becomes $2 = 3(5) - 12$, or $2 = 3$; eliminate (C). Choice (D) becomes $2 = 4(5) - 12$, or $2 = 8$; eliminate (D). The correct answer is (B).

3. **B** The question asks for a value given a specific situation. Since the question asks for a specific value and the answers contain numbers in increasing order, plug in the answers. Rewrite the answer choices on the scratch paper and label them "miles Irina cycled." Start with one of the values in the middle and try (B), 32. The question states that *Tiki cycled 13 fewer miles than Irina*. If Irina cycled 32 miles, Tiki cycled $32 - 13 = 19$ miles. The question also states that *the two of them cycled a total of 51 miles*. If Irina cycled 32 miles and Tiki cycled 19 miles, they cycled a combined $32 + 19 = 51$ miles. This matches the information in the question, so stop here. The correct answer is (B).

4. **1** The question asks for the value of the y-coordinate of the solution to a system of equations. One method is to enter both equations into the built-in calculator, and then scroll and zoom as needed to find the point of intersection. The lines intersect at (4, 1), so the y-coordinate is 1.

   To solve the system for the y-coordinate algebraically, find a way to make the x-coordinates disappear when stacking and adding the equations. Compare the x-terms: a common multiple of 8 and 5 is 40. Multiply the entire first equation by 5 to get $40x - 25y = 135$. Multiply the entire second equation by -8 to get the same coefficient with opposite signs on the x-terms. The second equation becomes $-40x - 80y = -240$. Now stack and add the two equations.

$$40x - 25y = 135$$
$$\underline{+\ -40x - 80y = -240}$$
$$-105y = -105$$

   Divide both sides of the resulting equation by -105 to get $y = 1$.

   Using either of these methods, the correct answer is 1.

5. **12**   The question asks for the value of a constant in a function. In function notation, the number inside the parentheses is the x-value that goes into the function, or the input, and the value that comes out of the function is the y-value, or the output. The question provides a point on the graph, which means that an input value of 4 has an output value of –2. Plug $x = 4$ and $g(x) = -2$ into the function to get $-2 = 2(4)^2 - 4k + 14$. Simplify the right side of the equation to get $-2 = 2(16) - 4k + 14$, then $-2 = 32 - 4k + 14$, and finally $-2 = 46 - 4k$. Subtract 46 from both sides of the equation to get $-48 = -4k$, and then divide both sides of the equation by –4 to get $12 = k$. The correct answer is 12.

6. **D**   The question asks for the interpretation of a term in context. Start by reading the final question, which asks for the meaning of –0.14. Rewrite the equation on the scratch paper. Then, label the parts of the equation with the information given, and eliminate answers that do not match the labels. The question states that *x represents the number of years since 2010*, and that *y is the total annual rainfall*. Thus, –0.14 has something to do with each year. Eliminate (A) and (B) because the total annual rainfall in one year is represented by y, not by x. Eliminate (C) because it is the difference between the y-value for 2010 and the y-value for 2020. Choice (D) describes something that occurs every year, and –0.14 is multiplied by the number of years, so this fits the information in the question. The correct answer is (D).

7. **10**   The question asks for the greatest possible x-value of the solution to a system of inequalities. According to the first inequality, $3y$ cannot be greater than 7. Plug in 7 for $3y$ in the second inequality to get $x < 7 + 4$, which becomes $x < 11$. The question asks for the greatest integer value of x, and the greatest integer less than 11 is 10. The correct answer is 10.

8. **C**   The question asks for the equation of a line that is perpendicular to the given line. Perpendicular lines have slopes that are negative reciprocals. The given equation and the equations in the answer choices are all in standard form, $Ax + By = C$. When a linear equation is in standard form, the slope is $-\frac{A}{B}$. The slope of the first equation is $-\frac{-3}{4}$, or $\frac{3}{4}$. The slope of a line perpendicular to this line will be $-\frac{4}{3}$. Determine the slope of each answer choice to see which one matches this value. For (A), the slope is $-\frac{3}{6}$, or $-\frac{1}{2}$. This is not equal to the target slope of $-\frac{4}{3}$, so eliminate (A). For (B), the slope is $-\frac{3}{8}$; eliminate (B). For (C), the slope is $-\frac{4}{3}$, which matches the target slope, so stop here. The correct answer is (C).

9. **C**   The question asks for an equation that represents a specific situation. The number of baseball cards in the collection is decreasing by a certain percent over time, so this question is about exponential decay. Write down the growth and decay formula, which is *final amount = (original amount)*$(1 \pm$ *rate*$)^{number\ of\ changes}$. The question states that the *original amount* is 6,500, and all of the answers include this piece. The question also states that the number *will decrease by 20 percent*. This is the *rate*, and

20% in decimal form is 0.2. Because the number of cards is decreasing, the value inside the parentheses is (1 − *rate*), which is (1 − 0.2) = 0.8. Eliminate (A) and (B) because they have the wrong value inside the parentheses. The number of cards decreases once every 6 months, and the exponents in the answer choices are in terms of *m* months. Plug in a value for *m*. After 12 months, the number of cards in the collection will decrease twice, so when *m* = 12, the *number of changes* is 2. Plug *m* = 12 into the exponent in (C) to get $\frac{12}{6}$ = 2; keep (C). Plug *m* = 12 into the exponent in (D) to get 6(12) = 72; eliminate (D). The correct answer is (C).

10.   **A**   The question asks for the surface area of a geometric figure. Draw a cube on the scratch paper as best as possible, or at least a square to represent one face of the cube. Next, write down the relevant formulas. Write down the formula for the volume of a cube, either from memory or after looking it up on the reference sheet. The reference sheet doesn't give the formula for the volume of a cube, but it does give the volume of a rectangular solid: *V* = *lwh*. All three dimensions of a cube have the same length, so the formula becomes $V = s^3$. There is a variable in the question and the answers, so plug a value for *c* into the equation given in the question to find the volume of the cube. Plug in *c* = 4 to get $V = \frac{1}{8}(4)^3$, then $V = \frac{1}{8}(64)$, and finally *V* = 8. Plug this volume into the volume formula for a cube to solve for the edge length: $8 = s^3$. Take the positive cube root of both sides of the equation to get 2 = *s*. Label this on the figure.

The surface area of a geometric figure is the sum of the areas of its sides. Since a cube has 6 sides that are identical squares, and the formula for the area of a square is $A = s^2$, the formula for the surface area of a cube is $SA = 6s^2$. Plug the edge length of 2 into the surface area formula to get $SA = 6(2)^2 = 6(4) = 24$. This is the target value; write it down and circle it. Now plug *c* = 4 into the answer choices and eliminate any that do not match the target value. Choice (A) becomes $6\left(\frac{4}{2}\right)^2 = 6(2)^2 = 6(4) = 24$. This matches the target value, so keep (A), but check the remaining answers just in case. Choice (B) becomes $6\left(\frac{4^2}{2}\right) = 6\left(\frac{16}{2}\right) = 6(8) = 48$. This does not match the target value, so eliminate (B). Choice (C) becomes $6(4)^2 = 6(16) = 96$; eliminate (C). Choice (D) will have an even larger result than (C), so eliminate (D). The correct answer is (A).

11. **B**   The question asks for the number of solutions to a system of equations. The most efficient method is to enter both equations into the built-in calculator, and then scroll and zoom as needed to see how many times, if at all, the two graphs intersect. There are two points of intersection, so the system of equations has two real solutions. The correct answer is (B).

12. **C**   The question asks for a change in value expressed as a percentage. One method is to ballpark. The number of units sold of both products increased, one by 50% and the other by 30%, so the total increase must be between 30% and 50%. Only (C) is within this range, so it must be correct.

Another method is to translate the English to math in bite-sized pieces. One piece of information says that the sales of laptops *increased by 50%* this week. Since *percent* means out of 100, translate 50% as $\frac{50}{100}$, and find 50% of the 90 laptops sold: $\frac{50}{100}$ (90) = 45. Add this to the number of laptops sold last week to get 90 + 45 = 135. Another piece of information says that the store sold 210 tablets last week and that the sales of tablets *increased by 30%*. Follow the same steps to get 210 + $\frac{30}{100}$ (210) = 210 + 63 = 273. The total number of units sold this week is 135 + 273 = 408. Add the number of laptops and tablets sold last week to get a total number of units sold last week of 90 + 210 = 300. Now, plug in the answer choices to see which percent increases the sales from 300 to 408. Start with (B), 25%. A 25% increase from 300 is 300 + $\frac{25}{100}$ (300) = 300 + 75 = 375. This is not 408, so eliminate (B). The result was too small, so also eliminate (A) and try (C) next. A 36% increase from 300 is 300 + $\frac{36}{100}$ (300) = 300 + 108 = 408. This matches the information in the question, so stop here and pick (C).

Using either of these methods, the correct answer is (C).

13. **D**   The question asks for the number of solutions to an equation. Distribute on both sides of the equation to get −10 + 18x = 18x + 24. Subtract 18x from both sides of the equation to get −10 = 24. This is not true, so the equation has no solutions, and (D) is correct.

It is also possible to answer this question using the built-in calculator. Enter each side of the equation into a separate entry field, and then scroll and zoom as needed to see that the lines are parallel. This means there are no solutions, and (D) is correct.

Using either of these methods, the correct answer is (D).

14. **123**   The question asks for a value based on means, or averages. For averages, use the formula $T = AN$, in which T is the *Total*, A is the *Average*, and N is the *Number of things*. When there are 6 people on the elevator, the *average* is 160.5 and the *number of things* is 6, so the equation becomes T = (160.5)(6), or T = 963. When the person with the lowest weight gets off the elevator, the *average* is 168

and the *number of things* is 5. The average equation becomes $T = (168)(5)$, or $T = 840$. To find the weight of the person with the lowest weight, subtract the two totals to get $963 - 840 = 123$. The correct answer is 123.

15. **D**   The question asks for the value of a constant in a quadratic. One method is to enter the equation into the built-in calculator. The slider for k does not appear, so subtract k from both sides of the equation to get $4x^2 - 5x - k = 0$. Delete the "= 0" part, and the slider appears. Either use the slider or enter each answer choice into the "$k =$" equation. Only when $k = -1$ does the graph of the system have exactly two real solutions, so (D) is correct.

To determine algebraically when a quadratic equation has two real solutions, use the discriminant. The discriminant is the part of the quadratic formula under the square root sign and is written as $D = b^2 - 4ac$. When the discriminant is positive, the quadratic has exactly two real solutions; when the discriminant is 0, the quadratic has exactly one real solution; and when the discriminant is negative, the quadratic has no real solutions. Thus, the discriminant of this quadratic must equal a positive number. First, put the quadratic in standard form, which is $ax^2 + bx + c = 0$, by subtracting k from both sides of the equation to get $4x^2 - 5x - k = 0$. Now that the quadratic is in standard form, $a = 4$, $b = -5$, and $c = -k$. Plug these into the discriminant formula to get $D = (-5)^2 - 4(4)(-k)$, or $D = 25 + 16k$. Since there are two real solutions, $25 + 16k > 0$. Subtract 25 from both sides of the inequality to get $16k > -25$, then divide both sides of the inequality by 16 to get $k > -1.5625$. The only answer choice greater than -1.5625 is -1. Using either method, the correct answer is (D).

16. **C**   The question asks for the product of the two coordinates of the solution to a system of equations. One method is to enter both equations into the built-in calculator, and then scroll and zoom as needed to find the points of intersection. The graph shows one point of intersection at $(0, 0)$, but the question states that $x < 0$. The other point of intersection is at $(-1, 1)$. Thus, $x = -1$, $y = 1$, and $xy = -1$, so (C) is correct.

To solve algebraically, substitute x^2 for y in the second equation to get $6x + 9 = -3(2x^2 - 3)$. Simplify the right side of the equation to get $6x + 9 = -6x^2 + 9$. Subtract 9 from both sides of the equation to get $6x = -6x^2$. Divide both sides of the equation by $-6x$ to get $-1 = x$. Plug $x = -1$ into the first equation to solve for y: $(-1)^2 = y$, so $y = 1$. Finally, solve for xy: $(-1)(1) = -1$, making (C) correct.

Using either of these methods, the correct answer is (C).

17. **B**   The question asks for a value given information about trigonometric functions. Redraw the figure, and then label it with information from the question. The question asks for a specific value and the answers contain numbers in increasing order, so plug in the answers. Rewrite the answer choices and label them "m." Start with one of the middle numbers and try (B), 7.5. If $m = 7.5$, the measure of angle A is $6(7.5) - 9 = 45 - 9 = 36$; label this on the figure. The measure of angle C is $8(7.5) - 6 = 60 - 6 = 54$; label this on the figure. Use a calculator in degree mode to get $\sin(36) \approx 0.588$ and $\cos(54) \approx 0.588$. The values are equal, which matches the information in the question, so stop here. The correct answer is (B).

18.   **D**   The question asks for a true statement based on the data. Use bite-sized pieces and process of elimination to tackle this question. The answer choices compare the ranges of the two data sets, and range is the difference between the greatest value and the least value, so start there. The range of the values in data set 1 is $9 - 3 = 6$, and the range of the values in data set 2 is $13 - 8 = 5$. Eliminate (B) and (C) because they say the ranges are equal, whereas the range of data set 1 is greater than the range of data set 2. Standard deviation is a measure of the spread of a group of numbers. A group of numbers close together has a small standard deviation, whereas a group of numbers spread out has a large standard deviation. The values in data set 1 are spread out almost equally among the numbers, whereas the values in data set 2 are clustered around 12. Thus, the standard deviation of data set 1 is greater than the standard deviation of data set 2. Eliminate (A) because it says that the standard deviation of data set 1 is less than that of data set 2. The correct answer is (D).

19. $\dfrac{17}{6}$ **or 2.833**

The question asks for the sum of two constants in a system of linear equations. When two linear equations have infinitely many solutions, the two equations represent the same line. Therefore, make the two equations look the same. First, put the equations in the same order by adding bx to both sides of the second equation to get $bx + 4y = 48$. Next, multiply the entire first equation by 3 to make both equations equal 48. The first equation becomes $\dfrac{3}{2}x + 3ay = 48$. Set the x-terms equal to each other to get $\dfrac{3}{2}x = bx$. Divide both sides of this equation by x to get $\dfrac{3}{2} = b$. Set the y-terms equal to each other to get $3ay = 4y$. Divide both sides of this equation by $3y$ to get $a = \dfrac{4}{3}$. Finally, add a and b: $\dfrac{3}{2} + \dfrac{4}{3}$. Either use a calculator or a common denominator of 6 to get $a + b = \dfrac{17}{6}$. The answer can also be entered in the fill-in box in decimal form, entering digits until there is no more room, as 2.833. The correct answer is $\dfrac{17}{6}$ or 2.833.

20.   **B**   The question asks for the value of a constant in an equation. When a quadratic is in standard form, which is $ax^2 + bx + c$, the shortcut to find the sum of the solutions is $-\dfrac{b}{a}$. In this quadratic, $a = 43$ and $b = (43d + e)$, so the sum of the solutions is $-\dfrac{(43d + e)}{43}$. The question states that the sum of the solutions can also be written as $k(43d + e)$, so set these values equal to each other: $-\dfrac{(43d + e)}{43} = k(43d + e)$. Multiply both sides of the equation by 43 to get $-(43d + e) = 43k(43d + e)$. Divide both sides of the equation by $(43d + e)$ to get $-1 = 43k$. Finally, divide both sides of the equation by 43 to get $-\dfrac{1}{43} = k$. The correct answer is (B).

21. **C** The question asks for the volume of a geometric figure. Find the volume of each piece of the capsule separately, and then add the volumes together. The figure is already drawn and labeled, but redraw it on the scratch paper if that makes it easier to see what's going on. Write down the relevant formulas, either from memory or after looking them up on the reference sheet. The formula for the volume of a cylinder is $V = \pi r^2 h$, and the formula for the volume of a sphere is $V = \frac{4}{3}\pi r^3$. The radius of the cylinder is given on the figure as 3, and the height is given as 12, so the volume of the cylinder is $V = \pi(3)^2(12)$, which becomes $V = \pi(9)(12)$, and then $V = 108\pi$. The two ends of the capsule make up one complete sphere, and the radius of the sphere is given on the figure as 3. The volume of the complete sphere is $V = \frac{4}{3}\pi(3)^3$, which becomes $V = \frac{4}{3}\pi(27)$, and then $V = 36\pi$. The volume of the entire capsule is $108\pi + 36\pi = 144\pi$. The correct answer is (C).

22. **6** The question asks for radius of a circle given an equation for its graph. The most efficient approach is to enter the equation into the built-in calculator. Click on the gray dots at the maximum and minimum y-values to see that the maximum y-value is at $(-2.5, 7.5)$, and the minimum y-value is at $(-2.5, -4.5)$. Since the two points have the same x-coordinate, the distance between them is the diameter of the circle. Find the difference to get a diameter of $7.5 - (-4.5) = 12$. The radius of a circle is half the diameter, so the radius is 6. The correct answer is 6.

Chapter 7
Practice Test 4

HOW TO EMULATE THE DIGITAL SAT ON PAPER

Practice Tests 5 and 6 are available in your online student tools in a digital, adaptive environment. The four tests in this physical book are printed on paper, but otherwise emulate the digital test in every way: test style, difficulty, and content. Please use the checklist below to ensure that you are able to emulate the adaptive nature of the test and get the preparation that you need for test day. Feel free to use the versions of Module 2 that you do not take during your test as additional practice.

- ☐ Take Reading and Writing (RW) Module 1, allowing yourself 32 minutes to complete it.

- ☐ Go to the answer key on page 404 and determine the number of questions you got correct in RW Module 1.

- ☐ If you get fewer than 15 questions correct, take RW Module 2 – Easier, which starts on page 357. If you get 15 or more questions correct, take RW Module 2 – Harder, which starts on page 367.

- ☐ Whichever RW Module 2 you take, start immediately and allow yourself 32 minutes to complete it.

- ☐ Take a 10-minute break between RW Module 2 and Math Module 1.

- ☐ Take Math Module 1, allowing yourself 35 minutes to complete it.

- ☐ Go to the answer key on page 404 and determine the number of questions you got correct in Math Module 1.

- ☐ If you get fewer than 14 questions correct, take Math Module 2 – Easier, which starts on page 386. If you get 14 or more questions correct, take Math Module 2 – Harder, which starts on page 394.

- ☐ Whichever Math Module you take, start it immediately and allow yourself 35 minutes to complete it.

- ☐ After you finish the test, check your answers to RW Module 2 and Math Module 2.

- ☐ Only after you complete the entire test should you read the explanations for the questions, which start on page 405.

Test 4—Reading and Writing
Module 1

Turn to Section 1 of your answer sheet to answer the questions in this section.

---

1 ☐ Mark for Review

The Chilean volcano Calabozos is located in _____ area. Therefore, the risk of loss of human life in the event of an eruption is minimal.

Which choice completes the text with the most logical and precise word or phrase?

- (A) a hazardous
- (B) an active
- (C) a mountainous
- (D) a remote

---

2 ☐ Mark for Review

Contemporaries of American modernist poet H.D. focused only on her important contributions to the Imagist movement in the 1920s, taking _____ view of her work. However, she wrote in a variety of forms and genres, from short, lyrical works to complex, book-length poems.

Which choice completes the text with the most logical and precise word or phrase?

- (A) an expansive
- (B) a limited
- (C) an imaginative
- (D) a complicated

CONTINUE →

3 🔖 Mark for Review

Since the 1950s, scientists have known that rapid eye movement, or REM, occurs when someone is sleeping. <u>Previous studies attempting to determine the meaning of these eye movements have been unsuccessful in part because these studies relied on human subjects recalling the content of their dreams.</u> A recent study by physiologists Yuta Senzai and Massimo Scanziani has avoided this issue by studying dreaming mice instead. Their results suggest that REM is correlated to changes in direction during the dream.

Which choice best describes the function of the second sentence in the overall structure of the text?

- (A) It names a problem in the approach taken by Senzai and Scanziani.

- (B) It introduces the difficulty that the study by Senzai and Scanziani was designed to bypass.

- (C) It presents the findings of studies done prior to the study by Senzai and Scanziani.

- (D) It clarifies how others studying REM sleep interpret the study by Senzai and Scanziani.

4 🔖 Mark for Review

Electroreception is the ability of an animal to sense the flow of electricity around it by using specialized organs known as electroreceptors. Most species known to use electroreception are fish, including many sharks, elephant fishes, and eels. <u>However, electroreception is not limited to fish.</u> Monotremes, a group of mammals that includes the platypus and some echidnas, have electroreceptors on or near their mouths to help locate prey. There is also some evidence that bees can detect static electricity on flowers.

Which choice best describes the function of the third sentence in the overall structure of the text?

- (A) It generalizes the phenomenon discussed beyond fishes.

- (B) It offers another explanation of electroreception that is different from the explanation of how electroreception is used by fishes.

- (C) It provides more examples of animals with electroreception.

- (D) It explains how electroreception evolved in monotremes and bees.

CONTINUE ➡

5 ☐ Mark for Review

Text 1

An animal is said to have a theory of mind when it is able to act according to the mental states of other individuals. Psychologists David Premack and Guy Woodruff studied whether chimpanzees have such a theory of mind. They showed videos of human actors struggling with various problems. The chimpanzees were able to select photographs that showed the best tool to solve each actor's problem.

Text 2

Biologist Daniel J. Povinelli and psychologists Kurt E. Nelson and Sarah T. Boysen have argued that previous research into whether chimpanzees have a theory of mind have not adequately addressed alternative explanations for the chimpanzees' behaviors. Specifically, it may be the case that chimpanzees are following learned behaviors in a known environment, rather than applying a theory of mind in a novel situation.

Based on the texts, how would Povinelli, Nelson, and Boysen (Text 2) most likely respond to Premack and Woodruff (Text 1)?

(A) They would argue that nonhuman primates other than chimpanzees, such as baboons and gorillas, may also have a theory of mind.

(B) They would argue that the chimpanzees would be able to solve the problems themselves without referencing the photographs by struggling with the situation themselves and eventually determining the correct solution.

(C) They would encourage Premack and Woodruff to show the same videos and photographs to other nonhuman primates and compare the other nonhuman primates' reactions to the chimpanzees' reactions.

(D) They would suggest that placing the chimpanzee subjects in novel environments, such as rooms distinct from the chimpanzees' regular enclosures, may help better ascertain whether chimpanzees have a theory of mind.

6 ☐ Mark for Review

The following text is from Oscar Wilde's 1890 novel *The Picture of Dorian Gray*. Dorian is seeing his portrait, painted by Basil Hallward, for the first time.

Dorian made no answer, but passed listlessly in front of his picture and turned towards it. When he saw it he drew back, and his cheeks flushed for a moment with pleasure. A look of joy came into his eyes, as if he had recognized himself for the first time. He stood there motionless and in wonder, dimly conscious that Hallward was speaking to him, but not catching the meaning of his words. The sense of his own beauty came on him like a revelation. He had never felt it before.

According to the text, what is true about Dorian?

(A) Dorian is distracted by the beauty of the painting.

(B) Dorian believes that what Hallward is saying is unimportant.

(C) Dorian does not recognize his own image.

(D) Dorian is prone to embarrassment.

CONTINUE ➤

7 ▢ Mark for Review

The following text is from Frederick Marryat's 1847 novel *The Children of the New Forest*.

The old forester lay awake the whole of this night, reflecting how he should act relative to the children; he felt the great responsibility that he had incurred, and was alarmed when he considered what might be the consequences if his days were shortened. What would become of them—living in so sequestered a spot that few knew even of its existence—totally shut out from the world, and left to their own resources?

Based on the text, what is true about the children?

(A) They are isolated from people other than the old forester.

(B) They are completely unable to take care of themselves.

(C) The old forester is resentful of having to take care of them.

(D) They attempt to help the old forester with his responsibilities.

8 ▢ Mark for Review

The following text is Baron George Gordon Byron's poem "Answer to _____'s Professions of Affection," written around 1814. The poem is addressed to an unknown person.

In hearts like thine ne'er may I hold a place
Till I renounce all sense, all shame, all grace—
That seat,—like seats, the bane of Freedom's realm,
But dear to those presiding at the helm—
Is basely purchased, not with gold alone;
Add Conscience, too, this bargain is your own—
'Tis thine to offer with corrupting art
The rotten borough of the human heart.

What is the main idea of the text?

(A) The speaker is expressing disapproval towards the unknown person.

(B) The speaker is unimportant to the unknown person.

(C) The speaker is thinking of purchasing a seat.

(D) The speaker holds a place in the heart of the unknown person.

CONTINUE ➡

9 ☐ Mark for Review

Sepsis is a life-threatening condition caused by the body's response to an infection. These infections are typically bacterial but may be fungal, parasitic, or viral. The body's response to these infections leads to increased inflammation and organ damage. This damage, in turn, results in a weakened immune system, which increases the likelihood of reinfection. In a recent study, a team of doctors and pharmacologists led by Shubham Soni claims that administering ketone esters can reduce inflammation and immune system weakening caused by sepsis.

Which finding from the team led by Soni, if true, would most directly support its claim?

(A) Patients with sepsis who were administered ketone esters had fewer signs of inflammation and less organ damage than those administered standard antibiotics.

(B) When administered, ketone esters are known to increase blood ketone levels, which in turn are a source of energy for the brain.

(C) Both those patients administered ketone esters and those administered standard antibiotics did not have reduced inflammation when treated with medication intended to reduce fever.

(D) Those sepsis patients administered ketone esters had reduced inflammation but greater organ damage than those administered standard antibiotics.

10 ☐ Mark for Review

Horses' Responses to Novel Objects
Based on Number of Handlers

	Only One Handler	Multiple Handlers
No reluctance	45%	25%
Mild reluctance	42%	49%
Strong reluctance	13%	26%

Horses have been domesticated for thousands of years. Therefore, they show great sensitivity to the emotions of humans. Biologist Océane Liehrmann from the University of Turku, Finland, led a team of researchers in a study of horses to determine the effect of the number of handlers (either only one person or multiple people) on the horses' responses to a novel object. The researchers determined that horses with only one handler were less reluctant to interact with the novel object than were horses with multiple handlers. For example, 45% of horses with only one handler had no reluctance when interacting with a novel object while

_____

Which choice most effectively uses data from the table to complete the example?

(A) 13% of horses with only one handler had strong reluctance.

(B) 25% of horses with multiple handlers had no reluctance.

(C) 26% of horses with multiple handlers had strong reluctance.

(D) 42% of horses with only one handler had mild reluctance.

CONTINUE ➡

11 ☐ Mark for Review

Indian Lok Sabha Results by Percentage of Seats Won, 1999–2019

Party	1999	2004	2009	2014	2019
Bharatiya Janata Party	33%	25%	21%	52%	56%
Indian National Congress	21%	27%	38%	8%	10%
Communist Party of India (Marxist)	6%	8%	4%	7%	4%
Other	40%	40%	37%	33%	30%

India is the largest democracy in the world, with over 614 million people voting in the 2019 election for the Lok Sabha, the parliament of the federal government. In the early years of Indian independence, from the first election in 1951–52 through the eighth Lok Sabha in 1984, each election resulted in one party winning the majority of seats. However, starting with the 1989 election, the party with the largest number of seats failed to win more than half of the total seats. This trend was eventually broken by the Bharatiya Janata Party, which _____

Which choice most effectively uses data from the graph to illustrate the claim?

(A) went from holding the second most seats among the top 3 parties in parliament in 2004 and 2009 to holding a majority of seats in 2014 and 2019.

(B) reached its highest percentage of seats the same year that the Indian National Congress had its lowest percentage of seats over the same time period.

(C) won a lower percentage of seats in the 2009 election than in the 2004 election.

(D) had a lower percentage of seats than the Indian National Congress in 2004 but a higher percentage of seats than the Indian National Congress in 1999.

CONTINUE ➡

12 ☐ Mark for Review

Changes in Indicators of Fatty Liver Disease
in Vitamin B12 and Placebo Groups

Indicator	Vitamin B12 Group	Control Group
steatosis values (dB/cm/MHz)	−0.41	−0.30
fibrosis values (kPa)	−0.35	0.10
fasting blood glucose (mg/dl)	−5.00	−1.50
fasting serum insulin (μU/ml)	−1.46	−0.21
homeostasis model assessment of insulin resistance (HOMA-IR)	−0.23	0.06

Fatty liver disease (FLD) occurs when excess fat builds up in the liver. While there are often few or no symptoms of FLD, if left untreated, it can lead to cirrhosis or liver cancer. Because FLD is often asymptomatic, doctors and researchers rely on indicators such as steatosis (retention of fat in the liver), fibrosis (scarring), blood glucose (sugar), serum insulin, and insulin resistance to measure and track the development of FLD. A group of researchers led by radiologist Hamid Reza Talari hypothesized that those who take vitamin B12 would experience improvements in fibrosis and insulin resistance when compared to a control group over the same time period.

Which choice best describes data from the table that support the researchers' hypothesis?

(A) Those in the control group had decreases in their steatosis values and fasting blood glucose but had increases in fibrosis values and HOMA-IR.

(B) Those in the vitamin B12 group had decreases in fibrosis values and HOMA-IR levels, whereas those in the control group had increases in these same values.

(C) Both those in the vitamin B12 group and the control group had decreases in their steatosis values.

(D) Those in the control group had a decrease in their fasting blood glucose, but those in the vitamin B12 group had an increase in their fasting blood glucose.

CONTINUE

---

13 ☐ Mark for Review

Mean Levels of Carbon Monoxide (ppm),
November 18–26, 1966

City	Day of the Month of November								
	18	19	20	21	22	23	24	25	26
Newark, NJ	16	14	15	21	23	28	32	27	21
New York, NY	4	3	1	2	3	6	7	13	8
Philadelphia, PA	6	0	0	0	1	6	9	10	6
Washington, D.C.	4	2	3	0	0	0	0	0	0

The air pollution produced in an area is only one factor in that area's air quality. Weather patterns, in particular wind and the movement of air masses, can affect the concentration of pollutants such as carbon monoxide. During a smog event that occurred in the northeastern United States in November 1966, levels of carbon monoxide were recorded in Newark, New Jersey, the origin of the smog event, as well as neighboring city New York, NY, and more distant cities such as Philadelphia, PA, and Washington, D.C. The localized nature of weather patterns during this event can be seen by comparing Newark, NJ, and New York, NY, with _____

Which choice most effectively uses data from the table to complete the statement?

(A) Washington, D.C., on the 18th and the 19th.

(B) Philadelphia, PA, on the 23rd and the 25th.

(C) Philadelphia, PA, on the 24th and the 26th.

(D) Washington, D.C., on the 23rd and the 24th.

---

14 ☐ Mark for Review

Neurons respond to stimuli from sensory organs or other neurons. Learning occurs when neurons change how they respond to stimuli based on previous experience, which is a property of memory. Electrical engineers seek to replicate similar processes in their development of computer memory. Recently, research by electrical engineer Mohammad Samizadeh Nikoo has demonstrated that vanadium dioxide (VO_2) has a similar memory property to that of neurons, suggesting that _____

Which choice most logically completes the text?

(A) VO_2 could be used in the development of computer memory.

(B) neurons use VO_2 when forming memories.

(C) VO_2 can learn to respond to stimuli from sensory organs.

(D) electrical engineers can now use neurons to develop computer memory.

CONTINUE ➤

15 ☐ Mark for Review

Uruguayan-Spanish author Carmen Posadas has written the children's books *Juego de Niños* (*Child's Play*) and *La Cinta Roja* (*The Red Ribbon*). Currently, _____ available in over fifty countries and thirty languages.

Which choice completes the text so that it conforms to the conventions of Standard English?

(A) some are

(B) this is

(C) they are

(D) it is

16 ☐ Mark for Review

During a meeting, a group of twelve young deaf people shared their feelings of isolation and their desire for support. In 1988, the group worked together to form Action Deaf Youth, an _____ provides services and programs for deaf children and youth throughout Northern Ireland.

Which choice completes the text so that it conforms to the conventions of Standard English?

(A) organization, that

(B) organization

(C) organization that

(D) organization,

17 ☐ Mark for Review

In 1986, after a 56-day expedition, Ann Bancroft became the first woman to reach the North Pole. Her experience as a physical education teacher and her leadership of the first all-female team to cross the ice to the South _____ her to create a foundation that supports girls in pursuing their dreams.

Which choice completes the text so that it conforms to the conventions of Standard English?

(A) Pole to inspire

(B) Pole that inspired

(C) Pole, inspiring

(D) Pole inspired

18 ☐ Mark for Review

American artist Simone Leigh creates art in various mediums, including sculptures, video, and _____ the themes and images in her artwork, Leigh has emphasized that Black women are her primary audience and that they would be familiar with the allusions in her work.

Which choice completes the text so that it conforms to the conventions of Standard English?

(A) performance. Discussing

(B) performance discussing

(C) performance and discussing

(D) performance, discussing

CONTINUE ➡

19 ☐ Mark for Review

Japanese origamist Akira Yoshizawa is considered the grandmaster of origami, creating more than 50,000 models as well as wet-folding, the most well-known of his invented techniques. _____ dampening the paper before folding, leading to origami models with rounder and more sculpted looks.

Which choice completes the text so that it conforms to the conventions of Standard English?

- Ⓐ It involves
- Ⓑ They involve
- Ⓒ One involves
- Ⓓ These involve

20 ☐ Mark for Review

Chinese artist Xu Bing is known for his art installations that showcase his printmaking skills and his creative use of languages and texts. His 1991 installation *A Book from the Sky*, for example, consists of volumes and scrolls printed with characters he invented, while his 2004 installation *The Glassy Surface of a* _____ uses the text of Henry David Thoreau's *Walden* to create the illusion of a lake.

Which choice completes the text so that it conforms to the conventions of Standard English?

- Ⓐ *Lake*:
- Ⓑ *Lake*
- Ⓒ *Lake*,
- Ⓓ *Lake*—

21 ☐ Mark for Review

Developed along with the swing style of jazz music in the 1920s, swing dance is a group of social dances that once comprised hundreds of styles. Not all of the styles survived beyond that time _____ the dances that are still popular today include Lindy Hop, Balboa, Collegiate Shag, and Charleston.

Which choice completes the text so that it conforms to the conventions of Standard English?

- Ⓐ period; however,
- Ⓑ period, however;
- Ⓒ period, however,
- Ⓓ period, however

22 ☐ Mark for Review

Evolutionary biologist Jonathan Calede may have discovered the oldest amphibious beaver species in the world. Calede first compared measurements of the beaver's ankle to those of almost 350 other rodent species to learn more about how it moved. _____ Calede dated the species to approximately 30 million years ago based on its location between rock and ash layers.

Which choice completes the text with the most logical transition?

- Ⓐ For example,
- Ⓑ In conclusion,
- Ⓒ Next,
- Ⓓ In fact,

CONTINUE

23 ☐ Mark for Review

Male and female American citizens had starkly different roles during World War II. Men served as soldiers or took part in the workforce to create weapons and other wartime materials. _____ women were responsible for maintaining the home and supporting the men. Some women also ventured into the workforce for the first time, and the famous "We Can Do It" poster featuring "Rosie the Riveter" was created to motivate women to pursue this new role.

Which choice completes the text with the most logical transition?

(A) Besides,

(B) Instead,

(C) Likewise,

(D) Meanwhile,

24 ☐ Mark for Review

While treatment for hearing loss is typically associated with the ears, some patients with damaged ear structures are not able to use traditional cochlear implants. _____ researchers are working to develop hearing aids anchored to patients' bones in order to combat hearing loss through vibrations in the skull.

Which choice completes the text with the most logical transition?

(A) Secondly,

(B) In addition,

(C) Finally,

(D) Hence,

25 ☐ Mark for Review

Korean artist Anicka Yi uses a unique process and materials to generate her art installations. Her materials are often perishable and biological, such as soap and flowers, and are not traditionally used for artwork. _____ Yi spends almost as much time transforming these substances into completely new materials as she does creating the actual art pieces.

Which choice completes the text with the most logical transition?

(A) Meanwhile,

(B) Instead,

(C) In fact,

(D) To conclude,

CONTINUE ➔

26 ☐ Mark for Review

While researching a topic, a student has taken the following notes:

- A writing system for expressing numbers is a numeral system.
- Two examples of numeral systems from history are Babylonian cuneiform numerals and Roman numerals.
- The Babylonian cuneiform numeral system is a base-60 system and lacks a zero digit.
- It's a positional numeral system in which the position of a digit affects its value.
- The Roman numeral system is a base-10 system and lacks a zero digit.
- It's a non-positional numeral system in which the position of a digit does not affect its value.

The student wants to emphasize a difference between the two numeral systems. Which choice most effectively uses relevant information from the notes to accomplish this goal?

Ⓐ Babylonian cuneiform numerals and Roman numerals are two writing systems for expressing numbers.

Ⓑ The Roman numeral system is a base-10 non-positional system that lacks a zero digit.

Ⓒ One system for expressing numbers is Babylonian cuneiform; however, another one is the Roman numeral system.

Ⓓ The Babylonian cuneiform numeral system is base-60 and positional, while the Roman numeral system is base-10 and non-positional.

27 ☐ Mark for Review

While researching a topic, a student has taken the following notes:

- Archaeologists studied the burial of an individual at the Newen Antug site in Argentinian Patagonia.
- The individual was buried in a wooden structure over 800 years ago.
- An analysis of the structure revealed that it was carved from a tree with excellent buoyancy.
- The wooden structure was a canoe, suggesting that canoes were used as coffins at that time.

The student wants to present the Newen Antug study and its conclusions. Which choice most effectively uses relevant information from the notes to accomplish this goal?

Ⓐ The burial site of an individual over 800 years ago was found at the Newen Antug site in Argentinian Patagonia.

Ⓑ Archaeologists studied the burial site of an individual who was buried at the Newen Antug site over 800 years ago.

Ⓒ An analysis of a burial site at the Newen Antug site in Argentinian Patagonia provided evidence that canoes were used as coffins over 800 years ago.

Ⓓ As part of a study of a burial site at the Newen Antug site in Argentinian Patagonia, a wooden structure buried with an individual was analyzed.

YIELD

Once you've finished (or run out of time for) this section, use the answer key to determine how many questions you got right. If you got fewer than 15 questions right, move on to Module 2—Easier, otherwise move on to Module 2—Harder.

Test 4—Reading and Writing
Module 2—Easier

Turn to Section 1 of your answer sheet to answer the questions in this section.

The questions in this section address a number of important reading and writing skills. Each question includes one or more passages, which may include a table or graph. Read each passage and question carefully, and then choose the best answer to the question based on the passage(s).

All questions in the section are multiple-choice with four answer choices. Each question has a single best answer.

---

1 ☐ Mark for Review

Shakespeare intentionally provided no stage directions for his play *Macbeth* regarding whether to have Banquo's ghost physically present on stage or simply to have Macbeth react fearfully to something invisible, thus providing future directors with the _____ to indulge their own artistic interpretations.

Which choice completes the text with the most logical and precise word or phrase?

- (A) confusion
- (B) dedication
- (C) instruction
- (D) liberty

2 ☐ Mark for Review

German-Dutch paleontologist Ralph von Koenigswald was the first to discover the fossilized remains of *Gigantopithecus blacki*, a gargantuan ape believed to have lived during the Pleistocene Epoch. Because the fossils were exclusively found in caves in southern China, many experts believe that the species was _____ that region—that is, anyone claiming to have found remains of *Gigantopithecus* elsewhere would be mistaken.

Which choice completes the text with the most logical and precise word or phrase?

- (A) restricted to
- (B) eliminated from
- (C) common in
- (D) unknown to

CONTINUE

---

3 ☐ Mark for Review

Computer scientist Ray Kurzweil _____ that although artificial intelligence will not displace human beings, it will undoubtedly become smarter than people within this generation. This possibility has been the domain of science fiction writers for decades, whose works explore the ramifications of just such a future.

Which choice completes the text with the most logical and precise word or phrase?

(A) proves

(B) requires

(C) predicts

(D) denies

4 ☐ Mark for Review

In psychology, it's critical not to generalize from the results of studies in which the subjects are not representative of the larger population. The infamous Stanford Prison Experiment _____ this principle: the participants, whose behavior supposedly demonstrated the "human" tendency towards alarming aggression in authoritarian situations, were a handful of male college-age individuals from the same private university in California rather than a diverse sampling of subjects.

Which choice completes the text with the most logical and precise word or phrase?

(A) illustrates

(B) refutes

(C) supersedes

(D) critiques

5 ☐ Mark for Review

Neurologists know that prosopagnosia—the _____ to recognize faces—involves a specific lesion in the brain and can be caused by disease or head injury. However, prominent author Dr. Oliver Sacks believes that this "face blindness" also has a definite genetic component.

Which choice completes the text with the most logical and precise word or phrase?

(A) capability

(B) incapacity

(C) tendency

(D) reluctance

6 ☐ Mark for Review

The shark's competitive advantage in the oceanic ecosystem is principally due to electroreception, or the ability to detect electrical impulses. Marine biologists believe that this heightened _____ to electrical stimuli allows the shark to easily find its prey, for as fish swim through water, their movement produces minute electrical signals.

Which choice completes the text with the most logical and precise word or phrase?

(A) allergy

(B) sensitivity

(C) indifference

(D) aversion

CONTINUE →

7 ☐ Mark for Review

The Voynich manuscript was written on vellum dating from the fifteenth century in a script that is not found in any other source. Since cryptographers have yet to demonstrably decipher any portion of the text, the meaning and purpose of the Voynich manuscript remain _____.

Which choice completes the text with the most logical and precise word or phrase?

Ⓐ enigmatic

Ⓑ venerable

Ⓒ multifarious

Ⓓ coherent

8 ☐ Mark for Review

It is commonly believed that, in the complex ecosystem of the Nile River in Africa, the crocodile and the Egyptian plover bird have formed an _____ relationship: the crocodile opens its mouth and keeps it open while the bird instinctively eats the food particles remaining in the crocodile's teeth, thus nourishing the bird while simultaneously promoting the crocodile's dental health.

Which choice completes the text with the most logical and precise word or phrase?

Ⓐ interdependent

Ⓑ inexplicable

Ⓒ enthralling

Ⓓ inarticulate

9 ☐ Mark for Review

The following text is from Herman Melville's 1924 short novel *Billy Budd* and pertains to Edward Vere, the captain of the ship on which Billy is sailing.

Captain the Honorable Edward Fairfax Vere, to give his full title, was a bachelor of forty or thereabouts, a sailor of distinction even in a time prolific of renowned seamen. Though allied to the higher nobility, his advancement had not been altogether owing to influences connected with that circumstance. He had seen much service, been in various engagements, always acquitting himself as an officer mindful of the welfare of his men, but never tolerating an infraction of discipline; thoroughly versed in the science of his profession, and intrepid to the verge of temerity, though never injudiciously so.

According to the text, what is true of Captain Vere?

Ⓐ He dislikes many of the men who serve under him.

Ⓑ He is proud of his aristocratic background.

Ⓒ He is a capable and evenhanded naval officer.

Ⓓ He prefers navy life to life outside the navy.

CONTINUE

10 ☐ Mark for Review

"I Remember, I Remember" is an 1844 poem by Thomas Hood. The poem conveys the speaker's sadness that his life as an adult does not compare favorably to his childhood: _____

Which quotation from the poem most effectively illustrates the claim?

(A) "The lilacs where the robin built, / And where my brother set / The laburnum on his birthday,— / The tree is living yet!"

(B) "I remember, I remember, / The house where I was born, / The little window where the sun / Came peeping in at morn."

(C) "I remember, I remember, / The roses, red and white, / The vi'lets, and the lily-cups, / Those flowers made of light!"

(D) "It was a childish ignorance,/ But now 'tis little joy / To know I'm farther off from heav'n / Than when I was a boy."

11 ☐ Mark for Review

Dracula is an 1897 novel by Bram Stoker. In the story, English lawyer Jonathan Harker has traveled to Transylvania to conduct business with Count Dracula at his castle. In his journal, Harker conveys his belief that he has become Dracula's prisoner: _____

Which quotation from Jonathan Harker's journal most effectively illustrates the claim?

(A) "What manner of man is this, or what manner of creature, is it in the semblance of man? I feel the dread of this horrible place overpowering me."

(B) "My lamp seemed to be of little effect in the brilliant moonlight, but I was glad to have it with me, for there was a dread loneliness in the place which chilled my heart and made my nerves tremble."

(C) "I start at my own shadow, and am full of all sorts of horrible imaginings. God knows that there is ground for my terrible fear in this accursed place!"

(D) "I rushed up and down the stairs, trying every door and peering out of every window I could find, but after a little the conviction of my helplessness overpowered all other feelings."

CONTINUE ➡

12 🔖 Mark for Review

"In Flanders Fields" is a 1915 poem written by Lieutenant-Colonel John McCrae, a Canadian military officer who died three years later in World War I. The poem is meant to be a plea towards others to join the war effort, as is evident by the following lines: _____

Which quotation from "In Flanders Fields" most effectively illustrates the claim?

- (A) "Loved and were loved and now we lie / In Flanders fields"

- (B) "In Flanders fields the poppies blow / Between the crosses row on row"

- (C) "To you from failing hands we throw / The torch; be yours to hold it high"

- (D) "We are the dead. Short days ago / We lived, felt dawn, saw sunset glow"

13 🔖 Mark for Review

The curator of a museum claims that a dress in his possession was worn by the wife of one of Lincoln's generals at the presidential inauguration in 1865. Radiocarbon dating, which dates organic material with an error range of about thirty years in either direction, was performed on the sleeves of the dress, revealing that they date back to the 1975–2005 period. If both the curator's claim and the radiocarbon dating analysis are correct, that would suggest that _____

Which choice most logically completes the text?

- (A) the dress was made sometime between 1835 and 1895 and then damaged sometime after 1975.

- (B) vintage dresses are more commonly recovered from the late twentieth and early twenty-first centuries than from the mid-nineteenth century.

- (C) over one hundred years after the dress was made, its sleeves were replaced.

- (D) the dress was made from material different from that used for most dresses in the nineteenth century.

CONTINUE ➡

14 ☐ Mark for Review

In the early 1900s, paleontologists largely believed that there were no undocumented prehistoric aquatic species that had survived to the present day because it would be impossible for such a species to have enough animals to sustain a breeding population while escaping detection in the modern era. However, a coelacanth, a large lobe-finned fish universally believed by scientists to have gone extinct sixty-six million years ago, was found off the coast of South Africa as recently as 1938. This event may suggest that _____

Which choice most logically completes the text?

(A) fewer coelacanths are required to sustain a breeding population than was previously thought.

(B) it is possible for a prehistoric species to go undiscovered for longer than expected.

(C) the scientists who determined that the coelacanth was extinct ignored critical evidence.

(D) the same environmental conditions that eliminated the dinosaurs nearly killed off the coelacanths.

15 ☐ Mark for Review

The *door-in-the-face* technique involves initially making an outrageous or unappealing request or offer, which the other person is highly likely to refuse, then following up with a more reasonable one. The subject is more likely to look favorably upon this second request or offer because it seems acceptable compared to the initial proposition. So, if an employee wants the best raise in annual salary from her boss that she can get, she might succeed by asking for a _____

Which choice most logically completes the text?

(A) 50% raise, then asking for a 5% raise.

(B) 3% raise, then asking for a 2% raise.

(C) 10% raise, then asking for a 50% raise.

(D) 3% raise, then asking for a 3% raise again.

CONTINUE

16 🔖 Mark for Review

The North American Free Trade Agreement (NAFTA) was an agreement among the United States, Canada, and Mexico that was in effect between 1994 and 2020. During this time, the number of manufacturing jobs in the United States and Canada declined, but the total number of manufacturing jobs in the countries covered by NAFTA increased. This suggests that, between 1994 and 2020, _____

Which choice most logically completes the text?

Ⓐ the number of manufacturing jobs in Mexico increased by a greater amount than the combined decreases in the United States and Canada.

Ⓑ NAFTA made it more difficult for manufacturers to establish factories in the United States and Canada.

Ⓒ the cost of manufacturing goods in the area covered by NAFTA decreased.

Ⓓ complex goods, such as automobiles and electronics, were increasingly manufactured in the United States, Canada, and Mexico.

17 🔖 Mark for Review

American chef Alice Waters is well-known for opening the restaurant Chez Panisse, which _____ the farm-to-table movement by serving local and seasonal food.

Which choice completes the text so that it conforms to the conventions of Standard English?

Ⓐ originating

Ⓑ to originate

Ⓒ having originated

Ⓓ originated

18 🔖 Mark for Review

American activists Dolores Huerta and Cesar Chavez founded the National Farm Workers Association in 1962 to defend the rights of farm workers through nonviolent organizing tactics, such as marches and boycotts. _____ organization merged with the Agricultural Workers Organizing Committee, led by Larry Itliong, to form United Farm Workers, a labor union that advocates on behalf of farm workers across the U.S.

Which choice completes the text so that it conforms to the conventions of Standard English?

Ⓐ Its

Ⓑ Their

Ⓒ It's

Ⓓ They're

CONTINUE →

---

19 ☐ Mark for Review

Researchers at the University of York found that people who are highly individualistic feel less connected to the natural world and engage in fewer activities to improve the environment; however, engaging with nature through activities such as walking and bird-watching can reconnect _____ to the natural world and encourage environmentally-friendly behaviors.

Which choice completes the text so that it conforms to the conventions of Standard English?

Ⓐ it

Ⓑ you

Ⓒ one

Ⓓ them

20 ☐ Mark for Review

National flags are designed to best represent and symbolize the individual _____ when countries share a history or culture, their flags are designed to look similar, thus creating a flag family that shares colors, shapes, or other elements.

Which choice completes the text so that it conforms to the conventions of Standard English?

Ⓐ country but

Ⓑ country,

Ⓒ country

Ⓓ country, but

21 ☐ Mark for Review

Scientists at the University of Illinois and the University of Lancaster observed that plants under very bright sunlight enter a protective mode for several minutes, during which they stop photosynthesizing and growing. If the crops were genetically modified to have a shorter time in protective mode, _____ The scientists resolved to find out.

Which choice completes the text so that it conforms to the conventions of Standard English?

Ⓐ could the crop yield increase?

Ⓑ the crop yield could increase?

Ⓒ the crop yield could increase.

Ⓓ could the crop yield increase.

22 ☐ Mark for Review

Take Our Daughters and Sons to Work Day originally started as a day focused on engaging girls with the workforce, Take Our Daughters to Work Day. On the national day, the fourth Tuesday in April, parents and caregivers go to work with their children; shadowing their parents or caregivers _____ children real-world experience and ideas for potential future careers.

Which choice completes the text so that it conforms to the conventions of Standard English?

Ⓐ offer

Ⓑ have offered

Ⓒ are offering

Ⓓ offers

CONTINUE ➡

23 ▢ Mark for Review

In order to allow olive ridley turtles to lay eggs on Versova Beach in Mumbai, community activist Afroz Shah organized a large group of volunteers to remove over 11 million pounds of trash. The beach now allows community members to connect with the natural world and _____ a healthy habitat for olive ridley turtles to use after a twenty-year absence.

Which choice completes the text so that it conforms to the conventions of Standard English?

Ⓐ provided

Ⓑ providing

Ⓒ provides

Ⓓ provide

24 ▢ Mark for Review

Yoga is an ancient discipline from India that aims to combine physical fitness with mental and spiritual control and calm and has expanded to become popular with many different cultures. _____ yoga is shifting into different forms to allow a wider range of people to participate. For example, accessible yoga provides opportunities for those with physical disabilities to access the health and mental benefits of the practice.

Which choice completes the text with the most logical transition?

Ⓐ Nevertheless,

Ⓑ Similarly,

Ⓒ Thus,

Ⓓ Currently,

25 ▢ Mark for Review

Scientists often disagree about what traits to use to place newly discovered species in the tree of life and debate different ways to organize evolutionary relationships. *Chimerarachne yingi*, _____ is an extinct arachnid species that is sometimes placed near modern spiders based on its acquisition of silk-spinning organs or near other arachnids based on its loss of a tail.

Which choice completes the text with the most logical transition?

Ⓐ as a result,

Ⓑ in comparison,

Ⓒ for example,

Ⓓ still,

26 ▢ Mark for Review

In 2011, a seismometer detected seismic activity from a magnitude 8.9 earthquake and automatically cut the power to all 30 bullet trains in Japan, potentially avoiding mass architectural damage to the tracks. _____ the cut to the power prevented citizens from being caught in a dangerous location during the earthquake and allowed riders to seek shelter.

Which choice completes the text with the most logical transition?

Ⓐ In addition,

Ⓑ In comparison,

Ⓒ For example,

Ⓓ Specifically,

CONTINUE ➡

27 🔖 Mark for Review

While researching a topic, a student has taken the following notes:

- The Endangered Species Act (ESA) was enacted in 1973 to recover species and prevent extinction.

- A species is listed under the ESA when it's determined that the species needs protection and delisted when the population has recovered.

- Only 54 of the over 1,000 listed species have been delisted from the ESA, raising concerns about the effectiveness of the ESA.

- Erich Eberhard, David Wilcove, and Andrew Dobson conducted an analysis of population trends of species listed under the ESA.

- They found that most species had to wait multiple years before being listed and by then their populations were already so low that recovery was much more difficult.

The student wants to make a generalization about the kind of study conducted by Eberhard, Wilcove, and Dobson. Which choice most effectively uses relevant information from the notes to accomplish this goal?

(A) Scientists have analyzed population trends to find out the impact of legal protections in the realm of conservation.

(B) Species listed under the ESA have low population levels when they are listed.

(C) Only 54 once-listed species have been delisted; many more species have not recovered and are still listed.

(D) Based on an analysis of population trends, Eberhard, Wilcove, and Dobson found that species listed under the ESA have very small populations when listed.

STOP
**If you finish before time is called, you may check your work on this module only.
Do not turn to any other module in the test.**

Test 4—Reading and Writing
Module 2—Harder

Turn to Section 1 of your answer sheet to answer the questions in this section.

DIRECTIONS

The questions in this section address a number of important reading and writing skills. Each question includes one or more passages, which may include a table or graph. Read each passage and question carefully, and then choose the best answer to the question based on the passage(s).

All questions in the section are multiple-choice with four answer choices. Each question has a single best answer.

---

1 ☐ Mark for Review

Dutch philosopher Baruch Spinoza argued as part of his rejection of dualism that all things, living or not, have the inclination to continue to exist and enhance themselves, a property he named "conatus." All things, he believed, had the tendency to _____ and would only cease to be if acted upon by outside forces.

Which choice completes the text with the most logical and precise word or phrase?

- Ⓐ deteriorate
- Ⓑ perish
- Ⓒ persevere
- Ⓓ disappear

2 ☐ Mark for Review

Many species demonstrate rescue behavior, a behavior in which an individual will help another in distress without any obvious benefit to the helper. In fact, this behavior _____ a recent study of Australian magpies when some birds in the study helped other birds remove the trackers that researchers had placed upon them, making it more difficult for the researchers to obtain data.

Which choice completes the text with the most logical and precise word or phrase?

- Ⓐ aided
- Ⓑ impeded
- Ⓒ clarified
- Ⓓ exposed

CONTINUE

3 ☐ Mark for Review

Dutch artist M.C. Escher's work uses _____ to engage viewers by employing mathematical and intuitive processes to create images of objects that at first appear normal but on closer inspection are, in fact, impossible.

Which choice completes the text with the most logical and precise word or phrase?

(A) geometry

(B) beauty

(C) paradox

(D) color

4 ☐ Mark for Review

Typically, pure water is not considered particularly _____, but a team of scientists led by Richard Zare has discovered how microdroplets of water can turn into caustic hydrogen peroxide. When microdroplets of water hit a solid surface, an electric charge jumps between the water and the solid, producing hydroxyl radicals that, in turn, combine with remaining oxygen to form hydrogen peroxide.

Which choice completes the text with the most logical and precise word or phrase?

(A) viable

(B) contaminated

(C) common

(D) reactive

5 ☐ Mark for Review

The Beat Generation, a literary subculture movement featured in works such as Allen Ginsberg's *Howl* (1956) and William S. Burroughs's *Naked Lunch* (1959), was characterized by its _____ the traditional values of the 1950s. The movement's central message of nonconformity would be criticized by American literary critic Manuel Luis Martinez, who believed that the Beat Generation's lack of attention to the politics of individualism undermined the movement's goals.

Which choice completes the text with the most logical and precise word or phrase?

(A) dissension from

(B) gratitude towards

(C) adherence to

(D) deference to

6 ☐ Mark for Review

The possibility of recycling used car tires as building materials is _____ indeed: the disposal of used tires is a major environmental problem, so potentially reusing them would be beneficial. Furthermore, initial studies have shown that walls made of used tires and dirt are more structurally robust than those made of concrete.

Which choice completes the text with the most logical and precise word or phrase?

(A) derivative

(B) ludicrous

(C) auspicious

(D) innovative

CONTINUE ➡

7 ☐ Mark for Review

The Voynich manuscript was written on vellum dating from the fifteenth century in a script that is not found in any other source. Since cryptographers have yet to demonstrably decipher any portion of the text, the meaning and purpose of the Voynich manuscript remain _____.

Which choice completes the text with the most logical and precise word or phrase?

(A) enigmatic

(B) venerable

(C) multifarious

(D) coherent

8 ☐ Mark for Review

Astronautics owes much to the _____ contributions of Charles E. Whitsett. His ground-breaking development of the manned maneuvering unit enabled the first spacewalks in which astronauts were not tethered to a spacecraft.

Which choice completes the text with the most logical and precise word or phrase?

(A) dubious

(B) futile

(C) galvanizing

(D) avant-garde

9 ☐ Mark for Review

The following text is adapted from Charles Dickens's 1859 novel *A Tale of Two Cities*. Mr. Lorry, traveling to France on business, is delivering some news to Miss Manette, the daughter of one of his friends.

"Miss Manette, I am a man of business. I have a business charge to acquit myself of. In your reception of it, don't heed me any more than if I was a speaking machine—truly, I am not much else. I will, with your leave, relate to you, miss, the story of one of our customers."

"Story!"

He seemed wilfully to mistake the word she had repeated, when he added, in a hurry, "Yes, customers; in the banking business we usually call our connection our customers. He was a French gentleman; a scientific gentleman; a man of great acquirements—a Doctor."

Based on the text, how does Mr. Lorry interact with Miss Manette?

(A) Although he claims to be uninterested in the news, he makes purposeful decisions during his conversation with Miss Manette.

(B) Although he is a professional, he misunderstands Miss Manette's interjection.

(C) Although he acts as if the news has no importance to him, he cannot keep the details of the story accurate.

(D) Although he is unthinkingly following directions, he is flustered by Miss Manette's rudeness.

CONTINUE →

10 ☐ Mark for Review

Nisga'a poet Jordan Abel addresses the experiences of Indigenous people as European settlers and their descendants took over North America. Abel's first book of poetry, *The Place of Scraps* (2014), uses *Totem Poles*, a 1929 book by anthropologist Marius Barbeau, as source material. Abel claims that his use of Barbeau's text shows how anthropological texts can be used to portray Indigenous people differently based on the author.

Which finding, if true, would most directly support Abel's claim?

- (A) Abel intersperses Barbeau's text with images of Indigenous people and personal anecdotes written in the third person.

- (B) Abel explains that Barbeau presented two chiefs feuding over constructing the largest pole as unreasonable, yet other anthropologists claim that such arguments between chiefs of Indigenous tribes were important political exchanges.

- (C) *The Place of Scraps* won the Dorothy Livesay Poetry Prize and was a finalist for the Gerald Lampert Award.

- (D) Before Abel wrote *The Place of Scraps*, other Indigenous writers had used texts from anthropologists in their works.

11 ☐ Mark for Review

In Japan, adults may be legally adopted into a family. The practice may have started as early as the 13th century CE, but widespread adult adoption dates from the Tokugawa shogunate, a military government that began around 1600 CE. During this time, members of the ruling class would adopt competent adult males, who would then ensure that the family's political and business interests would be sustained. While adult adoption remains a way for individuals to improve their economic and social status, the practice has its detractors as well, with some researchers arguing that it can lead to issues with the adoptee developing a firm sense of identity in his or her new environment.

Which of the following best illustrates the researchers' claim?

- (A) Adult adoptees are entitled to an inheritance from their adoptive families, strengthening the ties between them, which further encourages the adult adoptee to work to enhance the new family's prosperity.

- (B) While most adult adoptees typically report improved financial status after adoption, many of those same adoptees also experience higher-than-normal rates of depression and anxiety.

- (C) Elsewhere in East Asia, such as in China and Korea, families have a traditional obligation to adopt blood relatives who lack more closely-related living kin, but adoptions in Japan are almost exclusively between those with no blood relations.

- (D) Families with ancestors who were adult adoptees do not distinguish between those ancestors who were members of the family by birth and those who were adopted into the family.

CONTINUE →

12 ☐ Mark for Review

Neurologists have hypothesized that tau protein, the mutation of which is known to cause Alzheimer's disease, is key to controlling glutamate receptors, which are involved in the production of memories. Tau protein does not directly affect glutamate receptors but does inhibit NSF, an enzyme found in the brain.

Which finding, if true, would most directly support the neurologists' hypothesis?

Ⓐ Other studies have shown that an excess of NSF has been shown to lead to abnormal glutamate receptor behavior.

Ⓑ Patients with Alzheimer's disease have been found to have an excess of NSF in their brains during autopsies.

Ⓒ Neurologists do not yet know what causes mutations of tau protein; one hypothesis is that disease leads to these mutations.

Ⓓ Other types of dementia are not caused by mutations in tau protein but rather physical damage to the brain.

13 ☐ Mark for Review

From 1634 to 1637 CE, tulips in the Dutch Republic sold for extraordinarily high prices, sometimes as much as 10 times the annual wage of a skilled worker, in a phenomenon known as tulip mania. Some economists, such as Charles Kindleberger, argue that tulip mania was the first speculative bubble in history, during which the prices of a commodity (in this case tulip bulbs) do not follow the typical rules of economics. Others, such as Peter Garber, believe that tulip mania is explainable by fundamental economic concepts such as supply and demand.

Which finding, if true, would most directly support Garber's argument?

Ⓐ Tulips during this period were very rare, and demand for tulips was fueled in part by the ability to reproduce and sell bulbs, enabling some purchasers to make profits.

Ⓑ Some common bulbs, such as the Witte Croonen bulb, saw price increases as dramatic as those of rare bulbs.

Ⓒ The prices of tulip bulbs were much higher than could be supported by the banking system in place in 17th century Europe.

Ⓓ The tulip mania led to an increase of the supply of gold coins in the Dutch Republic.

CONTINUE →

14 ☐ Mark for Review

The use of pesticides in agriculture poses risks to both humans and the environment, so finding alternative methods of pest control is an important area of research. The use of ants to control pests in China goes back to at least the 4th century CE, and farmers in places such as Kenya, Ghana, and Canada have also used ants to control various organisms. Entomologist Diego Anjos and others have identified several positive effects (services) of ants, such as reducing both the abundance of non-honeydew-producing species and plant damage. However, ants also have negative effects, such as increasing the abundance of honeydew-producing species and spreading pathogens, suggesting that _____.

Which choice most logically completes the text?

- (A) ants may have unintended environmental consequences when used to control pests in certain circumstances.

- (B) other species may also be effective in providing services to farmers.

- (C) ants as pest control provide numerous services without serious ramifications.

- (D) scientists do not yet know whether using ants to control organisms is a net positive in any situation.

15 ☐ Mark for Review

Among many animals, such as mice, fruit flies, and humans, each odor that an animal can smell is detected by a particular kind of sensory neuron that has a particular kind of receptor; eliminating that receptor through illness or genetic manipulation results in the inability to smell that odor. A team led by neurobiologist Margo Herre tested whether mosquitoes modified to lack the receptor for smelling blood would be unable to find humans. These mosquitoes were still able to find humans, suggesting that _____.

Which choice most logically completes the text?

- (A) mosquitoes without damage to their odor receptors are more capable of finding humans than those with damage.

- (B) like mice, fruit flies, and humans, individual mosquitoes with damage to particular receptors will be unable to detect certain odors.

- (C) researchers cannot assume that mosquitoes have the same correlation between receptors and the ability to sense certain odors that mice, fruit flies, and humans have.

- (D) researchers can assume that interfering with mosquitoes' odor receptors is a potential way to prevent mosquitoes from feeding on humans.

CONTINUE

16 ◻ Mark for Review

The North American Free Trade Agreement (NAFTA) was an agreement among the United States, Canada, and Mexico that was in effect between 1994 and 2020. During this time, the number of manufacturing jobs in the United States and Canada declined, but the total number of manufacturing jobs in the countries covered by NAFTA increased. This suggests that, between 1994 and 2020, _____

Which choice most logically completes the text?

(A) the number of manufacturing jobs in Mexico increased by a greater amount than the combined decreases in the United States and Canada.

(B) NAFTA made it more difficult for manufacturers to establish factories in the United States and Canada.

(C) the cost of manufacturing goods in the area covered by NAFTA decreased.

(D) complex goods, such as automobiles and electronics, were increasingly manufactured in the United States, Canada, and Mexico.

17 ◻ Mark for Review

Researchers studying the recent eruption of Hunga Tonga–Hunga Ha'apai, a submarine volcano located near the islands of Tonga in the South Pacific, found that the volcanic cloud, compared to those of other eruptions, _____ the highest ever recorded.

Which choice completes the text so that it conforms to the conventions of Standard English?

(A) have been

(B) are

(C) was

(D) were

18 ◻ Mark for Review

Connectomes, extensive maps of neural connections in the brain, reveal that each person has a distinct pattern of connections known as a functional fingerprint. In a 2017 study, behavioral _____ found that about one-third of the functional fingerprint is unique to an individual and that other parts are inherited.

Which choice completes the text so that it conforms to the conventions of Standard English?

(A) neuroscientist, Damien Fair,

(B) neuroscientist Damien Fair

(C) neuroscientist Damien Fair,

(D) neuroscientist, Damien Fair

CONTINUE ⟶

19 ☐ Mark for Review

Throughout her career, Muscogee Nation member and poet Joy Harjo has edited multiple anthologies that have highlighted Native voices in the U.S. For example, a map showcasing 47 Native Nations poets _____ her signature project during her time as the U.S. Poet Laureate.

Which choice completes the text so that it conforms to the conventions of Standard English?

Ⓐ was

Ⓑ are

Ⓒ have been

Ⓓ were

20 ☐ Mark for Review

When bees pollinate flowers, they may be exposed to insecticides, potentially affecting their nervous systems. Recently, Dr. Rachel Parkinson of the University of Oxford added the common _____ to a sucralose solution to examine the insecticide's impact on honeybees' ability to walk in a straight line.

Which choice completes the text so that it conforms to the conventions of Standard English?

Ⓐ insecticide sulfoxaflor

Ⓑ insecticide, sulfoxaflor,

Ⓒ insecticide sulfoxaflor,

Ⓓ insecticide, sulfoxaflor

21 ☐ Mark for Review

In 1946, Juliet Rice Wichman acquired 1,000 acres on Kaua'i, one of the Hawaiian islands, to transform the land into a garden by removing grazing cattle and restoring terraces to grow taro. Wichman's work to preserve the culture of Kaua'i wasn't _____ as the first director of the Kaua'i Museum, she oversaw exhibits celebrating the history, culture, and art of Native Hawaiians.

Which choice completes the text so that it conforms to the conventions of Standard English?

Ⓐ finished though

Ⓑ finished. Though,

Ⓒ finished, though,

Ⓓ finished, though:

22 ☐ Mark for Review

Researchers studying bacteria have solved a 50-year mystery of how bacteria are able to move using appendages that are made of a single _____ the subunits of the protein can exist in 11 different shapes, allowing the appendages to "supercoil" into corkscrews that the bacteria use to propel themselves.

Which choice completes the text so that it conforms to the conventions of Standard English?

Ⓐ protein

Ⓑ protein while

Ⓒ protein,

Ⓓ protein:

CONTINUE →

23 ☐ Mark for Review

Fault tree analysis was originally used in engineering to enhance safety practices in high-risk fields, such as nuclear power and pharmaceuticals, but other fields are experimenting with ways to utilize this process to benefit their work. _____ fault tree analysis is also being used in low-risk fields, such as social services and software engineering.

Which choice completes the text with the most logical transition?

- (A) Increasingly,
- (B) Nevertheless,
- (C) Therefore,
- (D) In addition,

24 ☐ Mark for Review

When Monika Sosnowska began her career in Amsterdam as a painter, she never expected to branch out into other media. _____ she had primarily worked on canvas, but she quickly found her works evolving to include the three-dimensional space around her.

Which choice completes the text with the most logical transition?

- (A) Instead,
- (B) Consequently,
- (C) Previously,
- (D) Similarly,

25 ☐ Mark for Review

Fish sometimes appear in otherwise uninhabited bodies of water, seemingly emerging out of nowhere. Some scientists believe that the fish are carried to these locations in the beaks or talons of birds. _____ new research suggests that the fish eggs enter a state of hibernation and are actually eaten by birds and excreted out into the bodies of water.

Which choice completes the text with the most logical transition?

- (A) For instance,
- (B) Next,
- (C) Likewise,
- (D) Alternatively,

CONTINUE

26 ☐ Mark for Review

While researching a topic, a student has taken the following notes:

- To restore oyster reefs in Australia, limestone boulders are submerged to provide habitats, but baby oysters need help finding the boulders.
- A team from University of Adelaide looked into using sound as a way to encourage the baby oysters to attach to the boulders.
- The research team recorded sounds at the healthy Port Noarlunga Reef to play near the submerged boulders.
- Boulders in the area with the soundscape attracted around 17,000 more oysters per square meter compared to boulders without the soundscape.
- Soundscapes can indicate a healthy place for baby oysters to grow and can be a cost-effective way to restore oyster reefs.

The student wants to emphasize the aim of the research study. Which choice most effectively uses relevant information from the notes to accomplish this goal?

(A) Researchers obtained a soundscape at Port Noarlunga Reef to help in the restoration of oyster reefs in Australia.

(B) Researchers now know that the soundscape of a healthy marine ecosystem can attract baby oysters to attach to submerged limestone boulders.

(C) After they measured the number of oysters attracted to boulders in the soundscape area compared to no soundscape, researchers determined that the soundscape attracted more baby oysters.

(D) Researchers wanted to know whether a soundscape of a healthy marine ecosystem could encourage baby oysters to attach to submerged limestone boulders.

27 ☐ Mark for Review

While researching a topic, a student has taken the following notes:

- Neanderthals are an extinct species of humans who died out about 40,000 years ago and are the closest evolutionary relatives of present-day humans.
- Studying the genomes of Neanderthals provides insight into human evolution.
- Professor Svante Pääbo is a Swedish geneticist and the director of the Department of Genetics at the Max Planck Institute for Evolutionary Anthropology.
- His landmark study presented the first draft sequence of the Neanderthal genome.
- Laurits Skov of the Max Planck Institute for Evolutionary Anthropology has a doctorate in bioinformatics and studied evolutionary anthropology.
- One of his recent studies revealed the genomes of a family of Neanderthals.

The student wants to emphasize the affiliation and purpose of Pääbo's and Skov's work. Which choice most effectively uses relevant information from the notes to accomplish this goal?

(A) The closest evolutionary relatives of present-day humans, Neanderthals went extinct about 40,000 years ago.

(B) By studying the genomes of Neanderthals, Svante Pääbo and Laurits Skov of the Max Planck Institute for Evolutionary Anthropology provide insight into human evolution.

(C) Svante Pääbo and Laurits Skov study the genome of Neanderthals, an extinct species of humans.

(D) Studies by Svante Pääbo and Laurits Skov reveal information about Neanderthals, who died out about 40,000 years ago.

STOP
If you finish before time is called, you may check your work on this module only.
Do not turn to any other module in the test.

THIS PAGE LEFT INTENTIONALLY BLANK.

Test 4—Math
Module 1

Turn to Section 2 of your answer sheet to answer the questions in this section.

DIRECTIONS

The questions in this section address a number of important math skills.
Use of a calculator is permitted for all questions.

NOTES

Unless otherwise indicated:

- All variables and expressions represent real numbers.
- Figures provided are drawn to scale.
- All figures lie in a plane.
- The domain of a given function f is the set of all real numbers x for which $f(x)$ is a real number.

REFERENCE

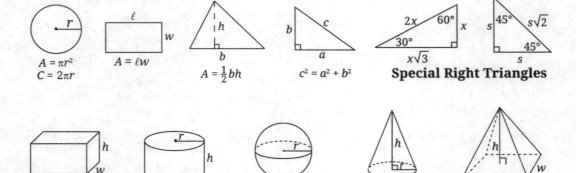

$A = \pi r^2$
$C = 2\pi r$

$A = \ell w$

$A = \frac{1}{2}bh$

$c^2 = a^2 + b^2$

Special Right Triangles

$V = \ell w h$

$V = \pi r^2 h$

$V = \frac{4}{3}\pi r^3$

$V = \frac{1}{3}\pi r^2 h$

$V = \frac{1}{3}\ell w h$

The number of degrees of arc in a circle is 360.
The number of radians of arc in a circle is 2π.
The sum of the measures in degrees of the angles of a triangle is 180.

CONTINUE

For multiple-choice questions, solve each problem, choose the correct answer from the choices provided, and then fill in the circle with the answer letter. Enter only one answer for each question. You will not get credit for questions with more than one answer entered or for questions with no answers entered.

For student-produced response questions, solve each problem and write your answer next to or under the question in the test book as described below.

- Once you've written your answer, circle it clearly. You will not receive credit for anything written outside the circle or for any questions with more than one circled answer.

- If you find **more than one correct answer**, write and circle only one answer.

- Your answer can be up to 5 characters for a **positive** answer and up to 6 characters (including the negative sign) for a **negative** answer, but no more.

- If your answer is a **fraction** that is too long (over 5 characters for positive, 6 characters for negative), write the decimal equivalent.

- If your answer is a **decimal** that is too long (over 5 characters for positive, 6 characters for negative), truncate it or round at the fourth digit.

- If your answer is a **mixed number** (such as $3\frac{1}{2}$), write it as an improper fraction (7/2) or its decimal equivalent (3.5).

- Don't enter **symbols** such as a percent sign, comma, or dollar sign in your circled answer.

CONTINUE ➔

1 ☐ Mark for Review

A data set containing only the values 2, 2, 9, 9, 9, 16, 16, 16, 16, 26, 26, and 26 is represented by a frequency table. Which of the following is the correct representation of this data set?

Ⓐ

Number	Frequency
2	4
9	27
16	64
26	78

Ⓑ

Number	Frequency
2	2
9	3
16	4
26	3

Ⓒ

Number	Frequency
2	2
3	9
4	16
3	26

Ⓓ

Number	Frequency
4	2
27	9
64	16
78	26

2 ☐ Mark for Review

The expression $x^2 - x - 56$ is equivalent to which of the following expressions?

Ⓐ $(x - 14)(x + 4)$

Ⓑ $(x - 7)(x + 8)$

Ⓒ $(x - 8)(x + 7)$

Ⓓ $(x - 4)(x + 14)$

3 ☐ Mark for Review

A carpenter hammers 10 nails per minute and installs 7 screws per minute during a project. Which of the following equations represents the scenario if the carpenter hammers nails for x minutes, installs screws for y minutes, and uses a combined total of 200 nails and screws?

Ⓐ $\frac{1}{10}x + \frac{1}{7}y = 200$

Ⓑ $\frac{1}{10}x + \frac{1}{7}y = 3,420$

Ⓒ $10x + 7y = 200$

Ⓓ $10x + 7y = 3,420$

CONTINUE ➡

4 Mark for Review

What is the measure of angle F in the triangle DEF, where angle D is 73° and angle E is 35°?

(A) 38°

(B) 72°

(C) 108°

(D) 126°

5 Mark for Review

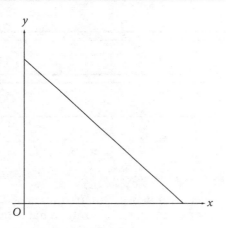

The total amount of plastic remaining to be recycled in a facility over x shifts is represented by the graph shown. Which of the following is the best interpretation of the y-intercept of the graph?

(A) The total amount of plastic remaining at any given time

(B) The number of shifts it will take to finish recycling the plastic

(C) The amount of plastic that is recycled per shift

(D) The initial amount of plastic to be recycled

6 Mark for Review

The table shows the condition and subject type for 200 textbooks at a bookstore.

	Biology	Chemistry	Physics	Anatomy	Total
Used	10	25	30	15	80
New	30	25	10	55	120
Total	40	50	40	70	200

What is the probability that a textbook chosen at random will be a new textbook? (Express your answer as a decimal or fraction, not as a percent.)

7 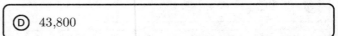 Mark for Review

A random sample of 5,000 students out of 60,000 undergraduate students at a university were surveyed about a potential change to the registration system. According to the survey results, 75% of the respondents did not support the existing registration system, with a 4% margin of error. Which of the following represents a reasonable total number of students who did not support the existing registration system?

(A) 1,250

(B) 3,750

(C) 13,800

(D) 43,800

CONTINUE

8 ☐ Mark for Review

What is the negative solution to the equation $\frac{32}{a} = a - 4$?

9 ☐ Mark for Review

After a hot air balloon is launched from a plateau 1,000 meters above sea level, it rises at a constant rate of 750 meters per minute. Which of the following best describes the function used to model the balloon's distance above sea level over time?

(A) Increasing linear

(B) Increasing exponential

(C) Decreasing linear

(D) Decreasing exponential

10 ☐ Mark for Review

What is the x-intercept of the function $f(x) = (22)^x - 1$ when it is graphed in the xy-plane, where $y = f(x)$?

(A) $(-1, 0)$

(B) $(0, 0)$

(C) $(21, 0)$

(D) $(22, 0)$

11 ☐ Mark for Review

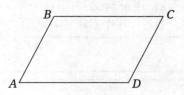

Note: Figure not drawn to scale.

In parallelogram $ABCD$ shown, the length of $\overline{AB}$ is one-third the length of $\overline{AD}$. The perimeter of the parallelogram is 64 inches. What is the length, in inches, of $\overline{AB}$?

(A) 8

(B) 16

(C) 24

(D) 32

12 ☐ Mark for Review

A triangle with an area of 18 square units has a base of $(m + 5)$ units and a height of m units. What is the value of m?

(A) 4

(B) 9

(C) 13

(D) 36

CONTINUE ➡

13 ☐ Mark for Review

Time (seconds)	Number of colonies of yeast
0	5
1	20
2	80
3	320

The table shows the exponential growth of a type of yeast over time s, in seconds. There are c total yeast colonies. What is the equation that represents this relationship, assuming that no yeast was added or removed after counting began?

Ⓐ $c = (1 + 3)^s$

Ⓑ $c = (1 + 5)^s$

Ⓒ $c = 3(1 + 5)^s$

Ⓓ $c = 5(1 + 3)^s$

14 ☐ Mark for Review

The equations $12x = y$ and $24x + 7 = 2y$ intersect at how many points when graphed in the xy-plane?

Ⓐ 0

Ⓑ 1

Ⓒ 2

Ⓓ 7

15 ☐ Mark for Review

Several tiles labeled with either an A or a B are placed in a bag, and tiles are worth a different point value depending on the label. The equation $15a + 10b = 100$ represents the situation when a of the A tiles and b of the B tiles are drawn from the bag for a total of 100 points. How many points would be earned by drawing one A tile and one B tile from the bag?

☐☐☐☐

16 ☐ Mark for Review

The amount of money remaining in a scholarship fund is reduced by one-fourth every year. The amount of money in the fund is represented by d and the number of years by y. If the fund starts with $10,000, which of the following equations represents this situation after y years?

Ⓐ $d = \frac{1}{4}(10,000)^y$

Ⓑ $d = \frac{3}{4}(10,000)^y$

Ⓒ $d = 10,000\left(\frac{1}{4}\right)^y$

Ⓓ $d = 10,000\left(\frac{3}{4}\right)^y$

CONTINUE

17 🔖 Mark for Review

What is the diameter, in millimeters (mm), of a cylinder with a volume of 144π mm^3 and a height of 4 mm?

(A) 6

(B) 9

(C) 12

(D) 36

18 🔖 Mark for Review

$$4x + 2y = 4$$
$$19x + 10y = 14$$

When graphed in the xy-plane, the linear equations shown above intersect at (a, b). What is the value of a?

(A) –20

(B) –10

(C) 6

(D) 14

19 🔖 Mark for Review

The longest side of right triangle ABC is opposite angle B. If $\sin(A) = \dfrac{9}{41}$, what is the value of $\sin(C)$?

20 🔖 Mark for Review

Function g reaches its maximum value when $x = a$. If $g(x) = -6x^2 - 30x - 24$, what is the value of a?

CONTINUE ➡

21 ☐ Mark for Review

$$f(x) = -\frac{1}{5}x - 3$$

The linear function $f(x)$, defined by the given equation, is perpendicular to linear function $g(x)$ when graphed in the xy-plane. If $g(0) = 0$, what is the value of $g(2)$?

22 ☐ Mark for Review

$$y = 5kx^2 + 2x + 3$$

$$\frac{y}{10} = -x$$

The given system of equations has exactly one solution. If k is a positive constant, what is the value of k?

YIELD
Once you've finished (or run out of time for) this section, use the answer key to determine how many questions you got right. If you got fewer than 14 questions right, move on to Module 2—Easier, otherwise move on to Module 2—Harder.

Test 4—Math
Module 2—Easier

Turn to Section 2 of your answer sheet to answer the questions in this section.

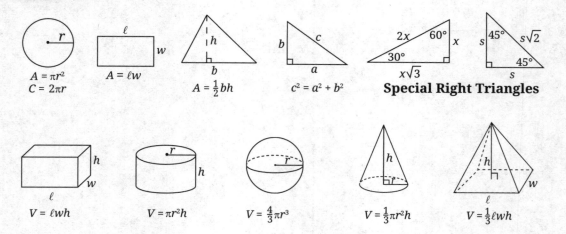
CONTINUE

For multiple-choice questions, solve each problem, choose the correct answer from the choices provided, and then fill in the circle with the answer letter. Enter only one answer for each question. You will not get credit for questions with more than one answer entered or for questions with no answers entered.

For student-produced response questions, solve each problem and write your answer next to or under the question in the test book as described below.

- Once you've written your answer, circle it clearly. You will not receive credit for anything written outside the circle or for any questions with more than one circled answer.
- If you find **more than one correct answer**, write and circle only one answer.
- Your answer can be up to 5 characters for a **positive** answer and up to 6 characters (including the negative sign) for a **negative** answer, but no more.
- If your answer is a **fraction** that is too long (over 5 characters for positive, 6 characters for negative), write the decimal equivalent.
- If your answer is a **decimal** that is too long (over 5 characters for positive, 6 characters for negative), truncate it or round at the fourth digit.
- If your answer is a **mixed number** (such as $3\frac{1}{2}$), write it as an improper fraction (7/2) or its decimal equivalent (3.5).
- Don't enter **symbols** such as a percent sign, comma, or dollar sign in your circled answer.

- -

1 ☐ Mark for Review

33, 34, 38, 41, 43, 44, 47

Which of the following is the median of the given data?

Ⓐ 38

Ⓑ 40

Ⓒ 41

Ⓓ 42

2 ☐ Mark for Review

What is the value of the solution to the equation $22 = y - 10$?

3 ☐ Mark for Review

A rectangle has a height of 23 inches (in) and a width of 9 in. What is its perimeter, in inches?

Ⓐ 32

Ⓑ 64

Ⓒ 207

Ⓓ 1,024

4 ☐ Mark for Review

$15a - (6a - 2a)$

Which of the following expressions is equivalent to the given expression?

Ⓐ $5a$

Ⓑ $7a$

Ⓒ $11a$

Ⓓ $23a$

5 ☐ Mark for Review

Which equation represents the relationship between the numbers a and b if a is half of b?

Ⓐ $a = \frac{1}{2}b$

Ⓑ $a = b - 2$

Ⓒ $a = b + 2$

Ⓓ $b = \frac{1}{2}a$

CONTINUE →

---

6 ☐ Mark for Review

For all positive values of y, the expression $\frac{3}{y+c}$ is equivalent to $\frac{15}{5y+30}$. What is the value of constant c?

Ⓐ 3

Ⓑ 6

Ⓒ 8

Ⓓ 150

---

7 ☐ Mark for Review

A total of 200 pets were adopted at an event. If 70% of the adopted pets were dogs, how many of the pets were dogs?

---

8 ☐ Mark for Review

James must drive 100 miles before he can take his driver's license test. He knows that when he drives around town running errands, he drives at an average speed of 20 miles per hour. If James maintains this average speed, how many hours must he drive to meet the requirement for his driver's license test?

Ⓐ 5

Ⓑ 20

Ⓒ 80

Ⓓ 100

---

9 ☐ Mark for Review

What is the value of $4y - 16$ if $y - 4 = 11$?

---

10 ☐ Mark for Review

The function g is defined as $g(x) = x^2 - 1$. What is the value of $g(x)$ when $x = 3$?

(A) 4

(B) 5

(C) 7

(D) 8

11 ☐ Mark for Review

The production cost $p(x)$, in dollars, to produce x units of an item when materials cost \$2 per item is given by $p(x) = 2x + 150$. What is the total cost to produce 2,000 units of this item?

(A) \$1,850

(B) \$2,300

(C) \$3,850

(D) \$4,150

12 ☐ Mark for Review

The function f is given as $f(x) = \frac{2}{3}x$. When $x = 6$, what is the value of $f(x)$?

(A) 2

(B) 4

(C) 6

(D) 9

13 ☐ Mark for Review

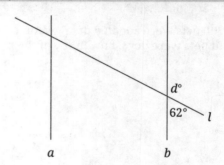

Note: Figure not drawn to scale.

In the given figure, what is the value of d if line a is parallel to line b?

CONTINUE

14 ☐ Mark for Review

$$3x - 4y = 17$$

In the xy-plane, the graph of a line with an x-intercept of $(c, 0)$ and a y-intercept of $(0, k)$, where c and k are constants, can be represented by the given equation. What is the value of $\frac{c}{k}$?

Ⓐ $-\frac{4}{3}$

Ⓑ $-\frac{3}{4}$

Ⓒ $\frac{3}{4}$

Ⓓ $\frac{4}{3}$

15 ☐ Mark for Review

A postal machine processes mail at a constant rate of 21 pieces of mail per minute. At this rate, how many pieces of mail would the machine process in 7 minutes?

Ⓐ 3

Ⓑ 14

Ⓒ 28

Ⓓ 147

16 ☐ Mark for Review

Stella had 211 invitations to send for an event. She has already sent 43 invitations and will send them all if she sends 24 each day for the next d days. Which of the following equations represents this situation?

Ⓐ $24d - 43 = 211$

Ⓑ $24d + 43 = 211$

Ⓒ $43d - 24 = 211$

Ⓓ $43d + 24 = 211$

17 ☐ Mark for Review

x	−1	0	1	2
$f(x)$	12	15	18	21

When the linear function $y = f(x)$ is graphed in the xy-plane, the graph contains the corresponding values of x and $f(x)$ shown in the table. Which of the following could represent function f?

Ⓐ $f(x) = 3x + 12$

Ⓑ $f(x) = 3x + 15$

Ⓒ $f(x) = 15x + 12$

Ⓓ $f(x) = 15x + 15$

CONTINUE

18 ☐ Mark for Review

The height of a rocket launched from a rooftop can be modeled by the equation $h = -16s^2 + 64s + 21$, where h is the height of the rocket above the ground, in feet, and s is the number of seconds since the rocket was launched. Which of the following represents the height, in feet, of the rooftop from which the rocket was launched?

(A) 0

(B) 16

(C) 21

(D) 64

19 ☐ Mark for Review

Function f is defined by $f(x) = x^3 + 1$. Which of the following tables gives three values of x and their corresponding values of y?

(A)

x	2	3	4
y	3	4	5

(B)

x	2	3	4
y	3	28	64

(C)

x	2	3	4
y	9	10	65

(D)

x	2	3	4
y	9	28	65

20 ☐ Mark for Review

If $h(-1) = 3$ and $h(0) = 5$ in linear function h, which of the following is the equation of function h?

(A) $h(x) = 2x + 5$

(B) $h(x) = 2x + 3$

(C) $h(x) = 2x$

(D) $h(x) = 3x + 5$

CONTINUE

21 ☐ Mark for Review

Which of the following equations correctly expresses r in terms of p and s if the relationship between the numbers p, r, and s can be expressed as $p = 13r - 6s$?

(A) $r = \dfrac{-6s - p}{13}$

(B) $r = 13p + 6s$

(C) $r = \dfrac{1}{13}p + 6s$

(D) $r = \dfrac{p + 6s}{13}$

22 ☐ Mark for Review

Right triangle ABC has sides of the following lengths: $AB = 165$, $BC = 280$, and $AC = 325$. Another triangle, LMN, is similar to ABC such that A corresponds to L and B corresponds to M. What is the value of $\cos(L)$?

(A) $\dfrac{33}{65}$

(B) $\dfrac{33}{56}$

(C) $\dfrac{56}{65}$

(D) $\dfrac{65}{33}$

STOP
**If you finish before time is called, you may check your work on this module only.
Do not turn to any other module in the test.**

Test 4—Math
Module 2—Harder

Turn to Section 2 of your answer sheet to answer the questions in this section.

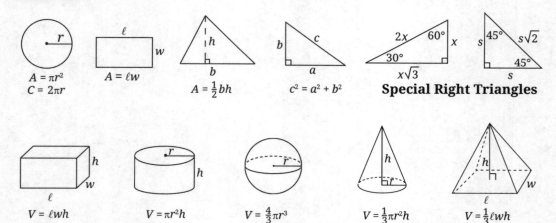
CONTINUE

For multiple-choice questions, solve each problem, choose the correct answer from the choices provided, and then fill in the circle with the answer letter. Enter only one answer for each question. You will not get credit for questions with more than one answer entered or for questions with no answers entered.

For student-produced response questions, solve each problem and write your answer next to or under the question in the test book as described below.

- Once you've written your answer, circle it clearly. You will not receive credit for anything written outside the circle or for any questions with more than one circled answer.

- If you find **more than one correct answer**, write and circle only one answer.

- Your answer can be up to 5 characters for a **positive** answer and up to 6 characters (including the negative sign) for a **negative** answer, but no more.

- If your answer is a **fraction** that is too long (over 5 characters for positive, 6 characters for negative), write the decimal equivalent.

- If your answer is a **decimal** that is too long (over 5 characters for positive, 6 characters for negative), truncate it or round at the fourth digit.

- If your answer is a **mixed number** (such as $3\frac{1}{2}$), write it as an improper fraction (7/2) or its decimal equivalent (3.5).

- Don't enter **symbols** such as a percent sign, comma, or dollar sign in your circled answer.

CONTINUE

1 ☐ Mark for Review

Which of the following is equivalent to $3a^3 - 5a^3 + 6a$?

Ⓐ $-2a^3 + 6a$

Ⓑ $3a^3 + a$

Ⓒ $4a$

Ⓓ $-15a^9 + 6a$

2 ☐ Mark for Review

In a shipment of $45,000,000$ shirts, $4,950,000$ are white. What percent of the shirts are white shirts?

Ⓐ 11%

Ⓑ 22%

Ⓒ 78%

Ⓓ 89%

3 ☐ Mark for Review

If $3(x - 8) - 16 = 8(x + 10) + x$, what is the value of $6x$?

4 ☐ Mark for Review

$$8(a - 3) - 17 = 9(a - 3)$$

In the given equation, what is the value of $a - 3$?

Ⓐ -20

Ⓑ -17

Ⓒ -14

Ⓓ 3

5 ☐ Mark for Review

A school classroom with a total of $4,200$ floor tiles is divided into a 30 square-foot lab area and an 80 square-foot seating area. The number of tiles on the entire classroom floor can be represented by the equation $30a + 80b = 4,200$. In this context, which of the following does b represent?

Ⓐ The average number of tiles per square foot in the lab area

Ⓑ The total number of tiles in the lab area

Ⓒ The average number of tiles per square foot in the seating area

Ⓓ The total number of tiles in the seating area

CONTINUE

6 ☐ Mark for Review

A triangle has a base that is 65% of its height. If the base were decreased by 13 inches, how would the height need to change to keep the same proportions?

Ⓐ It must increase by 13 inches.

Ⓑ It must increase by 20 inches.

Ⓒ It must decrease by 13 inches.

Ⓓ It must decrease by 20 inches.

7 ☐ Mark for Review

If $\frac{a}{3} = 10 - 7b$ and $a \neq 0$, which of the following correctly expresses b in terms of a?

Ⓐ $b = \frac{a - 21}{30}$

Ⓑ $b = \frac{30 - a}{21}$

Ⓒ $b = 10 + \frac{a}{3}$

Ⓓ $b = 10 + \frac{3}{a}$

8 ☐ Mark for Review

For all positive values of y, the expression $\frac{3}{y + c}$ is equivalent to $\frac{15}{5y + 30}$. What is the value of constant c?

Ⓐ 3

Ⓑ 6

Ⓒ 8

Ⓓ 150

9 ☐ Mark for Review

In the xy-plane, the equation $(x - 7)^2 + (y + 7)^2 = 64$ defines circle O, and the equation $(x - 7)^2 + (y + 7)^2 = c$ defines circle P. If the two circles have the same center, and the radius of circle P is three less than the radius of circle O, what is the value of constant c?

☐_____

CONTINUE ➤

10 ▢ Mark for Review

A school has received a donation of \$20,000 for the purchase of new laptops. If each laptop costs \$149, no tax is charged, and the laptop manufacturer offers a 7.5% discount on orders of at least 100 laptops, what is the maximum number of laptops the school can purchase with the donation?

Ⓐ 124

Ⓑ 134

Ⓒ 145

Ⓓ 146

11 ▢ Mark for Review

$$3x^2 - y - 26 = 0$$

$$y = -3x + 10$$

The point (a, b) is an intersection of the system of equations above when graphed in the xy-plane. What is a possible value of a?

Ⓐ -4

Ⓑ 6

Ⓒ 20

Ⓓ 26

12 ▢ Mark for Review

How many values for x satisfy the equation $-6(4x + 2) = 3(4 - 8x)$?

Ⓐ Zero

Ⓑ Exactly one

Ⓒ Exactly two

Ⓓ Infinitely many

13 ▢ Mark for Review

A parabola represents the graph of the function f in the xy-plane, where $y = f(x)$. If the vertex of the parabola is $(5, -4)$ and one of the x-intercepts is $(-1.5, 0)$, what is the other x-intercept?

Ⓐ $(-6.5, 0)$

Ⓑ $(1.5, 0)$

Ⓒ $(3.5, 0)$

Ⓓ $(11.5, 0)$

CONTINUE ➡

---

14 ☐ Mark for Review

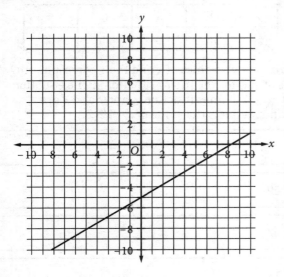

Which equation defines function g, if the graph of $y = g(x) - 10$ is shown?

Ⓐ $y = \frac{3}{5}x - 15$

Ⓑ $y = \frac{3}{5}x - 5$

Ⓒ $y = \frac{3}{5}x + 5$

Ⓓ $y = \frac{3}{5}x + 10$

15 ☐ Mark for Review

If c is a constant in the equation $10x^2 + c = -5x$, and the equation has no real solutions, what is the value of c?

Ⓐ -20

Ⓑ -5

Ⓒ 0

Ⓓ 1

16 ☐ Mark for Review

$$3x - 4y = 17$$

In the xy-plane, the graph of a line with an x-intercept of $(c, 0)$ and a y-intercept of $(0, k)$, where c and k are constants, can be represented by the equation above. What is the value of $\frac{c}{k}$?

Ⓐ $-\frac{4}{3}$

Ⓑ $-\frac{3}{4}$

Ⓒ $\frac{3}{4}$

Ⓓ $\frac{4}{3}$

CONTINUE ➡

17 Mark for Review

$$-7 + 2f = cg$$
$$21g + 21 = 6f - 15g$$

If c is a constant, and the system of equations shown above has infinitely many solutions, what is the value of c?

18 Mark for Review

Triangle A has angles measuring 30°, 60°, and 90°. What is the perimeter, in centimeters, of this triangle if the smallest side has a length of 15 centimeters?

(A) $15\sqrt{3}$

(B) $15 + 15\sqrt{3}$

(C) $45 + 15\sqrt{3}$

(D) $45\sqrt{3}$

19 Mark for Review

x	2	4	6	8
$g(x)$	46	0	−46	−92

The table shows values of x and their corresponding values of $g(x)$ for the linear function g. The equation $g(x) = cx + d$ defines function g, and c and d are constants. What is the value of $c + d$?

(A) −23

(B) 69

(C) 92

(D) 115

20 Mark for Review

114, 109, 106, 111

A data set consists of 5 positive integers greater than 101. What is the value of the smallest integer in the data set if the mean of the entire data set is an integer that is less than the mean of the four integers from the data set shown?

CONTINUE

21 ☐ Mark for Review

A teacher awards points to a class based on completed assignments. He gives 5 points per assignment for the first 50 completed assignments and 3 points for each additional completed assignment beyond 50. When $a \geq 50$, which function g gives the total number of points earned by the class for a completed assignments?

(A) $g(a) = 3a + 5$

(B) $g(a) = 3a + 100$

(C) $g(a) = 3a + 250$

(D) $g(a) = 8a - 150$

22 ☐ Mark for Review

In triangles ABC and XYZ, $AB = 22$, $XY = 11$, and angles A and X both measure 77°. Which of the following pieces of information, if any, would be enough to prove that the two triangles are similar to each other?

 I. Angle B measures 40°

 II. Angle Y measures 50°

 III. Angle Z measures 63°

(A) No additional information is necessary.

(B) Angle measures alone do not provide enough information.

(C) I and II together provide enough information.

(D) I and III together provide enough information.

STOP
If you finish before time is called, you may check your work on this module only.
Do not turn to any other module in the test.

Chapter 8
Practice Test 4:
Answers and
Explanations

PRACTICE TEST 4: ANSWER KEY

Reading and Writing		
Module 1	Module 2 (Easier)	Module 2 (Harder)
1. D	1. D	1. C
2. B	2. A	2. B
3. B	3. C	3. C
4. A	4. A	4. D
5. D	5. B	5. A
6. A	6. B	6. C
7. A	7. A	7. A
8. A	8. A	8. D
9. A	9. C	9. A
10. B	10. D	10. B
11. A	11. D	11. B
12. B	12. C	12. A
13. D	13. C	13. A
14. A	14. B	14. A
15. C	15. A	15. C
16. C	16. A	16. A
17. D	17. D	17. C
18. A	18. B	18. B
19. A	19. D	19. A
20. B	20. D	20. A
21. B	21. A	21. D
22. C	22. D	22. D
23. D	23. C	23. A
24. D	24. D	24. C
25. C	25. C	25. D
26. D	26. A	26. D
27. C	27. A	27. B

Math		
Module 1	Module 2 (Easier)	Module 2 (Harder)
1. B	1. C	1. A
2. C	2. 32	2. A
3. C	3. B	3. −120
4. B	4. C	4. B
5. D	5. A	5. C
6. $\frac{12}{20}$ or .6	6. B	6. D
7. D	7. 140	7. B
8. −4	8. A	8. B
9. A	9. 44	9. 25
10. B	10. D	10. C
11. A	11. D	11. A
12. A	12. B	12. A
13. D	13. 118	13. D
14. A	14. A	14. C
15. 25	15. D	15. D
16. D	16. B	16. A
17. C	17. B	17. 12
18. C	18. C	18. C
19. $\frac{40}{41}$ or .9756	19. D	19. B
20. −2.5	20. A	20. 105
21. 10	21. D	21. B
22. 2.4	22. A	22. D

PRACTICE TEST 4—READING AND WRITING EXPLANATIONS

Module 1

1. **D** This is a Vocabulary question, as it's asking for a *logical and precise word or phrase*. Read the passage and highlight what can help fill in the blank. The passage states that *the risk of loss of human life in the event of an eruption is minimal,* so the area surrounding Calabozos must not be very inhabited. A good word for the annotation box based on this information would be "isolated."

    - (A) and (B) are wrong because *hazardous* and *active* don't match "isolated."

    - (C) is wrong because *mountainous* is a **Beyond the Text trap**: mountainous regions are often isolated, but the passage does not support that the area surrounding Calabozos has any other mountains besides the volcano itself.

    - (D) is correct because *remote* matches "isolated."

2. **B** This is a Vocabulary question, as it's asking for a *logical and precise word or phrase*. Read the passage and highlight what can help fill in the blank. The passage states that H.D. *wrote in a variety of forms and genres,* yet her contemporaries *focused only on her important contributions to the Imagist movement.* Therefore, a good phrase for the annotation box based on this information would be that the contemporaries' view was "narrow."

    - (A) is wrong because *expansive* is the **Opposite** of "narrow."

    - (B) is correct because *limited* matches "narrow."

    - (C) and (D) are wrong because *imaginative* and *complicated* don't match "narrow."

3. **B** This is a Purpose question, as it's asking for the *function* of a sentence. Read the passage and highlight what can help understand the function of the second sentence. In the second sentence, *Previous studies…have been unsuccessful because these studies relied on human subjects.* In the third sentence, it states that *A recent study by physiologists Yuta Senzai and Massimo Scanziani has avoided this issue by studying dreaming mice instead.* Therefore, the second sentence must be describing an issue that the scientists in the third sentence avoided. Write "explain issue with previous studies" in the annotation box.

    - (A) is wrong because it is the **Opposite** of what the passage supports: *previous studies* ran into a *problem,* but the study by *Yuta Senzai and Massimo Scanziani has avoided this issue.*

    - (B) is correct because it's consistent with the relationship between the second and third sentences.

- (C) is wrong because it is **Half-Right:** the sentence mentions the studies before Senzai and Scanziani's but does not *present the findings* of those studies.

- (D) is wrong because the passage does not discuss anyone interpreting Senzai and Scanziani's study.

4. **A** This is a Purpose question, as it's asking for the *function* of a sentence. Read the passage and high-light what can help understand the function of the third sentence. In the third sentence, it states that *electroreception is not limited to fish*. Write "explain it's not just fish" in the annotation box.

- (A) is correct because it's consistent with the highlighting and annotation.

- (B) is wrong because it's **Half-Right:** the fourth sentence explains how monotremes use electroreception, but the earlier sentences do not explain how fish use electroreception, just that they have it.

- (C) is wrong because it is **Right Answer, Wrong Question:** the fourth and possibly the fifth sentence give more *examples* of animals with electroreception, not the third sentence, which is what the question asks about.

- (D) is wrong because the passage does not explain *how electroreception evolved* in any of the animals discussed.

5. **D** This is a Dual Texts question, as it asks how the scientists in Text 2 would *most likely respond* to those in Text 1. Read Text 1 and highlight the claim made by Premack and Woodruff regarding a theory of mind: after seeing videos of human actors struggling with various problems, *the chim-panzees were able to select photographs that showed the best tool to solve each actor's problem.* Read Text 2 and highlight Povinelli, Nelson, and Boysen's response to the same idea: *it may be the case that chimpanzees are following learned behaviors in a known environment, rather than applying a theory of mind in a novel situation.* Write in the annotation box for the highlighting in Text 2 that "Text 2 offers an alternate explanation."

- (A) and (C) are wrong because neither passage discusses any other *nonhuman primates* besides chimpanzees.

- (B) is wrong because it is **Recycled Language:** it's the human subjects in Text 1 that are described as *struggling* with a problem and Text 2 never suggests that the chimpanzees could solve problems by struggling through the problems on their own.

- (D) is correct because it would address the scientists in Text 2's main objection to the claim in Text 1: by placing the chimpanzees *in novel environments* that they *would have been unlikely to encounter* previously, Premack and Woodruff could better determine whether the chimpanzees have a theory of mind rather than are just *following learned behaviors in a known environment.*

6.   **A**   This is a Retrieval question, as it says *According to the text.* Read the passage and highlight what is said about Dorian. The passage mentions that *his cheeks flushed for a moment with pleasure* and *A look of joy came into his eyes* upon seeing his picture. He knows that *Hallward was speaking to him, but* he was *not catching the meaning of his words.* Lastly, *The sense of his own beauty came on him like a revelation.* The correct answer should be consistent with as many of these ideas as possible.

   - (A) is correct because it exactly describes what is occurring in the passage. Dorian cannot focus on what Hallward is saying because of the beauty of his own picture.

   - (B) is wrong because it is **Extreme Language:** Dorian can't focus on what Hallward is saying, but the passage never goes so far as to state that Dorian thinks it's *unimportant.*

   - (C) is wrong because it is the **Opposite** of the passage: not only does Dorian *recognize his own image,* but he is also immensely pleased by it.

   - (D) is wrong because nothing about how easily Dorian gets embarrassed is mentioned in the passage.

7.   **A**   This is a Retrieval question, as it says *Based on the text.* Read the passage and highlight what is said about the children. The passage states that the old forester wondered *What would become of them* (the children)—*living in so sequestered a spot that few even knew of its existence—totally shut out from the world, and left to their own resources?* The correct answer should be as consistent with this description of the children as possible.

   - (A) is correct because *isolated from people other than the old forester* is consistent with *totally shut out from the world.*

   - (B) is wrong because it is **Extreme Language:** while the forester is worried about what would happen to the children if left alone, the passage does not indicate that the children would be *completely unable* to take care of themselves.

   - (C) is wrong because it is the **Opposite** of the forester's feelings towards the children: he feels responsible for them, not *resentful* of them.

   - (D) is wrong because it is **Recycled Language:** the answer misuses the word *responsibility* from the passage and never indicates that the children help the forester with his tasks.

8.   **A**   This is a Main Idea question, as it asks for the *main idea* of the text. Read the passage and highlight the main phrases or lines that all of the other sentences seem to support. The citation states that the author is addressing an unknown person. The opening two lines state that the author will never *hold a place* in this person's (*thine*) heart until the author renounces *all sense, all shame, all grace.* The author also states at the end of the poem that this individual will make an *offer with corrupting*

art / The rotten borough of the human heart. The main idea would be that author's feelings towards this individual in this poem are negative, and the correct answer should be consistent with this.

- (A) is correct because it is consistent with the main idea and *disapproval towards the unknown person* is expressed several times in the poem.

- (B) and (D) are wrong because the poem never states what the unknown person feels towards the author, just what the author feels towards the unknown person. Choice (D) is also **Recycled Language** and warps the meaning of the opening line of the passage.

- (C) is wrong because it is **Recycled Language:** the author is not referring to a literal seat. Rather, the seat is a metaphor for the place the speaker may hold in the unknown person's heart.

9. **A** This is a Claims question, as it asks for what answer would support Soni and his team's claim. Read the passage and highlight the claim made by Soni's team, which is that *administering ketone esters can reduce inflammation and immune system weakening caused by sepsis.*

- (A) is correct because it shows *ketone esters* to be more effective at reducing inflammation and reducing damage to organs (which the passage states are connected to immune system response) than at least one other treatment, *standard antibiotics.*

- (B) is wrong because it does not address the items mentioned in the claim, referencing *blood ketone levels* and *energy* rather than *inflammation* and the *immune system* or *organ damage.*

- (C) is wrong because the passage does not mention *medication intended to reduce fever* or how such medication would affect the performance of *ketone esters.*

- (D) is wrong because it is **Half-Right:** patients treated with *ketone esters* should have *reduced inflammation*, but they should have *less* organ damage, not *greater* organ damage, than those treated with other treatments, such as standard antibiotics.

10. **B** This is a Charts question as it asks about *data from the table* that will complete an example. Read the table first and note the title and terms on the table. Then, read the passage and look for a claim and example that mentions those same terms. The fourth sentence states that *horses with only one handler were less reluctant to interact with the novel object than were horses with multiple handlers.* The example states that *45% of horses with only one handler had no reluctance when interacting with a novel object,* so a good completion of this example would compare that statistic to a statistic regarding *multiple handlers* while remaining consistent with the claim in the fourth sentence.

- (A) and (D) are wrong because they don't mention *multiple handlers,* which are needed to be consistent with the passage's claim.

- (B) is correct because it shows that horses with *multiple handlers* only had *no reluctance* towards interacting with the novel object 25% of the time, whereas horses with only one handler showed no reluctance 45% of the time, making them less reluctant overall as the claim states.

- (C) is wrong because the claim and the first half of the example address no reluctance rather than strong reluctance. It's best to compare two items from the same row or same column to complete comparisons, depending on what the problem is looking for.

11.   **A**   This is a Charts question as it asks about *data from the table* that will illustrate a claim. Read the table first and note the title and variables. Then, read the passage and look for a claim that mentions those same terms. The fourth sentence states that *starting with the 1989 election, the party which won the largest number of seats failed to win more than half of the total seats.* The final sentence claims that *This trend was eventually broken by the Bharatiya Janata Party.* The correct answer should offer evidence from the table that supports the Bharatiya Janata Party breaking the trend described in the fourth sentence.

- (A) is correct because it is consistent with the table for those years and shows the Bharatiya Janata Party holding both the largest number of seats *and* a majority of the total seats.

- (B), (C), and (D) are wrong because none of them mention the Bharatiya Janata Party winning a majority, or *more than half of the total seats,* as stated in the passage.

12.   **B**   This is a Charts question as it asks about *data from the table* that will support a hypothesis. Read the table first and note the title and terms. Then, read the passage and look for a hypothesis that mentions those same terms. The last sentence states that *A group of researchers…hypothesized that those who take vitamin B12 would experience improvements in fibrosis and insulin resistance when compared to a control group over the same time period.* The correct answer should use data from the table to support this idea.

- (A) is wrong because it only talks about the control group and not the Vitamin B12 group.

- (B) is correct because it references both groups and is consistent with the relationship between those groups stated by the claim in the passage.

- (C) and (D) are wrong because neither mentions the terms *fibrosis* and *insulin resistance* that were referenced by the claim.

13.   **D**   This is a Charts question as it asks about *data from the table* that will complete a statement. Read the table first and note the title and terms. Then, read the passage and look for a statement that mentions those same terms. The last sentence states that *The localized nature of weather patterns during this event can be seen by comparing Newark, NJ, and New York, NY, with _____.* The correct answer should complete this statement regarding localized weather patterns by showing a difference in mean levels of carbon monoxide in Newark and New York when compared to a more distant city.

- (A), (B), and (C) are wrong because the mean levels of carbon monoxide shown for Washington, D.C., and Philadelphia, PA, on the dates in each answer are similar or identical to the levels in New York, NY, on those dates. Farther cities from Newark showing similar levels to neighboring cities to Newark would not show the *localized nature of weather patterns during the smog event.*

- (D) is correct because Washington, D.C., shows zero carbon monoxide recorded on those dates, while Newark and New York show positive carbon monoxide level.

14. **A** This is a Conclusions question as it asks for an answer that *logically completes the text*. Read the passage and highlight the main ideas. The passage states that *neurons change how they respond to stimuli based on previous experience* and that *electrical engineers seek to replicate similar processes in their development of computer memory*. Lastly, *electrical engineer Mohammad Samizadeh Nikoo has demonstrated that vanadium dioxide (VO_2) has a similar memory property to that of neurons*. The correct answer should be consistent with these ideas and establish a logical link between them.

- (A) is correct because it establishes a link between VO_2 from the last sentence and the computer memory that electrical engineers are trying to work on from the second sentence.

- (B) and (C) are wrong because both are **Recycled Language.** For (B), it's never stated that neurons use VO_2 in any way, just that they have a similar memory property. Choice (C) takes the words *neurons, VO_2,* and *stimuli from sensory organs* and combines them in a way not supported by the passage.

- (D) is wrong because it uses **Extreme and Recycled Language:** it is VO_2, not neurons, that may be helpful for computer memory. Furthermore, the passage supports this as only a possibility, whereas the answer states that the engineers *can now use* it.

15. **C** In this Rules question, pronouns are changing in the answer choices, so it's testing consistency with pronouns. Find and highlight the word the pronoun refers back to, *books*, which is plural, so a plural pronoun is needed. Write an annotation saying "plural." Eliminate any answer that isn't consistent with *books*.

- (A) is wrong because *some* doesn't refer back to a specific thing.

- (B) and (D) are wrong because they are singular.

- (C) is correct because *they* is plural and is consistent with *books*.

16. **C** In this Rules question, commas and the word *that* are changing in the answers, which suggests that the question is testing the construction of describing phrases. The first part of the sentence says *In 1988, the group worked together to form Action Deaf Youth,* which is an independent clause followed by a comma. Eliminate any answer that isn't consistent with the first part of the sentence.

- (A) is wrong because a phrase starting with "that" is Specifying and never follows a comma.

- (B) and (D) are wrong because they both create a run-on sentence.

- (C) is correct because it creates a Specifying phrase with *that* and no punctuation.

17. **D** In this Rules question, verb forms are changing in the answer choices, so it's testing sentence structure. If the main verb is in the wrong form, the sentence won't be complete. The subject of the sentence is *Her experience*, but there is no main verb, so one is needed. Eliminate any answer that does not produce a complete sentence.

   - (A) is wrong because a "to" verb can't be the main verb in a sentence.

   - (B) is wrong because it lacks a main verb and thus creates an incomplete sentence.

   - (C) is wrong because an *-ing* verb can't be the main verb in a sentence.

   - (D) is correct because *inspired* is in the right form to be the main verb and make a complete sentence.

18. **A** In this Rules question, punctuation is changing in the answer choices, so look for independent clauses. The first part of the sentence says *American artist Simone Leigh creates art in various mediums, including sculptures, video, and performance*, which is an independent clause. The second part says *discussing the themes and images in her artwork, Leigh has emphasized that Black women are her primary audience…*, which is also an independent clause. Eliminate any answer that can't correctly connect two independent clauses.

   - (A) is correct because a period is appropriately used after an independent clause.

   - (B) is wrong because it creates a run-on sentence.

   - (C) and (D) are wrong because neither a coordinating conjunction by itself nor a comma by itself can connect two independent clauses.

19. **A** In this Rules question, pronouns are changing in the answer choices, so it's testing consistency with pronouns. Find and highlight the word the pronoun refers back to, *wet-folding*, which is singular, so a singular pronoun is needed. Write an annotation saying "singular." Eliminate any answer that isn't consistent with *wet-folding*.

   - (A) is correct because *it* is singular and is consistent with *wet-folding*.

   - (B) and (D) are wrong because they are plural.

   - (C) is wrong because *one* doesn't refer back to a specific thing.

20. **B** In this Rules question, punctuation is changing in the answer choices. Look for independent clauses. The first part of the sentence says *His 2004 installation The Glassy Surface of a Lake*. The verb (*uses*) comes right after this. A single punctuation mark can't separate a subject and a verb, so eliminate answers with punctuation.

   - (A), (C), and (D) are wrong because a single punctuation mark can't come between a subject and a verb.

   - (B) is correct because no punctuation should be used here.

21. **B** In this Rules question, punctuation with a transition is changing in the answer choices. The first part of the sentence says *Not all of the styles survived beyond that time*. There is an option to add *however* to this independent clause, and since it is contrasting with the previous idea, eliminate options that don't include *however* in the first part or are incorrectly punctuated.

- (A) is wrong because it doesn't put *however* with the first independent clause.

- (B) is correct because *however* is part of the first independent clause.

- (C) and (D) are wrong because a comma can't be used to connect two independent clauses.

22. **C** This is a Transitions question, so follow the basic approach. Highlight ideas that relate to each other. The previous sentence says *Calede first compared measurements of the beaver's ankle*, and the next sentence says *Calede dated the species to approximately 30 million years ago*. These ideas are different steps Calede took, so a same-direction transition is needed. Make an annotation that says "agree." Eliminate any answer that doesn't match.

- (A) is wrong because *for example* introduces an example not stated in the passage.

- (B) is wrong because *in conclusion* introduces a conclusion not present in the passage.

- (C) is correct because *next* introduces another step in a sequence.

- (D) is wrong because *in fact* is used to give more detail, which is not present.

23. **D** This is a Transitions question, so follow the basic approach. Highlight ideas that relate to each other. The previous part of the paragraph says *Male and female American citizens had starkly different roles during World War II* and lists the roles of men, and the sentence in question says *women were responsible for maintaining the home and supporting the men*. These ideas disagree, so an opposite-direction transition is needed. Make an annotation that says "disagree." Eliminate any answer that doesn't match.

- (A) and (C) are wrong because they are same-direction transitions.

- (B) is wrong because *instead* introduces an alternative, but the paragraph discusses the different roles of men and women, not alternative roles for men.

- (D) is correct because *meanwhile* shows that women had different roles during the same time period.

24. **D** This is a Transitions question, so follow the basic approach. Highlight ideas that relate to each other. The first sentence says *some patients with damaged ear structures are not able to use traditional cochlear implants*, and the next sentence tells what *researchers are working* on as a result of this problem. These ideas agree, so a same-direction transition is needed. Make an annotation that says "agree." Eliminate any answer that doesn't match.

- (A) is wrong because there is no first step in the paragraph.

- (B) is wrong because the last sentence is not an addition to the previous sentence.

- (C) is wrong because *finally* is used to indicate the last step or a conclusion.

- (D) is correct because *hence* suggests that the last sentence is an effect of the previous sentence.

25. **C** This is a Transitions question, so follow the basic approach. Highlight ideas that relate to each other. The previous sentence says *Her materials are often perishable and biological and are not traditionally used for artwork*, and the next sentence says *Yi spends almost as much time transforming these substances into completely new materials as she does creating the actual art pieces*. These ideas agree, so a same-direction transition is needed. Make an annotation that says "agree." Eliminate any answer that doesn't match.

- (A) and (B) are wrong because they are opposite-direction transitions.

- (C) is correct because *in fact* adds detail to the previous sentence.

- (D) is wrong because the last sentence is not a conclusion.

26. **D** This is a Rhetorical Synthesis question, so follow the basic approach. Highlight the goal(s) stated in the question: *emphasize a difference between the two numeral systems*. Eliminate any answer that doesn't fulfill this purpose.

- (A) is wrong because it states a similarity between the two numeral systems.

- (B) is wrong because it doesn't mention both *numeral systems*.

- (C) is wrong because it doesn't mention a *difference* between the systems.

- (D) is correct because it states differences between the two numeral systems and uses the contrast word *while*.

27. **C** This is a Rhetorical Synthesis question, so follow the basic approach. Highlight the goal(s) stated in the question: *present the Newen Antug study and its conclusions*. Eliminate any answer that doesn't fulfill this purpose.

- (A), (B), and (D) are wrong because they do not include a *conclusion*—what the researchers found.

- (C) is correct because *canoes were used as coffins* is a conclusion.

Module 2—Easier

1. **D** This is a Vocabulary question, as it's asking for a *logical and precise word or phrase*. Read the passage and highlight what can help fill in the blank. The passage states that *Shakespeare intentionally provided no stage directions* as to what should happen in a scene, so it's logical that he meant for *future directors* to use their *own artistic interpretations*. A good word for the annotation box based on this information would be "freedom."

   - (A) and (B) are wrong because *confusion* and *dedication* don't match "freedom."

   - (C) is wrong because it is the **Opposite** of what the passage states—Shakespeare *provided no stage directions*.

   - (D) is correct because *liberty* matches "freedom."

2. **A** This is a Vocabulary question, as it's asking for a *logical and precise word or phrase*. Read the passage and highlight what can help fill in the blank. The passage states that the *fossils were exclusively found in caves in southern China and that anyone claiming to have found the remains of Gigantopithecus elsewhere would be mistaken*. A good phrase for the annotation box based on this information would be "only in" that region.

   - (A) is correct because *restricted to* matches "only in."

   - (B) and (D) are wrong because *eliminated from* and *unknown to* are the **Opposite** of "only in."

   - (C) is wrong because *common in* doesn't match "only in."

3. **C** This is a Vocabulary question, as it's asking for a *logical and precise word or phrase*. Read the passage and highlight what can help fill in the blank. The passage states that *artificial intelligence will not displace human beings* but *will undoubtedly become smarter than people within this generation*. The next sentence calls this *a possibility*. A good word for the annotation box would be that Kurzweil "hypothesizes" what will happen.

   - (A) is wrong because *proves* is **Extreme Language:** it goes too far beyond "hypothesizes."

   - (B) and (D) are wrong because *requires* and *denies* don't match "hypothesizes."

   - (C) is correct because *predicts* matches "hypothesizes."

4.   **A**   This is a Vocabulary question, as it's asking for a *logical and precise word or phrase*. Read the passage and highlight what can help fill in the blank. The passage states that the Stanford Prison Experiment *supposedly demonstrated* an idea: *supposedly* means that the author does not think the experiment actually demonstrated that idea. The passage also notes that the individuals were of the same background *rather than* representing *a diverse sampling of subjects*. Since all of this supports the point made in the first sentence, a good word or phrase for the annotation box would be "shows" or "is an example of."

- (A) is correct because *illustrates* matches "shows."

- (B) and (D) are wrong because *refutes* and *critiques* are the **Opposite** tone of "shows."

- (C) is wrong because *supersedes*, which means "overrides," doesn't match "shows."

5.   **B**   This is a Vocabulary question, as it's asking for a *logical and precise word or phrase*. Read the passage and highlight what can help fill in the blank. The passage states that prosopagnosia is also called "*face blindness,*" so a good word for the annotation box would be the "inability" to recognize faces.

- (A) and (C) are wrong because *capability* and *tendency* are the **Opposite** of "inability."

- (B) is correct because *incapacity* matches "inability."

- (D) is wrong because *reluctance* suggests not wanting to do something, which isn't the same as "inability."

6.   **B**   This is a Vocabulary question, as it's asking for a *logical and precise word or phrase*. Read the passage and highlight what can help fill in the blank. The passage states that the shark has a *competitive advantage…due to electroreception, or ability to detect electrical impulses*. A good phrase for the annotation box based on this information would be "detection ability."

- (A) and (D) are wrong because *allergy* and *aversion* are the **Opposite** of the shark's "ability" being a *competitive advantage*.

- (B) is correct because *sensitivity* matches "detection ability."

- (D) is wrong because *indifference*, which means not having a preference, doesn't match "detection ability."

7.   **A**   This is a Vocabulary question, as it's asking for a *logical and precise word or phrase*. Read the passage and highlight what can help fill in the blank. The passage states that *cryptographers have yet to demonstrably decipher any portion of the text*, so a good word for the annotation box to describe *the meaning and purpose of the Voynich manuscript* would be "mysterious."

- (A) is correct because *enigmatic* matches "mysterious."

- (B) and (D) are wrong because *venerable* and *coherent* don't match "mysterious."

- (C) is wrong because it is a **Beyond the Text trap** answer. While *multifarious,* or complex, things can be *mysterious,* the words are not synonyms: mysterious things can be simple and complex things can be quite well known and understood.

8. **A** This is a Vocabulary question, as it's asking for a *logical and precise word or phrase.* Read the passage and highlight what can help fill in the blank. The passage states after the colon that the relationship between the crocodile and bird nourishes *the bird while simultaneously promoting the crocodile's dental health.* A good phrase for the annotation box based on this information would be "mutually beneficial."

    - (A) is correct because *interdependent* matches "mutually beneficial."

    - (B), (C), and (D) are incorrect because *inexplicable* (puzzling), *enthralling* (fascinating), and *inarticulate* (unclear) don't match "mutually beneficial."

9. **C** This is a Retrieval question, as it says *According to the text.* Read the passage and highlight what is said about Captain Vere. The passage states that he is a *sailor of distinction,* was *mindful of the welfare of his men, but never tolerating an infraction of discipline, versed in the science of his profession,* and *intrepid.* The correct answer should be as consistent with these qualities as possible.

    - (A) is wrong because it is the **Opposite** of the passage: Vere is *mindful* of his men's welfare.

    - (B) is wrong because it is **Recycled Language:** this answer misuses *nobility* from the passage, which never states that Vere has an *aristocratic background.*

    - (C) is correct because it is consistent with the Vere's qualities in the passage.

    - (D) is wrong because the passage doesn't state which lifestyle Vere *prefers.*

10. **D** This is a Claims question, as it asks for an illustration of the claim in the question. Read the passage and highlight the claim made, which is that the *poem conveys the speaker's sadness that his life as an adult does not compare favorably to his childhood.*

    - (A), (B), and (C) are wrong because they are all **Half-Right:** each focuses on some element or description from the speaker's childhood but makes no comparisons to the speaker's adult life.

    - (D) is correct because *'tis little joy* is consistent with sadness and *To know I'm farther off from heav'n / Than when I was a boy* is consistent with the speaker's life as an adult not comparing favorably to childhood.

11.   **D**   This is a Claims question, as it asks for an illustration of the claim in the question. Read the passage and highlight the claim made, which is that *Harker conveys his belief that he has become Dracula's prisoner.*

- (A), (B), and (C) are wrong because while in each of them the speaker expresses negative emotions toward a place *(dread, loneliness, fear)*, none of these answers support the idea that the speaker is *Dracula's prisoner.*

- (D) is correct because the speaker *rushed up and down the stairs, trying every door and peering out of every window* and after this still has a feeling of *helplessness.* This would be the best support toward the idea that the narrator is at least trapped or imprisoned.

12.   **C**   This is a Claims question, as it asks for an illustration of the claim in the question. Read the passage and highlight the claim made, which states that the *poem is meant to be a plea towards others to join the war effort.*

- (A), (B), and (D) are wrong because none of these answers include any call to an or group to fight or take any action.

- (C) is correct because the answer describes a *torch* that is being thrown to someone from those with *failing hands*, with the hope that the new holder would hold the torch high. These lines best support *a plea towards others* even if they don't directly reference any war effort.

13.   **C**   This is a Conclusions question as it asks for an answer that *logically completes the text.* Read the passage and highlight the main ideas. The passage states that *The curator of a museum claims* that the dress was worn *at the presidential inauguration in 1865. Radiocarbon dating,* on the other hand, reveals that the *sleeves of the dress…date back to the 1975–2005 period.* If both are assumed to be correct, as the passage says, the correct answer to the question must be consistent with both claims.

- (A) is wrong because it is **Recycled Language:** it's applying the *error range of about thirty years* to the year 1865, but the error range is mentioned when discussing radiocarbon dating in a completely separate part of the passage.

- (B) is wrong because it is a **Beyond the Text trap:** as logical as it is that dresses would be recovered more frequently from modern times than from older times, the passage does not state anything to this regard.

- (C) is correct because it shows how both claims could be correct, offering a possible reason for the contradictory statements made by the claims.

- (D) is wrong because the passage never discusses what material was used to make the dress or whether it was different from the materials used for most other dresses.

14. **B** This is a Conclusions question as it asks for an answer that *logically completes the text*. Read the passage and highlight the main ideas. The passage states that *paleontologists largely believed that there were no undocumented prehistoric aquatic species that had survived* to the early 1900s. However, just such a species *was found off the coast of South Africa as recently as 1938*. These two claims indicate that there is indeed at least one undocumented species that survived. The correct answer should be consistent with this idea.

- (A) is wrong because it is **Recycled Language:** this answer mentions *breeding population* from the passage, but no numbers regarding breeding population for the coelacanth are given.

- (B) is correct because the *coelacanth* from the second sentence did indeed go *undiscovered longer than* the 1900's paleontologists expected it would—they had thought there were *no undocumented prehistoric aquatic species* in their era.

- (C) is wrong because the passage never states that the scientists *ignored* any evidence.

- (D) is wrong because it is a **Beyond the Text trap:** it uses outside knowledge of when the dinosaurs went extinct to make an assumption regarding a similar fate for most coelacanths.

15. **A** This is a Conclusions question, as it asks for an answer that *logically completes the text*. Read the passage and highlight the main idea: *The door-in-the-face technique involves initially making an outrageous or unappealing offer, which the other person is likely to refuse, then following up with a more reasonable one.* The concluding sentence to the passage must be consistent with this main idea.

- (A) is correct because the second amount requested is comparatively much smaller than the first.

- (B) is wrong because the first request of 3% is unlikely to be considered *outrageous* when compared to 2%.

- (C) is wrong because according to the door-in-the-face technique in the passage, the more *outrageous* amount should be asked for first.

- (D) is wrong because the two amounts are the same and therefore neither one would be considered *outrageous* compared to the other.

16. **A** This is a Conclusions question, as it asks for an answer that *logically completes the text*. Read the passage and highlight the main ideas. The focus of the passage is on *NAFTA* and its relation to *manufacturing jobs*. During the interval from 1994 to 2020, the second sentence states that *the number of manufacturing jobs in the United States and Canada declined, but the total number of manufacturing jobs in the countries covered by NAFTA increased*. Therefore, a logical conclusion would explain how this might be possible.

- (A) is correct because if an increase in *the number of manufacturing jobs in Mexico*, which is also covered by NAFTA, was greater than the *combined decreases in the United States and Canada*, this would explain the seemingly contradictory data in the second sentence.

- (B), (C), and (D) are wrong because none of them offers a reason as to how the number of manufacturing jobs in the United States and Canada declined, but the total number of manufacturing jobs in all three countries increased.

17. **D** In this Rules question, verb forms are changing in the answer choices, so it's testing sentence structure. If the main verb is in the wrong form, the sentence won't be complete. The subject of the clause is *which*, but the clause has no verb, so the verb in the answers must be the main verb of the clause. Eliminate any answer that does not produce a complete sentence.

- (A) and (C) are wrong because an *-ing* verb can't be the main verb in a sentence.

- (B) is wrong because a "to" verb can't be the main verb in a sentence.

- (D) is correct because it's in the right form to make a complete sentence.

18. **B** In this Rules question, pronouns and apostrophes are changing in the answer choices, so it's testing consistency with pronouns. Find and highlight the word that the pronoun refers back to: *activists*. This is plural, so in order to be consistent, a plural pronoun is needed. Make an annotation saying "plural." Eliminate any answer that isn't consistent with *activists* or is incorrectly punctuated.

- (A) and (C) are wrong because *its* and *it's* are singular.

- (B) is correct because *their* is plural and possessive.

- (D) is wrong because *they're* means "they are."

19. **D** In this Rules question, pronouns are changing in the answer choices, so it's testing consistency with pronouns. Find and highlight the word the pronoun refers back to, *people*, which is plural, so a plural pronoun is needed. Write an annotation saying "plural." Eliminate any answer that isn't consistent with *people*.

- (A) and (C) are wrong because they are singular.

- (B) is wrong because *you* is not appropriate to refer to *people* in this context.

- (D) is correct because *them* is plural and is consistent with *people*.

20. **D** In this Rules question, punctuation is changing in the answer choices, so look for independent clauses. The first part of the sentence says *National flags are designed to best represent and symbolize the individual country*, which is an independent clause. The second part of the sentence says *when countries share a history or culture, their flags are designed to look similar...*, which is also an independent clause. Eliminate any answer that can't correctly connect two independent clauses.

- (A) and (B) are wrong because neither a comma by itself nor a coordinating conjunction by itself can connect two independent clauses.

- (C) is wrong because it creates a run-on sentence.

- (D) is correct because a comma + a coordinating conjunction (FANBOYS) can connect two independent clauses.

21.   **A**   In this Rules question, periods and question marks are changing in the answer choices, so it's testing questions versus statements. The last sentence says *The scientists resolved to find out*, which suggests that the previous sentence was a question. Eliminate answers that aren't correctly written as questions.

- (A) is correct because it's correctly written as a question.

- (B) is wrong because it has a question mark but is written as a statement.

- (C) and (D) are wrong because they are statements.

22.   **D**   In this Rules question, verbs are changing in the answer choices, so it's testing consistency with verbs. Find and highlight the subject, *shadowing*, which is singular, so a singular verb is needed. Write an annotation saying "singular." Eliminate any answer that is not singular.

- (A), (B), and (C) are wrong because they are plural.

- (D) is correct because it's singular.

23.   **C**   In this Rules question, verbs are changing in the answer choices, so it's testing consistency with verbs. In this case, the verb is part of a list of two things that the beach does, the first of which is *allows community members to connect with the natural world*. Highlight the word *allows*, which the verb in the answer should be consistent with. Eliminate any answer that isn't consistent with *allows*.

- (A), (B), and (D) are wrong because *provided*, *providing*, and *provide* aren't consistent with *allows*.

- (C) is correct because *provides* is in the same tense and form as *allows*.

24.   **D**   This is a Transitions question, so follow the basic approach. Highlight ideas that relate to each other. The first sentence says *Yoga is an ancient discipline that…has expanded to become popular with many different cultures*, and the next sentence says *yoga is shifting into different forms to allow a wider range of people to participate*. These ideas agree, so a same-direction transition is needed. Make an annotation that says "agree." Eliminate any answer that doesn't match.

- (A) is wrong because it is an opposite-direction transition.

- (B) is wrong because the second sentence is not about a separate but similar topic.

- (C) is wrong because *thus* indicates a conclusion.

- (D) is correct because *currently* suggests a change, which is consistent with *yoga is shifting*.

25. **C** This is a Transitions question, so follow the basic approach. Highlight ideas that relate to each other. The first sentence says *Scientists often disagree about what traits to use to place newly discovered species in the tree of life*, and the second sentence describes a species that *is sometimes placed near modern spiders based on its acquisition of silk-spinning organs or near other arachnids based on its loss of a tail*. These ideas agree, so a same-direction transition is needed. Make an annotation that says "agree." Eliminate any answer that doesn't match.

- (A) is wrong because *as a result* suggests a conclusion that is not stated in the passage.

- (B) and (D) are wrong because they are opposite-direction transitions.

- (C) is correct because *Chimerarachne yingi* is an example of the previous sentence.

26. **A** This is a Transitions question, so follow the basic approach. Highlight ideas that relate to each other. The first sentence says that the seismometer's detection potentially avoided *mass architectural damage*, and the second sentence says *the cut to the power prevented citizens from being caught in a dangerous location during the earthquake and allowed riders to seek shelter*. These ideas agree, so a same-direction transition is needed. Make an annotation that says "agree." Eliminate any answer that doesn't match.

- (A) is correct because allowing *riders to seek shelter* is another way the cut to power was beneficial.

- (B) is wrong because it is an opposite-direction transition.

- (C) and (D) are wrong because the second sentence is an additional point, not an example or specification.

27. **A** This is a Rhetorical Synthesis question, so follow the basic approach. Highlight the goal(s) stated in the question: *make a generalization about the kind of study conducted by Eberhard, Wilcove, and Dobson*. Eliminate any answer that doesn't *make a generalization*.

- (A) is correct because it provides a *generalization about the kind of study* conducted by the scientists: analyzing *population trends to find out the impact of legal protections*.

- (B), (C), and (D) are wrong because they don't provide a *generalization* or a broader way of explaining the type of study.

Module 2—Harder

1. **C** This is a Vocabulary question, as it's asking for a *logical and precise word or phrase*. Read the passage and highlight what can help fill in the blank. The passage states that *all things, living or not, have the inclination to exist and enhance themselves*. A good word or phrase for the annotation box based on this information would be "exist" or "hold on."

    - (A), (B), and (D) are wrong because *deteriorate, perish*, and *disappear* are the **Opposite** of "exist" or "hold on."

    - (C) is correct because *persevere* matches with "exist" or "hold on."

2. **B** This is a Vocabulary question, as it's asking for a *logical and precise word or phrase*. Read the passage and highlight what can help fill in the blank. The passage states that the birds' behavior in the study made it *more difficult for the researchers to obtain data*. A good word for the annotation box based on this information would be "hindered."

    - (A) and (C) are wrong because *aided* and *clarified* are the **Opposite** of "hindered."

    - (B) is correct because *impeded* matches "hindered."

    - (D) is wrong because *exposed* doesn't match "hindered."

3. **C** This is a Vocabulary question, as it's asking for a *logical and precise word or phrase*. Read the passage and highlight what can help fill in the blank. The passage states that the objects that M.C. Escher creates *first appear normal but on closer inspection are, in fact, impossible*. A good phrase for the annotation box based on this information would be "confusing objects."

    - (A), (B), and (D) are wrong because *geometry, beauty,* and *color* don't match "confusing objects."

    - (C) is correct because *paradox* best matches "confusing objects."

4. **D** This is a Vocabulary question, as it's asking for a *logical and precise word or phrase*. Read the passage and highlight what can help fill in the blank. The passage states that *When microdroplets of water hit a solid surface, an electric charge* produces *hydroxyl radicals that in turn combine with remaining oxygen to form hydrogen peroxide*. This information describes a chain of events started by water, so a good phrase for the annotation box would be "likely to trigger something."

    - (A), (B), and (C) are wrong because *viable, contaminated,* and *common* don't match "likely to trigger something."

    - (D) is correct because *reactive* matches "likely to trigger something."

5.   **A**   This is a Vocabulary question, as it's asking for a *logical and precise word or phrase*. Read the passage and highlight what can help fill in the blank. The passage states that *The Beat Generation* had a *central message of nonconformity*, meaning that they would reject *the traditional values of the 1950s*. A good word for the annotation box based on this information would be "rejection of."

- (A) is correct because *dissension from* matches "rejection of."

- (B), (C), and (D) are wrong because *gratitude, adherence,* and *deference* all imply a positive attitude toward or at least an acknowledgment of traditional values, which is the **Opposite** of "rejection of."

6.   **C**   This is a Vocabulary question, as it's asking for a *logical and precise word or phrase*. Read the passage and highlight what can help fill in the blank. In regard to *recycling used car tires*, the passage states *potentially reusing them would be beneficial* and that *walls made of used tires and dirt* are *structurally robust*, or strong. A good word for the annotation box based on this information would be that the author considers the possibility of recycling used car tires as building materials to be "promising."

- (A) and (B) are wrong because both *derivative* and *ludicrous* are negative words that are the **Opposite** tone of "promising."

- (C) is correct because *auspicious* matches with "promising."

- (D) is wrong because *innovative* is a **Beyond the Text trap** answer: the passage doesn't actually say reusing tires as what the passage describes would be a new idea or has not been done before.

7.   **A**   This is a Vocabulary question, as it's asking for a *logical and precise word or phrase*. Read the passage and highlight what can help fill in the blank. The passage states that *cryptographers have yet to demonstrably decipher any portion of the text*, so a good word for the annotation box to describe *the meaning and purpose of the Voynich manuscript* would be "mysterious."

- (A) is correct because *enigmatic* matches "mysterious."

- (B) and (D) are wrong because *venerable* and *coherent* don't match "mysterious."

- (C) is wrong because it is a **Beyond the Text trap** answer. While *multifarious*, or complex, things can be *mysterious*, the words are not synonyms: mysterious things can be simple, and complex things can be quite well known and understood.

8.   **D**   This is a Vocabulary question, as it's asking for a *logical and precise word or phrase*. Read the passage and highlight what can help fill in the blank. The passage describes Whitsett's *ground-breaking development* and states that astronautics *owes much to him*. A good word for the annotation box based off this information would be "innovative."

- (A) and (B) are wrong because *dubious* (doubtful) and *futile* (hopeless) are the **Opposite** tone of "innovative."

- (C) is wrong because *galvanizing*, which means "stimulating," doesn't match "innovative."

- (D) is correct because *avant-garde* means "pioneering," which matches "innovative."

9. **A** This is a Retrieval question, as it says *Based on the text*. Read the passage and highlight what is said about Mr. Lorry in his interaction with Miss Manette. Mr. Lorry states that he is *a man of business* and *not much else* before telling Miss Manette he wants to tell her a story. After her repetition of the word *story*, the passage states that *He seemed willfully to mistake the word she had repeated* and acts as if she had repeated the word *customers* instead of *story*. The correct answer should be as consistent with these two descriptions of Mr. Lorry as possible.

    - (A) is correct because it is consistent with the description of Mr. Lorry before and after Miss Manette's reply.

    - (B) and (C) are wrong because they are **Half-Right:** In (B), Mr. Lorry does not misunderstand Miss Manette's interjection; he intentionally focuses on a different word. Similarly, in (C), it's never stated that he *cannot keep the details of the story accurate*.

    - (D) is wrong because the passage never indicates that Miss Manette is *rude*, nor does it state that Mr. Lorry is *unthinking* in his actions.

10. **B** This is a Claims question, as it asks what finding would support a claim. Read the passage and highlight the claim made, which is that *Abel claims that his use of Barbeau's text shows how anthropological texts can be used to portray Indigenous people differently based on the author*.

    - (A), (C), and (D) are wrong because they do not contain *different* portrayals of Indigenous peoples.

    - (B) is correct because it focuses on one anthropologist, Marius Barbeau, choosing to portray the chiefs' feud *over constructing the largest pole as unreasonable,* while the *other anthropologists* offer a reason as to why *larger totem poles* may have been culturally important to a tribe.

11. **B** This is a Claims question, as it asks for an illustration of a claim. Read the passage and highlight the claim made, which is that *While adult adoption remains a way for individuals to improve their economic status, the practice has its detractors as well, with some researchers arguing that it can lead to issues with the adoptee developing a firm sense of identity in his or her new environment*. The correct answer should be consistent with this claim and support both the positive and negative viewpoints toward adult adoption.

    - (A) and (D) are wrong because they are **Half-Right:** both express positive opinions toward adult adoptees but fail to account for the negative opinions towards adult adoption stated in the second half of the passage.

    - (B) is correct because it is consistent with both the positive and negative outcomes of adult adoption discussed in the claim.

    - (C) is wrong because the distinction made in the passage is between positive and negative outcomes of adult adoption, not the status of adult adoption in different East Asian countries.

12. **A** This is a Claims question, as it asks for support for a hypothesis. Read the passage and highlight the hypothesis, which states that *tau protein, the mutation of which is known to cause Alzheimer's disease, is key to controlling glutamate receptors.* It's also important to note the last sentence, which clarifies that *Tau protein does not directly affect glutamate receptors but does inhibit NSF.* The correct answer should be consistent with these two sentences.

   • (A) is correct because if *an excess of NSF has been shown to lead to abnormal glutamate receptor behavior,* and *tau protein…does inhibit NSF,* this would support the link made between tau proteins and glutamate receptors made in the hypothesis.

   • (B) and (D) are wrong because even if true, they either disregard or do not mention *tau protein* and *glutamate receptors,* the main components of the hypothesis.

   • (C) is wrong because the hypothesis is not about *what causes mutations of tau protein,* but how tau protein controls glutamate receptors.

13. **A** This is a Claims question, as it asks for support for an argument. Read the passage and highlight Garber's argument, which states that *tulip mania is explainable by fundamental economic concepts such as supply and demand.* The correct answer will be as consistent as possible with this claim.

   • (A) is correct because it discusses supply and demand, which is consistent with Garber's claim.

   • (B) and (C) are wrong because even though they focus on the price of tulip bulbs, they don't discuss supply and demand.

   • (D) is wrong because Garber's argument does not mention any connection between tulip bulbs and the *supply of gold coins in the Dutch republic.*

14. **A** This is a Conclusions question as it asks for an answer that *logically completes the text.* Read the passage and highlight the main ideas. The focus of the passage is on *the use of ants to control pests.* The third sentence identifies *several positive effects,* but the last sentence mentions that *ants also have negative effects.* Therefore, a logical conclusion to the passage should expand upon the negative effects introduced in the final sentence.

   • (A) is correct because it references *unintended environmental consequences,* which relate back to the negative effects described in the first half of the last sentence when ants are *used to control pests.*

   • (B) and (D) are wrong because they do not focus on *negative effects* that ants may have as pest control.

   • (C) is wrong because it is the **Opposite** of what the last sentence states: there are indeed *ramifications,* or negative effects, to using ants as pest control.

15.   **C**   This is a Conclusions question as it asks for an answer that *logically completes the text*. Read the passage and highlight the main ideas. The focus of the passage is on *a receptor* related to *odor*. The first sentence states that *eliminating that receptor...results in the inability to smell that odor*. The second sentence states that *mosquitoes modified to lack the receptor for smelling blood would be unable to find humans,* but the third sentence says they *were still able to find humans*. Therefore, a logical conclusion to the passage should make some claim about how mosquitoes may be different from other animals.

- (A) is wrong because no comparison between *mosquitoes without damage* and *those with damage* is made in the passage.

- (B) and (D) are wrong because they are the **Opposite** of what is stated in the passage: in both cases, mosquitoes with damage to their odor receptors were still able to find humans, so there is no evidence they could not detect certain odors or would be prevented from feeding.

- (C) is correct because it indicates that mosquitoes may not *have the same correlation between receptors and the ability to sense certain odors* that other animals do.

16.   **A**   This is a Conclusions question as it asks for an answer that *logically completes the text*. Read the passage and highlight the main ideas. The focus of the passage is on *NAFTA* and its relation to *manufacturing jobs*. During the interval from 1994 to 2020, the second sentence states that *the number of manufacturing jobs in the United States and Canada declined, but the total number of manufacturing jobs in the countries covered by NAFTA increased*. Therefore, a logical conclusion would explain how this might be possible.

- (A) is correct because if an increase in *the number of manufacturing jobs in Mexico*, which is also covered by NAFTA, was greater than the *combined decreases in the United States and Canada*, this would explain the seemingly contradictory data in the second sentence.

- (B), (C), and (D) are wrong because none of them offers a reason as to how the number of manufacturing jobs in the United States and Canada declined, but the total number of manufacturing jobs in all three countries increased.

17.   **C**   In this Rules question, verbs are changing in the answer choices, so it's testing consistency with verbs. Find and highlight the subject, *cloud*, which is singular, so a singular verb is needed. Write an annotation saying "singular." Eliminate any answer that is not singular.

- (A), (B), and (D) are wrong because they are plural.

- (C) is correct because it's singular.

18.   **B**   In this Rules question, punctuation is changing in the answer choices. The words *behavioral neuroscientist* are a title for *Damien Fair*, so no punctuation should be used. Eliminate answers that use punctuation.

- (A), (C), and (D) are wrong because a comma isn't used before or after a title.

- (B) is correct because titles before names have no punctuation

19. **A**   In this Rules question, verbs are changing in the answer choices, so it's testing consistency with verbs. Find and highlight the subject, *map*, which is singular, so a singular verb is needed. Write an annotation saying "singular." Eliminate any answer that is not singular.

- (A) is correct because it's singular.

- (B), (C), and (D) are wrong because they are plural.

20. **A**   In this Rules question, punctuation is changing in the answer choices. The words *common insecticide* are a title for *sulfoxaflor*, so no punctuation should be used. Eliminate answers that use punctuation.

- (A) is correct because titles before names have no punctuation.

- (B), (C), and (D) are wrong because a comma isn't used before or after a title.

21. **D**   In this Rules question, punctuation with a transition is changing in the answer choices. Look for independent clauses. The first part of the sentence says *Wichman's work to preserve the culture of Kaua'i wasn't finished*. There is an option to add *though* to this independent clause, and since it's contrasting with the previous idea, the transition should be added. Eliminate options that don't have *though* in the first part.

- (A) and (C) are wrong because they create a run-on sentence.

- (B) is wrong because it puts *Though* with the second independent clause.

- (D) is correct because *though* is part of the first independent clause.

22. **D**   In this Rules question, punctuation is changing in the answer choices, so look for independent clauses. The first part of the sentence says *Researchers studying bacteria have solved a 50-year mystery of how bacteria are able to move using appendages that are made of a single protein*, which is an independent clause. The second part of the sentence says *the subunits of the protein can exist in 11 different shapes…*, which is also an independent clause. Eliminate any answer that can't correctly connect two independent clauses.

- (A) and (C) are wrong because two independent clauses can't be linked with a comma by itself or with no punctuation at all.

- (B) is wrong because *while* is used for a contrast or for simultaneous events, which isn't the case here.

- (D) is correct because a colon can connect two independent clauses and is appropriately used when the second part explains the first.

23. **A** This is a Transitions question, so follow the basic approach. Highlight ideas that relate to each other. The first part of the sentence says *Fault tree analysis was originally used…in high-risk fields…but other fields are experimenting* with using it, and the second part of the sentence says *fault tree analysis is also being used in low-risk fields*. These ideas agree, so a same-direction transition is needed. Make an annotation that says "agree." Eliminate any answer that doesn't match.

- (A) is correct because *increasingly* supports the change from fault tree analysis's original use to where it is begun to be used.

- (B) is wrong because it is an opposite-direction transition.

- (C) is wrong because the second sentence isn't a conclusion.

- (D) is wrong because the second sentence isn't an additional point.

24. **C** This is a Transitions question, so follow the basic approach. Highlight ideas that relate to each other. The first part of the sentence says *she had primarily worked on canvas*, and the second part of the sentence says *but she quickly found her works evolving to include the three-dimensional space around her*. These ideas disagree, so an opposite-direction transition is needed. Make an annotation that says "disagree." Eliminate any answer that doesn't match.

- (A) is wrong because *instead* implies that the contrast is between the first and second sentence, but the contrast is between the two parts of the sentence.

- (B) and (D) are wrong because they are same-direction transitions.

- (C) is correct because *previously* is opposite-direction and supports the shift described in the sentence.

25. **D** This is a Transitions question, so follow the basic approach. Highlight ideas that relate to each other. The previous sentence says *Some scientists believe that the fish are carried to these locations in the beaks or talons of birds*, and this sentence describes what *new research suggests* as a different way the fish travel. These ideas disagree, so an opposite-direction transition is needed. Make an annotation that says "disagree." Eliminate any answer that doesn't match.

- (A), (B), and (C) are wrong because they are same-direction transitions.

- (D) is correct because *alternatively* is an opposite-direction transition.

26. **D** This is a Rhetorical Synthesis question, so follow the basic approach. Highlight the goal(s) stated in the question: *emphasize the aim of the research study*. Eliminate any answer that doesn't fulfill this purpose.

- (A), (B), and (C) are wrong because they don't mention the *aim of the research study*—what researchers wanted to accomplish.

- (D) is correct because it mentions the *aim of the research study* by stating what researchers *wanted to know*.

27. **B** This is a Rhetorical Synthesis question, so follow the basic approach. Highlight the goal(s) stated in the question: *emphasize the affiliation and purpose of Pääbo's and Skov's work*. Eliminate any answer that doesn't fulfill this purpose.

- (A), (C), and (D) are wrong because they don't mention the *affiliation*—the group or institution the scientists are associated with.

- (B) is correct because it states the *affiliation* (*Max Planck Institute for Evolutionary Anthropology*) and *purpose* (*provide insight into human evolution*).

PRACTICE TEST 4—MATH EXPLANATIONS

Module 1

1. **B** The question asks for the frequency table that correctly represents a list of numbers. A frequency table has two columns: the left-hand column contains the values, and the right-hand column contains the number of times each value occurs, or its frequency. Work in bite-sized pieces and eliminate answer choices that do not match the data. The number 2 occurs twice in the list, so its frequency is 2. Eliminate (A) because it shows a frequency of 4 for the number 2. Eliminate (D) because it does not include the number 2 at all. Next, the number 9 occurs three times in the list, so its frequency is 3. Eliminate (C) because it shows the number 3 occurring 9 times instead of the number 9 occurring 3 times. Choice (B) shows the correct frequency for each value. The correct answer is (B).

2. **C** The question asks for an equivalent form of an expression. One approach is to use the built-in calculator. Enter the expression given in the question, and then enter the expressions from the answer choices one at a time and stop when one of the answers produces the same graph. Only the graph of the expression in (C) matches, so it is correct.

   Since the question asks for an equivalent expression and the answer choices contain variables, another approach is to plug in. Make $x = 2$, and plug it into the expression to get $2^2 - 2 - 56$, which becomes $4 - 58$, and then -54. This is the target value; write it down and circle it. Next, plug $x = 2$ into each answer choice and eliminate any that do not equal the target value. Choice (A) becomes $(2 - 14)(2 + 4)$, then $(-12)(6)$, and finally -72. This does not match the target value, so eliminate (A). Choice (B) becomes $(2 - 7)(2 + 8)$, then $(-5)(10)$, and finally 50; eliminate (B). Choice (C) becomes $(2 - 8)(2 + 7)$, then $(-6)(9)$, and finally -54. This matches the target value, so keep (C), but check (D) just in case. Choice (D) becomes $(2 - 4)(2 + 14)$, then $(-2)(16)$, and finally -32; eliminate (D). Only (C) matched the target value, so it is correct.

   Finally, when given a quadratic in standard form, which is $ax^2 + bx + c$, another approach is to factor it. Find two numbers that multiply to -56 and add to -1. These are -8 and 7, so the factored form of the quadratic is $(x - 8)(x + 7)$, which is (C).

   Using any of these methods, the correct answer is (C).

3. **C** The question asks for an equation that represents a specific situation. Translate the information in Bite-Sized Pieces and eliminate after each piece. One piece of information says that the carpenter *hammers 10 nails per minute*, and another piece says that the carpenter *hammers nails for x minutes*. Multiplying the rate of 10 nails per minute by the number of minutes gives the number of nails: $\left(\dfrac{10 \text{ nails}}{1 \text{ minute}}\right)(x \text{ minutes}) = 10x$ nails. Eliminate (A) and (B) because they multiply the number of minutes by $\dfrac{1}{10}$ instead of by 10. Compare the remaining answer choices. The difference between (C) and (D) is the number on the right side of the equation. Since the carpenter *uses a combined total of 200 nails and screws*, the equation must equal 200. Eliminate (D) because it equals 3,420. The correct answer is (C).

4. **B** The question asks for the value of the measure of an angle on a figure. Use the Geometry Basic Approach. Start by drawing a triangle on the scratch paper. Next, label the figure with the given information. Label angle D as 73°, angle E as 35°, and angle F without a number. Since the measures of the angles in a triangle have a sum of 180°, set up the equation $73° + 35° + F = 180°$, which becomes $108° + F = 180°$. Subtract 108° from both sides of the equation to get $F = 72°$. The correct answer is (B).

5. **D** The question asks about a graph representing a certain situation. In a linear graph that represents an amount over time, the y-intercept represents the initial amount. In this case, it represents the amount of plastic remaining to be recycled when $x = 0$. After 0 shifts, no plastic has been recycled yet, so the y-intercept represents the initial amount of plastic to be recycled. The correct answer is (D).

6. $\dfrac{12}{20}$ **or 0.6**

   The question asks for a probability based on data in a table. Probability is defined as $\dfrac{\# \text{ of outcomes that fit requirements}}{\text{total } \# \text{ of outcomes}}$. Read the table carefully to find the numbers to make the probability. There are 200 total textbooks, so that is the *total # of outcomes*. Of these 200 textbooks, 120 are new textbooks, so that is the *# of outcomes that fit requirements*. Therefore, the probability that a textbook chosen at random is a new textbook is $\dfrac{120}{200}$. This cannot be entered into the fill-in box, which only accepts 5 characters when the answer is positive. All equivalent answers that fit will be accepted, so reduce the fraction or convert it to a decimal. The correct answer is $\dfrac{12}{20}$, 0.6, or another equivalent form.

7. **D** The question asks for a reasonable number based on survey results and a margin of error. Work in bite-sized pieces and eliminate after each piece. A margin of error expresses the amount of random sampling error in a survey's results. Start by applying the percent of respondents who did not support the existing registration system to the entire population of undergraduate students. Take 75% of the entire undergraduate student population to get $\frac{75}{100}(60,000) = 45,000$ students. Eliminate (A) and (B) because they are not close to this value and do not represent a reasonable number of students who did not support the existing registration system. The margin of error is 4%, meaning that results within a range of 4% above and 4% below the estimate are reasonable. A 4% margin of error will not change the result by very much, and (D) is the only answer choice close to 45,000. To check, calculate the lower limit of the range based on the margin of error, since 43,800 is less than 45,000. To find the lower limit, subtract 4% from 75% to get 71%, and then find 71% of the total population to get a lower limit of $\frac{71}{100}(60,000) = 42,600$. The value in (C) is less than the lower limit, so it is not a reasonable number. Choice (D) contains a value between 42,600 and 45,000, so it is reasonable. The correct answer is (D).

8. **−4** The question asks for the negative solution to an equation. One method is to enter the equation into the built-in calculator, replacing a with x in order to see a graph of the equation. The values of x are shown by vertical lines; scroll and zoom as needed to see that these cross the x-axis at −4 and 8. The question asks for the negative solution, which is −4.

   To solve for a algebraically, start by multiplying both sides of the equation by a to get $32 = a(a − 4)$. Next, distribute on the right side of the equation to get $32 = a^2 − 4a$. Subtract 32 from both sides of the equation to get $0 = a^2 − 4a − 32$. Now that the equation is a quadratic in standard form, which is $ax^2 + bx + c$, factor it to find the solutions. Find two numbers that multiply to −32 and add to −4. These are 4 and −8, so the factored form of the quadratic is $0 = (a + 4)(a − 8)$. Now set each factor equal to 0 to get two equations: $a + 4 = 0$ and $a − 8 = 0$. Subtract 4 from both sides of the first equation to get $a = −4$. Add 8 to both sides of the second equation to get $a = 8$. Therefore, the negative solution to the given equation is −4.

   Using either of these methods, the correct answer is −4.

9. **A** The question asks for a description of a function that models a specific situation. Compare the answer choices. Two choices say the function is increasing, and two say it is decreasing. Since the balloon is rising, its distance above sea level is increasing over time. Eliminate (C) and (D) because they describe a decreasing function. The difference between (A) and (B) is whether the function

is linear or exponential. Since the distance above sea level changes by a constant amount during each unit of time, the relationship between the balloon's distance above sea level and time is linear. Eliminate (B) because it describes an exponential function. The correct answer is (A).

10. **B** The question asks for the *x*-intercept of a function. An *x*-intercept is a point where $y = 0$. In function notation, the number inside the parentheses is the *x*-value that goes into the function, or the input, and the value that comes out of the function is the *y*-value, or the output. Together, they represent points on the graph of the function. The answers are points that could be the *x*-intercept, so plug in the answers. Start with (A), and plug $x = -1$ and $y = 0$ into the function, keeping in mind that $f(x) = y$. The equation becomes $0 = (22)^{-1} - 1$. Add 1 to both sides of the equation to get $1 = (22)^{-1}$. Either use a calculator or know how to work with a negative exponent. A negative exponent means to raise the value to the positive exponent and take the reciprocal, so $(22)^{-1}$ becomes $\frac{1}{22^1}$. The equation then becomes $1 = \frac{1}{22^1}$. This is not true, so eliminate (A). Next, try (B) and plug $x = 0$ and $y = 0$ into the function to get $0 = (22)^0 - 1$. Add 1 to both sides of the equation to get $1 = (22)^0$. Any number raised to the power of 0 is 1, so the equation becomes $1 = 1$. This is true, so stop and pick (B).

It is also possible to answer this question using the built-in calculator. Enter the equation of the function, and then scroll and zoom as needed to see that the *x*-intercept is at $(0, 0)$, making (B) correct.

Using either of these methods, the correct answer is (B).

11. **A** The question asks for the length of a side of a geometric figure. Use the Geometry Basic Approach. Start by redrawing the figure on the scratch paper, and then label it with information from the question. Since the question asks for a specific value and the answers contain numbers in increasing order, plug in the answers. Write the answers on the scratch paper, label them as "side $\overline{AB}$," and start with a middle number. Try (B) and make $\overline{AB} = 16$. The question states that *the length of $\overline{AB}$ is one-third the length of $\overline{AD}$*. Given this, if $\overline{AB} = 16$, $\overline{AD} = 3(16) = 48$. The perimeter of a geometric shape is the sum of the lengths of the sides, so the perimeter of this figure is $16 + 48 + 16 + 48 = 128$. This does not match the perimeter of 64 given in the question, so eliminate (B). The result was too big, and a longer side length will make the perimeter even bigger, so eliminate (C) and (D) as well. The correct answer is (A).

12. **A** The question asks for a value based on a geometric figure. Use the Geometry Basic Approach. Start by drawing a triangle on the scratch paper, and then label the figure with the given information. The question gives the area of the triangle, so write out the formula for the area of a triangle, $A = \frac{1}{2}bh$, and plug in the given area to get $18 = \frac{1}{2}bh$. Since the question asks for a specific value and the answers contain numbers in increasing order, plug in the answers. Write the answers on the scratch paper, label them as "m," and start with a middle number. Try (B), 9. If $m = 9$, the base of the triangle is $9 + 5 = 14$, and the height of the triangle is 9. Plug these numbers into the area formula to get $18 = \frac{1}{2}(14)(9)$. Simplify the right side of the equation to get $18 = 63$. This is not true, so eliminate (B). The result was too big, and a larger value of m will make the area even bigger, so eliminate (C) and (D) as well. The correct answer is (A).

13. **D** The question asks for the equation that represents the relationship between two variables. When given a table of values and asked for the correct equation, plug values from the table into the answer choices to see which one works. Plugging in 0 or 1 is likely to make more than one answer work, so start with the third row of the table and plug in $s = 2$ and $c = 80$. Choice (A) becomes $80 = (1 + 3)^2$, then $80 = 4^2$, and finally $80 = 16$. This is not true, so eliminate (A). Choice (B) becomes $80 = (1 + 5)^2$, then $80 = 6^2$, and finally $80 = 36$; eliminate (B). Choice (C) becomes $80 = 3(1 + 5)^2$, and then $80 = 3(6)^2$. Continue simplifying to get $80 = 3(36)$, and then $80 = 108$; eliminate (C). Choice (D) becomes $80 = 5(1 + 3)^2$, and then $80 = 5(4)^2$. Continue simplifying to get $80 = 5(16)$, and then $80 = 80$. This is true, so keep (D). The correct answer is (D).

14. **A** The question asks for the number of points of intersection in a system of equations. One method is to use the built-in calculator. Enter each equation into a separate entry field, and then scroll and zoom as needed to see where, if at all, they intersect. The lines are parallel and do not intersect, making (A) correct.

Another method is to use algebra. Substitute $12x$ for y in the second equation to get $24x + 7 = 2(12x)$. Simplify the right side of the equation to get $24x + 7 = 24x$. Subtract $24x$ from both sides of the equation to get $7 = 0$. This is not true, so the system of equations has no solution. This means the lines are parallel and do not intersect, and (A) is correct.

Using either of these methods, the correct answer is (A).

15. **25** The question asks for a value given a specific situation. Translate the information in bite-sized pieces. The question states that the *equation 15a + 10b = 100 represents the situation when a of the A tiles and b of the B tiles are drawn for a total of 100 points.* Since the sum of $15a$ and $10b$ is the number of points, and a and b are numbers of tiles, 15 and 10 must be the point values of one A tile and one B tile, respectively. To find the number of points earned by drawing 1 of each type of tile, plug in 1 for a and 1 for b to get $15(1) + 10(1) = 15 + 10 = 25$. The correct answer is 25.

16. **D** The question asks for an equation that represents a specific situation. The value of the fund is decreasing by a certain fraction over time, so this question is about exponential decay. Write down the growth and decay formula: *final amount* = (*original amount*)(1 ± *rate*)^*number of changes*. In this case, *d* is the final amount, and the question states that the original amount was $10,000. Eliminate (A) and (B) because they do not have 10,000 as the original amount in front of the parentheses. Since this situation involves a decrease, the original amount must be multiplied by (1 – *rate*), and the rate here is $\frac{1}{4}$, so the value in parentheses should be $1 - \frac{1}{4}$ or $\frac{3}{4}$. Eliminate (C), which does not have this rate. The only remaining answer is (D), and it matches the growth formula, so (D) is correct.

Without this formula, it is still possible to answer this question. Plug in a value of *y* to see how the fund amount decreases over time. After one year, the fund will have $\frac{1}{4}$ less than the initial $10,000. The value of the account will then be $\$10,000 - \frac{1}{4}(\$10,000) = \$10,000 - \$2,500 = \$7,500$. After another year, the fund will have $\frac{1}{4}$ less than $7,500, so the value will be $\$7,500 - \frac{1}{4}(\$7,500) = \$7,500 - \$1,875 = \$5,625$. Plug *y* = 2 into the answer choices to see which results in a value of 5,625 for *d*. Only (D) works, so it is correct.

Using either of these methods, either method, the correct answer is (D).

17. **C** The question asks for the measurement of part of a geometric figure. Use the Geometry Basic Approach. Start by drawing a cylinder on the scratch paper as best as possible, and then label the figure with the given information. Write down the formula for the volume of a cylinder, either from memory or after looking it up on the reference sheet: $V = \pi r^2 h$. Plug in the values given in the question for the volume and the height to get $144\pi = \pi r^2(4)$. Divide both sides of the equation by 4π to get $36 = r^2$. Take the positive square root of both sides of the equation to get $6 = r$. Read carefully: the question asks for the diameter, not the radius. The diameter of a circle is twice the radius, so $d = 2(6)$, or $d = 12$. The correct answer is (C).

18. **C** The question asks for the value of the *x*-coordinate of the solution to a system of equations. The most efficient method is to enter both equations into the built-in calculator, and then scroll and zoom as needed to find the point of intersection. The point is (6, –10), so the *x*-coordinate, or *a*, is 6, and (C) is correct.

To solve algebraically for the *x*-coordinate of the point of intersection, find a way to make the *y*-coordinates disappear when stacking and adding the equations. Compare the *y*-terms: the larger coefficient, 10, is 5 times the smaller one, 2. Multiply the entire first equation by –5 to get the same coefficient with opposite signs on the *y* terms. The first equation becomes $-5(4x + 2y) = -5(4)$ and then $-20x - 10y = -20$. Now stack and add the two equations.

$$
\begin{array}{r}
-20x - 10y = -20 \\
+\ 19x + 10y = \ \ 14 \\
\hline
-x \qquad\quad = -6
\end{array}
$$

Divide both sides of the resulting equation by -1 to get $x = 6$, making (C) correct.

Using either of these methods, the correct answer is (C).

19. $\dfrac{40}{41}$ The question asks for the value of a trigonometric function. Use the Geometry Basic Approach. Begin by drawing a triangle and labeling the vertices. The largest angle in a right triangle is the 90° angle, and the largest angle is opposite the longest side, so label angle *B* as a right angle. The drawing should look something like this:

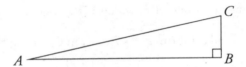

Next, write out SOHCAHTOA to remember the trig functions. The SOH part defines the sine as $\dfrac{\text{opposite}}{\text{hypotenuse}}$, and the question states that $\sin(A) = \dfrac{9}{41}$, so label the side opposite angle *A*, which is $\overline{BC}$, as 9 and the hypotenuse, which is $\overline{AC}$, as 41. To find the length of the third side, use the Pythagorean Theorem: $a^2 + b^2 = c^2$. Plug in the known values to get $9^2 + b^2 = 41^2$. Square the numbers to get $81 + b^2 = 1{,}681$, and then subtract 81 from both sides of the equation to get $b^2 = 1{,}600$. Take the positive square root of both sides of the equation to get $b = 40$.

With all three side lengths labeled, the drawing looks like this:

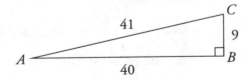

To find $\sin(C)$, use the SOH part of SOHCAHTOA again. The side opposite angle *C* is 40, and the hypotenuse is 41, so $\sin(C) = \dfrac{40}{41}$. On fill-in questions, a fractional answer can also be entered as a decimal. When the answer is positive, there is room in the fill-in box for five characters, including the decimal point. In this case $\frac{40}{41} = .\overline{97560}$, which is too long. Either stop when there's no more room and enter .9756, or round the last digit, which in this case is also .9756. It is allowed but not required to put a 0 in front of the decimal point, which would make the answer 0.975 or 0.976, but do not shorten it more than that. The correct answer is $\frac{40}{41}$ or an equivalent form.

20. **−2.5** The question asks for the value when a quadratic function reaches its maximum. A parabola reaches its minimum or maximum value at its vertex, so find the x-coordinate of the vertex. One method is to enter the equation into the built-in calculator, and then scroll and zoom as needed to find the vertex. The vertex is at (−2.5, 13.5), so the value of the x-coordinate is −2.5.

To solve algebraically, find the value of h, which is the x-coordinate of the vertex (h, k). When a quadratic equation is in standard form, $ax^2 + bx + c$, find h using the formula $h = -\frac{b}{2a}$. Since $a = -6$ and $b = -30$, $h = -\frac{-30}{2(-6)}$. This becomes $h = -\frac{-30}{-12}$, and then $h = -\frac{30}{12}$. When the answer is negative, there is room in the fill-in box for six characters, including the negative sign. This fraction fits, so either enter it, reduce the fraction, or convert it to a decimal.

Using either of these methods, the correct answer is −2.5 or an equivalent form.

21. **10** The question asks for the value of a function. The question states that the graph of function f and the graph of function g are perpendicular lines, which means they have slopes that are negative reciprocals of each other. The question gives the equation of line f, so find the slope of that line. This function is in the form $y = mx + b$, in which m is the slope and b is the y-intercept, so the slope of line f is $-\frac{1}{5}$. The negative reciprocal of $-\frac{1}{5}$ is 5, so the slope of line g is 5. In function notation, the number inside the parentheses is the x-value that goes into the function, or the input, and the value that comes out of the function is the y-value, or the output. Together, they represent points on the graph of the function. Thus, if $g(0) = 0$, that means line g contains the point (0, 0). Thus, the y-intercept, or b, is 0. Now plug $x = 2$, $m = 5$, and $b = 0$ into $y = mx + b$ to get $y = 5(2) + 0$, or $y = 10$. The correct answer is 10.

22. **2.4** The question asks for a value in a system of equations. One method is to use the built-in calculator. Enter each equation into a separate entry field, and then click on the slider for k. Move the slider left and right until the line intersects the parabola exactly once. It might be hard to see when this happens, so scroll and zoom as needed and click on one of the equations to see a gray dot at the point of intersection. There is one point of intersection when $k = 2.4$.

To solve for k algebraically, start by simplifying the second equation by multiplying both sides of the equation by 10 to get $y = -10x$. Now that both equations are equal to y, set them equal to each other to get $-10x = 5kx^2 + 2x + 3$. Add $10x$ to both sides of the equation to get $5kx^2 + 12x + 3 = 0$. The question states that the system *has exactly one solution*. To determine the number of solutions to a quadratic, use the discriminant. The discriminant is the part of the quadratic formula under the square root sign, and it can be written as $D = b^2 - 4ac$. When the discriminant is positive, the quadratic has exactly two real solutions; when the discriminant is 0, the quadratic has exactly one real solution; and when the discriminant is negative, the quadratic has no real solutions. Since this quadratic has exactly one real solution, the discriminant must equal 0. The quadratic is now in standard form, $ax^2 + bx + c = 0$, so $a = 5k$, $b = 12$, and $c = 3$. Plug these into the discriminant formula, along with $D = 0$, to get $0 = 12^2 - 4(5k)(3)$, which becomes $0 = 144 - 60k$. Add $60k$ to both sides of the equation to get $144 = 60k$, and then divide both sides of the equation by 60 to get $2.4 = k$.

Using either of these methods, the correct answer is 2.4.

Module 2—Easier

1. **C** The question asks for the median of a set of data. The median of a list of numbers is the middle number when the numbers are arranged in order. In lists with an even number of numbers, the median is the average of the two middle numbers. Count to see that there are 7 numbers in the list. Since there is an odd number of numbers, the median is the middle number. Since this list is already in order, cross out one number at a time from each end until only the middle number is left, like so: ~~33~~, ~~34~~, ~~38~~, 41, ~~43~~, ~~44~~, ~~47~~. The middle number is 41, so the median is 41, and (C) is correct.

It is also possible to calculate the median of a list of numbers using the built-in calculator. Type the word *median* followed by the list of numbers inside parentheses, and the calculated median will appear in the lower right corner of the entry field. The calculator shows the median as 41, so (C) is correct.

Using either of these methods, the correct answer is (C).

2. **32** The question asks for the value of a variable based on an equation. Isolate the variable by moving everything else to the other side of the equation. Since the right side of the equation has −10, add 10 to both sides of the equation. The equation becomes $32 = y$. The correct answer is 32.

3.   **B**   The question asks for the perimeter of a rectangle. Use the Geometry Basic Approach. Start by drawing a rectangle on the scratch paper. Next, label the figure with information from the question. In a rectangle, opposite sides are equal, so this rectangle has two sides that are 23 inches long and two sides that are 9 inches long. The drawing should look something like this:

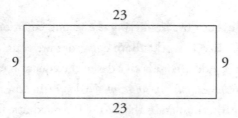

The perimeter of a geometric shape is the sum of the lengths of the sides. Add all four side lengths to get 9 + 23 + 9 + 23 = 64. The correct answer is (B).

4.   **C**   The question asks for an equivalent form of an expression. Every term includes the variable a multiplied by a different number, called a coefficient. Work with the coefficients, and remember the order of operations, PEMDAS, which stands for Parentheses, Exponents, Multiply, Divide, Add, Subtract. Start inside the parentheses: $6a - 2a = 4a$. The expression becomes $15a - 4a$. Subtract the coefficients to get $15a - 4a = 11a$. The correct answer is (C).

5.   **A**   The question asks for an equation that represents the relationship between two variables. Translate the English to math in bite-sized pieces. Translate *is* as equals, or =. Translate *half* as $\frac{1}{2}$. Translate *of* as times, or ×. Thus, *a is half of b* translates to $a = \frac{1}{2} \times b$. The multiplication sign is not needed when multiplying a number by a variable, so this can be written as $a = \frac{1}{2}b$. The correct answer is (A).

6.   **B**   The question asks for the value of a constant given two equivalent expressions. Start by rewriting the expressions with an equals sign between them to get $\frac{3}{y + c} = \frac{15}{5y + 30}$. Next, start to solve by cross-multiplying. The equation becomes $(y + c)(15) = (3)(5y + 30)$. Distribute on both sides of the equation to get $15y + 15c = 15y + 90$. Subtract $15y$ from both sides of the equation to get $15c = 90$. Divide both sides of the equation by 15 to get $c = 6$. The correct answer is (B).

7.   **140**   The question asks for a value based on a percent. One method is to use the built-in calculator. The calculator automatically adds "of" after the percent sign, so enter "70%" and then "200" into an entry field. The result in the lower right corner of the entry field is 140, which is correct.

Another method is to translate the English to math in bite-sized pieces. *Percent* means out of 100, so translate 70% as $\dfrac{70}{100}$. Translate *how many* as a variable, such as *d* for dogs. Translate *of* as times, or ×. Translate *the pets* as 200. The equation becomes $d = \left(\dfrac{70}{100}\right)(200)$. Solve the equation by hand or on a calculator to get *d* = 140.

Using either of these methods, the correct answer is 140.

8. **A**   The question asks for a value given a rate. Begin by reading the question to find information about the rate. The question states that James *drives at an average speed of 20 miles per hour*. Set up a proportion to determine how many hours it will take James to drive 100 miles. The proportion is $\dfrac{20 \text{ miles}}{1 \text{ hour}} = \dfrac{100 \text{ miles}}{x \text{ hours}}$. Cross-multiply to get (20)(*x*) = (1)(100), or 20*x* = 100. Divide both sides of the equation by 20 to get *x* = 5. The correct answer is (A).

9. **44**   The question asks for the value of an expression given an equation. When an SAT question asks for the value of an expression, there is usually a straightforward way to solve for the expression without needing to completely isolate the variable. Since 4*y* is four times *y* and 16 is four times 4, multiply the entire equation by 4 to get (4)(*y* − 4) = (4)(11). The equation becomes 4*y* − 16 = 44. The correct answer is 44.

10. **D**   The question asks for the value of a function. In function notation, the number inside the parentheses is the *x*-value that goes into the function, or the input, and the value that comes out of the function is the *y*-value, or the output. The question provides an input value, so plug *x* = 3 into the function to get $g(3) = 3^2 - 1$, which becomes *g*(3) = 9 − 1, and then *g*(3) = 8. The correct answer is (D).

11. **D**   The question asks for the value of a function that represents a situation. In function notation, the number inside the parentheses is the *x*-value that goes into the function, or the input, and the value that comes out of the function is the *y*-value, or the output. The question provides the number of items, which is represented by *x*, so plug *x* = 2,000 into the function to get *p*(2,000) = 2(2,000) + 150, which becomes *p*(2,000) = 4,000 + 150, and then *p*(2,000) = 4,150. The correct answer is (D).

12. **B**   The question asks for the value of a function. In function notation, the number inside the parentheses is the *x*-value that goes into the function, or the input, and the value that comes out of the function is the *y*-value, or the output. The question provides an input value, so plug *x* = 6 into the function to get $f(6) = \dfrac{2}{3}(6)$, which becomes *f*(6) = 4. The correct answer is (B).

13. **118** The question asks for the value of an angle on a figure. Use the Geometry Basic Approach. Start by redrawing the figure on the scratch paper, and then label the figure with the given information. The fact that two of the lines are parallel will be important on some questions about lines and angles, but here it's unnecessary information. Instead, since d and 62 make up a straight line and there are 180° in a line, $d + 62 = 180$. Subtract 62 from both sides of the equation to get $d = 118$. The correct answer is 118.

14. **A** The question asks for the value of an expression given the equation of a graph in the xy-plane. One method is to use the built-in calculator. Enter the equation of the line, and then scroll and zoom as needed to find the intercepts. The x-intercept is at (5.667, 0), and the y-intercept is at (0, −4.25). Thus, $c = 5.667$, $k = -4.25$, and $\dfrac{c}{k} = \dfrac{5.667}{-4.25} = -1.33$. This is the same value as $-\dfrac{4}{3}$, which makes (A) correct.

To solve algebraically, plug the given points into the equation of the line. Plug in $x = c$ and $y = 0$ to get $3c - 4(0) = 17$, or $3c = 17$. Divide both sides of the equation by 3 to get $c = \dfrac{17}{3}$. Next, plug in $x = 0$ and $y = k$ to get $3(0) - 4k = 17$, or $-4k = 17$. Divide both sides of the equation by −4 to get $k = -\dfrac{17}{4}$. Finally divide c by k to get $\dfrac{c}{k} = \dfrac{\frac{17}{3}}{-\frac{17}{4}}$. When dividing fractions, multiply the reciprocal of the fraction in the denominator by the fraction in the numerator. This becomes $\dfrac{c}{k} = \left(\dfrac{17}{3}\right)\left(-\dfrac{4}{17}\right)$, and then $\dfrac{c}{k} = -\dfrac{4}{3}$, and (A) is correct.

Using either of these methods, the correct answer is (A).

15. **D** The question asks for a value given a rate. Begin by reading the question to find information about the rate. The question states that the machine *processes mail at a constant rate of 21 pieces of mail per minute*. Set up a proportion to determine how many pieces of mail the machine will process in 7 minutes, being sure to match up units. The proportion is $\dfrac{21 \text{ pieces of mail}}{1 \text{ minute}} = \dfrac{x \text{ pieces of mail}}{7 \text{ minutes}}$. Cross-multiply to get $(1)(x) = (21)(7)$, or $x = 147$. The correct answer is (D).

16. **B** The question asks for an equation that represents a specific situation. Translate the information in bite-sized pieces and eliminate after each piece. One piece of information says that Stella will send 24

invitations *each day for the next d days*. Since d represents the number of days, it should be multiplied by 24. Eliminate (C) and (D) because they multiply d by 43 instead of 24. Compare the remaining answer choices. The difference between (A) and (B) is whether 43 is added to $24d$ or subtracted from $24d$. Since Stella *has already sent 43 invitations* and will send a total of 211 invitations, 43 should be added to $24d$ and set equal to 211. Eliminate (A) because it uses subtraction. The correct answer is (B).

17. **B**   The question asks for the function that represents values given in a table. In function notation, the number inside the parentheses is the x-value that goes into the function, or the input, and the value that comes out of the function is the y-value, or the output. Together, they represent points on the graph of the function. The table shows pairs of values for x and $f(x)$, and the correct function must work for every point on the graph. Plug in values from the table and eliminate functions that don't work. Since plugging in 0 or 1 is likely to make more than one answer work, start with the fourth column in the table and plug in $x = 2$ and $f(x) = 21$. Choice (A) becomes $21 = 3(2) + 12$, then $21 = 6 + 12$, and finally $21 = 18$. This is not true, so eliminate (A). Choice (B) becomes $21 = 3(2) + 15$, then $21 = 6 + 15$, and finally $21 = 21$. This is true, so keep (B), but check the remaining answers with this pair of values. Choice (C) becomes $21 = 15(2) + 12$, then $21 = 30 + 12$, and finally $21 = 42$; eliminate (C). Choice (D) becomes $21 = 15(2) + 15$, then $21 = 30 + 15$, and finally $21 = 45$; eliminate (D). Only the equation in (B) worked with this pair of values, so stop here. The correct answer is (B).

18. **C**   The question asks for the term in an equation that represents a specific part of a scenario. The question states that s represents *the number of seconds since the rocket was launched* and asks for the height when the rocket was launched. No time had elapsed at the instant the rocket was launched, so plug $s = 0$ into the equation. The equation becomes $h = -16(0)^2 + 64(0) + 21$. Simplify the right side of the equation to get $h = 0 + 0 + 21$, or $h = 21$. Since the height at the time of 0 seconds is 21 feet, that number represents the initial height, or the height of the rooftop, and (C) is correct.

Another method is to enter the equation into the built-in calculator, and then scroll and zoom as needed to find the y-intercept, which represents the height of the rocket 0 seconds after launch. Click on the gray dot to see that the coordinates are $(0, 21)$, so the height of the rooftop is 21, and (C) is correct.

Using either of these methods, the correct answer is (C).

19. **D**   The question asks for correct values in a function. In function notation, the number inside the parentheses is the x-value that goes into the function, or the input, and the value that comes out of the function is the y-value, or the output. When given a function and asked for the table of values, plug values from the answer choices into the function and eliminate answers that don't work. Start with $x = 2$ because two answers pair it with $y = 3$, and two pair it with $y = 9$, so this will eliminate half of the answer choices. Plug $x = 2$ into the function to get $f(2) = 2^3 + 1$, which becomes $f(2) = 8 + 1$, and then $f(2) = 9$. Eliminate (A) and (B) because they both have $y = 3$ for this x value. The third pair of values is the same in (C) and (D), so try the second pair of values and plug $x = 3$ into the function. The function becomes $f(3) = 3^3 + 1$, then $f(3) = 27 + 1$, and then $f(3) = 28$. Eliminate (C). The correct answer is (D).

20.   **A**   The question asks for the equation that defines a function. In function notation, the number inside the parentheses is the *x*-value that goes into the function, or the input, and the value that comes out of the function is the *y*-value, or the output. The question provides two pairs of input and output values, so plug those into the answer choices and eliminate answers that don't work with both pairs. Start by plugging *x* = –1 and *h*(*x*) = 3 into the answer choices. Choice (A) becomes 3 = 2(–1) + 5, then 3 = –2 + 5, and finally 3 = 3. This is true, so keep (A), but check the remaining answers with the first pair of values. Choice (B) becomes 3 = 2(–1) + 3, then 3 = –2 + 3, and finally 3 = 1. This is not true, so eliminate (B). Choice (C) becomes 3 = 2(–1), and then 3 = –2; eliminate (C). Choice (D) becomes 3 = 3(–1) + 5, then 3 = –3 + 5, and finally 3 = 2; eliminate (D). Only the equation in (A) worked with the first pair of values, so stop here. The correct answer is (A).

21.   **D**   The question asks for an equation in terms of a specific variable. The question asks about the relationship among variables and there are variables in the answer choices, so one option is to plug in. That might get messy with three variables, and all of the answer choices have *r* by itself, so the other option is to solve for *r*. To begin to isolate *r*, add 6*s* to both sides of the equation to get *p* + 6*s* = 13*r*. Divide both sides of the equation by 13 to get $\frac{p + 6s}{13} = r$. Flip the sides of the equation to get $r = \frac{p + 6s}{13}$. The correct answer is (D).

22.   **A**   The question asks for the value of a trigonometric function. Use the Geometry Basic Approach. Start by drawing two right triangles that are similar to each other, meaning they have the same proportions but are different sizes. Be certain to match up the corresponding angles that are given in the question, and put the longest side opposite the right angle. Next, label the sides of triangle *ABC* with the lengths given in the question. The drawing should look something like this:

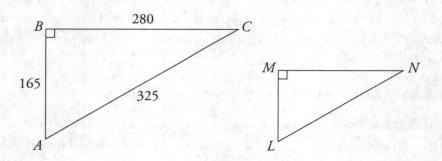

The question asks for the cosine of angle *L*, which corresponds to angle *A*. Trig functions are proportions, so cos(*L*) = cos(*A*), and it is possible to answer the question without knowing any of the side lengths of triangle *LMN*. To find cos(*A*), use SOHCAHTOA to remember the trig functions. The CAH part of the acronym defines the cosine as $\frac{\text{adjacent}}{\text{hypotenuse}}$. The side adjacent to *A* is

165, and the hypotenuse is 325, so $\cos(A) = \dfrac{165}{325}$. Since $\cos(L) = \cos(A)$, $\cos(L)$ is also $\dfrac{165}{325}$. To

match the result with an answer choice, either use a calculator to find the decimal equivalent or

reduce the fraction. Using a calculator, $\dfrac{165}{325} \approx 0.5077$ and $\dfrac{33}{65} \approx 0.5077$. To reduce the fraction,

notice that both numbers are multiples of 5, so divide the numerator and denominator by 5 to get

$\cos(L) = \dfrac{33}{65}$. Either way, the correct answer is (A).

Module 2—Harder

1. **A** The question asks for an equivalent form of an expression. Use Bite-Sized Pieces and the Process of Elimination to tackle this question. The only term with a single a is $6a$, so it cannot be combined with any other terms and must appear in the correct answer. Eliminate (B) and (C) because they do not include $6a$. Combine the two terms with a^3 to get $3a^3 - 5a^3 = -2a^3$. Eliminate (D) because it does not include $-2a^3$. The correct answer is (A).

2. **A** The question asks for a percent based on the information provided. Start by ballparking: 10% of 45,000,000 is 4,500,000, so 4,950,000 is a little more than 10%. Eliminate (C) and (D) because they are much too large. Choice (A) is likely correct, but to check, plug in 11%. *Percent* means out of 100, so 11% can be represented as $\dfrac{11}{100}$. Multiply this by the total number of shirts to get $\dfrac{11}{100}(45,000,000) = 4,950,000$. This matches the number of white shirts given in the question. The correct answer is (A).

3. **–120** The question asks for the value of an expression based on an equation. When an SAT question asks for the value of an expression, there is usually a straightforward way to solve for the expression without needing to completely isolate the variable. Start solving by distributing on both sides of the equation. The equation becomes $3x - 24 - 16 = 8x + 80 + x$. Simplify both sides of the equation to get $3x - 40 = 9x + 80$. Subtract $3x$ from both sides of the equation to get $-40 = 6x + 80$, and then subtract 80 from both sides of the equation to get $-120 = 6x$. The question asked for the value of $6x$, so stop here and enter -120.

Another method is to enter the equation as written into the built-in calculator, and then scroll and zoom as needed to see the value of x represented by a vertical line at $x = -20$. Read carefully: the question asks for the value of $6x$, which is $6(-20)$, or -120.

Using either of these methods, the correct answer is -120.

4. **B** The question asks for the value of an expression based on an equation. When an SAT question asks for the value of an expression, there is usually a straightforward way to solve for the expression without needing to completely isolate the variable. Start by subtracting $8(a - 3)$ from both sides of the equation to get $-17 = 9(a - 3) - 8(a - 3)$. Combine the terms with $(a - 3)$ to get $-17 = (9 - 8)$ $(a - 3)$, which becomes $-17 = 1(a - 3)$, or $-17 = a - 3$, making (B) correct.

Another method is to enter the equation into the built-in calculator, changing every a to x in order to see a graph, and then scroll and zoom as needed to see the value of a represented by a vertical line at $x = -14$. Read carefully: the question asks for the value of a $- 3$, which is $-14 - 3$, or -17, and (B) is correct.

Using either of these methods, the correct answer is (B).

5. **C** The question asks for the meaning of a constant in context. Start by reading the final question, which asks for the meaning of the constant b. Next, label the parts of the equation with the information given. The question states that the lab area is 30 square feet, the seating area is 80 square feet, and the total number of floor tiles is 4,200. Rewrite the equation with these labels: (lab area size)(a) + (seating area size)(b) = total tiles. Next, use Process of Elimination to get rid of answer choices that are not consistent with the labels. Since b is multiplied by the size of the seating area, eliminate (A) and (B) because they refer to the lab area, not the seating area. Compare the remaining answer choices. The difference is between the average number of tiles and the total number of tiles. Since b is multiplied by the number of square feet in the seating area, it must represent a value per square foot, not a total value. Keep (C) because it is consistent with this information, and eliminate (D) because it refers to a total number. The correct answer is (C).

6. **D** The question asks for the change in a value given a proportion. Use the Geometry Basic Approach. Start by drawing two triangles, one with a smaller base than the other. The question asks about the height, so draw a line for the height. This figure should look something like this:

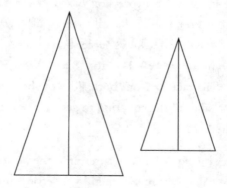

Next, label the figure with the information given. Since no specific numbers are given for the base and the height, plug in. Make the height of the larger triangle 100, so the base would be 65% of 100, which is 65. If the base decreased by 13 inches, the new base would be $65 - 13 = 52$ inches.

Label this information on the figure, which now looks like this:

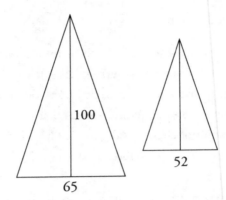

Since the base is smaller and the proportions stay the same, the height must also be smaller. Eliminate (A) and (B) because they would both make the height larger. To find the length of the new height, set up a proportion for $\frac{\text{base}}{\text{height}}$: $\frac{65}{100} = \frac{52}{x}$. Cross-multiply to get $(100)(52) = (65)(x)$. Simplify both sides of the equation to get $5,200 = 65x$. Divide both sides of the equation by 65 to get $80 = x$. Since the original height was 100, the change is $100 - 80 = 20$. The new height is less than the original height, so it decreased by 20. The correct answer is (D).

7. **B** The question asks for an equation in terms of a specific variable. Since the question is about the relationship between variables and the answers contain variables, plug in. The fraction on the left side of the equation could make the numbers awkward, so start on the right side of the equation and make $b = 2$. The equation becomes $\frac{a}{3} = 10 - 7(2)$, then $\frac{a}{3} = 10 - 14$, and finally $\frac{a}{3} = -4$. Multiply both sides of the equation by 3 to get $a = -12$. Now plug $a = -12$ and $b = 2$ into the answer choices and eliminate any that do not work. Choice (A) becomes $2 = \frac{-12 - 21}{30}$, and then $2 = -\frac{33}{30}$. This is not true, so eliminate (A). Choice (B) becomes $2 = \frac{30 - (-12)}{21}$, then $2 = \frac{42}{21}$, and finally $2 = 2$. This is true, so keep (B), but check the remaining answers just in case. Choice (C) becomes $2 = 10 + \frac{-12}{3}$, then $2 = 10 + (-4)$, and finally $2 = 6$; eliminate (C). Choice (D) becomes $2 = 10 + \frac{3}{-12}$, then $2 = 10 + \left(-\frac{1}{4}\right)$, and finally $2 = 9\frac{3}{4}$; eliminate (D). The correct answer is (B).

8. **B** The question asks for the value of a constant given two equivalent expressions. Start by rewriting the expressions with an equal sign between them to get $\frac{3}{y + c} = \frac{15}{5y + 30}$. Next, start to solve by cross-multiplying. The equation becomes $(y + c)(15) = (3)(5y + 30)$. Distribute on both sides of the

equation to get $15y + 15c = 15y + 90$. Subtract $15y$ from both sides of the equation to get $15c = 90$. Divide both sides of the equation by 15 to get $c = 6$. The correct answer is (B).

9. **25** The question asks for the value of a constant given information about circles in the coordinate plane. The equation of a circle in standard form is $(x - h)^2 + (y - k)^2 = r^2$, where (h, k) is the center and r is the radius. In the equation given for circle O, $r^2 = 64$. Take the positive square root of both sides of the equation to get $r = 8$. The question states that *the radius of circle P is three less than the radius of circle O*, so the radius of circle P is $8 - 3 = 5$. Plug $r = 5$ into the equation of circle P to get $(x - 7)^2 + (y + 7)^2 = 5^2$, or $(x - 7)^2 + (y + 7)^2 = 25$. Thus, $c = 25$. The correct answer is 25.

10. **C** The question asks for a maximum value given a specific situation. Since the question asks for a specific value and the answers contain numbers in increasing order, plug in the answers. Rewrite the answer choices on the scratch paper and label them "number of laptops." Next, pick a value to start with. Since the question asks for the maximum, start with the largest number, 146. The question states that *each laptop costs $149*, so multiply that by the number of laptops to get ($149)(146) = $21,754. The question also states that there is *a 7.5% discount on orders of at least 100 laptops*. Since 146 is more than 100, the discount applies. Take 7.5% of the cost and subtract the result from the cost to get $\$21,754 - \left(\dfrac{7.5}{100}\right)(\$21,754) = \$20,122.45$. This is greater than the donation of $20,000, so eliminate (D). The result was close, so plug in the next largest value, 145, for the number of laptops. The initial cost becomes ($149)(145) = $21,605. Apply the 7.5% discount to get $\$21,605 - \left(\dfrac{7.5}{100}\right)(\$21,605) \approx \$19,984.63$. This is less than the donation of $20,000, so the school can purchase 145 laptops. The correct answer is (C).

11. **A** The question asks for the value of the x-coordinate of the solution to a system of equations. The most efficient method is to enter both equations into the built-in calculator, and then scroll and zoom as needed to find the points of intersection. The graph shows two points of intersection: (3, 1) and (−4, 22), so the x-coordinate is either 3 or −4. Only −4 is in an answer choice, so choose (A).

To solve the system for the x-coordinate algebraically, substitute $-3x + 10$ for y in the first equation to get $3x^2 - (-3x + 10) - 26 = 0$. Distribute the negative sign to get $3x^2 + 3x - 10 - 26 = 0$, and then combine like terms to get $3x^2 + 3x - 36 = 0$. Factor out 3 to get $3(x^2 + x - 12) = 0$. Factor the quadratic to get $3(x + 4)(x - 3) = 0$. Set each factor equal to 0 and solve to get $x = -4$ and $x = 3$. Only −4 is in an answer choice, so choose (A).

Using either of these methods, the correct answer is (A).

12. **A** The question asks for the number of solutions to an equation. Distribute on both sides of the equation to get $-24x - 12 = 12 - 24x$. Add $24x$ to both sides of the equation to get $-12 = 12$. This is not true, so the equation has no solutions, and (A) is correct.

It is also possible to answer this question using the built-in calculator. Enter each side of the equation into a separate entry field, and then scroll and zoom as needed to see that the lines are parallel. This means there are no solutions, and (A) is correct.

Using either of these methods, the correct answer is (A).

13. **D** The question asks for an x-intercept of a parabola. Sketch a graph using the given points, and label those points. The vertex of a parabola is on the axis of symmetry, so the axis of symmetry of this parabola is the line $x = 5$; add this line to the graph. The graph should look something like this:

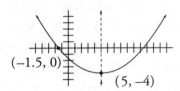

The two x-intercepts are an equal distance from the line of symmetry. The x-coordinate of the given x-intercept is -1.5, so the distance from the line of symmetry is $5 - (-1.5) = 6.5$. The x-coordinate of the other x-intercept is thus $5 + 6.5 = 11.5$. The correct answer is (D).

14. **C** The question asks for an equation that represents a graph. One approach is to enter the equation from each answer choice into the built-in calculator. Since the graph shown in the question has been translated, or shifted, down 10 units from the graph of $g(x)$, the correct answer should result in a graph that is 10 units up from the graph shown in the question. The graph of the equation in (C) does this, so (C) is correct.

Another approach is to compare features of the graph to the answer choices. The answer choices all take the form $y = mx + b$, in which m is the slope and b is the y-intercept. All of the answer choices have the same slope, so focus on the y-intercept. The graph shown in the question has been translated from the graph of function g. Adding or subtracting outside the parentheses shifts the graph up or down. Thus, the given graph of $g(x) - 10$ is shifted 10 units down from the graph of $g(x)$. Undo this by adding 10 to transform the given graph back to $g(x)$. The graph of $g(x) - 10$ has its y-intercept at $(0, -5)$. Move the point up 10 units to get a y-intercept of $(0, 5)$. Eliminate (A), (B), and (D) because the equations have the wrong y-intercept, leaving (C) as correct.

Using either of these methods, the correct answer is (C).

15. **D** The question asks for the value of a constant in a quadratic equation. One method is to use the built-in calculator, although it will take some experimentation. Start by entering the equation into an entry field. The slider for c does not appear, so add $5x$ to both sides of the equation to get $10x^2 + 5x + c = 0$. It might be necessary to delete "= 0" to show the slider and then add it back to see the graph. Click on the slider for c, and then either move the slider left and right or enter each answer choice into the "$c =$" equation one at a time. The parabola does not intersect the x-axis when $c = 1$, meaning there are no real solutions and (D) is correct.

To determine algebraically when a quadratic equation has no real solutions, use the discriminant. The discriminant is the part of the quadratic formula under the square root sign and is written as $D = b^2 - 4ac$. When the discriminant is positive, the quadratic has exactly two real solutions; when the discriminant is 0, the quadratic has exactly one real solution; and when the discriminant is negative, the quadratic has no real solutions. Thus, the discriminant of this quadratic must equal a negative number. First, put the quadratic in standard form, which is $ax^2 + bx + c = 0$, by adding $5x$ to both sides of the equation to get $10x^2 + 5x + c = 0$. Now $a = 10$, $b = 5$, and $c = c$. Plug these into the discriminant formula to get $D = (5)^2 - 4(10)(c)$, or $D = 25 - 40c$. Next, plug in the values from the answer choices to see which value of c makes the discriminant negative. Start with a middle answer and try (C), 0. If $c = 0$, the discriminant becomes $D = 25 - 40(0)$, or $D = 25$. This is not negative, so eliminate (C). It might not be clear whether a larger or smaller number is needed, so pick a direction and try (D), 1. If $c = 1$, the discriminant becomes $D = (5)^2 - (4)(10)(1)$, or $D = 25 - 40$, and then $D = -15$. This is negative, so stop here and pick (D).

Using either of these methods, the correct answer is (D).

16. **A** The question asks for the value of an expression given the equation of a graph in the xy-plane. One method is to use the built-in calculator. Enter the equation of the line, and then scroll and zoom as needed to find the intercepts. The x-intercept is at $(5.667, 0)$, and the y-intercept is at $(0, -4.25)$. Thus, $c = 5.667$, $k = -4.25$, and $\dfrac{c}{k} = \dfrac{5.667}{-4.25} = -1.33$. This is the same value as $-\dfrac{4}{3}$, which makes (A) correct.

To solve algebraically, plug the given points into the equation of the line. Plug in $x = c$ and $y = 0$ to get $3c - 4(0) = 17$, or $3c = 17$. Divide both sides of the equation by 3 to get $c = \dfrac{17}{3}$. Next, plug in $x = 0$ and $y = k$ to get $3(0) - 4k = 17$, or $-4k = 17$. Divide both sides of the equation by -4 to get $k = -\dfrac{17}{4}$. Finally divide c by k to get $\dfrac{c}{k} = \dfrac{\frac{17}{3}}{-\frac{17}{4}}$. When dividing fractions, multiply the reciprocal of the fraction in the denominator by the fraction in the numerator. This becomes

$\frac{c}{k} = \left(\frac{17}{3}\right)\left(-\frac{4}{17}\right)$, and then $\frac{c}{k} = -\frac{4}{3}$, and (A) is correct.

Using either of these methods, the correct answer is (A).

17. **12** The question asks for the value of a constant in a system of equations. When a system of linear equations has infinitely many solutions, the two equations form the same line and are equivalent to each other. Since c is a coefficient of g, look for a way to cancel the f terms and the constants when stacking and adding the equations. First, put the two equations in the same order by subtracting $21g$ from both sides of the second equation to get $21 = 6f - 36g$, and then subtracting $6f$ from both sides of the second equation to get $21 - 6f = -36g$. The f term and constant of the second equation are both 3 times the equivalent terms in the first equation with opposite signs, so multiply the first equation by 3 to get $-21 + 6f = 3cg$. Now stack and add the equations.

$$-21 + 6f = 3cg$$
$$\underline{+\ 21 - 6f = -36g}$$
$$0 + 0\ = 3cg - 36g$$

Add $36g$ to both sides of the resulting equation to get $36g = 3cg$. Divide both sides of the equation by $3g$ to get $12 = c$. The correct answer is 12.

18. **C** The question asks for the perimeter of a triangle. Use the Geometry Basic Approach. Start by drawing a triangle on the scratch paper with a right angle and one of the remaining angles twice the size of the other. Next, label the figure with the information given, and label the shortest side as 15. The drawing should look something like this:

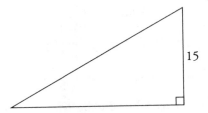

A 30:60:90 triangle is one of the special right triangles that has a specific proportional relationship among the sides. The proportion can be found by clicking open the reference sheet, and it is $x : x\sqrt{3} : 2x$. Since the smallest side is 15, $x = 15$. The other sides are $15\sqrt{3}$ and $2(15) = 30$. Label the figure with this information; the figure now looks like this:

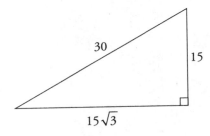

The perimeter of a geometric shape is the sum of the lengths of all of the sides. Add all three side lengths to get $15 + 15\sqrt{3} + 30 = 45 + 15\sqrt{3}$. The correct answer is (C).

19. **B**   The question asks for the value of an expression based on information about a function. In function notation, the number inside the parentheses is the x-value that goes into the function, or the input, and the value that comes out of the function is the y-value, or the output. The table gives four pairs of input and output values for the function. To solve for the constants c and d, start by plugging in one of the pairs from the table. Plug $x = 2$ and $g(x) = 46$ into the function to get $46 = 2c + d$. There is no way to solve for $c + d$ using only this equation, so plug in a second pair of values. Plug $x = 4$ and $g(x) = 0$ into the function to get $0 = 4c + d$. There are now two equations with two constants, so find a way to make one of the constants disappear when stacking and adding the equations. Multiply the second equation by -1 to get $0 = -4c - d$. The d-terms are now the same with opposite signs, so stack and add the two equations.

$$\begin{array}{r} 46 = 2c + d \\ +\ \ 0 = -4c - d \\ \hline 46 = -2c \end{array}$$

Divide both sides of the resulting equation by -2 to get $c = -23$. Plug $c = -23$ into the first equation to get $46 = 2(-23) + d$, or $46 = -46 + d$. Add 46 to both sides of the equation to get $92 = d$. Add the values of the two constants to get $c + d = -23 + 92 = 69$, so (B) is correct.

Another method is to recognize that the equation is in slope-intercept form, $y = mx + b$, in which m is the slope and b is the y-intercept. In this case, the constant c is the slope and the constant d is the y-intercept. Find the slope by putting two points from the table, such as $(2, 46)$ and $(4, 0)$, into the formula $slope = \dfrac{y_2 - y_1}{x_2 - x_1}$. The formula becomes $slope = \dfrac{46 - 0}{2 - 4}$, then $slope = \dfrac{46}{-2}$, and finally $slope = -23$. Thus, $c = -23$. To find the y-intercept, note that the values of $g(x)$ in the table decrease by 46 each time the x-value increases by 2. The reverse will also be true: when x decreases by 2 to be 0, $g(x)$ will increase by 46 to be 92. This means that the y-intercept is $(0, 92)$, and $d = 92$. If $c = -23$ and $d = 92$, the value of $c + d$ is $-23 + 92$, or $c + d = 69$, making (B) correct.

Using either of these methods, the correct answer is (B).

20. **105**   The question asks for a value given information about the mean, or average, of a data set. One method is to use the built-in calculator. Type "*mean(114,109,106,111)*" to see the mean of the original data set in the lower right corner. The mean is 110, so the mean of the new data set must be an integer less than 110. Add a fifth integer to the list of numbers in parentheses until the conditions of the question are met. The question asks for the smallest integer and states that the integers are greater than 101, so start with 102. Add 102 to the list of number in parentheses, and the mean becomes 108.4. This is not an integer, so keep going. When the new integer is 103, the mean is 108.6. When the new integer is 104, the mean is 108.8. When the new integer is 105, the mean is 109. Thus, 105 is the smallest integer that results in a mean that is an *integer that is less than the mean of the four integers*. Be careful to enter the new integer, 105, not the new mean, 109. The correct answer is 105.

Another method is to use the formula $T = AN$, in which T is the *Total*, A is the *Average*, and N is the *Number of things*. Start by finding the mean of the four integers given in the question. There are 4 values, so $N = 4$. Find the *Total* by adding the four integers to get $T = 114 + 109 + 106 + 111 = 440$. The average formula becomes $440 = (A)(4)$. Divide both sides of the equation by 4 to get $A = 110$. The question asks for the smallest integer that results in the full data set having an average less than that of the four integers shown, which is 110. Start with the next smallest integer, 109, for the average, and solve for the fifth integer in the data set. The average formula becomes $T = (109)(5)$, so $T = 545$. The total of the first four integers was 440, so the fifth integer is $545 - 440 = 105$. The question also states that *the mean of the entire data set is an integer* and that all of the integers are *greater than 101*, and 105 meets both of these conditions. To see whether a smaller integer meets all of the conditions given in the question, try an average of 108. The *Total* is now $T = (108)(5) = 540$, and the fifth integer is $540 - 440 = 100$. This is not greater than 101, so 100 is too small. Thus, 105 is the smallest integer that meets the conditions, and it is correct.

Using either of these methods, the correct answer is 105.

21. **B**   The question asks for the function that represents a certain situation. There are variables in the answer choices, and the question asks about the relationship between the number of points and the number of assignments, so plug in. Make $a = 51$ to include the 5-point assignments and at least one 3-point assignment. The first 50 completed assignments earn 5 points each, for a total of $(50)(5) = 250$ points. The additional completed assignment earns 3 points. The total number of points earned for the 51 completed assignments is $250 + 3 = 253$. This is the target value; write it down and circle it. Now plug $a = 51$ into the answer choices and eliminate any that do not match the target value. Choice (A) becomes $g(51) = 3(51) + 5$, then $g(51) = 153 + 5$, and finally $g(51) = 158$. This does not match the target value, so eliminate (A). Choice (B) becomes $g(51) = 3(51) + 100$, then $g(51) = 153 + 100$, and finally $g(51) = 253$. This matches the target, so keep (B), but check the remaining answers just in case. Choice (C) becomes $g(51) = 3(51) + 250$, then $g(51) = 153 + 250$, and finally $g(51) = 403$; eliminate (C). Choice (D) becomes $g(51) = 8(51) - 150$, then $408 - 150$, and finally $g(51) = 258$; eliminate (D). The correct answer is (B).

22.   **D**   The question asks for information that will provide proof of similar triangles. Use the Geometry Basic Approach. Triangles are similar when they have the same angle measures and proportional side lengths, so draw two triangles on the scratch paper that look similar but are different sizes. Then label the figures with information from the question: label *AB* as 22, *XY* as 11, and angles *A* and *X* as 77°. The drawing should look something like this.

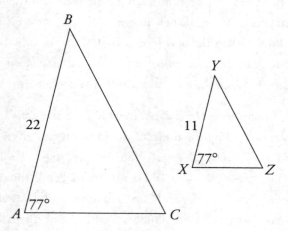

Next, evaluate the Roman numeral statements. They all give information about angles, so focus on the rule that similar triangles have the same three angle measures. The question only provides enough information to know that one angle measure is the same in both triangles, so more information is necessary; eliminate (A). Angle measures alone do provide enough information if all three angles have the same measure, so eliminate (B).

Check the remaining answers one at a time to see whether one shows that all three angles have the same measure. Try (C), and label angle *B* as 40° and angle *Y* as 50°. Find the measure of the third angle in each triangle. All triangles contain 180°, so set up equations: 77° + 40° + *C*° = 180°, and 77° + 50° + *Z*° = 180°. Simplify the first equation to get 117° + *C*° = 180°, and then subtract 117° from both sides of the equation to get *C* = 63°. Simplify the second equation to get 127° + *Z*° = 180°, and then subtract 127° from both sides of the equation to get *Z* = 53°.

Label the figures with this information, and they now look like this:

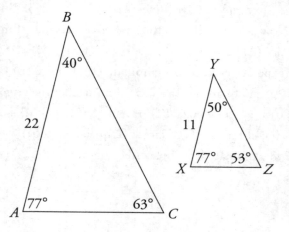

The triangles do not have the same three angle measures, so they are not similar; eliminate (C). Try (D) and follow the same steps. Label angle B as 40° and angle Z as 63°. Angle C is again 63°. Solve for angle Y: 77° + Y° + 63° = 180°, 140° + Y° = 180°, and Y° = 40°. Label the triangles with this information to see that the triangles now have the same three angle measures. The correct answer is (D).

6 Practice Tests for the Digital SAT
Practice Test 1

The Princeton Review®

© 2024 by TPR Education IP Holdings, LLC.

YOUR NAME: _____
(Print)   Last   First   M.I.

SIGNATURE: _____ DATE: ___/___/___

HOME ADDRESS: _____
(Print)   Number and Street

_____
City   State   Zip Code

PHONE NO.: _____
(Print)

DATE OF BIRTH: ___/___/___
(Print)   Month / Day / Year

For both the Reading and Writing and the Math, be sure to only fill in the bubbles for the version of Module 2 that you took. If you took the Easier Module 2, only fill in the answers in the Easier column. If you took the Harder Module 2, only fill in the answers in the Harder column.

Section 1: Module 1
Reading and Writing

1. Ⓐ Ⓑ Ⓒ Ⓓ
2. Ⓐ Ⓑ Ⓒ Ⓓ
3. Ⓐ Ⓑ Ⓒ Ⓓ
4. Ⓐ Ⓑ Ⓒ Ⓓ
5. Ⓐ Ⓑ Ⓒ Ⓓ
6. Ⓐ Ⓑ Ⓒ Ⓓ
7. Ⓐ Ⓑ Ⓒ Ⓓ
8. Ⓐ Ⓑ Ⓒ Ⓓ
9. Ⓐ Ⓑ Ⓒ Ⓓ
10. Ⓐ Ⓑ Ⓒ Ⓓ
11. Ⓐ Ⓑ Ⓒ Ⓓ
12. Ⓐ Ⓑ Ⓒ Ⓓ
13. Ⓐ Ⓑ Ⓒ Ⓓ
14. Ⓐ Ⓑ Ⓒ Ⓓ
15. Ⓐ Ⓑ Ⓒ Ⓓ
16. Ⓐ Ⓑ Ⓒ Ⓓ
17. Ⓐ Ⓑ Ⓒ Ⓓ
18. Ⓐ Ⓑ Ⓒ Ⓓ
19. Ⓐ Ⓑ Ⓒ Ⓓ
20. Ⓐ Ⓑ Ⓒ Ⓓ
21. Ⓐ Ⓑ Ⓒ Ⓓ
22. Ⓐ Ⓑ Ⓒ Ⓓ
23. Ⓐ Ⓑ Ⓒ Ⓓ
24. Ⓐ Ⓑ Ⓒ Ⓓ
25. Ⓐ Ⓑ Ⓒ Ⓓ
26. Ⓐ Ⓑ Ⓒ Ⓓ
27. Ⓐ Ⓑ Ⓒ Ⓓ

Section 1: Module 2 (Easier)
Reading and Writing

1. Ⓐ Ⓑ Ⓒ Ⓓ
2. Ⓐ Ⓑ Ⓒ Ⓓ
3. Ⓐ Ⓑ Ⓒ Ⓓ
4. Ⓐ Ⓑ Ⓒ Ⓓ
5. Ⓐ Ⓑ Ⓒ Ⓓ
6. Ⓐ Ⓑ Ⓒ Ⓓ
7. Ⓐ Ⓑ Ⓒ Ⓓ
8. Ⓐ Ⓑ Ⓒ Ⓓ
9. Ⓐ Ⓑ Ⓒ Ⓓ
10. Ⓐ Ⓑ Ⓒ Ⓓ
11. Ⓐ Ⓑ Ⓒ Ⓓ
12. Ⓐ Ⓑ Ⓒ Ⓓ
13. Ⓐ Ⓑ Ⓒ Ⓓ
14. Ⓐ Ⓑ Ⓒ Ⓓ
15. Ⓐ Ⓑ Ⓒ Ⓓ
16. Ⓐ Ⓑ Ⓒ Ⓓ
17. Ⓐ Ⓑ Ⓒ Ⓓ
18. Ⓐ Ⓑ Ⓒ Ⓓ
19. Ⓐ Ⓑ Ⓒ Ⓓ
20. Ⓐ Ⓑ Ⓒ Ⓓ
21. Ⓐ Ⓑ Ⓒ Ⓓ
22. Ⓐ Ⓑ Ⓒ Ⓓ
23. Ⓐ Ⓑ Ⓒ Ⓓ
24. Ⓐ Ⓑ Ⓒ Ⓓ
25. Ⓐ Ⓑ Ⓒ Ⓓ
26. Ⓐ Ⓑ Ⓒ Ⓓ
27. Ⓐ Ⓑ Ⓒ Ⓓ

Section 1: Module 2 (Harder)
Reading and Writing

1. Ⓐ Ⓑ Ⓒ Ⓓ
2. Ⓐ Ⓑ Ⓒ Ⓓ
3. Ⓐ Ⓑ Ⓒ Ⓓ
4. Ⓐ Ⓑ Ⓒ Ⓓ
5. Ⓐ Ⓑ Ⓒ Ⓓ
6. Ⓐ Ⓑ Ⓒ Ⓓ
7. Ⓐ Ⓑ Ⓒ Ⓓ
8. Ⓐ Ⓑ Ⓒ Ⓓ
9. Ⓐ Ⓑ Ⓒ Ⓓ
10. Ⓐ Ⓑ Ⓒ Ⓓ
11. Ⓐ Ⓑ Ⓒ Ⓓ
12. Ⓐ Ⓑ Ⓒ Ⓓ
13. Ⓐ Ⓑ Ⓒ Ⓓ
14. Ⓐ Ⓑ Ⓒ Ⓓ
15. Ⓐ Ⓑ Ⓒ Ⓓ
16. Ⓐ Ⓑ Ⓒ Ⓓ
17. Ⓐ Ⓑ Ⓒ Ⓓ
18. Ⓐ Ⓑ Ⓒ Ⓓ
19. Ⓐ Ⓑ Ⓒ Ⓓ
20. Ⓐ Ⓑ Ⓒ Ⓓ
21. Ⓐ Ⓑ Ⓒ Ⓓ
22. Ⓐ Ⓑ Ⓒ Ⓓ
23. Ⓐ Ⓑ Ⓒ Ⓓ
24. Ⓐ Ⓑ Ⓒ Ⓓ
25. Ⓐ Ⓑ Ⓒ Ⓓ
26. Ⓐ Ⓑ Ⓒ Ⓓ
27. Ⓐ Ⓑ Ⓒ Ⓓ

6 Practice Tests for the Digital SAT
Practice Test 1

The **Princeton Review**®

© 2024 by TPR Education IP Holdings, LLC.

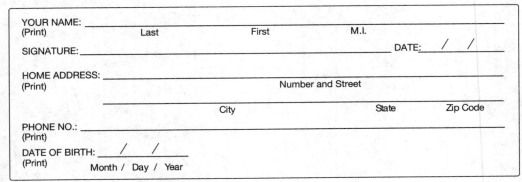

YOUR NAME: _____
(Print)   Last   First   M.I.

SIGNATURE: _____ DATE: __/__/__

HOME ADDRESS: _____
(Print)   Number and Street

_____
City   State   Zip Code

PHONE NO.: _____
(Print)

DATE OF BIRTH: __/__/__
(Print)   Month / Day / Year

For both the Reading and Writing and the Math, be sure to only fill in the bubbles for the version of Module 2 that you took. If you took the Easier Module 2, only fill in the answers in the Easier column. If you took the Harder Module 2, only fill in the answers in the Harder column.

Section 2: Module 1
Math

1. Ⓐ Ⓑ Ⓒ Ⓓ
2. _____
3. Ⓐ Ⓑ Ⓒ Ⓓ
4. Ⓐ Ⓑ Ⓒ Ⓓ
5. _____
6. Ⓐ Ⓑ Ⓒ Ⓓ
7. Ⓐ Ⓑ Ⓒ Ⓓ
8. Ⓐ Ⓑ Ⓒ Ⓓ
9. Ⓐ Ⓑ Ⓒ Ⓓ
10. _____
11. Ⓐ Ⓑ Ⓒ Ⓓ
12. Ⓐ Ⓑ Ⓒ Ⓓ
13. _____
14. Ⓐ Ⓑ Ⓒ Ⓓ
15. _____
16. _____
17. Ⓐ Ⓑ Ⓒ Ⓓ
18. Ⓐ Ⓑ Ⓒ Ⓓ
19. Ⓐ Ⓑ Ⓒ Ⓓ
20. Ⓐ Ⓑ Ⓒ Ⓓ
21. Ⓐ Ⓑ Ⓒ Ⓓ
22. Ⓐ Ⓑ Ⓒ Ⓓ

Section 2: Module 2 (Easier)
Math

1. Ⓐ Ⓑ Ⓒ Ⓓ
2. Ⓐ Ⓑ Ⓒ Ⓓ
3. Ⓐ Ⓑ Ⓒ Ⓓ
4. _____
5. Ⓐ Ⓑ Ⓒ Ⓓ
6. Ⓐ Ⓑ Ⓒ Ⓓ
7. _____
8. _____
9. Ⓐ Ⓑ Ⓒ Ⓓ
10. _____
11. Ⓐ Ⓑ Ⓒ Ⓓ
12. Ⓐ Ⓑ Ⓒ Ⓓ
13. Ⓐ Ⓑ Ⓒ Ⓓ
14. Ⓐ Ⓑ Ⓒ Ⓓ
15. Ⓐ Ⓑ Ⓒ Ⓓ
16. Ⓐ Ⓑ Ⓒ Ⓓ
17. Ⓐ Ⓑ Ⓒ Ⓓ
18. _____
19. Ⓐ Ⓑ Ⓒ Ⓓ
20. Ⓐ Ⓑ Ⓒ Ⓓ
21. Ⓐ Ⓑ Ⓒ Ⓓ
22. Ⓐ Ⓑ Ⓒ Ⓓ

Section 2: Module 2 (Harder)
Math

1. Ⓐ Ⓑ Ⓒ Ⓓ
2. Ⓐ Ⓑ Ⓒ Ⓓ
3. Ⓐ Ⓑ Ⓒ Ⓓ
4. Ⓐ Ⓑ Ⓒ Ⓓ
5. Ⓐ Ⓑ Ⓒ Ⓓ
6. Ⓐ Ⓑ Ⓒ Ⓓ
7. _____
8. _____
9. Ⓐ Ⓑ Ⓒ Ⓓ
10. Ⓐ Ⓑ Ⓒ Ⓓ
11. _____
12. Ⓐ Ⓑ Ⓒ Ⓓ
13. _____
14. Ⓐ Ⓑ Ⓒ Ⓓ
15. Ⓐ Ⓑ Ⓒ Ⓓ
16. Ⓐ Ⓑ Ⓒ Ⓓ
17. Ⓐ Ⓑ Ⓒ Ⓓ
18. _____
19. _____
20. Ⓐ Ⓑ Ⓒ Ⓓ
21. Ⓐ Ⓑ Ⓒ Ⓓ
22. Ⓐ Ⓑ Ⓒ Ⓓ

6 Practice Tests for the Digital SAT
Practice Test 2

© 2024 by TPR Education IP Holdings, LLC.

YOUR NAME: _____
(Print)　　　　Last　　　　First　　　　M.I.

SIGNATURE: _____　　DATE: ___ / ___ / ___

HOME ADDRESS: _____
(Print)　　　　　　　　Number and Street

_____
City　　　　　　State　　　Zip Code

PHONE NO.: _____
(Print)

DATE OF BIRTH: ___ / ___ / ___
(Print)　　Month / Day / Year

For both the Reading and Writing and the Math, be sure to only fill in the bubbles for the version of Module 2 that you took. If you took the Easier Module 2, only fill in the answers in the Easier column. If you took the Harder Module 2, only fill in the answers in the Harder column.

Section 1: Module 1
Reading and Writing

1. Ⓐ Ⓑ Ⓒ Ⓓ
2. Ⓐ Ⓑ Ⓒ Ⓓ
3. Ⓐ Ⓑ Ⓒ Ⓓ
4. Ⓐ Ⓑ Ⓒ Ⓓ
5. Ⓐ Ⓑ Ⓒ Ⓓ
6. Ⓐ Ⓑ Ⓒ Ⓓ
7. Ⓐ Ⓑ Ⓒ Ⓓ
8. Ⓐ Ⓑ Ⓒ Ⓓ
9. Ⓐ Ⓑ Ⓒ Ⓓ
10. Ⓐ Ⓑ Ⓒ Ⓓ
11. Ⓐ Ⓑ Ⓒ Ⓓ
12. Ⓐ Ⓑ Ⓒ Ⓓ
13. Ⓐ Ⓑ Ⓒ Ⓓ
14. Ⓐ Ⓑ Ⓒ Ⓓ
15. Ⓐ Ⓑ Ⓒ Ⓓ
16. Ⓐ Ⓑ Ⓒ Ⓓ
17. Ⓐ Ⓑ Ⓒ Ⓓ
18. Ⓐ Ⓑ Ⓒ Ⓓ
19. Ⓐ Ⓑ Ⓒ Ⓓ
20. Ⓐ Ⓑ Ⓒ Ⓓ
21. Ⓐ Ⓑ Ⓒ Ⓓ
22. Ⓐ Ⓑ Ⓒ Ⓓ
23. Ⓐ Ⓑ Ⓒ Ⓓ
24. Ⓐ Ⓑ Ⓒ Ⓓ
25. Ⓐ Ⓑ Ⓒ Ⓓ
26. Ⓐ Ⓑ Ⓒ Ⓓ
27. Ⓐ Ⓑ Ⓒ Ⓓ

Section 1: Module 2 (Easier)
Reading and Writing

1. Ⓐ Ⓑ Ⓒ Ⓓ
2. Ⓐ Ⓑ Ⓒ Ⓓ
3. Ⓐ Ⓑ Ⓒ Ⓓ
4. Ⓐ Ⓑ Ⓒ Ⓓ
5. Ⓐ Ⓑ Ⓒ Ⓓ
6. Ⓐ Ⓑ Ⓒ Ⓓ
7. Ⓐ Ⓑ Ⓒ Ⓓ
8. Ⓐ Ⓑ Ⓒ Ⓓ
9. Ⓐ Ⓑ Ⓒ Ⓓ
10. Ⓐ Ⓑ Ⓒ Ⓓ
11. Ⓐ Ⓑ Ⓒ Ⓓ
12. Ⓐ Ⓑ Ⓒ Ⓓ
13. Ⓐ Ⓑ Ⓒ Ⓓ
14. Ⓐ Ⓑ Ⓒ Ⓓ
15. Ⓐ Ⓑ Ⓒ Ⓓ
16. Ⓐ Ⓑ Ⓒ Ⓓ
17. Ⓐ Ⓑ Ⓒ Ⓓ
18. Ⓐ Ⓑ Ⓒ Ⓓ
19. Ⓐ Ⓑ Ⓒ Ⓓ
20. Ⓐ Ⓑ Ⓒ Ⓓ
21. Ⓐ Ⓑ Ⓒ Ⓓ
22. Ⓐ Ⓑ Ⓒ Ⓓ
23. Ⓐ Ⓑ Ⓒ Ⓓ
24. Ⓐ Ⓑ Ⓒ Ⓓ
25. Ⓐ Ⓑ Ⓒ Ⓓ
26. Ⓐ Ⓑ Ⓒ Ⓓ
27. Ⓐ Ⓑ Ⓒ Ⓓ

Section 1: Module 2 (Harder)
Reading and Writing

1. Ⓐ Ⓑ Ⓒ Ⓓ
2. Ⓐ Ⓑ Ⓒ Ⓓ
3. Ⓐ Ⓑ Ⓒ Ⓓ
4. Ⓐ Ⓑ Ⓒ Ⓓ
5. Ⓐ Ⓑ Ⓒ Ⓓ
6. Ⓐ Ⓑ Ⓒ Ⓓ
7. Ⓐ Ⓑ Ⓒ Ⓓ
8. Ⓐ Ⓑ Ⓒ Ⓓ
9. Ⓐ Ⓑ Ⓒ Ⓓ
10. Ⓐ Ⓑ Ⓒ Ⓓ
11. Ⓐ Ⓑ Ⓒ Ⓓ
12. Ⓐ Ⓑ Ⓒ Ⓓ
13. Ⓐ Ⓑ Ⓒ Ⓓ
14. Ⓐ Ⓑ Ⓒ Ⓓ
15. Ⓐ Ⓑ Ⓒ Ⓓ
16. Ⓐ Ⓑ Ⓒ Ⓓ
17. Ⓐ Ⓑ Ⓒ Ⓓ
18. Ⓐ Ⓑ Ⓒ Ⓓ
19. Ⓐ Ⓑ Ⓒ Ⓓ
20. Ⓐ Ⓑ Ⓒ Ⓓ
21. Ⓐ Ⓑ Ⓒ Ⓓ
22. Ⓐ Ⓑ Ⓒ Ⓓ
23. Ⓐ Ⓑ Ⓒ Ⓓ
24. Ⓐ Ⓑ Ⓒ Ⓓ
25. Ⓐ Ⓑ Ⓒ Ⓓ
26. Ⓐ Ⓑ Ⓒ Ⓓ
27. Ⓐ Ⓑ Ⓒ Ⓓ

6 Practice Tests for the Digital SAT
Practice Test 2

YOUR NAME: _____
(Print)　　　　Last　　　　　First　　　　　M.I.

SIGNATURE: _____　DATE: ___/___/___

HOME ADDRESS: _____
(Print)　　　　　　　　　Number and Street

_____
City　　　　　　　　State　　　Zip Code

PHONE NO.: _____
(Print)

DATE OF BIRTH: ___/___/___
(Print)　　Month / Day / Year

For both the Reading and Writing and the Math, be sure to only fill in the bubbles for the version of Module 2 that you took. If you took the Easier Module 2, only fill in the answers in the Easier column. If you took the Harder Module 2, only fill in the answers in the Harder column.

Section 2: Module 1 Math

1. Ⓐ Ⓑ Ⓒ Ⓓ
2. Ⓐ Ⓑ Ⓒ Ⓓ
3. Ⓐ Ⓑ Ⓒ Ⓓ
4. _____
5. Ⓐ Ⓑ Ⓒ Ⓓ
6. Ⓐ Ⓑ Ⓒ Ⓓ
7. Ⓐ Ⓑ Ⓒ Ⓓ
8. Ⓐ Ⓑ Ⓒ Ⓓ
9. Ⓐ Ⓑ Ⓒ Ⓓ
10. Ⓐ Ⓑ Ⓒ Ⓓ
11. _____
12. Ⓐ Ⓑ Ⓒ Ⓓ
13. Ⓐ Ⓑ Ⓒ Ⓓ
14. _____
15. _____
16. Ⓐ Ⓑ Ⓒ Ⓓ
17. _____
18. Ⓐ Ⓑ Ⓒ Ⓓ
19. Ⓐ Ⓑ Ⓒ Ⓓ
20. Ⓐ Ⓑ Ⓒ Ⓓ
21. _____
22. Ⓐ Ⓑ Ⓒ Ⓓ

Section 2: Module 2 (Easier) Math

1. Ⓐ Ⓑ Ⓒ Ⓓ
2. Ⓐ Ⓑ Ⓒ Ⓓ
3. _____
4. _____
5. _____
6. Ⓐ Ⓑ Ⓒ Ⓓ
7. Ⓐ Ⓑ Ⓒ Ⓓ
8. Ⓐ Ⓑ Ⓒ Ⓓ
9. Ⓐ Ⓑ Ⓒ Ⓓ
10. Ⓐ Ⓑ Ⓒ Ⓓ
11. _____
12. Ⓐ Ⓑ Ⓒ Ⓓ
13. Ⓐ Ⓑ Ⓒ Ⓓ
14. Ⓐ Ⓑ Ⓒ Ⓓ
15. Ⓐ Ⓑ Ⓒ Ⓓ
16. Ⓐ Ⓑ Ⓒ Ⓓ
17. _____
18. _____
19. Ⓐ Ⓑ Ⓒ Ⓓ
20. Ⓐ Ⓑ Ⓒ Ⓓ
21. Ⓐ Ⓑ Ⓒ Ⓓ
22. Ⓐ Ⓑ Ⓒ Ⓓ

Section 2: Module 2 (Harder) Math

1. Ⓐ Ⓑ Ⓒ Ⓓ
2. Ⓐ Ⓑ Ⓒ Ⓓ
3. Ⓐ Ⓑ Ⓒ Ⓓ
4. Ⓐ Ⓑ Ⓒ Ⓓ
5. Ⓐ Ⓑ Ⓒ Ⓓ
6. Ⓐ Ⓑ Ⓒ Ⓓ
7. Ⓐ Ⓑ Ⓒ Ⓓ
8. Ⓐ Ⓑ Ⓒ Ⓓ
9. _____
10. _____
11. Ⓐ Ⓑ Ⓒ Ⓓ
12. Ⓐ Ⓑ Ⓒ Ⓓ
13. Ⓐ Ⓑ Ⓒ Ⓓ
14. Ⓐ Ⓑ Ⓒ Ⓓ
15. _____
16. _____
17. Ⓐ Ⓑ Ⓒ Ⓓ
18. Ⓐ Ⓑ Ⓒ Ⓓ
19. Ⓐ Ⓑ Ⓒ Ⓓ
20. _____
21. Ⓐ Ⓑ Ⓒ Ⓓ
22. Ⓐ Ⓑ Ⓒ Ⓓ

6 Practice Tests for the Digital SAT
Practice Test 3

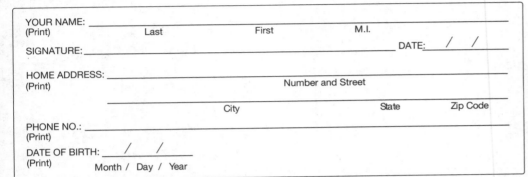

YOUR NAME: _____
(Print)   Last   First   M.I.

SIGNATURE: _____ DATE: __/__/__

HOME ADDRESS: _____
(Print)   Number and Street

_____
          City   State   Zip Code

PHONE NO.: _____
(Print)

DATE OF BIRTH: __/__/__
(Print)   Month / Day / Year

For both the Reading and Writing and the Math, be sure to only fill in the bubbles for the version of Module 2 that you took. If you took the Easier Module 2, only fill in the answers in the Easier column. If you took the Harder Module 2, only fill in the answers in the Harder column.

Section 1: Module 1
Reading and Writing

1. Ⓐ Ⓑ Ⓒ Ⓓ
2. Ⓐ Ⓑ Ⓒ Ⓓ
3. Ⓐ Ⓑ Ⓒ Ⓓ
4. Ⓐ Ⓑ Ⓒ Ⓓ
5. Ⓐ Ⓑ Ⓒ Ⓓ
6. Ⓐ Ⓑ Ⓒ Ⓓ
7. Ⓐ Ⓑ Ⓒ Ⓓ
8. Ⓐ Ⓑ Ⓒ Ⓓ
9. Ⓐ Ⓑ Ⓒ Ⓓ
10. Ⓐ Ⓑ Ⓒ Ⓓ
11. Ⓐ Ⓑ Ⓒ Ⓓ
12. Ⓐ Ⓑ Ⓒ Ⓓ
13. Ⓐ Ⓑ Ⓒ Ⓓ
14. Ⓐ Ⓑ Ⓒ Ⓓ
15. Ⓐ Ⓑ Ⓒ Ⓓ
16. Ⓐ Ⓑ Ⓒ Ⓓ
17. Ⓐ Ⓑ Ⓒ Ⓓ
18. Ⓐ Ⓑ Ⓒ Ⓓ
19. Ⓐ Ⓑ Ⓒ Ⓓ
20. Ⓐ Ⓑ Ⓒ Ⓓ
21. Ⓐ Ⓑ Ⓒ Ⓓ
22. Ⓐ Ⓑ Ⓒ Ⓓ
23. Ⓐ Ⓑ Ⓒ Ⓓ
24. Ⓐ Ⓑ Ⓒ Ⓓ
25. Ⓐ Ⓑ Ⓒ Ⓓ
26. Ⓐ Ⓑ Ⓒ Ⓓ
27. Ⓐ Ⓑ Ⓒ Ⓓ

Section 1: Module 2 (Easier)
Reading and Writing

1. Ⓐ Ⓑ Ⓒ Ⓓ
2. Ⓐ Ⓑ Ⓒ Ⓓ
3. Ⓐ Ⓑ Ⓒ Ⓓ
4. Ⓐ Ⓑ Ⓒ Ⓓ
5. Ⓐ Ⓑ Ⓒ Ⓓ
6. Ⓐ Ⓑ Ⓒ Ⓓ
7. Ⓐ Ⓑ Ⓒ Ⓓ
8. Ⓐ Ⓑ Ⓒ Ⓓ
9. Ⓐ Ⓑ Ⓒ Ⓓ
10. Ⓐ Ⓑ Ⓒ Ⓓ
11. Ⓐ Ⓑ Ⓒ Ⓓ
12. Ⓐ Ⓑ Ⓒ Ⓓ
13. Ⓐ Ⓑ Ⓒ Ⓓ
14. Ⓐ Ⓑ Ⓒ Ⓓ
15. Ⓐ Ⓑ Ⓒ Ⓓ
16. Ⓐ Ⓑ Ⓒ Ⓓ
17. Ⓐ Ⓑ Ⓒ Ⓓ
18. Ⓐ Ⓑ Ⓒ Ⓓ
19. Ⓐ Ⓑ Ⓒ Ⓓ
20. Ⓐ Ⓑ Ⓒ Ⓓ
21. Ⓐ Ⓑ Ⓒ Ⓓ
22. Ⓐ Ⓑ Ⓒ Ⓓ
23. Ⓐ Ⓑ Ⓒ Ⓓ
24. Ⓐ Ⓑ Ⓒ Ⓓ
25. Ⓐ Ⓑ Ⓒ Ⓓ
26. Ⓐ Ⓑ Ⓒ Ⓓ
27. Ⓐ Ⓑ Ⓒ Ⓓ

Section 1: Module 2 (Harder)
Reading and Writing

1. Ⓐ Ⓑ Ⓒ Ⓓ
2. Ⓐ Ⓑ Ⓒ Ⓓ
3. Ⓐ Ⓑ Ⓒ Ⓓ
4. Ⓐ Ⓑ Ⓒ Ⓓ
5. Ⓐ Ⓑ Ⓒ Ⓓ
6. Ⓐ Ⓑ Ⓒ Ⓓ
7. Ⓐ Ⓑ Ⓒ Ⓓ
8. Ⓐ Ⓑ Ⓒ Ⓓ
9. Ⓐ Ⓑ Ⓒ Ⓓ
10. Ⓐ Ⓑ Ⓒ Ⓓ
11. Ⓐ Ⓑ Ⓒ Ⓓ
12. Ⓐ Ⓑ Ⓒ Ⓓ
13. Ⓐ Ⓑ Ⓒ Ⓓ
14. Ⓐ Ⓑ Ⓒ Ⓓ
15. Ⓐ Ⓑ Ⓒ Ⓓ
16. Ⓐ Ⓑ Ⓒ Ⓓ
17. Ⓐ Ⓑ Ⓒ Ⓓ
18. Ⓐ Ⓑ Ⓒ Ⓓ
19. Ⓐ Ⓑ Ⓒ Ⓓ
20. Ⓐ Ⓑ Ⓒ Ⓓ
21. Ⓐ Ⓑ Ⓒ Ⓓ
22. Ⓐ Ⓑ Ⓒ Ⓓ
23. Ⓐ Ⓑ Ⓒ Ⓓ
24. Ⓐ Ⓑ Ⓒ Ⓓ
25. Ⓐ Ⓑ Ⓒ Ⓓ
26. Ⓐ Ⓑ Ⓒ Ⓓ
27. Ⓐ Ⓑ Ⓒ Ⓓ

YOUR NAME: _____
(Print)   Last   First   M.I.

SIGNATURE: _____   DATE: ___/___/___

HOME ADDRESS: _____
(Print)   Number and Street

_____
           City   State   Zip Code

PHONE NO.: _____
(Print)

DATE OF BIRTH: ___/___/___
(Print)   Month / Day / Year

For both the Reading and Writing and the Math, be sure to only fill in the bubbles for the version of Module 2 that you took. If you took the Easier Module 2, only fill in the answers in the Easier column. If you took the Harder Module 2, only fill in the answers in the Harder column.

Section 2: Module 1 Math

1. Ⓐ Ⓑ Ⓒ Ⓓ
2. Ⓐ Ⓑ Ⓒ Ⓓ
3. _____
4. Ⓐ Ⓑ Ⓒ Ⓓ
5. Ⓐ Ⓑ Ⓒ Ⓓ
6. Ⓐ Ⓑ Ⓒ Ⓓ
7. Ⓐ Ⓑ Ⓒ Ⓓ
8. Ⓐ Ⓑ Ⓒ Ⓓ
9. Ⓐ Ⓑ Ⓒ Ⓓ
10. Ⓐ Ⓑ Ⓒ Ⓓ
11. Ⓐ Ⓑ Ⓒ Ⓓ
12. Ⓐ Ⓑ Ⓒ Ⓓ
13. _____
14. Ⓐ Ⓑ Ⓒ Ⓓ
15. Ⓐ Ⓑ Ⓒ Ⓓ
16. Ⓐ Ⓑ Ⓒ Ⓓ
17. Ⓐ Ⓑ Ⓒ Ⓓ
18. Ⓐ Ⓑ Ⓒ Ⓓ
19. _____
20. _____
21. Ⓐ Ⓑ Ⓒ Ⓓ
22. Ⓐ Ⓑ Ⓒ Ⓓ

Section 2: Module 2 (Easier) Math

1. Ⓐ Ⓑ Ⓒ Ⓓ
2. Ⓐ Ⓑ Ⓒ Ⓓ
3. _____
4. _____
5. Ⓐ Ⓑ Ⓒ Ⓓ
6. Ⓐ Ⓑ Ⓒ Ⓓ
7. _____
8. Ⓐ Ⓑ Ⓒ Ⓓ
9. _____
10. Ⓐ Ⓑ Ⓒ Ⓓ
11. Ⓐ Ⓑ Ⓒ Ⓓ
12. Ⓐ Ⓑ Ⓒ Ⓓ
13. Ⓐ Ⓑ Ⓒ Ⓓ
14. Ⓐ Ⓑ Ⓒ Ⓓ
15. _____
16. _____
17. Ⓐ Ⓑ Ⓒ Ⓓ
18. Ⓐ Ⓑ Ⓒ Ⓓ
19. Ⓐ Ⓑ Ⓒ Ⓓ
20. Ⓐ Ⓑ Ⓒ Ⓓ
21. Ⓐ Ⓑ Ⓒ Ⓓ
22. Ⓐ Ⓑ Ⓒ Ⓓ

Section 2: Module 2 (Harder) Math

1. Ⓐ Ⓑ Ⓒ Ⓓ
2. Ⓐ Ⓑ Ⓒ Ⓓ
3. Ⓐ Ⓑ Ⓒ Ⓓ
4. _____
5. _____
6. Ⓐ Ⓑ Ⓒ Ⓓ
7. _____
8. Ⓐ Ⓑ Ⓒ Ⓓ
9. Ⓐ Ⓑ Ⓒ Ⓓ
10. Ⓐ Ⓑ Ⓒ Ⓓ
11. Ⓐ Ⓑ Ⓒ Ⓓ
12. Ⓐ Ⓑ Ⓒ Ⓓ
13. Ⓐ Ⓑ Ⓒ Ⓓ
14. _____
15. Ⓐ Ⓑ Ⓒ Ⓓ
16. Ⓐ Ⓑ Ⓒ Ⓓ
17. Ⓐ Ⓑ Ⓒ Ⓓ
18. Ⓐ Ⓑ Ⓒ Ⓓ
19. _____
20. Ⓐ Ⓑ Ⓒ Ⓓ
21. Ⓐ Ⓑ Ⓒ Ⓓ
22. _____

6 Practice Tests for the Digital SAT
Practice Test 4

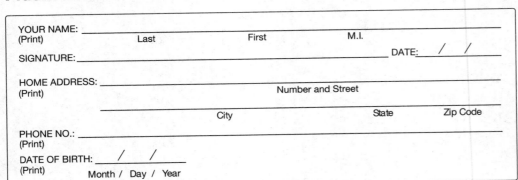

YOUR NAME: _____
(Print)   Last   First   M.I.

SIGNATURE: _____ DATE: ___/___/___

HOME ADDRESS: _____
(Print)   Number and Street

_____
City   State   Zip Code

PHONE NO.: _____
(Print)

DATE OF BIRTH: ___/___/___
(Print)   Month / Day / Year

For both the Reading and Writing and the Math, be sure to only fill in the bubbles for the version of Module 2 that you took. If you took the Easier Module 2, only fill in the answers in the Easier column. If you took the Harder Module 2, only fill in the answers in the Harder column.

Section 1: Module 1
Reading and Writing

1. Ⓐ Ⓑ Ⓒ Ⓓ
2. Ⓐ Ⓑ Ⓒ Ⓓ
3. Ⓐ Ⓑ Ⓒ Ⓓ
4. Ⓐ Ⓑ Ⓒ Ⓓ
5. Ⓐ Ⓑ Ⓒ Ⓓ
6. Ⓐ Ⓑ Ⓒ Ⓓ
7. Ⓐ Ⓑ Ⓒ Ⓓ
8. Ⓐ Ⓑ Ⓒ Ⓓ
9. Ⓐ Ⓑ Ⓒ Ⓓ
10. Ⓐ Ⓑ Ⓒ Ⓓ
11. Ⓐ Ⓑ Ⓒ Ⓓ
12. Ⓐ Ⓑ Ⓒ Ⓓ
13. Ⓐ Ⓑ Ⓒ Ⓓ
14. Ⓐ Ⓑ Ⓒ Ⓓ
15. Ⓐ Ⓑ Ⓒ Ⓓ
16. Ⓐ Ⓑ Ⓒ Ⓓ
17. Ⓐ Ⓑ Ⓒ Ⓓ
18. Ⓐ Ⓑ Ⓒ Ⓓ
19. Ⓐ Ⓑ Ⓒ Ⓓ
20. Ⓐ Ⓑ Ⓒ Ⓓ
21. Ⓐ Ⓑ Ⓒ Ⓓ
22. Ⓐ Ⓑ Ⓒ Ⓓ
23. Ⓐ Ⓑ Ⓒ Ⓓ
24. Ⓐ Ⓑ Ⓒ Ⓓ
25. Ⓐ Ⓑ Ⓒ Ⓓ
26. Ⓐ Ⓑ Ⓒ Ⓓ
27. Ⓐ Ⓑ Ⓒ Ⓓ

Section 1: Module 2 (Easier)
Reading and Writing

1. Ⓐ Ⓑ Ⓒ Ⓓ
2. Ⓐ Ⓑ Ⓒ Ⓓ
3. Ⓐ Ⓑ Ⓒ Ⓓ
4. Ⓐ Ⓑ Ⓒ Ⓓ
5. Ⓐ Ⓑ Ⓒ Ⓓ
6. Ⓐ Ⓑ Ⓒ Ⓓ
7. Ⓐ Ⓑ Ⓒ Ⓓ
8. Ⓐ Ⓑ Ⓒ Ⓓ
9. Ⓐ Ⓑ Ⓒ Ⓓ
10. Ⓐ Ⓑ Ⓒ Ⓓ
11. Ⓐ Ⓑ Ⓒ Ⓓ
12. Ⓐ Ⓑ Ⓒ Ⓓ
13. Ⓐ Ⓑ Ⓒ Ⓓ
14. Ⓐ Ⓑ Ⓒ Ⓓ
15. Ⓐ Ⓑ Ⓒ Ⓓ
16. Ⓐ Ⓑ Ⓒ Ⓓ
17. Ⓐ Ⓑ Ⓒ Ⓓ
18. Ⓐ Ⓑ Ⓒ Ⓓ
19. Ⓐ Ⓑ Ⓒ Ⓓ
20. Ⓐ Ⓑ Ⓒ Ⓓ
21. Ⓐ Ⓑ Ⓒ Ⓓ
22. Ⓐ Ⓑ Ⓒ Ⓓ
23. Ⓐ Ⓑ Ⓒ Ⓓ
24. Ⓐ Ⓑ Ⓒ Ⓓ
25. Ⓐ Ⓑ Ⓒ Ⓓ
26. Ⓐ Ⓑ Ⓒ Ⓓ
27. Ⓐ Ⓑ Ⓒ Ⓓ

Section 1: Module 2 (Harder)
Reading and Writing

1. Ⓐ Ⓑ Ⓒ Ⓓ
2. Ⓐ Ⓑ Ⓒ Ⓓ
3. Ⓐ Ⓑ Ⓒ Ⓓ
4. Ⓐ Ⓑ Ⓒ Ⓓ
5. Ⓐ Ⓑ Ⓒ Ⓓ
6. Ⓐ Ⓑ Ⓒ Ⓓ
7. Ⓐ Ⓑ Ⓒ Ⓓ
8. Ⓐ Ⓑ Ⓒ Ⓓ
9. Ⓐ Ⓑ Ⓒ Ⓓ
10. Ⓐ Ⓑ Ⓒ Ⓓ
11. Ⓐ Ⓑ Ⓒ Ⓓ
12. Ⓐ Ⓑ Ⓒ Ⓓ
13. Ⓐ Ⓑ Ⓒ Ⓓ
14. Ⓐ Ⓑ Ⓒ Ⓓ
15. Ⓐ Ⓑ Ⓒ Ⓓ
16. Ⓐ Ⓑ Ⓒ Ⓓ
17. Ⓐ Ⓑ Ⓒ Ⓓ
18. Ⓐ Ⓑ Ⓒ Ⓓ
19. Ⓐ Ⓑ Ⓒ Ⓓ
20. Ⓐ Ⓑ Ⓒ Ⓓ
21. Ⓐ Ⓑ Ⓒ Ⓓ
22. Ⓐ Ⓑ Ⓒ Ⓓ
23. Ⓐ Ⓑ Ⓒ Ⓓ
24. Ⓐ Ⓑ Ⓒ Ⓓ
25. Ⓐ Ⓑ Ⓒ Ⓓ
26. Ⓐ Ⓑ Ⓒ Ⓓ
27. Ⓐ Ⓑ Ⓒ Ⓓ

6 Practice Tests for the Digital SAT
Practice Test 4

YOUR NAME: _____
(Print)   Last   First   M.I.

SIGNATURE: _____   DATE: __/__/__

HOME ADDRESS: _____
(Print)   Number and Street

_____
City   State   Zip Code

PHONE NO.: _____
(Print)

DATE OF BIRTH: __/__/__
(Print)   Month / Day / Year

For both the Reading and Writing and the Math, be sure to only fill in the bubbles for the version of Module 2 that you took. If you took the Easier Module 2, only fill in the answer in the Easier column. If you took the Harder Module 2, only fill in the answers in the Harder column.

Section 2: Module 1 Math

1. Ⓐ Ⓑ Ⓒ Ⓓ
2. Ⓐ Ⓑ Ⓒ Ⓓ
3. Ⓐ Ⓑ Ⓒ Ⓓ
4. Ⓐ Ⓑ Ⓒ Ⓓ
5. Ⓐ Ⓑ Ⓒ Ⓓ
6. _____
7. Ⓐ Ⓑ Ⓒ Ⓓ
8. _____
9. Ⓐ Ⓑ Ⓒ Ⓓ
10. Ⓐ Ⓑ Ⓒ Ⓓ
11. Ⓐ Ⓑ Ⓒ Ⓓ
12. Ⓐ Ⓑ Ⓒ Ⓓ
13. Ⓐ Ⓑ Ⓒ Ⓓ
14. Ⓐ Ⓑ Ⓒ Ⓓ
15. _____
16. Ⓐ Ⓑ Ⓒ Ⓓ
17. Ⓐ Ⓑ Ⓒ Ⓓ
18. Ⓐ Ⓑ Ⓒ Ⓓ
19. _____
20. _____
21. _____
22. _____

Section 2: Module 2 (Easier) Math

1. Ⓐ Ⓑ Ⓒ Ⓓ
2. _____
3. Ⓐ Ⓑ Ⓒ Ⓓ
4. Ⓐ Ⓑ Ⓒ Ⓓ
5. Ⓐ Ⓑ Ⓒ Ⓓ
6. Ⓐ Ⓑ Ⓒ Ⓓ
7. _____
8. Ⓐ Ⓑ Ⓒ Ⓓ
9. _____
10. Ⓐ Ⓑ Ⓒ Ⓓ
11. Ⓐ Ⓑ Ⓒ Ⓓ
12. Ⓐ Ⓑ Ⓒ Ⓓ
13. _____
14. Ⓐ Ⓑ Ⓒ Ⓓ
15. Ⓐ Ⓑ Ⓒ Ⓓ
16. Ⓐ Ⓑ Ⓒ Ⓓ
17. Ⓐ Ⓑ Ⓒ Ⓓ
18. Ⓐ Ⓑ Ⓒ Ⓓ
19. Ⓐ Ⓑ Ⓒ Ⓓ
20. Ⓐ Ⓑ Ⓒ Ⓓ
21. Ⓐ Ⓑ Ⓒ Ⓓ
22. Ⓐ Ⓑ Ⓒ Ⓓ

Section 2: Module 2 (Harder) Math

1. Ⓐ Ⓑ Ⓒ Ⓓ
2. Ⓐ Ⓑ Ⓒ Ⓓ
3. _____
4. Ⓐ Ⓑ Ⓒ Ⓓ
5. Ⓐ Ⓑ Ⓒ Ⓓ
6. Ⓐ Ⓑ Ⓒ Ⓓ
7. Ⓐ Ⓑ Ⓒ Ⓓ
8. Ⓐ Ⓑ Ⓒ Ⓓ
9. _____
10. Ⓐ Ⓑ Ⓒ Ⓓ
11. Ⓐ Ⓑ Ⓒ Ⓓ
12. Ⓐ Ⓑ Ⓒ Ⓓ
13. Ⓐ Ⓑ Ⓒ Ⓓ
14. Ⓐ Ⓑ Ⓒ Ⓓ
15. Ⓐ Ⓑ Ⓒ Ⓓ
16. Ⓐ Ⓑ Ⓒ Ⓓ
17. _____
18. Ⓐ Ⓑ Ⓒ Ⓓ
19. Ⓐ Ⓑ Ⓒ Ⓓ
20. _____
21. Ⓐ Ⓑ Ⓒ Ⓓ
22. Ⓐ Ⓑ Ⓒ Ⓓ